HERIOT-WATT UNIVERSITY

38O07 00043205 5

THE
ELE...

BANKING

Femi A. Adekanye

Graham Burn
28d High Street
Leighton Buzzard
Bedfordshire
LU7 7EA
United Kingdom

R113393 8

DEDICATED TO AMOKE

*My devoted and loving wife, whose encouragement and support
in many ways made this work possible.*

First Published: April 1983
© Graham Burn

No part of this book may be reproduced, stored in a retrieval system or transmitted in any form, by any means, electronic, mechanical, photocopying, microfilming, recording or otherwise, without the written permission of the publisher.

ISBN 0 907721 06 0

Published in the U.K. by:
GRAHAM BURN
28d High Street
Leighton Buzzard
Bedfordshire
LU7 7EA
Tel: Leighton Buzzard (0525) 377963
Telex: 825562 CHACOM G BURNPUB

Typesetting & Artwork:
Graham Burn
Advertising Studios
Leighton Buzzard
Bedfordshire
Printed by:
Amplion Press
Rickmansworth
Hertfordshire

First Published April 1983
Graham Burn

No part of this book may be reproduced, stored in a retrieval system or transmitted in any form by any means, electronic, mechanical, photocopying, microfilming, recording or otherwise, without the written permission of the publisher.

ISBN 0 907721 06 6

Published in the U.K. by:
GRAHAM BURN
284 High Street
Leighton Buzzard
Bedfordshire
LU7 7EA
Tel: Leighton Buzzard (0525) 372965
Telex 825852 CHACOM G BURNPUB

Typesetting & Artwork
Graham Burn
Advertising Studios
Leighton Buzzard
Bedfordshire
Printed by:
Amplion Press
Rickmansworth
Hertfordshire

FOREWORD

Books written by Nigerians were conspicuous by their absence in banking and finance literature in Nigeria up to the mid-1970's. This presented immense problems to both teachers and students. These problems were aggravated by the increase in the number of institutions of higher learning and the emergence of many professional bodies in the country. Today, the position is fairly different. Nigerians have risen up to the challenge and a number of books on Nigerian banking and finance now exist. Mr. Adekanye's *Elements of Banking* is one of such books.

Written from a practitioner's point of view and with a good deal of inside knowledge, *Elements of Banking* is the first of its kind in the country. Mr. Adekanye has carefully combined theory with practice in discussing banking in Nigeria and students and teachers will, no doubt, find the sections dealing with services offered by banks particularly very helpful. Surely, the book is a boon not only to the student and the teacher, but also to the practitioner and businessman in the insight it has given into the intricacies of banking in the country.

In writing this book, Mr. Adekanye, a practising banker, has no doubt demonstrated that textbook writing is not a monopoly of the academics in institutions of higher learning. It is hoped that other practitioners can accept the challenge.

Professor G. O. Nwankwo
Executive Director (Monetary & Banking Policy)
Central Bank of Nigeria.

1st Vice President, Nigerian Institute of Bankers.

ACKNOWLEDGEMENT

In writing this book I received help from several people, too numerous to mention. However, I wish specially to thank Professor G. O. Nwankwo, Professor of Finance and Executive Director, Monetary & Banking Policy, Central Bank of Nigeria and First Vice-President Nigerian Institute of Bankers, to whom I am deeply indebted for his detailed work on the manuscript. His helpful criticism and comments necessitated my re-writing some chapters, and restructuring the book. It is with a deep sense of appreciation that I note the improvement to this book brought about through Professor Nwankwo's suggestions. I also extend my profound gratitude to Alhaji S. O. A. Sule, Managing Director, Nigerian/Arab Bank Ltd and President of the Nigerian Institute of Bankers and Alhaji A. O. G. Otiti, Deputy Governor, Central Bank of Nigeria and immediate past President of the Nigerian Institute Bankers, for their assistance in reading through the whole manuscript, despite their busy schedule and making useful suggestions for improvement.

I am indebted to my good friend Emmanuel Ihemedu who, apart from reviewing the whole manuscript, was particularly incisive in his constructive criticism of the chapters on money and the overall structure of the book. I also thank O. Ohore who helped me to gather and collate useful materials and data from several financial institutions.

J. A. Adeniji, O. Fashedemi, S. K. A. Adebowale, Ayo Akingbade, T. O. Agbelusi and M. S. Udom also read the manuscript or sections of it and made helpful comments which were very useful to me in the preparation of the final draft for publication. No word can adequately express my deep sense of appreciation to these gentlemen.

I wish to acknowledge the assistance given to me by Messrs A. A. Adenubi and S. O. Dada, Executive Secretary and Director of Studies, respectively, of the Nigerian Institute of Bankers who gave me free access to past examination questions of the Institute.

I would like to thank Graham Burn, the Publisher, for his patience and understanding as we compiled this book.

At this juncture, I must add that I have endeavoured to correct all the mistakes to which my attention was drawn, but any other errors of omission or commission must remain my sole responsibility.

Finally, I wish to express my gratitude to my former secretary, Mrs. Oluremi Abike Akinsunmi, who spent her leisure time and weekends to type the manuscript speedily and accurately. My thanks also go to the following stenographers and typists who helped in the typing work — Mrs. O. A. Doherty, Mrs. K. Bello, Mrs. R. O. Aluko, Miss Justina Alozie and Stanely O. Nduka.

Femi A. Adekanye
Lagos
January 1983

CONTENTS

CONTENTS

LIST OF TABLES

PREFACE

Elements of Banking is an introduction to the study of practical banking with particular reference to Nigeria. The book has been written specifically for students preparing for the professional examinations of the Nigerian Institute of Bankers. At present, even though the Institute's examination papers on Elements of Banking and Economics II contain mainly questions relating to the local environment, there is no comprehensive textbook sufficiently localized for the use of students. I believe that this book will enable the Nigerian Institute of Bankers and other higher educational institutions to continue to test students on syllabus contents which are orientated to domestic needs, with the emphasis on local banking problems and issues, as they will now be doing so with the assurance that students have the necessary tool to work with.

I am not in any way advocating that Nigerian students should not study foreign banking systems any more. This will be done in the final examinations when students study Monetary Economics, Finance of International Trade and Practice of Banking. Banking business is, after all, international in nature and we cannot afford to be cut off from the mainstream of developments in techniques and operational procedures. However, it is my contention that every Nigerian banking student and practising banker must be knowledgeable in local banking systems, history, evolution of local money and the peculiar problems facing local bankers and the monetary authorities in a developing economy like Nigeria. If this book makes a contribution in any small way by awakening the interest of professionals and helping students in their understanding of these local problems, it will have served its purpose.

Today, the only books available on Elements of Banking are written by British authors specifically on the British banking system. Students are compelled to study these and make them applicable to Nigeria. This is a daunting task. It is my hope that this book will adequately fill the existing gap.

The book is divided into 26 chapters and six principal parts. Part I covers the theories, concepts and evolution of money and the history of monetary policy in Nigeria.

Part II is devoted to the Nigerian banking system, covering central banking and commercial, merchant and development banking. Part III examines the services offered by banks in Nigeria ranging from normal banking services to special services like exchange control and foreign exchange services. Part IV discusses the Nigerian Money and Capital Markets including the Nigerian Securities and Exchange Commission. Finally, Part V discusses international banking. The book is rounded up with a summary chapter which also examines banking education in Nigeria in some detail.

Thus, the Nigerian Institute of Bankers syllabus for Elements of Banking in Part I, Section I is fully covered; while Economics II in Part I, Section II is also partly covered. Chapters Nine and Ten in Part II and Fifteen and Sixteen in Part III are slightly beyond the normal requirements of the Institute's Part I (Intermediate) syllabus. These Chapters and the whole of Parts I and V will serve as introductory reading for students preparing for the professional examinations (Part II — Final) of the Nigerian Institute of Bankers in Monetary Economics and Practice of Banking.

The book will also be useful to students studying for any other Nigerian professional examination which contains a paper on Banking (e.g. the Institute of Chartered Accountants of Nigeria and full-time students of Banking, Accountancy and Business Management in Universities, Colleges of Technology and Polytechnics).

To assist students further and to encourage practice, each Chapter of the book ends with a number of questions, with suggested answers given at the end of the book. Most of the questions are selected from past examination papers set by both the Institute of Bankers, London, and the Nigerian Institute of Bankers. It must be emphasised that the suggested answers are meant to serve merely as a guide and are neither official answers nor have they any connection with either the Institute of Bankers in the U.K. or in Nigeria.

I sincerely hope that the book will prove useful to students, lecturers, practising bankers, other professionals, businessmen and general readers.

Femi A. Adekanye
Lagos
January 1983

AUTHOR'S NOTE

Now, a few words of caution.

The Questions & Answers in the book have been included for the use of lecturers in class discussions and to give the student the opportunity to gain experience and confidence through constant practice at answering examination questions. This book gives ample opportunity for such practice.

The questions are designed to test the student's understanding of the subject covered in each Chapter. Unless a Chapter has been read, digested and fully understood, it is advisable not to attempt the questions. The temptation to read the suggested answer before any serious attempt is made to tackle the question must be also resisted. They will be extremely useful for revision purposes after the whole syllabus has been adequately covered.

It may be helpful to quote from the Institute of Bankers, London, Students Guide on Examination Technique which every student must endeavour to follow:

> "1. Make sure that your preparation covers the whole syllabus and includes a thorough study of previous papers and reports, and practice at answering questions.
>
> 2. In the examination room, read the question paper through and spend five to ten minutes deciding which questions you are going to answer.
>
> 3. Allocate your time to the required number of questions.
>
> 4. Tackle first the question which you know best — build up confidence.
>
> 5. Plan your answer by setting down the main points and arranging them in their logical order before beginning to write in detail.
>
> 6. Be brief and relevant — you will get no marks for irrelevant material, however well it is expressed.
>
> 7. Answer the right number of questions. If you are required to answer four then the examiner will mark the first four you

have done and will ignore anything else.

8. *If you have to satisfy the examiner in each of the sections, then deal with one question from each section before going on to the second — don't run the risk of spending too much time on two sections and having to rush the third.*

9. *Finally, read what you have written, correct as necessary, and cut out anything which does not make sense."*

F. A. Adekanye
Lagos
January, 1983

PART I

MONEY AND MONETARY

SYSTEM

CHAPTER ONE

THE BASIC CONCEPTS OF MONEY

1-1 ORIGIN OF MONEY

Exchange can be carried out by a direct bartering of goods and services (i.e. exchange of goods for goods or exchange of service for service). However, this system of direct bartering has many shortcomings, including:

i) Lack of common unit of measure. An inventory of many kinds or qualities of various goods can only be ascertained by listing the different commodities that made up the inventory. For example, instead of recording goods and services in terms of naira and kobo, pounds and pence, or dollars and cents, goods are listed as the number of yams, goats, tables, types of services rendered, etc.

ii) Double coincidence of wants. Trade by barter becomes cumbersome because of the existence of a double coincidence of wants between buyers and sellers. For example, a man wanting to exchange goats for yams may spend several days before he finds anyone who has yams for sale and at the same time happens to want goats. Money is the only common factor that can avoid this incovenience, as the seller of goats can sell his goats for money and keep the proceeds until such a time he wants yams.

iii) Future contracts (which form the basis of modern business activities) are impossible. Wages, salaries, interest or rents which extend over a period of time are contractual arrangements. Even if future contracts were feasible under barter, there are many more questions to be settled (e.g. the type of goods, the quality, quantity, etc).

iv) There is no means of storing wealth or value since the value of the wealth cannot be ascertained. Even where wealth is designated in a particular commodity, the problem of storage facilities arises, whilst the goods are also subject to spoilage and the risks of being stolen.

In spite of all these inconveniences pertaining to direct barter, early societies survived and carried out their daily activities using bartering. However, as specialisation and trade increased and as societies grew from small groups to large nations, money was needed if specialisation and production were to be optimised. As Chandler [1] put it: *"money is productive, in the sense that it is an essential part of the modern exchange mechanism and thereby facilitates specialisation and production ..."*

Indeed, crude barter was highly inefficient and unsuitable as agent of trade. The extreme inconvenience of exchange by direct barter made people to seek 'something' that would eliminate the disadvantages enumerated above.

1-2 FUNCTIONS OF MONEY

The basic purpose of money is to serve as *"the great wheel of circulation, the great instrument of commerce"*[2]. Virtually all economists recognise four major functions of money:

i)   a unit of value;

ii) a medium of exchange;

iii) a standard of deferred payment; and,

iv) a store of value.

The first two can be classified as primary or basic functions of money, while the last two are derivative or secondary functions, having been derived from the primary functions.

1-2.1 Money as a Unit of Value

Many names have been given to this function of money: unit of value, standard of value, unit of account, common denominator of value, etc. One common idea is significant in all these names *"that monetary unit serves as the unit in terms of which the value of all goods and services is measured and expressed"*[3]. With the development of a common monetary unit, the individual member of the economy has to have some common denominator with which he measures the relative values of different goods and services. Money has, therefore, become the standard for measuring value in the same manner as feet or metres are standards for measuring distance or length. Every country has evolved its own unit of account which circulates within the national

---

[1] Chandler. L.V. *The Economics of Money and Banking* Harper International Edition, New York, 1973 pg. 7.

[2]*Ibid.*

[3] Chandler *op. cit. p. 7*

4

boundary (e.g. naira and kobo in Nigeria, dollars and cents in America, pounds and pence in Britain). All values are, therefore, expressed in monetary units of the country concerned.

The existence of a unit of account has some distinct advantages. For instance, the practice simplifies the question of ascertaining the exchange value of commodities in any market (e.g. one orange costs fifteen kobo, one yam costs one naira fifty kobo, a bag of rice costs sixty naira, etc.).

Second, we can compare prices in monetary terms between one city and another and one country and another. For example, a 3-bedroom flat in Lagos costs ₦3,600, while the same in Ibadan costs ₦1,440 or a 17-inch colour T.V. set which costs the equivalent of ₦250 in Britain, when converted in terms of naira costs about ₦750 in Nigeria.

Finally, accounting is made simple through the use of a unit of account. Instead of listing our inventory in terms of items like machinery, furniture, buildings or stocks, a unit of account helps us to give the value of assets in a single monetary aggregate.

1-2.2 Money as a Medium of Exchange

Once a particular commodity is used as a unit of account, it becomes convenient to serve also as a means of exchange. This brings us to the second primary function of money. It is in performance of this function that money acquired the notion of general acceptability. Anything that is generally (not universally, but commonly) accepted by people in exchange of goods and services is regarded as a *means of exchange.* This 'thing' may be salt, cowries, gold, copper, pieces of cloth or book entries by the commercial banks.

The essential requirement of this object is the general willingness of people to accept it in exchange for goods and services. By accepting this commodity in exchange for other goods and services, this payment mechanism saves time and encourages further specialisation and production. The shoemaker can now concentrate on his shoe-making with the hope of selling the shoe and obtaining the other commodities which he needs without having to search for somebody who wants shoes in exchange. Similarly, a bank worker can concentrate on his services and use the salary paid to him to buy goods of his choice.

in short the double coincidence of wants has been eliminated, as whoever possesses money, possesses "generalized purchasing power"[4]. He can exchange the money for other goods without any inconvenience.

1-2.3 Money as a Standard of Deferred Payment

Once money serves the two primary functions stated above, it invariably becomes the unit in terms of which all future or deferred payments are stated.

The existence of contracts of various forms cannot be over-emphasised in modern business. The contracts may be for wages, the payment of interest and debts, dividends, long-leases on property, hire purchase, pensions, etc. These contracts may range from one month to several years.

Money as a standard of deferred payments cannot function well if it does not maintain a constant purchasing power throughout the period of deferred payment. Experience has shown, however, that it is difficult for money to maintain a constant purchasing power over a long time. For example, 5 cups of garri in 1960 cost one shilling (10k), today the same 5 cups of garri cost ₦1.50. One room in Lagos 10 years ago could be rented at ₦10.00, but today the same room costs ₦50.00. We could enumerate here the different ways in which the purchasing power of money has changed within the same country and between countries, but further discussion of this changing purchasing power of money will be made later.

The instability in the purchasing power of money has certain implications and affects different interests in various ways. For example, if money increases in value over time, it hurts anyone who has entered into a contract to pay fixed sums of money in the future and favours those who receive fixed amounts like pensioners and wage earners. This is, however, a rare phenomenon, except in periods of depression or recession.

If, on the other hand, the purchasing power of money declines over time — a more common occurrence — it injures those who have agreed to receive fixed amounts and lightens the burden of payers. For

---

[4] Chandler, *op. cit.*

example, wage earners, pensioners or lenders will lose, while manufacturers who borrow money to set up a business based on instalment repayments will gain.

In the realm of finance, investors who expect to receive dividends or interest have become so aware of this eroding power of money over time that they have derived a method of moderating the negative effect. This is done by calculating in advance what one unit of money invested today will earn in, say, five years time at a given interest rate and by calculating the present value or equivalent today of an amount that is expected to be earned in the future. This is known as the Discounted Cash Flow (DCF) method of computing the NTV (Net Terminal Value) and the NPV (Net Present Value), but the mechanics and formula for these calculations are beyond the scope of this book. (The interested reader should consult an advanced text on management accounting [5].)

1-2.4 Money as a Store of Value

As soon as money comes to be used as a unit of value and as a generally acceptable means of payment, it is certain to be widely used as a means of storing value, because whoever holds money holds *"a generalized purchasing power"* which he can spend at his convenience and on a commodity of his choice.

The holder knows that it will be accepted at any time for any goods and services. Money is a good store of value for the purposes of meeting contingencies and the payment of debts that are fixed in terms of money. As in the case of money as a means of deferred payment, money can only serve as a good store of value if the value of money remains stable over a fairly long time. For example, during a period of inflation, the value of money will fall in real terms although the money value will still be the same. If a man stores ₦100 in the current account of a commercial bank during a period of 20 percent inflation, one year later the account will still read ₦100, but the man would have lost ₦20 in *purchasing power*.

---

[5] For instance *"Management Accounting: Theory & Application"* C.S.Ola, Graham Burn, 1982.

There are, however, other alternatives to money as a store of value, some of these assets include promissory notes, bonds, mortgages, stocks, houses, furniture, land or other valuables. On the one hand, the other assets which serve as a store of value have some advantages over money (e.g. because they yield an income in the form of interests, profits or rent and sometimes appreciate in terms of monetary value), while on the other hand, these assets have some inherent disadvantages as a store of value, (e.g. storage costs, depreciation in terms of money and illiquidity of varying degrees).

However, the decision to store wealth in any form depends upon individual expectations, preferences or circumstances. It is assumed that the individual being an 'economic being' will distribute his wealth in such a manner as to optimise the return from these assets (e.g. in an unstable environment such as during the Nigerian Civil War, people prefer to carry their wealth in liquid form because of uncertainty).

We shall examine later (during our discussion of demand for money) the factors that determine the distribution of wealth between money and other assets.

1-3 DEFINITION OF MONEY

Having identified the origin and functions of money, we shall now attempt to define money. It is difficult to find a clear-cut definition of the term 'money'. The definition of money depends on what constitutes the money supply (i.e. stock of money) and what things should be included or excluded. Through the ages different 'things' have served different societies as money. These range from food items (e.g. salt, corn or rice), implements (e.g. hoes), metals (e.g. copper, iron, or gold), paper money and book entries by commercial banks.

The only common factor about these items that served as money was the general acceptability by that particular society as a means of payment. Money can, therefore, have many definitions: some authorities focus attention on legal definitions and others on the functional or operational definition of money. The problem of definition of money is still a source of debate and controversy among economists.

1-3.1 Legal Definition

According to Chandler[6], *"money is what the law says it is"*. He went on to say that *"a thing is likely to have difficulty in achieving general acceptability in payments if the law prohibits its use for this purpose"*. Laws can, therefore, help a thing to achieve general acceptability by proclaiming it to be money and may even endow it with 'legal tender' attributes. Chandler argues, however, that legal definitions are unsatisfactory for purposes of economic analysis. This is because people may refuse to accept things that are legally defined as money and even refuse to sell goods and services to those who offer legal tender in payment.

On the other hand, things not legally defined as money may come to be generally acceptable in payment and even to become a major part of circulating medium (e.g. current accounts deposits with banks). On the basis of the above facts, Chandler concluded that legal provisions are necessary but not sufficient to determine things that do or do not serve as money.

1-3.2 Functional Definition of Money

In economic analysis what counts is the functional or operational definition of money. There is a general concensus by all economists that the money supply should include all those 'things' that are generally acceptable in payment of debts and as payment for goods and services. We can, therefore, conclude that anything that is generally acceptable in payment and generally used as a medium of payment is money, no matter what its legal status.

Applying this criterion to Nigeria, the money stock can be narrowly defined as the currency in circulation (coins and notes) plus private sector demand deposits at commercial banks and the Central Bank. This is popularly referred to as M1. Sometimes the definition can be extended to a broader concept called M2 which includes deposits with non-bank financial intermediaries and investments in government stocks such as Treasury Bills and Certificates, development stocks and savings bonds, etc. However, the monetary authorities in Nigeria use the narrow definition of money supply M1.

---

[6] Chandler, *op. cit.*

All coins and paper money are generally acceptable and endowed with full legal tender status for the settlement of debts, but demand deposit claims against banks are not legal tender, although are generally acceptable as payment.

In economies that are highly monetised and which have acquired banking habits, about 90% of all payments are made through cheques. In contrast, in developing countries like Nigeria, coins and bank notes constitute the major payment mechanism. The reasons for this behaviour are well-known. They include poor banking habits, the existence of a large rural sector which has little or no banking facilities and a lack of confidence in cheques as means of final payments. (A detailed analysis of the factors affecting money supply in the economy will be discussed later in this book.) In the meantime, we shall take a cursory look at the development of different types of money that have been used.

1-4 TYPES OF MONEY

The discussion of the different types of money is important because the type of money employed can and does influence the money supply in a country, the purchasing power of money and the ability of any monetary authority to control the money supply effectively. It is also necessary briefly to examine the characteristics of money in order to see the qualities that money must possess in order to discharge its functions satisfactorily.

1-4.1 Coins

Before the introduction of coins, many commodities such as rice, tobacco, wool or cattle were used as mediums of exchange. Their value as commodities for non-monetary purposes was as great as their value as money. However, the early 'commodity money' failed to pass some of the test of a good medium of exchange. The discovery of coins derived from metals was the most convenient form of money ever used in that it passed almost all qualities discussed below. The most popular of this metallic money were those based on silver and gold.

The issue of silver or gold coins was not necessarily the responsibility of governments. This function of issue was done mainly by private enterprises though they were regulated as to the purity and weight of the coins to prevent cheating. As time went on, governments took over the issue of coins and in doing this they had to define the value of the monetary unit. That meant, the stipulation of the gold content of the monetary units. As a further development, it meant that governments would, at the stipulated price, purchase all the metal that is offered and turn it into coin without charge. This prevented the market price of gold from falling below the mint buying price.

1-4.2 Convertible and Inconvertible Paper Money

Paper money had its origin in the Middle Ages when goldsmiths in England, by the nature of their business, had good storage systems for gold and other valuables. People resorted to lodging their raw gold with the goldsmiths and were issued receipts in different denominations. These bearer receipts could be used by the holder in exchange for goods and, whoever possessed the receipt, had a claim over the gold lodged with the goldsmith. This was how a rudimentary banking was evolved.

The receipts were a type of IOU, showing that the goldsmith (generally called banker) owed the bearer of the note a stated sum of money, the banker being expected to redeem that promise printed on his note and exchange it on demand for actual cash or gold coins. As the practice of bearer notes gained confidence, and as the banker recognised that the demand to convert the notes to real gold declined, it was natural for him to employ some of the excess cash profitably.

To avoid the proliferation of bankers and the attendant inability to meet the demands of the depositors, the question of issue of convertible paper money was centralised in the Bank of England. If a bank note can be exchanged on demand for gold or silver coins, it is said to be convertible. The earliest bank notes had to be convertible because people were only prepared to accept them in the belief that they would be converted to gold or silver coins on demand. The convertible bank note was not, in itself, money, but a substitute for money or 'token' money.

The implication of convertible paper money was that the State limited the amount of paper money in circulation. In fact, the paper money in circulation was directly tied to the amount of gold available for exchange on demand. However, as it was not possible to meet the demand for money due to the growth in business activities, the State devised a means of partial backing. The sole authority to print paper money having been invested in the State, it was easy for the State to determine the proportion of the paper money which was to be fully backed (depending upon the quantity of gold available) and the fraction that was not backed, although this is only practicable if the population as a whole retains confidence in the State. This fraction that was not backed by gold was known as *fiduciary issue*. With the device of fractional backing, the government was able to meet the demand for money, especially to cover its own expenditure.

Thus, the historical promise to pay on demand the sum stated on the bank note no longer exists in practice. Nowadays, paper money is valuable because of its general acceptability. The fact that it can no longer be converted into anything that possesses intrinsic value (like gold) has no effect on its functions as a medium of exchange. This conforms with the operational definition given earlier — that anything that is generally acceptable in payment and generally used as a medium of payment is money.

1-4.3 Deposit Money Withdrawable by Cheque

Deposit money is 'created' by the commercial banking system[7]. In our discussion of paper money, we noted how bank notes were more of promissory notes to pay gold on demand and how banks were able to create money by printing and putting into circulation many more notes than they could actually redeem in gold. Today, customers still deposit money with banks and banks give a promise to pay on demand the amount deposited by the customers. The customer can withdraw all this money in cash for the purpose of settling his debts or he can issue cheques which ask the bank to transfer the stated sum from his deposit to a beneficiary. The use of cheques to settle debts and for purposes of exchanging goods and services ensures that this instrument can be classified as money.

We can pay for most things by cheque, although cheques are not generally accepted as much as notes and coins. Since demand deposits are a means of exchange and cheques are generally (though not always) accepted, we can regard demand deposits as part of money supply. In Nigeria and in most less developed countries,

---

[7] Lipsey, R.G. *An Introduction to Positive Economics* English Language Book Society, Fourth Edition, 1975. p. 594.

cheques are not usually accepted as a means of payment by individuals. However, corporate entities make use of cheques as a medium of payment and they constitute the major users of cheques for purposes of money transmission.

1-5 HOW BANKS 'CREATE' MONEY

A typical illustration of money creation by banks will be of help to the reader. If for example Mr A deposits ₦5,000 in his bank, the bank credits his account by the same amount and has entered into contract to pay Mr A the sum of ₦5,000 cash on demand. Mr A can now make use of this bank entry to pay Mr B, say, ₦2,000 by issuing him a cheque. Mr B can either cash this cheque and have his money in cash or he may decide to have this cheque paid into his own account in the bank. If Mr B cashed ₦2,000, the effect will be a decrease in the bank deposit of Mr A by the amount of ₦2,000 and at the same time an outward flow of money from the bank to the same value. However, if Mr B did not want cash, the bank will pass a book entry crediting his account with ₦2,000. Hence, the total deposit balance of the bank remains the same, the transfers notwithstanding. The recording of the transactions becomes more complex if Mr B does not bank with A's bank. The banking system has developed a method of settling their claims against each other through the system of clearing and that makes the payment mechanism easy. (The clearing mechanism will be dealt with later.)

Lipsey argues that the modern deposit is the equivalent of the old bank note: *"a promise on the bank's behalf to pay out on demand the money at any time"*[8]. He goes on to say that the passing of the bank note from hand to hand transferred ownership of the claim against the bank, and this is now done by means of cheques i.e. an order to the bank telling it to transfer from one individual to another its obligation to pay cash.

As was the practice in the days of goldsmiths or early bankers, modern banks know that only a small proportion of their customers wish to have their money in cash at any one time. The banks now create money by granting loans or overdrafts which far exceed the actual cash available. When an overdraft is granted the bank allows the customer to issue cheques in excess of his deposit in payment of debts. In the case of loans, the bank enters into a contract to grant a customer a

---

[8]Lipsey, *op. cit.* p. 595.

fixed sum of money, even where he had no deposit with the bank. In each case, the bank credits the account of the customer involved with the agreed amount. By granting credit to customers, the bank has created deposits (or money).

Thus, the principal process by which the banking system creates deposits is the granting of loans and overdrafts. Every loan and overdraft approved by a bank creates a new deposit. Upon the granting of a bank facility, the customer can draw a cheque to effect a payment. Usually, the cheque will be paid to another bank account. After the cheque has been cleared, there is an increase in the total deposits in the banking system as a new deposit has been created.

Illustration

In Nigeria banks generally lend up to a maximum of 70% of their total deposits. The remaining 30% is held in liquid assets to meet depositors' demands for cash.

A practical example will show clearly how this process works:

Alpha Bank Ltd. grants a ₦10,000 overdraft to its customer Okoro to enable him to pay for some merchandise purchased from Ahmed & Sons, a wholesaler. Okoro writes a cheque for ₦10,000 and delivers the cheque to Ahmed & Sons, who pays the cheque into their account with Omega Bank Ltd. Omega Bank keeps 30% of the deposit (₦3,000) as reserves and proceeds to give out 70% (₦7,000) as loan to its customer Adebayo.

Adebayo issues his cheque for ₦7,000 to Toro Motors to pay for the cost of a new saloon car. Toro Motors pays the cheque into its current account with Premier Bank Ltd. Premier Bank also lends 70% of the deposit (₦4,900) to its customer Abass, who issues a cheque for this amount, thus creating another deposit within the banking system.

This process goes on and on and can be measured by the credit creation multiplier[9] which is calculated as follows:

$$\frac{\text{Total Amount of New Deposits Created}}{\text{Amount of Original Advance}}$$

[9] Based on the formula of David Cox *Success in Elements of Banking* John Murray, 1981 p. 18

In our example the multiplier can be calculated as follows:—

Original Loan .. .. ₦10,000   ₦

Cheque drawn and deposit created		—	10,000
Overdraft granted: 70% of	₦10,000	—	7,000
" " " "	7,000	—	4,900
" " " "	4,900	—	3,430
" " " "	3,430	—	2,401
" " " "	2,401	—	1,681
" " " "	1,681	—	1,176
" " " "	1,176	—	824
" " " "	824	—	576
" " " "	576	—	404
" " " "	404	—	282
" " " "	282	—	198
" " " "	198	—	138
" " " "	138	—	97
" " " "	97	—	68
" " " "	68	—	48
" " " "	48	—	33
" " " "	33	—	23
" " " "	23	—	16
" " " "	16	—	11
" " " "	11	—	8
" " " "	8	—	6
" " " "	6	—	4
" " " "	4	—	3 Approx.
" " " "	3	—	2 "
" " " "	2	—	1 "

TOTAL   33,330

Note: Assume that 30% of deposits is kept in the form of reserves.

$$\frac{\text{Total Amount of New Deposits Created}}{\text{Amount of Original Advance}} = \frac{₦33,330}{10,000} = 3.3$$

Thus the credit multiplier =   3.3

1-6 QUASI-MONEY OR NEAR MONEY

The question of a conclusive definition of money is still a matter of debate in modern economics. The debate stems from the fact that in defining money it was said that anything that serves as a medium of exchange can also serve as a store of value, but we have seen that the reverse is not the case. While many things can serve as a temporary store of value (e.g. time and savings deposits with banks and non-bank financial intermediaries, investments in Treasury Bills, stocks and shares, postal/money orders, etc), they may not qualify as a medium of exchange. These assets which adequately fulfil the function of store of value, but do not fulfil the medium of exchange function are called near money or *quasi-money*. While some economists argue that quasi-money should constitute part of the money stock, others argue that they should not be included because they do not perform the most important function of money — a medium of payment.

This controversy has led to two definitions of money. The *narrow* definition (M1) focusses attention on the means of payment functions, while the *broad* definition includes all assets which have some direct relationship with changes in spending in any given economy.

The bone of contention is that near-money, though not acceptable as a medium of exchange or final payment of debts, can nevertheless indirectly perform this function. For example, time and fixed deposits can be converted into money with little or no difficulty. Also, with the existence of stock exchanges, financial assets are highly liquid in that they can be easily traded in exchange for money.

Arising from the above debate, modern economists now distinguish at least two concepts of money[10]:

i) M1 (the narrow definition of money) defines money as the currency in circulation outside the banks plus private sector demand deposits in the banks.

ii) M2 (the broader definition of money) defines money as M1 plus time and savings deposits with commercial banks and non-bank financial institutions, such as the Federal Mortgage Bank, some finance houses and the Federal Savings Bank and investment in

[10] The wider definition of money is called M2 in Nigeria, and America, but is called M3 in Britain.

other financial assets such as government securities, Treasury Bills and Certificates, stocks and savings bonds, etc.

The first definition focusses attention on the medium of exchange function, while the broader definition which adds time deposits with banks focusses attention on the store of value function and the fact that these deposits are convertible instantly into a medium of exchange without any loss of time or value.

1-7 CHARACTERISTICS OF MONEY

For money to perform its functions satisfactorily, it must possess the following qualities:

i) General Acceptability. *"No commodity can successfully serve as money unless it is widely acceptable within the given community as money. This acceptability can derive from the customs of the people or the usage of trade."* [11] Thus, gold and silver become generally acceptable as money through custom and trade. However, the government can also impose acceptability by law, as in the case of paper notes issued by almost every country in the world today. The government of Nigeria changed the currency from pounds, shillings and pence to naira and kobo and gave it the force of law and this new currency became legal tender with general acceptability in January 1973.

ii) Durability. For anything to serve as money it must be durable. It must not be a living thing that can die or a thing that can break easily: it must be a thing that will last for a long time. This is why precious metals (i.e. silver and gold coins) have remained one of the best forms of money. However, they do lack other qualities (see iv below).

Notes can be destroyed by fire or mutilation. Book entries can not be destroyed, except the books in which they are recorded.

iii) Divisibility. It must be possible to sub-divide money into smaller units as payments have to be made in various amounts.

iv) Portability. Money must be easy and convenient to carry about. This is the quality that precious metals (silver and gold) and other

---

[11] G.O. Nwankwo *Basic Economics* Cambridge University Press 1977 p. 188

commodity monies lack. On the other hand, bank notes and bank deposits possess this quality in abundance.

v) Homogeneity. This means that one unit of money is identical to another unit of the same value and that one can be exchanged for the other: a 50k note is the same anywhere in Nigeria.

vi) Scarcity. To be generally acceptable, the supply of anything being used as money must be restricted. It must neither be too plentiful nor too scarce. Now that paper money is the order of the day, the supply is strictly controlled by the Central Bank.

REVIEW QUESTIONS

1.1 Discuss the qualities which anything should possess if it is to be used as money.

1.2 How do banks create money? What factors limit their ability to create money?

1.3 What are the disadvantages of the barter system?

1.4 Describe the main functions of money.

1.5 Define the following:
   i)   Near-money (or quasi-money)
   ii) Legal tender
   iii) The fiduciary issue.

CHAPTER TWO

THEORIES OF MONEY

2-1 INTRODUCTION

We have discussed the origin, functions, types and characteristics of money in Chapter One. In this Chapter we shall examine the significance of money in the economy. An attempt will be made to show the role of money in the economic system. It is now a known fact that money is causally related to the behaviour of employment, the rate of output, the level of prices and the distribution of national income. For example, during the 1930's, the world was faced with the problems of *deflation* and *depression,* climaxing in a decline in output, job opportunities and prices. Later a different situation was faced by the world — this time it was *inflation* (i.e. rising living costs). Since then many problems emanating from money have plagued the world from time to time. Money is so pervasive that we must neither under-estimate nor overestimate the influence of money and monetary policies on the functioning of any economic system.

2-2 THE THEORIES OF DEMAND FOR MONEY

Two special characteristics of money that set it apart from other goods include:

i) acceptability as a means of exchange for goods and services as its value is more predictable; and,

ii) relative liquidity: money is the most liquid of assets though some other assets possess liquidity to a certain degree.

Money is always readily acceptable in any transaction, so people prefer to hold money rather than any other wealth creating assets, despite the loss of income and value by holding money, because of the costs incurred in buying and selling earning assets and because the price of such assets is uncertain, as it is not always easy or possible to dispose of assets at will.

In micro-economic theory, a good is demanded because of the satisfaction or utility one derives from the particular good, but there is an exception to this general theory of demand. A separate demand theory for money has evolved due to the special characteristics mentioned above.

There are, however, divergent theories of the demand for money. While some focus attention on the transactionary demand for money and draw conclusions based on these motives, others focus attention on money as an *"excellent hedge against the risks inherent in holding other assets,"[1]* and on the basis of this draw their own conclusions and models. Yet others argue that there is no need for a separate theory of money, because there has not been any empirical evidence to show that money *per se* has no utility. To this group, money possesses psychological satisfaction, so has utility.

Resulting from these varying ideas of why people demand money, many approaches to the demand for money have evolved. However, three main developments can be discerned in the theory of the demand for money:

i) The Classical Quantity Theory of Money — the Classical School.

ii) The Keynesian Monetary Economics — the Keynesian School.

iii) The Modern Quantity Theory — the Monetarist School or the Chicago School.

2-2.1 The Classical Theory of the Demand for Money

As far back as the 17th century, it was observed that there was a connection between the quantity of money in circulation and the general level of prices. Hence, the formulation of the crude quantity theory of money. This stated that an increase in the quantity of money would lead to a proportionate rise in prices.

However, in 1920, Professor Irving Fisher reviewed this idea by introducing the concept of circulation. He argued that money circulates from hand to hand. For example, Mr A spends ₦1 to buy oranges from B, who uses the same ₦1 to buy kolanuts from Mr C and Mr C finally uses the money to buy bread from Mr A. The ₦1 in Fisher's example has been used for four separate transactions (i.e. ₦1 did the work of ₦4.00). He emphasised, therefore, the transactionary velocity of the circulation of money. He began his analysis with a simple identity that states that *"in every transaction there are both a buyer and a seller, and hence for the aggregate economy the value of sales must equal the value of receipts".[2]*

---

[1] Laidler D.E.W. *The Demand for Money* Harper & Row, 2nd Edition 1977 p. 53.
[2] *Ibid.* p. 44.

Translated into another form, the value of sales must be equal to the number of transactions undertaken over any time period multiplied by the average price at which they take place. On the other hand, the value of purchases must be equal to the amount of money in circulation in the economy times the average of times it changes hands over the same time period i.e.:

$$MV = PT$$

where
M = quantity of money
V = number of times it turns over (or its transaction velocity of circulation)
P = the price level
T = the volume of transactions

Though Irving Fisher's equation of exchange is a mere *identity* (i.e. it states the obvious), Fisher used this as a stepping-stone to other variations about the theory of the demand for money. He argued that the quantity of money was determined independently of any of the other three variables in the identity. T, the volume of transactions, and V, the velocity of circulation, were equally independent. P, the price level, was the only variable that depends upon the interaction of the other three.

If V and T were taken as constants, Fisher made the proposal that the price level was determined solely by, and was proportional to, the quantity of money.

Fisher's equation was criticised because some of its basic assumptions were regarded as simplistic (e.g. the assumption of full employment as the only equilibrium for the economy and the assumption that the demand for money was insensitive to the rate of interest).

2-2.2 Modification of the Traditional Quantity Theory of Money by the Cambridge School of Thought

The Cambridge School introduced the concept of the *opportunity cost of money* into the theory of the demand for money. While they did not disagree with Fisher's idea about transactions demand (i.e. medium of exchange), they added the idea that money could serve as a store of wealth. They argued that nobody would like to hold cash balances in excess of those needed for their immediate use, because there were some advantages to be derived from the alternatives (i.e. income yielding) which cash balances did not offer. This opportunity cost (or alternatives forgone) for holding money balances determines the distribution of wealth between idle cash balances and income earning assets, since sometimes these other assets might result in capital gains or losses.

Therefore, while the Cambridge School accepted the transactions demand for money, it added that the demand for money depended also on the level of income, the opportunity cost of holding money (i.e. the income foregone by not holding other assets) and finally on the price level.

Consequently, the Cambridge School formulated its own theory by saying that *"the demand for money would be proportional to the level of income for each individual and hence for the aggregate economy as well"[3]*. In simple terms, the Cambridge School looked at the problem of cash balances held by individuals in the economy from the point of view of the alternatives foregone (e.g. wealth, the rate of interest and the expectations about future events, etc). All these, it claimed, exerted some influence on one's decisions to hold money. Unlike Irving Fisher, there was no attempt to claim any fixed relationship between these variables.

From the foregoing, we can discern one significant difference between the Fisher proposition and the Cambridge proposition. Fisher propounded the idea that the rate of interest had no significant effect on the demand for money, while the Cambridge School regarded interest rate as one of the factors affecting the demand for money. However, they could not precisely say how the interest rate affected demand for money. (Their successors — the Keynesian School — were left to investigate the effect of interest rates on demand for money.)

On the whole, it can be said that the Classical School is primarily of historical interest, as few economists today subscribe to their theory. However, their ideas serve as a useful introduction to set in perspective the two views which are now most widely held — *Keynesianism* and *Monetarism*.

2-2.3 The Keynesian Theory of Demand for Money

J.M. Keynes in his *"General Theory of Employment, Interest and Money"* developed the Cambridge School of thought as far as the

---

[3] *Ibid.* p. 49.

problem of the demand for money is concerned and this in micro-economics is called *"Keynesian Monetary Theory"*.

Keynes went beyond the transaction motive which was the major focus of attention for his predecessors — Fisher and the Cambridge School. He, more than his predecessors, re-affirmed that the level of transactions undertaken by an individual and society as a whole had a stable relationship to the level of income. Consequently, he postulated that the transaction demand for money was proportional to the level of income (i.e. the transaction motive bridged the gap between receipts and planned regular payments). Apart from this gap-bridging, he added another motive — the *precautionary motive.* As far as he was concerned, those classes of payments that could not be regarded as regular and planned (e.g. payment of unexpected bills, making purchases at unexpectedly favourable price or meeting other emergencies that are caused by accidents or ill-health), would mean that people would consider it necessary to have some additional cash balances, because other assets are not instantly usable as money. As in the transaction motive the precautionary motive also depends, among other factors, upon the level of income.

Keynes added yet another factor to why people hold cash balances. This, he termed, the *speculative motive.* In order to speculate on the course of future events, companies and individuals like to hold money. If they think prices are very low now and perhaps will rise in future, there is the tendency to buy now and to sell when prices rise or vice versa. For the purpose of simplicity, Keynes chose as an example bonds, a financial asset which is a close substitute for money.

If the price of bonds is very high in relation to what people think is the normal price (i.e. the rate of interest is thought to be low), people will tend to sell bonds now and postpone intended purchases until prices have come down. In such a situation, large quantities of money may be held in anticipation of a more favourable chance to purchase bonds in future. On the other hand, if the price of bonds is very low in relation to what is thought to be normal price (i.e. the rate of interest is high), the tendency will be to buy bonds now and postpone sales until a more favourable price can be obtained. In this case, the tendency will be to hold as little cash as possible and hold bonds instead.

From the above illustration, we can see that while the transaction and precautionary motives focus on money's role as a medium of exchange, the speculative motive emphasises its role as a store of wealth.

Summarising the Keynesian theory of the demand for money, we can make two deductions:

i)   The demand for money varies directly with the level of income (i.e. the higher the level of income, the larger the amount of money held for transaction and precautionary purposes).

ii) The demand for money varies inversely with the rate of interest (i.e. the interest rate reflects the opportunity cost of holding money in idle balances). Thus, the higher the rate of interest, the higher the cost of holding money and hence the less money is held in idle balances. (This relationship between the demand for money and the rate of interest is often called the *liquidity preference* in economic theory.)

2-2.4 Modern Quantity Theory of the Chicago School

In the 1960's, there emerged a monetarist school (led by Professor Milton Friedman of the University of Chicago) which put forward a doctrine resembling the old quantity theory in some essentials, but which left out the simplistic assumptions made by that theory.

Friedman's contribution to monetary theory is precise, because it does not waste any time trying to explain the motives for holding money — rather he analysed the factors that determine how much money people will want to hold under various circumstances. However, the only essential difference between Keynesians and Monetarists lies in the notion of money being a close substitute for financial assets. Whereas the Keynesians hold the belief that money is a close substitute for financial assets because of the latter's relative liquidity, the monetarists argue that money is not a particularly close substitute for any specific range of assets.

Based on their belief, the Keynesians would expect that there was a close relationship between the demand for money and the yield (i.e. rate of interest) on money substitutes. On the other hand, the Monetarists would expect no significant relationship because of their belief that money is a substitute for all assets alike. Empirical evidence has, however, shown that there is a definite relationship between the demand for money and interest rate, although this is not as strong as the Keynesian theory suggests.

The issue of various definitional and conceptual problems of money has compounded the efficacy of the two extreme views so far as monetary policy is concerned. As a result of this, the empirical evidence on the demand for money can never be conclusive. The differences between the two extreme views of money will be reflected during our discussion on the role of monetary policy in the economy.

2-3 THE SUPPLY OF MONEY

The concept of money supply presents little difficulty unlike the concept of demand for money. The supply of money at any moment is the sum of all the money holdings of all members of the society. Put in another form, money supply can be defined as the stock or quantity of money the society wishes to hold at any time. This could be either M1 or M2 in Nigeria or M1, M3 in Britain. As we mentioned earlier, M1 (i.e. notes and coins issued by the Central Bank of Nigeria plus bank deposits held on current accounts and transferable by cheque) is used to define money supply in Nigeria. M2 (the broader definition of money) defines money as M1 plus time and savings deposits with banks and non-bank financial institutions like the Federal Mortgage Bank, the Federal Savings Bank, Finance Houses, etc, plus investments in other financial assets such as Treasury Bills, Treasury Certificates, stocks and savings bonds, etc. While M1 focusses attention on the medium of exchange function, M2 focusses attention on the store of value function. (M3 is not applicable to Nigeria: it is used in place of M2 in Britain.)

2-3.1 Factors that Determine Money Supply

There are two extreme views about the supply of money in the economy. On the one hand, some economists argue that money supply is determined by the credit policy of the monetary authorities. On the basis of this view, money supply is said to be exogenously determined and is independent of ups and downs in business activity in the economy. On the other hand, the view at the other extreme argues that money supply is determined by the happenings in the economy, especially by the level of business activity and rates of interest and is totally independent of the monetary authorities, In this case, money supply is said to be endogenously determined (i.e. the size of the money supply is not imposed from outside by monetary authorities, but is determined by what is happening within the economy).

In practice it is a combination of these factors that influence the supply of money. The supply of money is partly endogenous, because commercial banks can change the money supply in response to their own profit motives, by granting credits beyond the limits set by monetary authorities; and partly exogenous because the Central Bank sets limits beyond which commercial banks are unable to increase the money supply without incurring penalties.

Thus, in the Nigerian context, there are three major factors determining money supply. First, the monetary base — changes in the monetary base by the authorities account for a large part of the cyclical variations in the money stock. Second, and perhaps lesser in force, are the banks' ratio of reserves to deposits. The ratio falls when loan demand is strong and rises when loan demand is low. Third, the public's ratio of currency to deposits: during periods of business expansion there is a shift in money holdings from businesses to consumers. Since consumers typically have higher currency-to-deposit ratios than businesses, the aggregate currency-to-deposit ratio would rise. Thus, money balances of businesses would become relatively small and those of consumers relatively large.

REVIEW QUESTIONS

2.1 What are the motives for holding money?

2.2 Outline and explain the connection between the supply of money in Nigeria and the rate of inflation.

2.3 Write a short note on the determinants of the value of money.

2.4 State briefly the narrow and the broad definitions of the money supply as used by the CBN.

2.5 In Nigeria banks are the only financial institutions whose liabilities rank as money. Discuss.

CHAPTER THREE

MONETARY POLICY IN NIGERIA

3-1 INTRODUCTION

In Chapter Two we discussed the differences between the Keynesian and Monetarists on the importance of the money supply in economic policy. In this Chapter[1] we shall take a further look at its implications and the significance on monetary policy, beginning with the two extreme views of Keynesians and Monetarists.

The term monetary policy is defined as a *"policy which deals with the discretionary control of money supply by the monetary authorities in order to achieve stated or desired economic goals".*[2] But why do governments attempt to control the money supply? Because most governments believe that its rate of growth has something to do with the rate of inflation.

While the Keynesian view is that monetary policy should be directed at interest rates rather than money supply and that monetary policy should at all times be subsidiary to fiscal policy, the Monetarists recommend that control of money supply should be the major concern of the monetary authorities.

How will changes in interest rates affect economic activity? The Keynesian economist argues that since inflation is a sign of an economy overheating, a rise in interest rates will tend to cool it down by checking investment and, hence, overall demand. Conversely, in a period of recession, economic activities could be stimulated by lowering interest rates. Thus, the Keynesian economist argues that the level of activity is determined by the level of injections and withdrawals in the economic system (i.e. income and expenditure). The Keynesians assume that investment expenditures are influenced by changes in interest rates since capital formation results mainly through the issue of equities or through borrowing from banks and this is more attractive

---

[1] For the development of this Chapter, I am indebted to Chief S.B. Falegan, formerly Director of Research at the Central Bank of Nigeria and currently Managing Director of the Federal Mortgage Bank.

[2] S.B. Falegan; "Instruments of Monetary Policy: Their Application and Effectiveness in Nigeria". A paper presented at the symposium on "Role of Monetary Policy in Developing Countries" February 1978 at Banjul, Gambia.

when interest rates are lower. They argue that monetary policy will be more effective if the authorities aim to control interest rates directly rather than indirectly through the money supply.

Monetary policy to the Keynesians is not as crucial as fiscal policy, because, while fiscal policy has a direct impact on economic activity through government expenditure and taxation, monetary policy only affects economic activity indirectly by linking interest rates and investment.

The Monetarists view money as substitutes for all assets, financial or real. This assumption leads the Monetarists to conclude that an increase in the money supply directly brings about an increase in prices as a consequence of increased purchases of all types of goods and services. On the basis of this, the Monetarists conclude that the rapid fluctuations in the money supply are the cause of economic instability. The best policy, according to the Monetarists, is for the monetary authorities to aim at a steady and slow growth in the money supply. For example, they maintain that following the sharp rise in oil prices in the early 1970's, most governments allowed the money supply to rise proportionately, resulting in a worldwide inflation.

On the whole, the Keynesian versus Monetarists' debate gives conflicting advice to governments on the role and effectiveness of monetary policy. The Keynesians argue that the interest rate is the most important variable as a tool for the monetary authorities to control the economy, so they argue that monetary policy should be subsidiary to fiscal policy. On the other hand, the Monetarists argue that a steady growth in the money supply is the best policy to follow and that monetary policy directed to control of money supply is of paramount inportance.

The essence of citing and explaining these two views is to see how they have influenced the conduct of monetary policy in Nigeria since the inception of the Central Bank.

3-2 PHASES OF MONETARY POLICY IN NIGERIA

The major objectives of monetary policy in Nigeria since the inception of the Central Bank of Nigeria include:

i) The maintenance of relative stability in domestic prices.

ii) The maintenance of a healthy balance of payments.

iii) The acceleration of the pace of economic development.

Different phases of monetary policies have evolved since 1959, namely:

i)   Formative years and passive monetary policy (July 1959 - March 1962).

ii) Cheap money policy (April 1962 - September 1964).

iii) Credit restraint policy (October 1964 - October 1966).

iv) Monetary ease policy (November 1966 - June 1969).

v)   Moderate monetary restraint policy (July 1969 - March 1972).

vi) Monetary ease policy (April 1972 - March 1976).

vii) Monetary restraint policy (April 1976 - December 1981).

viii) Stringent monetary restraint policy (January 1982 to date).

Each of the above phases carried with it a particular set of instruments deemed fit by the Central Bank of Nigeria in order to attain the desired objective of the monetary authorities. The various instruments used include:

a) variable discount rates and interest rate structure;

b) variable liquid asset ratio;

c) moral suasion;

d) selective credit control;

e) cash ratio and cash reserve requirements;

f) special deposits; and,

g) exchange rate control.

3-2.1 Formative Years: July 1959 - March 1962

In this period, the major concern of the monetary authorities was the need for a strong local credit base and establishment of the domestic financial infrastructure such as the money and capital markets. During this period, the Nigerian Currency was launched (prior to this time Nigeria was part of the West African Currency Board System), the first money market instrument was introduced (the Treasury Bill), the Lagos Stock Exchange and bank clearing facilities were both established.

The most active instruments during this period were interest rates and moral suasion. The rediscount rate and the Treasury Bill rate were revised 10 and 13 times respectively between April 1960 and December 1961. The use of this instrument coupled with moral suasion was aimed at encouraging the commercial banks to repatriate short-term funds from London and hold them in Nigeria, in order to 'Nigerianise the credit base'. The periodic revision of the interest rates was designed to make the rates more favourable for banks to invest their short-term funds in Nigeria rather than in London Money Market.

The two instruments discussed above — variable rediscount rate and moral suasion — could be regarded as successful in that commercial banks' investments abroad declined, while their investments in Nigeria rose.

3-2.2 Cheap Money Policy: April 1962 – September 1964

During the second phase which coincided with the launching of the Second National Development Plan in 1962, the interest rate and variable liquid asset policies aimed to provide "cheap money" for development purposes.

During the same period there were institutional changes leading to the establishment of the Call Money Fund in July 1962. This provided an outlet for the investment of the commercial banks' surplus short-term funds. The issue of Treasury Bills became more regular on a weekly basis. The issue rate was reduced from 4½% to 4% and further to 3½%, in accordance with the reduction of the rediscount rate from 5¼% to 4½% and 4% respectively in 1963 and 1964. The result was an appreciable increase in credit to the economy by the banking system.

3-2.3 Credit Restraint Policy: October 1964 – October 1966

The aim of the monetary policy in this phase was to defend the balance of payments, as the cheap money policy of the second phase had led to a drain of the country's foreign reserves as a result of the increased demand for imports. In order to achieve this objective of restoring the balance of payments, credit restraint was adopted. The instruments used were direct credit control, interest rate, moral suasion and variable liquid assets. For example, a ceiling of a 15 percent annual growth rate was imposed on commercial bank lending. In addition, by moral suasion, commercial banks were enjoined to maintain restraint in granting loans to imports and consumption goods.

To strengthen further the policy of credit restraint and to discourage circumvention of the restriction on import finance by the commercial banks utilising their foreign assets, the share of their foreign assets that could be included in the calculation of their liquidity ratio was reduced from 7½% to 3%. In addition, the minimum rediscount rate was raised from 4% to 5% in 1965, while other rates went up accordingly. For example, the Treasury Bills issue rate was increased from 3½% to 4½%, while minimum lending rates moved from 7% to 7½% and maximum deposit rates raised from 3% to 4%.

The results of the policy adopted during this phase were a reduction in domestic credit, a reduction of import demand and an improvement in the balance of payments position which moved from a deficit of ₦62.0 million to a surplus of ₦23.9 million.

However, while trying to restrain import demand, the domestic price level began to rise. Also, as a result of the adverse balance on the services accounts, which more than offset the favourable balance of trade account, the credit restraint policy was slightly modified.

The social and political disturbances that erupted in 1966 brought signs of recession as a result of lack of confidence in the economy and consequent flight of capital from the economy. There was a greater need for credit by the government to finance the shortfall in revenue and the deepening of the disturbance caused considerable disruption in the patterns of domestic transportation and communication, while the in-flow of foreign capital fell drastically.

3-2.4 Monetary Ease Policy: November 1966 – June 1969

The social and political disturbances continued into the third quarter of 1966 and this worsened the state of the economy. The government was forced to change its monetary policy, because of the continuing recessional trends. There was a need to stimulate economic activity. Thus, monetary policy during this period focussed on the use of interest rates and moral suasion. The credit ceiling was relaxed, but banks were persuaded to continue to maintain some restraint in financing non-essential imports, especially consumption goods and to extend their credit to the more productive sectors of the economy (mainly agriculture, manufacturing, real estate and construction, transportation and communication).

In May 1968, the rediscount rate was lowered from 5% to 4½% and other rates were reduced by a half percentage point. The action was to facilitate the anticipated increase in government borrowing. The effect of the above action was an increase in bank credit mainly because of increased government borrowing. However, due to the substantial deficit in government financing and the disruption in economic activity, an inflationary trend set in.

3-2.5 Moderate Monetary Restraint Policy: July 1969 – March 1972

The major economic problem during this period was to increase domestic production in order to meet the expected increase in demand for goods as the war was coming to an end. By increasing production it was hoped that inflation would come down. Thus, it was recognised that the continued policy of credit ease would aggravate the inflationary trend. Selective credit control, moral suasion and a partial upward revision of interest rates were the instruments used to carry out the monetary policy of this period.

The outcome of the selective credit control was that the share of the less-preferred sectors (especially consumption and imports) fell, while the share of the preferred sectors rose. At the same time, government finances improved, especially as spending on war reconstruction had reduced. During the same period, there was a substantial overall budget surplus for the first time since 1960. Also, due to increased domestic production, the pressure on the balance of payments had eased and an appreciable increase was made in the external reserves of the country.

3-2.6 Monetary Ease Policy: April 1972 – March 1976

Expansion of domestic production was the major economic issue, while countering inflation was another major concern of the government. Sectoral credit allocation was the instrument used, although interest rates and exchange rate measures were introduced later during the period. The improved foregin reserves and government finance resulting from earnings from oil led to rapid increases in the money supply and excess liquidity in the economy. This was followed by an increased demand for consumer goods. These developments resulted, therefore, in the introduction of changes in interest rates and the exchange rate. The change in exchange rate meant severing the attachment of the Nigerian currency to the U.S. dollar and allowing it to appreciate against the dollar and sterling according to the relative strength of the two. The wage increases in 1975, coupled with increases in government expenditure led to large increases in bank credit, money supply and the demand for consumer goods and consequently in the inflation rate. There was, therefore, a need for change in monetary policy. Stabilisation Securities and the Bankers' Unit Fund were introduced by the CBN to mop up excess liquidity in the economy.

3-2.7 Moderate Restraint Policy: April 1976 — December 1981

The policy during this period was the reduction of the excess liquidity of the banks. A combination of instruments were used: direct credit ceiling, cash reserve requirements, stabilisation securities, exclusion of deposits against letters of credit from eligible liquid assets and interest rate changes.

3-2.8 Stringent Monetary Restraint Policy: 1981 to 1982

The current policy is geared towards conservation of our foreign reserves. Measures taken to slow down the amount of foreign exchange disbursements include the re-introduction of pre-shipment inspection of raw materials and spare parts, the re-introduction of pre-import deposits ranging from 10% to 250%, an outright ban on a variety of commodities and increases in import duties on others and reductions of travel allowances etc. In addition, interest rates were raised by 1% across the board. Banks were required to turn over all pre-import deposits to the CBN. There has been a noticeable recession in the economy and banks are compelled to curb credit expansion due to tight liquidity.

3-2.9 Conclusion

Tight money policy was followed by easy money policy and so on from one period to the other. Credit control (through the credit ceiling and interest rates) was the most prominent instrument. The policies succeeded in varying degrees, depending upon the co-operation of the banks and government. The use of the annually-determined credit guidelines have continued to be the major instrument of monetary control. (These are discussed later in the book.)

Finally, unlike the two extreme views of Keynes and Friedman, the monetary authorities relied on both control of money supply in the economy and the use of interest rates and at all times monetary policies were complemented by fiscal policies in order to stabilise the economy.

REVIEW QUESTIONS

3.1 Assess the efficacy of the various instruments and controls used by the CBN to implement monetary policy.

3.2 What are the objectives of monetary policy? Is it possible to achieve all of them simultaneously?

3.3 Outline the monetary policy pursued by Nigeria during the past 5 years.

CHAPTER FOUR

THE EVOLUTION OF THE MONEY SYSTEM IN NIGERIA

4-1 INTRODUCTION

Before the arrival of Arab and European (Portuguese) traders in Nigeria in the 18th century, trade within the country was carried on by barter, so items like coral beads, ivory, ornaments and cowries were commonly in use as money. The Portuguese — the first Europeans to visit West Africa — popularised the use of cowry and the manilla in their trading activities in the ancient Kingdom of Benin. These two monetary instruments were first introduced into West Africa by Arab traders from North Africa from 1870. The Portuguese monopoly of trade in West Africa was broken by the British who arrived a few years later.

The extension of European trading enterprises and British rule into West Africa encouraged the use of currency which greatly facilitated exchange and diminished the use of barter. This process was further accelerated by the introduction of banking, with the opening of the African Banking Corporation in 1892, the forerunner of the Bank of British West Africa which took over its assets in 1894. The process of monetising the economy was carried a stage further by the unification of the currency system in West Africa in 1912. The West African Currency Board introduced the West African Pound to replace the varieties of circulating media of exchange in these territories.

4-2 EARLY CURRENCY SYSTEM

There was no monetary system in Nigeria before 1912 when the West African Currency Board (WACB) was established. What existed prior to that time was a "mixed barter-money" economy. At first, the West African Currency Board used United Kingdom silver coins, but later the Board minted its own coins for circulation in all four British territories in West Africa. The West African currency notes were issued in 1916 to augment the silver coins which were in short supply during the First World War. Initially, the notes did not form part of the reserve money. The notes and coins were tied to sterling and were easily convertible to sterling.

Prior to the introduction of this rudimentary monetary system, the pattern of commercial and economic activities carried out were mainly among Africans on the one hand and between Europeans and Africans on the other. The African to African trading activities were mainly by barter, while commodity money was commonly used in trade between Africans and Europeans/Arabs. Commodity money used included coral beads, cowries, manillas, brass and copper rods, bottles, cases of gin, livestock and slaves who served more as beast of burden.

The later decades of the 19th century saw the use of foreign coins alongside the native currencies, among these were the eagle and doubloon of USA which circulated freely in Lagos in 1891 and the Maria Theresa dollars, an Australian coin, which circulated freely in Northern Nigeria.

4-3 WEST AFRICAN CURRENCY BOARD

4-3.1 Origin

The eventual successful introduction of the British currency saw West Africa absorbing about 25% of Royal Mint output. By 1886, total British silver coins amounted to £550 (₦1,100), but averaged £24,500 (₦49,000) per annum between 1886 and 1890. The above situation resulted in a pressure from West African Colonial Governments demanding among other things:

i) A share of *seigniorage* (i.e. a form of royalty to West African governments for the issue of British coins to West African territories).

ii) Replacement of the British silver coin by a West African issued coin.

iii) Establishment of banks in the area.

Responding to the above pressure, Rt. Hon. Joseph Chamberlain, the then UK Secretary of State for the Colonies, set up the Barbour Committee to investigate the desirability of the first and second claims enumerated above. The Barbour Committee recommended that the British silver coins should continue to circulate in West Africa, while the UK Treasury should undertake to pay 50 percent of the seigniorage to the Colonial dependencies. This recommendation was rejected as the Treasury was not ready to undertake to share the seigniorage.

The African Banking Corporation enjoyed the monopoly of distributing British silver coins between 1891 and 1893. This monopoly was transferred to the Bank of British West Africa (BBWA) in 1894. It enjoyed this till 1911 when the Secretary of State for the Colonies set up the Lord Emmott Committee to report on the desirability of introducing a West African silver coinage and joint issue of the currency in British West African Countries (i.e. Nigeria, Ghana, Sierra Leone and the Gambia).

The Committee recommended that:

i) A Currency Board be set up in London to buy bullion and mint coins to be issued on face value on behalf of British West African territories.

ii) Seigniorage derived to be accumulated in a fund set up to guarantee the convertibility of the new currency.

The above recommendation gave birth in 1912 to the West African Currency Board (WACB). This implied the repatriation of the British currencies to West Africa. A year later (1913), special silver coins common to the four countries were introduced in denominations of 3d, 6d, 1/- and 2/- with the proclamation of the required legislation on 26th June of that year.

It was discovered at that time that the natives did not like paper money. However, in 1920 when the silver coin was replaced with an alloy of little intrinsic value, the problem of aversion to paper money appeared to be solved.

4-3.2 Operations

The West African Currency Board (WACB) was not designed to be a Monetary Authority (i.e. it was not designed to exercise discretionary control over the money stock). Its essence was convertibility of West African Currency on demand into sterling. The currency it issued was only in exchange for sterling. Thus, the WACB was only a passive money exchanger. The issue and redemption was automatic, so the reduction or increase of the money supply was strictly determined by the balance of payments. The WACB was not initially allowed to hold government securities, but later was allowed to do so.

Although the WACB was allowed to distribute its income among the four countries, in practice all its income was kept in a Currency Reserve Fund in London. WACB throughout its life span maintained a policy of keeping the reserve fund at a level greater than the currency in circulation.

4-3.3 Advantages and Shortcomings

From the operations of the West African Currency Board (WACB), the following advantages could be identified:

i) it provided a unified system that commanded confidence;

ii) it relieved the colonial government of the problem of currency management; and,

iii) it eliminated the danger of locally created inflation or foreign exchange crises.

However, the following shortcomings could also be noted:

i) It did not provide the required flexibility and elasticity required of a currency that could serve developing countries.

ii) It was not designed to, and hence did not, train Africans in the art of money management.

iii) The idea of over 100% sterling backing stipulated for the issue of local currency turned the Board into a mere cloakroom where output is always equal to input.

iv) The issuing of the same currency for four different territories was self-defeating as the countries moved steadily towards self-government.

As more and more of the West African Countries gained independence, it became inperative that nothing short of a Central Bank for each country's monetary and financial development was needed.

REVIEW QUESTIONS

4.1 Trace the development of money in Nigeria from commodity money in the 18th century to the present day bank note.

4.2 Write short notes on:

i) The West African Currency Board,

ii) Seigniorage.

4.3 Compare the functions of the West African Currency Board with that of the Central Bank of Nigeria.

PART II

THE BANKING SYSTEM

CHAPTER FIVE

CENTRAL BANKING

5-1 THE ESTABLISHMENT AND GROWTH OF THE CENTRAL BANKING OF NIGERIA (CBN)

The banking failures of the early 1950's led to the power of control of banking being vested in the Financial Secretary. This triggered off two opposing camps. The Nationalists who were of the view that a Central Bank was needed to perform this and other traditional Central Banking functions; and the Colonials who believed that it was premature to introduce a Central Bank in a country where there was no financial system. To resolve the opposing views, a total of three studies were commissioned:

i) J.L. Fisher's Report, 1953.

ii) I.B.R.D. Mission Report, 1955.

iii) J.B. Loyne's Report, 1957.

Fisher based his study on orthodox banking principles and reported that it was not feasible to establish a Central Bank on the grounds that the financial environment did not exist and that it would be impossible to find the local staff to man it. He also contended that the West African Currency Board was equal to the task of promoting savings and capital formation.

As an alternative, Fisher recommended:

i)   The formation of a development corporation by the government.

ii) The issue of Treasury Bills.

iii) Establishment of an institution by government to lend to co-operative societies.

iv) The use of Post Office Savings for development purposes.

He also recommended a three step programme leading to the development of a Central Bank:

i)   Transfer of the operation of WACB to Africa so that its management would eventually be indigenised after the local people have acquired the necessary experience.

ii) Establishment of a Nigerian Currency Board and a separate Nigerian currency to take over Nigeria's share of WACB assets.

iii) Establishment of a Bank of Issue as the embryo of a future Central Bank.[1]

As was expected, Fisher's recommendations were supported in 1955 by the World Bank Mission. However, the IBRD Mission recommended a State Bank of Nigeria to take over the banking control functions of the Financial Secretary.

Contrary to the above two reports, that of J.B. Loynes in 1957 favoured the establishment of a Central Bank in Nigeria and by 17th March 1958 the CBN Ordinance was promulgated and became fully operational on the 1st July 1959.

The main provisions of the Act so far as the Central Bank of Nigeria was concerned were:

i)   Issuance of legal tender currency in Nigeria.

ii) Maintenance of external reserves in order to safeguard the internal value of the currency.

iii) Promotion of monetary stability and a sound financial structure.

iv) Banker to other banks in Nigeria and abroad.[2]

The functions of the Central Bank will be discussed later in this book.

5-2 WHAT IS A CENTRAL BANK?

A Central Bank stands at the apex of the banking system of every country. It is the government representative in the banking sector and acts mainly as banker to the government. It has a very close association with both the government and the banking sector of the economy, advising the government on monetary policy and implementing the policy on behalf of the government.

---

[1] J.L. Fisher's *Report on the Desirability and Practicability of Establishing a Central Bank in Nigeria for Promoting the Economic Development of theCountry* Government Printer, Lagos, Nigeria 1953 p. 17

[2] See Central Bank of Nigeria Act, 1959 (cap 30) (as amended 1962-69) paragraph 4 p. 6 and paragraph 83 p. 24

The main differences between the Central Bank and a commerical bank can be summarised as follows:

i) The maximisation of profits is one of the main objectives of a commercial bank, but a Central Bank does not aim to maximise profits.

ii) Commercial Banks serve as bankers to their customers, while the Central Bank serves as banker to commercial banks, acting as lender of last resort to the banking system.

iii) Apart from serving as banker to commercial banks, the Central Bank has a supervisory role over the commercial banks and other financial institutions.

iv) By virtue of the statutory powers delegated to the Central Bank by the government, it controls the actions of the banks and other financial institutions, particularly with regard to lending.

v) The control and issue of currency notes and coins are vested in the Central Bank, thus giving it the power to regulate the supply of money.

iv) In view of its privileged position the Central Bank does not normally compete for business with the commerical banks. Apart from the Federal and State Government accounts which are usually maintained by it, the Central Bank of Nigeria does not provide banking service for personal and commercial customers which is the main business of commercial and merchant banks.

5-3 STRUCTURE OF CENTRAL BANK BALANCE SHEET

5-3.1 Introduction

The Central Bank of Nigeria issues a monthly Return of Assets and Liabilities of the Bank. The Return as at close of business on 30th July 1982 is shown in Table 5-1 overleaf.

Table 5-1

Central Bank of Nigeria

Return of Assets and Liabilities as at the Close of Business on 30th July 1982

Liabilities	₦	₦
Capital Subscribed and Paid up	3,000,000	
General Reserve	88,000,000	
Currency in Circulation		4,228,397,619
Deposits:		
Federal and State Governments	1,140,310,989	
Bankers	756,650,600	
Others	1,022,738,706	
		2,919,700,295
Other Liabilities		1,819,074,681
		9,058,172,595

Assets	₦	₦
Gold		19,009,430
Convertible Currencies:		
Foreign Government Securities and Balances with Foreign Banks	821,504,696	
I.M.F. Gold Tranche	–	
Special Drawing Rights	–	
Total External Reserve		840,514,126
Federal Government Securities		4,825,583,294
Other Securities		289,905,655
Rediscounts and Advances		2,681,603,821
Other Assets		420,565,699
		9,058,172,595

Source: Central Bank of Nigeria.

5-3.2 Assets

i) Gold. This is the value of the gold bars held in the Bank's vault in Lagos as at the date of the balance sheet (₦19,009,430).

ii) Foreign Government Securities and Balances with Foreign Banks (₦821,504,696). This includes the Bank's total investments in foreign government securities like Treasury Bills, Treasury Certificates, other foreign bonds and stocks, and balances held in convertible foreign currencies on time deposits and current accounts. These are used mainly as working balances for international trade payments.

iii) I.M.F. Gold Tranche and Special Drawing Rights. Balances held on these two accounts are Nigeria's contribution in convertible currencies to the International Monetary Fund. Countries with temporary balance of payments problems are allowed to withdraw their contributions. Nigeria is presently going through such problems: hence, the two accounts have been completely drawn down. The sum of the balances held as gold and convertible currencies equals the total external reserve held by the Bank on behalf of the Federal Government of Nigeria.

iv) Federal Government Securities. On the date of the Return, the Bank's holding of Ferderal Government securities amounted to ₦4,825,583,294. Government securities are of two categories: short-dated securities like Treasury Bills, Treasury Certificates and government stocks with maturities ranging from 2 years to 25 years or over. The holdings of the Bank include those securities purchased as 'buyer of last resort' of stocks not absorbed by the capital market.

v) Other Securities (₦289,905,665). This is the value of the Bank's other investments especially in development banks like the Nigerian Industrial Development Bank, the Nigerian Bank for Commerce and Industries and the Nigerian Agricultural and Cooperative Bank.

vi) Rediscounts and Advances (₦2,681,603,821). These include temporary loans and advances made to the Federal Government as Ways and Means Advances, loans to Commodity Boards, advances granted to banks and discount houses in its role as 'lender of last resort'and the rediscount of government and commercial bills, etc.

vii)Other Assets. Items under other assets include premises, equipment and other miscellaneous assets.

5-3.3 Liabilities

i) Capital. The bank's authorised and paid-up capital which was originally fixed at £1.5m (₦3 million) has remained at that level since 1959. It is held by the Federal Government.

ii) General Reserve. The General Reserve has steadily grown to the present level of ₦88 million from a Nil balance at the inception of the Bank in 1959. The balance will continue to increase every year by 1/16th of the net profit made at the end of each financial year. (The CBN Act provided that the Bank should maintain a General Reserve Fund. Each year 1/8th of the net profit of the bank was allocated to the fund until it was equal to the paid-up capital. Thereafter 1/16th of the net profits of the year was allocated to the fund.)

iii) Currency in circulation (₦4,228,397,619). One of the main liabilities of the Bank is the currency in circulation (i.e. notes and coins issued by the Bank).

iv) Deposits (₦2,919,700,295). Balances held on deposits by Federal and State governments, banks, corporations and parastatals also form a major item of liability. Deposits by banks include compulsory deposits required for the maintenance of the statutory cash ratio, deposits required as cover for Letters of Credits, etc. and working balances on banks' accounts.

v) Other Liabilities. Items under Other Liabilities include provision for taxation, accrued interest, provision for currency fluctuations and allocation of Special Drawing Rights, etc.

REVIEW QUESTIONS

5.1 What were the foundations for Central Banking in Nigeria?

5.2 Outline the main similarities and differences between a commercial bank and the Central Bank of Nigeria.·

5.3 Write short notes on:

    i) Reserve ratios of banks in Nigeria.

    ii) Lender of last resort.

5.4 What are the major differences between the Balance Sheet of the CBN and that of a typical commerical bank?

5.5 How does central banking in Nigeria resemble or differ from central banking in the United States of America?

CHAPTER SIX

THE FUNCTIONS OF THE CENTRAL BANK OF NIGERIA

6-1 BANKING FUNCTIONS

6-1.1 Introduction

The main banking functions of the Central Bank include:

i)   Currency Issue;

ii) Banker and Adviser to Government; and,

iii) Banker to, and Supervisor of, Commercial/Merchant Banks and other Financial Institutions.

These functions, which are discussed in detail in the following pages, are performed by various specialised departments working under the overall control of the Board of Directors. The Board comprises of the Governor of the Bank as Chairman, the Deputy Governor, three Executive Directors and eight other Directors, all of whom are appointed by the Federal Government for five years (in the case of the Governor, his Deputy and three Executive Directors) and three years (for the other Directors). (A detailed organisation chart for the Central Bank of Nigeria is shown overleaf.)

6-1.2 Issuing of Currency

The Central Bank of Nigeria has the monopoly of the note issue in Nigeria. The first truly Nigerian currency was issued on 1st July 1959, the day the Central Bank was officialy opened. At that time the W.A.C.B. notes were withdrawn from circulation.

Further issues were made in 1965, 1968 and 1973. When Nigeria became a Republic in 1963, it was decided that the existing Federation of Nigeria notes be replaced. A total of ₦137m was redeemed between 1st July 1965 and June 1966.

The Nigerian Currency was again changed in 1968 during the period of the Nigerian Civil War. The Central Bank (Currency Conversion) Decree No. 51 was promulgated on 30th December 1967 aimed at achieving three objectives:

Table 6 - 1

Organisation Chart of the Central Bank of Nigeria

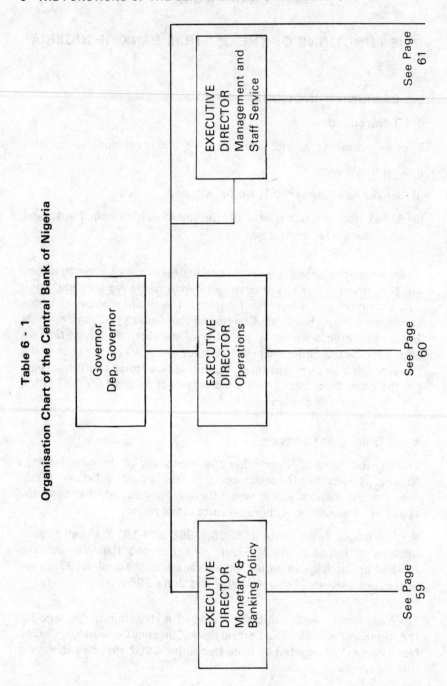

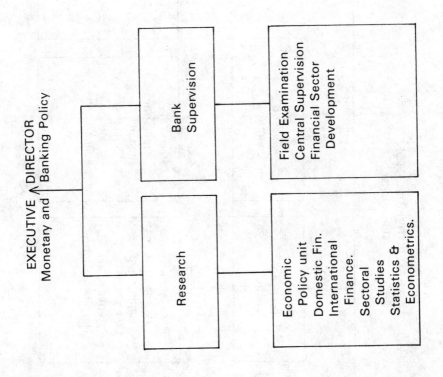

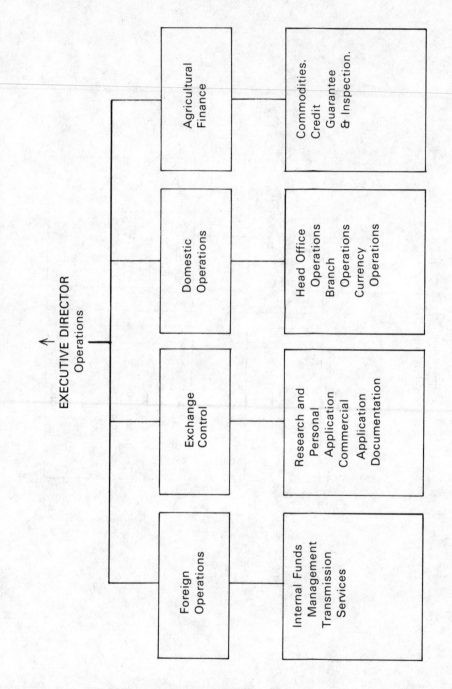

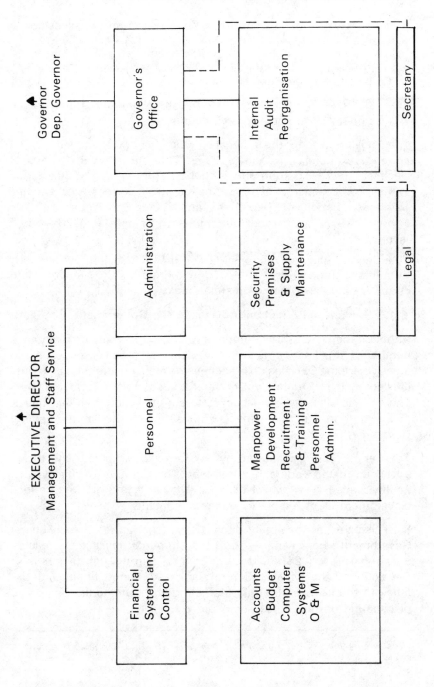

i) To ensure the success of the trade embargo on the secessionist areas.

ii) To forestall the use of mint notes stolen from CBN vaults in Enugu, Port Harcourt and Benin.

iii) To frustrate the illegal trafficking in the Nigerian currency which was going on in some foreign countries.[1]

The decision to adopt the decimal currency system resulted in another currency exchange in January 1973. This started with 2 units of decimal coins — 5 kobo and 10 kobo — introduced in July 1972, while the full exchange of new notes for the old currency was effected in 4 denominations of 50k, ₦1, ₦5, and ₦10 on 2nd January 1973. In February 1976, the largest denomination of note — ₦20 — was issued.

The Central Bank is responsible for the distribution of currency throughout the country. This is done through CBN branches and currency centres to the commercial banks.

6-1.3 Banker and Financial Adviser to the Government

Although the Federal Government and State Governments maintain a number of small accounts with the commercial banks, especially in areas where the CBN has no branches, the main government accounts are kept with the Central Bank of Nigeria, Lagos and its State branches. The CBN is also the main banker to statutory corporations, quasi-government institutions, especially those established by the Federal Government.

The Central Bank is required by law to make temporary short-term advances to the Federal Government. The granting of this type of facility, called *Ways and Means Advances,* is to assist the Federal Government meet temporary budgetary deficits.

It is also the responsibility of the Bank to arrange all the Federal Government's borrowing — short-term through the issue of Treasury Bills and Treasury Certificates and longer-term through the issue of Development Stocks. (The Central Bank also renders financial assistance to the various statutory Marketing and Commodity Boards by discounting of their bills.)

---

[1] See *Twenty years of Central Banking in Nigeria: 1959-79.* Research Department, C.B.N. p.78

The Bank has, therefore, to advise the government on the terms of issue of government debt instruments and the state of the Money and Capital Markets, as well as contributing to the preparation ,of the Federal Government Budget.

Apart from managing the internal public debt, the Central Bank also manages the external debt of the country. The Central Bank's role includes the collection of proceeds from investors and the prompt repayment of such loans as they fall due.

6-1.4 Banker to, and Supervisor of, Banks and Other Financial Institutions

The Central Bank of Nigeria acts as banker to the commercial banks, merchant banks, development banks and other financial institutions. Every bank in Nigeria keeps an account with the Central Bank. Strictly speaking, this is not a statutory requirement, but rather a necessity, as no bank can operate successfully without having some business relationship with other banks. Such business transactions invariably result in one form of inter-bank settlement or the other, so are best handled through the Central Bank.

As the Central Bank stands at the apex of the banking system in Nigeria, it shoulders the statutory responsibility for promoting a sound financial structure and ensuring that the operations of banks and other financial institutions are kept within the provisions of the law. The Banking Act, 1969, as amended in 1979, and the series of Monetary Policy Circulars issued by the Central Bank at the beginning of each government fiscal year, contain a number of regulations and directives for banking operations in the country. Some of the areas covered include liquidity ratios, interest rate structure and sectoral allocations of loans and advances. These will be discussed in more detail later in this book.

The Banking Supervision Department of the Central Bank pays periodic visits to all banks to examine and scrutinise their books, in order to ensure that banking regulations are not contravened. The banks themselves are also required to render bi-monthly, monthly and annual returns to the Central Bank. These include a Monthly Statement of Assets and Liabilities (First Schedule), a Monthly Report on Loans and Advances (Second Schedule), the Annual Audited Accounts -

Balance Sheet and Profit & Loss (Third Schedule), the Auditors' Report (Fourth Schedule) and the Auditors' Analysis of Doubtful Advances (Fifth Schedule).

In turn, the Central Bank is obliged to provide a cheap and efficient clearing facility and outlets for the investment of banks' temporary surplus funds.

As the lender of the last resort, the Central Bank is prepared to lend to banks by granting them short-term direct advances or through rediscounting eligible bills presented by them.

6-2 MONETARY FUNCTIONS

6-2.1 Introduction

The Central Bank of Nigeria has a primary responsibility for formulating monetary policy. The Central Bank's monetary policy proposals, after they have been reviewed and accepted by the Federal Government, are normally incorporated into the Federal Government budget each year. A few days after the budget has been released, the Central Bank of Nigeria issues a Monetary Policy Circular which spells out the revised monetary regulations in detail. (The most recent Monetary Policy Circular — No. 16: Central Bank Credit Guidelines for 1983 Fiscal Year — is examined later in this Chapter.)

At present, the Central Bank attempts to use six instruments of monetary policy to control the banks in Nigeria. These are:

i) open market operations;

ii) discount rate system;

iii) direct regulation of interest rates;

iv) moral suasion;

v) reserve requirements; and,

vi) direct control.

Each of these instruments will now be considered in detail.

6-2.2 Open Market Operations

Open market operations mean the buying and selling of short and long-term government securities in the money market and capital market by the Central Bank of Nigeria in order to increase or restrict bank lending. When the Central Bank buys securities on the market, payments are made to individuals and companies from whom they have been purchased. When the payment cheques issued by the CBN are credited to the sellers' accounts in various commercial banks, additional deposits are made in the banking system and the banks are then in a position to create more money by increasing their lending. On the other hand, when the CBN sells securities in the market the following will be the result: the buyers issue their cheques which are debited to their various accounts with commercial or merchant banks, thus reducing the deposit base of these banks. As a result, the banks will be compelled to reduce their lending. Open market operations can be conducted both on the money market (for short-term securities like Treasury Bills and Treasury Certificates) and on the capital market (for long dated government stocks). These operations also help the monetary authorities influence rates and/or maintain stability on the market.

At this juncture, it is pertinent to mention that a precondition for the successful application of this instrument of monetary policy is the existence of well-developed money and capital markets. We do not presently have this in Nigeria. In practice, therefore, the CBN cannot effectively use this instrument. For instance, interest rate movements are strictly controlled by the monetary authorities, so they are not responsive to market forces.

In the light of this problem, this instrument has never been used by the Central Bank due to non-existence of highly developed money and capital markets. Other more direct control systems which will accelerate the rate of economic development and growth, while at the same time sustaining monetary stability and more commonly used.

6-2.3 Discount Rate System — Lender of Last Resort

As the lender of last resort, the Central Bank is prepared to lend to banks by granting them short-term direct advances or by re-discounting eligible bills presented by them. However, in performing this function, the Central Bank has to take full consideration of the economic condition of the country. Thus, the rate at which the Central Bank will lend to a commercial bank depends on the prevailing economic policy at the time. At the beginning of each financial year, the Central Bank fixes a minimum rediscount rate. This is usually a penal rate as banks are expected to use it only as a last resort. Furthermore, such borrowings by banks must be adequately secured by Treasury Bills or other government stocks. It is to be noted that all interest rates are pegged to this Discount Rate.

In developed economies, this is a very effective instrument of monetary control. An increase in the rate is a signal for a credit squeeze, while a decrease gives the opposite indication. Again, due to the lack of developed money and capital markets, the discount rate policy has not been sufficiently effective in Nigeria and has been used sparingly. Moreover, owing to the high returns on investments in Nigeria, a rise or fall in interest rates has little or no impact on borrowers.

6-2.4 Direct Regulation of Interest Rates

Unlike the economies of developed countries where interest rates are only indirectly influenced by official policy action, the interest rate structure in Nigeria is directly controlled and managed by the Central Bank. Every year the Central Bank fixes the ranges within which both the deposit and the lending rates are to be maintained. The rates are controlled for three reasons:

i) to promote orderly growth of the financial markets;

ii) to combat inflation;

iii) to lessen the burden of internal debt servicing on the government.

6-2.5 Interest Rate Structure 1983 (January)

The interest rates (deposits and lending) as at January, 1983 were:

	per cent
Minimum Re-discount Rate	8
Treasury Bill Issue Rate	7
Treasury Certificate (1 year)	7½
Treasury Certificate (2 years)	8
Federal Government Stock	9–9¾
4–7 Years maturity	9
9–14 '' ''	9¼
15–20 '' ''	9½
21–25 '' ''	9¾

Deposit Rates:

Commercial Banks' Savings Deposit	7½
Time Deposit with 7 days notice	6½
" " for one month	7
" " for 1–3 months	7¼
" " for 3–6 months	7½
" " for 6–12 months	7¾
" " for 12 months	8

Lending Rates:

Minimum	9½
Maximum	13
Preferred Sectors Maximum	11½
Less-preferred Sectors Maximum	13
Agricultural Credit Guarantee Scheme	6–7
Residential Housing costing not more than ₦100,000	
Agricultural production	7

Specialised Institutions:

Federal Savings Bank — Savings Deposit Rate	7½
Nig. Ind. Dev. Bank (Lending Rates)	10½–13
Nig. Bank for Commerce and Ind. (Lending Rates)	10½–13

Nig. Agricultural & Cooperative Bank:

Lending Rates for Agric. Production	6–7
" " " Commodities Marketing	10–13

Federal Mortgage Bank:

Savings Rate	7½–8½
Lending Rates:	7–13
Residential Housing	7
Commercial Property	9½–13

Source: Central Bank of Nigeria

6-2.6 Moral Suasion

This is an instrument frequently used by the Central Bank of Nigeria. The Governor of the Central Bank tries, in a friendly manner, to persuade banks to reduce their lending activities when there is need for such restraint. Banks generally co-operate realising that the Central Bank has wide statutory powers to regulate the banking system. Moral suasion has been found to be a very effective instrument of monetary control.

6-2.7 Reserve Requirements

In Nigeria all banks are required to maintain two major reserve ratios: a *cash ratio* and liquid assets reserves otherwise known as a *liquidity ratio*.

i) The Cash Ratio

Each commercial bank maintains a minimum amount of cash deposits with the CBN Banking Office, Lagos. The cash deposit is expressed as a ratio of each bank's total demand deposit liabilities. For this purpose, banks are grouped into four classes, based on the amount of total deposit liabilities. The classes and the new minimum ratio of cash to demand deposits which the commercial banks are required to maintain with the CBN in 1982 were:

Class	Total Deposit Liabilities	Ratio of Cash to Demand Deposit (Per Cent)
A	₦300 million or more	5.0
B	₦100 million or more, but less than ₦300 million	4.0
C	₦30 million or more, but less than ₦100 million	3.0
D	Less than ₦30 million	2.0

This discriminatory pattern is to ensure that large and small banks feel the impact of the scheme equally.

ii) Liquidity Ratio

All banks are required to maintain a minimum of 25% of their deposits in cash or approved securities. Apart from this statutory requirement, a bank must retain in liquid, or readily realisable form, sufficient funds to meet an abnormal or unforeseen demand by depositors for the repayment of their deposits. Hence, apart from protecting the depositors, it is also an effective instrument of monetary control in Nigeria.

While the ratio has remained at 25% for many years, the composition of qualifying assets has been changed several times. For instance, the introduction of sectoral distribution of loans and advances with certain fixed percentages allocated to agriculture and residential building construction, banks are now required to deposit any shortfalls in their loans to agricultural and residential building construction with the CBN. However, such deposits do not count for the purpose of computing liquidity ratio. Similarly, cash balances for meeting the statutory cash reserves do not qualify for liquidity ratio computation. Advance Deposits for imports are also excluded from the computation. Deposits made with the CBN in respect of compulsory advance deposits for imports do not count in the liquidity ratio computation.

The following are the currently specified liquid assets:

a) vault cash;

b) balances with the CBN;

c) net inter-bank balances;

d) money at call;

e) Treasury Bills/Certificates;

f) bills discounted;

g) eligible development stock;

h) Bankers Unit Fund; and,

i) Negotiated Certificates of Deposit.

As mentioned earlier, the CBN has the power to alter the required liquidity ratio and its composition, thereby directly reducing the banks' ability to create credit. An increase in the ratio will compel the banks to reduce lending and transfer funds to reserve assets. A decrease in the ratio will have the opposite effect.

The CBN can also call on the banks to make *Special Deposits* which have the effect of reducing their liquidity. Such deposits are usually frozen and do not form part of their eligible liquid assets. Lastly, the CBN can issue stabilisation securities to banks in order to mop-up excess liquidity. This category of monetary control instrument has been found to be quite effective in a developing economy such as Nigeria. It forms part of the overall direct control instrument discussed below.

6-2.8 Direct Control

It has been confirmed by the authorities of the CBN that this is the most effective control instrument and the one which is most compatible with the economic goals and aspirations of the nation and the attainment of government objectives. This covers the sectoral distribution of loans and advances by commercial and merchant banks, loans to indigenous borrowers, loans to rural areas, reserve requirements, interest rate structure, prudential ratios and statistics. Quantitative ceilings on the overall and/or sectoral distribution of credit can also be imposed, while the Central Bank can prescribe the minimum ratios of loans and advances which the commercial banks should grant to indigenous persons and companies.

At the beginning of the fiscal year, immediately after the presentation of the budget, the CBN issues what is now popularly known as Monetary Policy Circulars (i.e. CBN Credit Guidelines) to all banks informing them about the details of the monetary policy to be pursued by the government in the new fiscal year. This circular is usually comprehensive and covers all aspects of the lending activities of banks. (The text of the Monetary Policy Circular issued in 1983 is given in Appendix 3 at the end of the book).

The Guidelines contain directives in the following areas:

i) Aggregate Credit

Banks are restricted to a certain growth rate per annum in loans and advances. For example in 1983, the aggregate loans and advances of banks were not permitted to rise by more than 25% except in the case of new banks or small banks with total loans and advances not exceeding ₦100 million as at 31st December 1982, which were permitted to grow by up to 35%, or 60% of their total deposit liabilities (excluding government deposits maturing earlier than 6 months) which ever was higher. However, in the calculation of the growth rate, loans granted for the purchase of shares by Nigerians under the indigenisation scheme, for buying motor cars by workers both in the public and private sectors and for agriculture and residential building construction, over and above the prescribed minimum, were excluded from the credit ceiling.

ii) Sectoral Distribution of Loan and Advances

The economy is classified into two major sectors - the preferred and the less preferred sectors:

a) The preferred sector consist mainly of those activities which are on the priority list of the government and are, therefore, to be encouraged. They include manufacturing to promote industrialisation, agriculture and housing, public utilities, transportation and communication, exports and Development Finance Institutions.

b) The less preferred sector consists mainly of credits extended to finance general commerce (imports and domestic trade) and personal loans, etc.

Each item is allocated a percentage share — minima in the case of the preferred sector and maxima in the case of the less preferred sector. The total for the preferred sector should not be less than 76%, while that of the less preferred sector should not exceed 24% of the total, although banks may exceed the targets for the preferred sectors within the overall ceiling.

iii) Loans to Indigenous Borrowers

The guidelines also allocate the minimum credit that must be extended to indigenous borrowers. In the year 1983 this was retained at the 1982 level (80%). It was also stipulated that at least 16% of the 80% must go to small scale enterprises wholly owned by Nigerians.

iv) Loans to Rural Areas

In pursuit of the government policy on rural banking, banks are required to lend not less than 30% of the total deposits collected in the rural areas to borrowers in the respective rural areas. This policy is intended to accelerate the economic growth of the rural areas and to spread the banking habit and development in the country.

v) Reserve Requirements

A cash deposit expressed as a ratio of each bank's total demand deposit liabilities is stipulated. For this purpose, banks are classified into four groups. (The classes and the new minimum ratio of cash to demand deposits which they are to maintain with the Central Bank was discussed earlier.)

vi) Compulsory Advance Deposits for Imports

Importers are required to make compulsory deposits in respect of goods imported under letters of credit, usance bills or bills for collection. Such deposits are transferred to the Central Bank and do not form part of the banks' liquid resources.

vii) Liquidity Ratio

The minimum specified liquidity ratio remained at 25% in 1983. As in previous years, deposits made with the Central Bank in respect of compulsory advance deposits and shortfalls in loans to agriculture and residential building construction and cash holdings for meeting cash reserves requirements, discussed earlier on, do not count for the purpose of computing liquidity ratio.

viii) Interest Rate Structure

The interest rate structure was also reviewed in 1983. The range of lending rates for the preferred sector/subsectors for loans maturing within 3 years was 9½% to 11½%, but loans to these sectors maturing after 3 years could carry interest rates up to a maximum of 13%, the maximum rate applicable to the less preferred sector.

6-2.9 Other Prudential Ratios

i) Legal Lending Limit — Aggregate Credit

A bank in Nigeria cannot lend in aggregate more than 10 times its adjusted capital fund or 70% of its total deposit liabilities (i.e. time, savings and demand deposits). The computation of an adjusted capital fund is shown in iii) below.

ii) Legal Lending Limit — Lending to One Borrower

Not more than 33½% of the sum of paid-up capital and statutory reserves of a bank shall be lent to an individual borrower (i.e. the aggregate lending to the group must not exceed 33½% of the bank's capital plus statutory reserves). This ceiling is of particular importance when the bank is dealing with a company with subsidiaries or associates maintaining accounts in one or more branches.

iii) Capital Funds

Except with the approval of the Central Bank, a bank may not apply its funds for payment of dividends to its shareholders unless the bank maintains a ratio of not less than 1:12 between its adjusted capital funds and its total loans and advances (i.e. the former should not be less than 8⅓% of the latter).

Provision for bad and doubtful debts should be netted out of loans and advances before the calculation of the ratio. Adjusted capital funds are computed as follows:

Issued and fully-paid up capital

plus statutory reserve

plus undivided profit or general reserve

plus Profit and Loss Account balance

plus reserve for possible loan losses (as per bank's books)

less reserve for possible loan losses (recommended by CBN examiners)

= ADJUSTED CAPITAL FUNDS

6-3 THE DEVELOPMENT FUNCTIONS

6-3.1 The Nigerian Money and Capital Markets

To promote economic development the Central Bank of Nigeria has contributed immensely to the creation and development of financial markets to mobilise and channel savings for economic growth. The Central Bank has created and nurtured the money and capital markets. In order to aid the development of the money market, the CBN introduced Treasury Bills in 1960 and Treasury Certificates in 1968. Since the creation of these money market instruments, the CBN has been directly involved in their management. Other money market instruments handled at one time or the other include Certificates of Deposit, Bankers' Unit Fund and the Call Money Fund. The bank also established clearing houses in Lagos and other urban centres to facilitate inter-bank settlements and enhance the effectiveness of money market transactions.

The CBN has been directly involved in the creation and the development of the capital market institutions such as the Nigerian Stock Exchange and the Nigerian Securities and Exchange Commission.

6-3.2 CBN's Role in Other Government-Sponsored Financial Institutions

The Central Bank has played an active role in the promotion of development-orientated banks such as the Nigerian Industrial Development Bank (N.I.D.B) and the Nigerian Bank for Commerce and Industry (N.B.C.I).

The Nigerian Industrial Development Bank was established in January, 1964 and specialises in the provision of medium and long-term finance for industries, either by way of loans or by taking up equity shares.

The Nigerian Bank for Commerce and Industry established in 1973 was set up to provide medium and long-term finance by loans or equity participation to indigenous enterprises engaged in industry and commerce.

Other development financial institutions include the Nigerian Agricultural and Co-operative Bank and the Federal Mortgage Bank. The Central Bank subscribes to the equity capital of these government-sponsored financial institutions which will be examined in more detail in Chapter Eleven.

6-3.3 CBN's Role in National Economic Policy Formulation

Every year the Central Bank of Nigeria makes concrete contributions to the Federal budget through the Ministry of Finance. The Governor of the Central Bank is a member of the National Economic Advisory Council and the Productivity Prices and Incomes Policy Board. The Bank also makes important contributions to the development of the Nigerian economy in the area of economic research through its Research Department. In addition, it assists the government implement its rural banking programme, which has helped considerably to spread the banking habit and development in the country.

6-3.4 Maintaining External Reserves

The country's external reserves are managed by the Central Bank. The Bank was required initially to maintain an external reserve level *"not less than the aggregate of an amount representing 60% of the Bank's notes and coins in circulation together with an amount representing*

35% of the bank's other demand liabilities".[2] Later (in 1959) the Bank was required to maintain not less than 80% of its assets in the form of external reserves to back the new Nigerian Pound to be issued just before independence.

The reserve/demand liabilities ratio was later reduced to 40% while for foreign exchange reserves the Bank now aims to achieve a minimum of foreign exchange reserves equal to the cost of the nation's imports for four months.

6-3.5 Exchange Control

The major reason for exchange control is to conserve a country's foreign exchange reserves. The authorities aim to achieve effective utilisation of these scarce foreign reserves by ensuring that only essential imports are allowed into the country.

An Exchange Control Act was enacted in 1962. Under the Act, the Federal Ministry of Finance is vested with overall responsibility for the administration of exchange control. The CBN has since been appointed its principal agent, while commercial banks, merchant banks, investment banks and some financial houses were appointed authorised dealers with powers to deal in foreign exchange in accordance with the directives and instructions issued by the Central Bank. Major hotels have also been appointed to act as authorised buyers. (Exchange control regulations are discussed in detail in Chapter Nineteen.)

[2]CBN Ordinance 1958 section 26(a).

REVIEW QUESTIONS

6.1 What functions are carried out by the Central Bank of Nigeria?

6.2 What are the main features of the Monetary Policy Circulars (Credit Guidelines) issued annually by the Central Bank of Nigeria?

6.3 Write short notes on:

i) Legal lending limit - aggregate credit.

ii) Lending to one borrower - limits on large loans.

6.4 Explain briefly why the CBN cannot effectively use open market operations to control the lending of banks.

REVIEW QUESTIONS

8.1 What functions are carried out by the Central Bank of Nigeria?

8.2 What are the main features of the Monetary Policy Circulars (Credit Guidelines) issued annually by the Central Bank of Nigeria?

8.3 Write short notes on:

i) legal lending limit - aggregate credit

ii) lending to one borrower - limits on large loans

8.4 Explain briefly why the CBN cannot effectively use open market operations to control the lending of banks.

CHAPTER SEVEN

COMMERCIAL BANKING

7-1 DEVELOPMENT OF COMMERCIAL BANKING IN NIGERIA

7-1.1 Brief History

i) British Bank of West Africa

The first commercial bank — the African Banking Corporation — opened its first branch in Lagos in 1892. Messrs. Elder Dempster & Co., a shipping firm based in Liverpool, was instrumental in its formation. The bank experienced some initial difficulties and eventually decided to transfer its interest to Elder Dempster & Co. in 1893. This led to the formation of a new bank known as the British Bank of West Africa (BBWA) in 1893 with £10,000 capital later increased to £100,000 during the same year. It was registered in London as a limited liability company in March 1894 and the first Lagos branch was opened in the same year. Other branches were opened in major West African cities like Accra, Freetown and Bathurst. The bank opened its second Nigerian branch in Old Calabar in 1900.

Another bank called the Anglo-African Bank was established in 1899 in Old Calabar by the Royal Niger Company (now UAC) to compete with BBWA. The bank later changed its name to Bank of Nigeria and established branches in Burutu, Lokoja and Jebba. However, due to fierce competition and the monopoly for the importation of silver from the Royal Mint enjoyed by BBWA, they sold out to BBWA in 1912.

ii) Barclays Bank DCO (Dominion, Colonial and Overseas)

This bank opened its first branch in Lagos 1917. (It is now known as The Union Bank.) Soon after, 9 other branches were opened.

The Nigerian banking scene was, therefore, dominated by these two British banks — BBWA and Barclays Bank DCO between 1894 and 1933.

iii) British and French Bank

The British and French Bank, now called United Bank for Africa Ltd., was established in 1949 making it the third expatriate bank to dominate early Nigerian commercial banking.

The foreign banks came principally to render services in connection with international trade, so their relations at that time were chiefly with the expatriate trading companies and with the government. They largely ignored the development of local African entrepreneurship.

Together these 3 banks controlled close to 90% of aggregate bank deposits. From 1914 to the early 1930's, several abortive attempts were made to establish locally owned and managed banks to break the foreign monopoly.

iv) Indigenous Banks

In 1929, the Industrial and Commercial Bank was set up by a handful of patriotic Nigerians. It folded up in 1930 due to under-capitalisation, poor management and aggressive competition from the expatriate banks. In 1931 another indigenous bank, the Nigerian Merchantile Bank was established. Like its predecessor, it went into liquidation in 1936. With greater courage and planning, the same group of pioneers in 1933 launched the National Bank of Nigeria Limited, which was the first indigenous bank to survive. The next private indigenous bank to be established was the Agbonmagbe Bank founded by Chief Okupe in 1945. This bank was taken over by the Western State Government in 1969 and its name was changed to Wema Bank. The fifth Bank, the Nigerian Penny Bank, set up in the early 1940's collapsed in 1946 under the weight of mismanagement. This was followed by the Nigerian Farmers & Commercial Bank in 1947 which failed in 1953. The Merchants Bank opened for business in 1952 and closed in 1960.

Indeed, this was a period of free-for-all banking. Between 1947 and 1952 a total of 22 banks were registered in Nigeria according to a study conducted by the CBN. However, a figure as high as 185 banks was quoted from government records and was confirmed by the Financial Secretary as the number actually registered as banking companies between 1947 and 1952, of which 145 were registered in 1947 and 40 in 1952.[1] Most of these banks however, merely registered without actually commencing operations. The next successfully established indigenous bank was the African Continental Bank founded by Dr. Nnamdi Azikiwe in 1947.

The need for legislation for the control of banking in Nigeria became very apparent if only to protect depositors. The Colonial Government,

---

[1] G. O. Nwankwo, *The Nigerian Financial System,* Macmillan 1980, p. 47

therefore, set up a commission of inquiry — the Paton Commission. Consequent upon the report of the Commission the first banking legislation was passed in 1952.

In spite of the enactment of the Banking Ordinance of 1952, banks were still indulging in some malpractices which the Act could not effectively control. Therefore, the necessity of establishing a Central Bank to supervise and control the banks became more apparent and pressing. Thus, the Central Bank came into being in 1959.

A new Banking Ordinance was promulgated in 1958. Through this Act, the conditions for establishing new banks were tightened and the capital requirements, especially for foreign banks, were doubled from ₦200,000 under the 1952 Act to ₦400,000. This was again increased to ₦1.5 million in 1969.

Nigeria now has 22 commercial banks with over 918 branches. In July 1981, the Federal Government of Nigeria granted licenses for the establishment of seven additional commercial banks:

Ibile Bank (Lagos State)
Lobi Bank (Benue State)
Progress Bank (Imo State)
Co-operative Bank (Ondo State)
Owena Bank (Ondo State)
Co-operative Bank (Borno State)
Co-operative Bank (Sokoto State)

All the seven are State government sponsored banks.

In April 1982, new banking licenses were issued to the following commercial banks:

— Credit Commercial de France Bank (Nigeria) Limited.
— Habib Nigeria Bank Limited.

Only two of the newly approved banks (Owena and Progress) were opened in 1982.

The conditions for approval of licenses are:

i) that the training and succession programme for Nigerian officers should be fully supplied to the satisfaction of the Minister of Finance;

ii) that the names and curricula vitae of the shareholders and top management of the bank be submitted to the Minister for vetting;

Table 7.1

Commercial Banks Registered in Nigeria From 1892 - 1982

	Commercial Banks	Date Established	Remarks
1.	African Banking Corporation	1892	Merged with BBWA
+2.	Bank of British West Africa	1894	Now First Bank of Nigeria Limited.
+3.	Barclays Bank DCO	1917	Now Union Bank of Nigeria Limited.
4.	The Industrial & Commercial Bank	1929	Failed 1930
5.	The Nigerian Mercantile Bank	1931	Failed 1936
+6.	National Bank of Nigeria	1933	
7.	Agbonmagbe Bank	1945	Now Wema Bank
+8.	The Nigerian Penny Bank	?	Failed 1946
+9.	African Continental Bank	1947	
10.	The Nigerian Farmers & Commercial Bank	1947	Failed 1953
+11.	British and French Bank	1948	Now United Bank for Africa Limited.
12.	Merchants Bank	1952	Failed 1960
13.	Pan Nigerian Bank	1951	Failed 1954
14.	Standard Bank of Nigeria	1951	Failed 1954
15.	Premier Bank	1951	Failed 1954
16.	Nigerian Trust Bank	1951	Failed 1954
17.	Afroseas Credit Bank	1951	Failed 1954
18.	Onward Bank of Nigeria	1951	Failed 1954
*19.	Central Bank of Nigeria	1951	Failed 1954
20.	Provincial Bank of Nigeria	1952	Failed 1954
21.	Metropolitan Bank of Nigeria	1952	1
22.	Union Bank of British Africa	1952	Failed 1954
23.	United Commercial (Credit) Bank	1952	1
24.	Cosmopolitan Credit Bank	1952	1
25.	Mainland Bank	1952	1
26.	Group Credit & Agricultural Bank	1952	1

No.	Bank	Year	Status
27.	Industrial Bank	1952	Failed 1954
28.	West African Bank	1952	Failed 1954
29.	Muslim Bank	1958	?
+30.	Banque de L'Afrique Quidentale	1959	Now I.B.W.A. Ltd.
31.	Bank of Lagos	1959	Surrendered its licence in 1965.
32.	Berini (Beirut-Riyad) Bank	1959	" " "
+33.	Bank of the North Limited	1959	" " "
+34.	Bank of America NT & SA	1960	Now Savannah Bank of Nigeria Limited.
35.	Chase Manhattan Bank	1961	Merged with Bank of West Africa (now First Bank in 1965).
+36.	Bank of India	1962	Now Allied Bank of Nigeria Limited.
+37.	Arab Bank	1962	Now Nigeria-Arab Bank Ltd.
+38.	Co-operative Bank of W/Nigeria	1962	Now Co-operative Bank Ltd.
+39.	Co-operative Bank of E/Nigeria	1962	Now Co-operative and Commerce Bank (Nig) Ltd.
+40.	Mercantile Bank Ltd.	1971	
+41.	Pan African Bank Ltd.	1971	
+42.	Kaduna Co-operative Bank	1974	
+43.	Kano Co-operative Bank	1976	
+44.	Societe Generale Bank	1977	
+45.	Bank of Credit & Commerce International (Nig) Limited	1979	
+46.	New Nigerian Bank Ltd.	1971	
+47.	Owena Bank Ltd.	1982	
+48.	Progress Bank Ltd.	1982	

* No connection with the Central Bank of Nigeria.

+ Existing Commercial Banks - 1982.

Source: Adapted from *The Nigerian Financial System*, G.O. Nwankwo.

iii) that the promoters must not be public officers; and,

iv) that ownership must reflect Federal character.

7-2 STRUCTURE

The structure of commercial banking in Nigeria is tailored towards that prevailing in the United Kingdom. Other countries in the Commonwealth, and indeed most countries of the Western World, have the same structure which can be described as the *branch banking system*. This is characterised by a few large banks with a wide network of branches extending throughout the country. For instance, the U.K. has only eight clearing banks (commercial banks) with over 12,000 numerous branches serving the banking needs of the country.

However, the United States of America has a unique banking structure with a *unit banking system* (i.e. numerous individual local banks) instead of the branch banking system. As a result, the U.S. has about 15,000 individual banks, operating approximately 25,000 branch offices, all of which, with minor exceptions, are at least confined to the state boundaries of the parent company and often restricted to an even greater degree depending on the governing state legislation. The U.S. banking system has been described as a dual system, meaning that banks are subject to either Federal or State regulatory control, and in some matters both.

Commercial banking institutions in Nigeria can be classified into two: the purely indigenous banks, owned 100% by Nigerians — (governments and individuals) and the mixed banks, with a majority indigenous shareholding (at least 60% equity), and minority foreign interests. (Nigerian law does not any longer allow the establishment of foreign banks with a majority foreign interest).

7-3 FUNCTIONS OF COMMERCIAL BANKS IN NIGERIA

The primary functions of a commercial bank are:

i)   acceptance and safe-keeping of deposits;

ii) granting loans and overdrafts to customers;

iii) transferring of funds on the instructions of their customers;

iv) management of customers' investments;

v) acting as executor and the trustee of wills;

vi) providing facilities for safe-keeping of important documents and title deeds;

vii) providing foreign exchange facilities to travellers;

viii) advising customers on insurance matters;

ix) providing services to the importer and exporter (e.g. documentary credits);

x) providing night safe facilities;

xi) buying and selling of stocks and shares for their customers; and,

xii) providing business status reports and references.

These functions are examined in more detail in Chapter Fourteen.

7-4 GOVERNMENT PARTICIPATION IN NIGERIAN BANKING

7-4.1 Origin

While there is no doubt that the Nigerian government is currently participating in Nigerian Banking, when actual government participation started is less obvious. Some observers argue that government participation started with the signing of the participation agreement in September 1976 by the Federal Ministry of Finance and the Expatriate Banks. Others date government participation back to 1959 when the Central Bank of Nigeria was established. They would maintain that the Nationalist argument in support of government participation in banking made direct reference to central banking and government control. In an attempt to resolve the above divergent views about when government participation started, we will examine the rationale for government participation.

7-4.2 Rationale for Government Participation

It is necessary to point out that government participation in banking is not a new phenomenon. Major banks in France, Italy and India are owned by the government. Without the Bank of England, which itself is owned by the British government, the Industrial Commercial Finance Corporation (ICFC) Ltd. and the Finance Corporation for Industry (IFCI) would probably not have been established. Similarly, the Industrial Development Bank of Canada and the Indian Industrial Development

85

Bank Limited are all government owned. Viewed against the above background, government participation in banking in Nigeria could be said to be following trends already consolidated in other countries.

It is a matter of fact, that without government participation, there would have been no indigenous banking in Nigeria today. The crucial questions, however, are:

Why did the government decide to participate in Nigerian banking?

What objectives do the authorities wish to achieve in the process? Is the approach adopted by the government the only and best way of achieving these objectives?

Given the objectives and the strategy adopted, what is the structure of a balance sheet of the achievement of government participation in Nigerian banking?

It is easy to identify two aspects of government participation in banking in Nigeria. One is the Regional/State Government participation and the other is the Federal Government participation.

The State Government participation dates back to 1954. In that year, only three of the mushroom banks of the late 1940's and early 1950's were still in existence. It was, however, a very fragile and shaky existence. They faced imminent closure because the three years' grace allowed them for licensing under the 1952 Banking Ordinance was fast expiring. It was to save them from this fate that the then Eastern Region Government pumped public money into the ACB Limited. The Western Regional Government also salvaged the National Bank Limited and later the Agbonmagbe Bank, now the Wema Bank. The Federal Government interest in banking dates back to the early 1950's. This was evident in the passing of the first Banking Ordinance in 1952 and in the adoption of a private member's motion in the House of Representatives which led eventually to the establishment of the Central Bank of Nigeria in 1959.

In conclusion, the rationale for government participation, indeed of indigenous banking in Nigeria, as advanced by the Nationalists, could be summed up by the following:

i) to break the monopoly power and discriminatory practices of the expatriate banks in the granting of loans and advances;

ii) to give financial assistance to indigenous banks so that they are able to provide credit facilities to Nigerian businessmen and women; and,

iii) to provide an avenue for indigenous banking by lending weight to the required cushion against the shock of confidence arising from the collapse of the banking boom of the late 1940's.[2]

It is necessary to state that these were a *sine qua non* given the bitter experience with the then indigenous banks.

7-4.3 The Participation Process

The forerunner of the participation process was the declared objective in the Second National Development Plan ". . . *to control the commanding heights of the economy"*. The aim of this participation is for government to get intimately involved in commercial banking in order to guide it to operate to the maximum benefit of the economy. This is as much in its own interest as it is in the interest of the economy. Government participation, which was initially fixed at 40%, was extended to 60% in 1976 with the signing of the participation agreement which provided for the following:

i) The Federal Government appointing a number of Nigerian citizens and some officials to represent her interest on the Boards of Directors.

ii) Mandating the Nigerian Directors to ensure that the management of the bank operate within the broad policy guidelines of the government.

iii) Ensuring that the banks should to the extent consistent with banking prudence:

a) increasingly undertake more medium and long-term lending designated as such;

b) conform to avowed national objectives and identify fully with Nigerian aspiration by taking a more active part in the financing of the economic programmes of priority;

---

[2] G.O. Nwankwo: "British Overseas Banks in Developing Countries" *Institute of Banker's Journal June 1972.*

c) be brought under Nigerian Control in ownership and management (i.e. decision-making in the commercial banking sector must be localised); and,

d) that a significant part of their profits be used to improve the quality of the services offered.

In pursuance of the above provisions in the participating agreement, corporate objectives were spelt out for the banks to achieve under their new Boards of Directors. The objectives, which are essentially in harmony with national interest, include:

i)   achievement of optimal growth rate in terms of deposits, assets and branch network;

ii) promotion of public confidence in the ability of banks to meet their deposit obligations;

iii) development of a well integrated and competent Nigerian staff;

iv) promotion of employment opportunities;

v)   development of export orientated industries, particularly those in the non-oil sectors; and,

vi) establishment of units in the banks to assist in the development of agriculture and small and medium scale industries.

It is essentially against the above background that a balance sheet of achievement could be drawn up and analysed, in an attempt to appraise government participation in Nigerian banking.

Those who argued against government participation in commercial banking, especially in developing countries, and Nigeria in particular, often entertained the fear that a government element in the commercial banks would impair their efficiency. They also believed that confidence would erode, mediocrity would set in and the banks would become other sick babies of the government like the numerous corporations (e.g. The Nigerian Railways, Airways, the Post and Telegraph Departments to name but a few).

Table 7-2
Deposit Liabilities

₦ (million)	1977	1978	1979	1980	1981
First Bank of Nig. Ltd.	1,229	1,217	1,693	2,742	2,262
Union Bank of Nig. Ltd.	1,071	823	1,282	1,625	2,318
United Bank for Africa Ltd.	890	992	1,133	1,576	2,407
Total	3,190	3,032	4,108	5,343	6,987

The table above shows an upward trend in the deposit liabilities of the major former expatriate banks where the Federal Government has acquired 60% participation. This negates the fear of eroding confidence in the banks. Between 1977 and 1981, the total deposits of these banks increased by ₦3,797 million or 119%. This represents an annual average growth rate of 23.8%. Thus, it is obvious that government participation has, in fact, increased the confidence and efficiency of the banks contrary to the fear of those against it. However, it must also be stated that, in spite of their huge investment in the banks, the Federal Government has not in any way interfered in their day-to-day administration. This appears to be the main reason for the success attained so far.

Table 7-3
Loans and Advances

₦ (million)	1977	1978	1979	1980	1981
First Bank of Nig. Ltd.	547	691	739	1,039	1,339
Union Bank of Nig. Ltd.	536	658	634	932	1,396
United Bank for Africa Ltd.	445	582	703	865	1,167
Total	1,528	1,931	2,076	2,836	3,902

Like the performance in the deposit mobilisation section, the performance in the loans and advances section has again proved that government participation could, and in fact has been, a blessing and is in the interest of the banks and the government.

The argument that there are no investment avenues locally in Nigeria and that Nigerians do not come forward for banking facilities because of a poor banking habit has been defeated in the face of the performance in loans and advances shown above. With the Nigerianisation of the credit base in 1960 and the introduction of selective credit controls, it was feared that if 70% of loans and advances must go to indigenous borrowers, then the total loans and advances would fall. On the contrary, total loans and advances of the big three increased by ₦2,374 million or 155.4% from ₦1,528 million in 1977 to ₦3,902 million in 1981. This represents an annual growth rate of 21.4%.

7-5 THE ORGANISATION STRUCTURE OF A NIGERIAN COMMERCIAL BANK:

One common feature in the organisational structure of all major banks in Nigeria is the fact that their Head Offices are located in Lagos or in a State Capital, with Area Regional offices in major cities up-country. The Area Offices have a number of branches under their control.

As in any other company, the shareholders are the owners of the bank. The Chairman and the other directors of Banks are appointed by the Federal and State Governments which own majority share holdings in nearly all the banks in Nigeria. The directors usually meet periodically to formulate the policy of the bank. This includes discussing management reports, approving changes in top management personnel, approving budgets and large loans and discussing other problems and policies with the management of the bank.

The Managing Director and the Executive Directors are usually the top management of the bank. They conduct the day-to-day affairs of the bank. Other members of the Board of Directors are not full time employees of the bank. There is normally one Managing Director assisted by 2 to 4 Executive Directors depending on the size of the bank. The Managing Director and the Executive Directors are full time employees of the bank, appointed by the Federal or State Government. For banks controlled by the Federal Government, the appointments are made by the Federal Ministry of Finance. After the Managing Director and Executive Directors come the Heads of Departments who report to the appropriate Executive Director. (Heads of Department are called Assistant or Deputy General managers in some banks.) Examples of Heads of Departments are: The Financial Controller or Assistant General Manager (Finance), The Chief Inspector, the Credit Administrator or Head of Advances Department, The Head of Operations Administration, The Chief Personnel Manager, The Assistant General Manager (Computer).

Table 7 – 4
Organisation Chart of a typical Nigerian bank

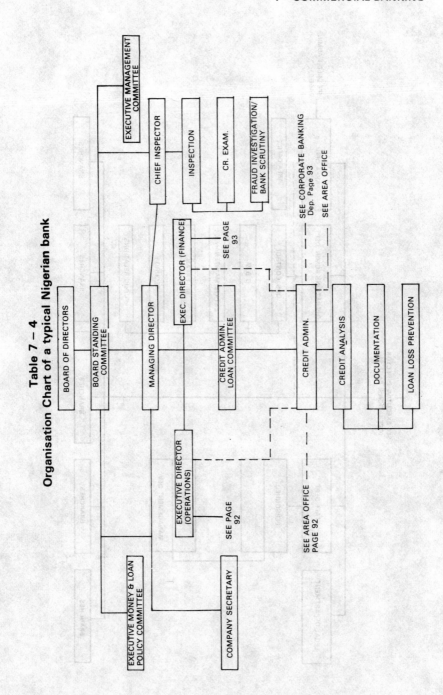

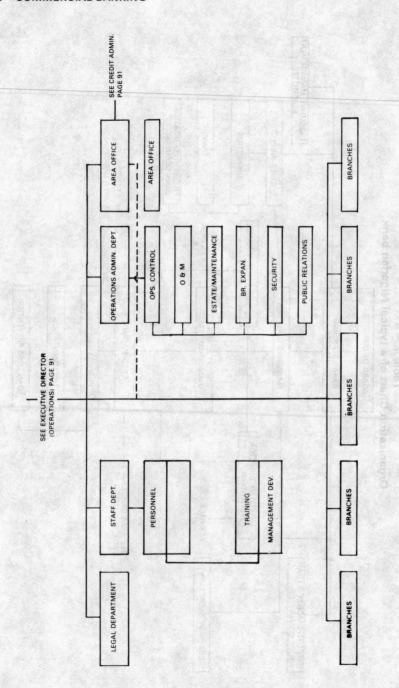

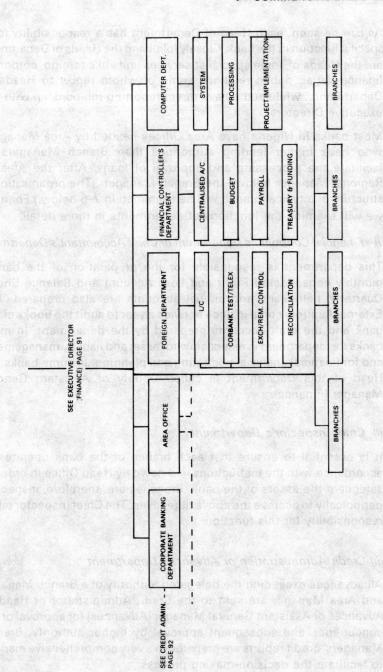

As can be seen, each Head of Department has a responsibility for a specific function in the bank. Closely following the Heads of Department are the Heads of some specialist services units like foreign, corporate finance, legal, public relations some of whom report to Heads of Departments, while some have direct reporting relationship with the executive Directors.

Most banks in Nigeria have Area Offices headed by Area Managers who have higher lending authorities than Branch Managers to facilitate the processing and approval of loans. After the Area or Regional Manager follows the Branch Manager. (The organisational structure of a typical branch will be examined in 7-6 below.) For now we will examine the functions of departments in more detail.

i) Financial Controller's Department or Chief Accountant's Department

This department is responsible for the preparation of the bank's monthly consolidated Profit and Loss Account and Balance Sheet. Quarterly, half-yearly and annual accounts are also prepared. The External Auditors come in once or twice a year to audit the books of the bank and the draft accounts prepared by the department. In most banks the department is responsible for asset and liability management, and for financial analysis, budgeting and planning. In some banks the Head of this Department is called Deputy or Assistant General Manager (Finance).

ii) Chief Inspector's Department

It is essential to ensure that each branch of the bank operates in accordance with the instructions laid down by Head Office in order to safeguard the assets of the bank. Branches are, therefore, inspected periodically to achieve the above objectives. The Chief Inspector takes responsibility for this function.

iii) Credit Administration or Advances Department

All advances exceeding the delegated authority of a Branch Manager and Area Manager are sent to the Credit Administrator or Head of Advances or Assistant General Manager (Advances) for approval or for concurrence and subsequent approval by higher authority. Branch Managers' credit reports are prepared in a very comprehensive manner to facilitate the decision-making process.

iv) Head of Operations Administration Department

This includes branch administration, operations and control, branch expansion, stationery supplies and purchasing, maintenance and security. The Operations Department ensures that branches operate in accordance with standard banking practices, principles and the Nigerian Law.

v) Staff Department

This department is concerned with recruitment, training and deployment of staff.

vi) Computer Department

A number of banks have introduced Electronic Data Processing systems into their operations in order to enhance efficiency and, as a result, Computer Departments have been created.

7-6 BRANCH ORGANISATION

i) The Branch Manager

At branch level the most senior official of a commercial bank is the Branch Manager. The Branch Manager is usually an experienced banker, versatile in banking operations generally and credit analysis and appraisal in particular.

Apart from receiving funds from and lending money to deserving customers of the bank, every Branch Manager is a potential salesman for his bank. Gone are the days when the branch manager used to do his work almost entirely within his branch, expecting his customers (or even potential customers) to come to see him. Today's business environment and keen competition in banking compels the Branch Manager to go outside and actively solicit business, to visit factories and to speak to varied groups.

Another important role which every Branch Manager is expected to play is that of an adviser. As the branch manager's daily routine brings him into close contact with all classes of people and all trades and professions, his views are likely to be more broadly based and in better perspective than those people with narrower interests and responsibilities. Apart from his own knowledge and experience, the Branch Manager relies on a number of experts in Head Office, subsidiaries, affiliates and associated banks and companies, to help him advise his customers. Areas where the Branch Manager has traditionally given advice to his customers include other sources of finance, especially when the bank itself cannot grant a request, maximum utilisation of surplus funds, investments and portfolio management, wills and trusts, insurance, tax matters and even family affairs. In addition to the above, corporate customers may seek advice on capital raising, balance sheet structure, mergers, leasing, factoring and international trade, etc.

Depending on the size of the branch and the experience of the Branch Manager, a lending limit is given up to which he can lend without reference to his Regional/Area Office or Head Office. Thus, the Branch Manager is able to approve certain loans on the spot, so the customer is not kept waiting anxiously for an Area Office or Head Office decision.

The overall responsibility for the running of a branch in accordance with Head Office instructions devolves on the Manager. In large branches he has one or more assistant managers.

ii) The Accountant

In some banks, especially those with an American origin, this official is called the Operations Officer. He is responsible for the day-to-day organisation and administration of the branch. His area of responsibility is restricted to branch operations and the accounting side of the branch. He is usually not involved with credit matters, except requests for small loans and overdrafts from personal rather than business customers. Thus, his main responsibility is to ensure the smooth and efficient running of the branch. To achieve this objective, he is usually responsible for staff recruitment and training and the preparation and balancing of the branch books. He may have one or more assistant accountants, depending on the size of the branch.

iii) Other Staff

The other staff in a branch include security clerks, who are responsible for the processing of security for bank loans and advances and investments for customers; foreign clerks, who handle foreign exchange, travellers' cheques, remittances, Letters of Credit, etc; the cashiers who receive and pay out funds and the accounting staff who carry out the accounting functions of the branch.

REVIEW QUESTIONS

7.1 Compare and contrast the commercial banking systems in Nigeria and America.

7.2 State briefly the main functions of commercial banks in Nigeria.

7.3 Classify the different types of banks in Nigeria, giving brief details of their main functions.

7.4 Outline the development of banking in Nigeria from 1982 – 1952.

CHAPTER EIGHT

STRUCTURE OF A BANK'S BALANCE SHEET

8-1 INTRODUCTION

Every student of banking should be able to analyse the Balance Sheet of a bank. Students are, therefore, advised to study the Annual Report and Accounts of their own banks. In the example below, the Balance Sheet of a medium sized Nigerian commercial bank is analysed item by item. It is hoped that this will give an insight into the peculiarities of a bank balance sheet.

Balance Sheet

30th September, 1982

		1982	1981
		₦	₦
Employment of Funds			
a)	Cash and short term funds	57,848,754	31,433,504
b)	Statutory & other deposits with Central Bank	70,295,864	36,990,014
c)	Government securities	26,240,000	23,200,000
d)	Investment with other banks	50,000,000	22,000,000
e)	Loans and advances	540,321,558	387,138,950
f)	Other assets	24,662,762	77,062,578
g)	Fixed assets	43,327,670	38,967,388
		812,696,608	616,792,434
Financed by:			
h)	Share capital	20,000,000	18,000,000
i)	Statutory reserve }	13,468,000	11,840,000
j)	Undistributed profit	11,460,360	8,059,388
	Shareholders' funds	44,928,360	37,899,388
k)	Customers' deposit	489,039 818	351,687,148
l)	Other liabilities	263,728,430	227,205,898
m)	Debenture stock	15,000,000	
		812,696,608	616,792,434
n)	Acceptances, guarantees and other obligations for account of customers (and customers liability thereof).	193,443,636	166,116,892

101

8-2 ASSETS: USE OF FUNDS

Unlike the usual company Balance Sheet which lists assets in order of illiquidity (that is, commencing with fixed assets and ending with cash), Nigerian banks attempt to place emphasis on liquidity by listing the more liquid assets first, so that customers can see that they hold sufficient cash and other liquid assets to meet depositors' demands. This is the practice in most countries.

8-2.1 Cash and Short-Term Funds

i) Cash

This is the amount of notes and coins held in the strong-rooms of all branches of the bank and in the Head Office to meet customers' demands for cash withdrawals. Cash kept in the strong-rooms of banks are regarded as idle funds, since they cannot earn interest. Therefore efforts are made to keep the balances low.

Banks know from experience what amount to keep in their strong rooms as cash. Should there be an unusually high demand for cash at any time either money is transferred from one branch to another branch or cash is withdrawn from the bank's account with the Central Bank.

ii) Short-Term Funds

This refers to items in course of collection within Nigeria as well as balances with banks abroad.

Any cheque credited to an account and drawn by another customer of the same branch is debited to the drawer's account on the same day. However, most of the cheques credited to customers' accounts are drawn on other banks or branches of the bank. Such cheques need to be 'cleared' before the payee can receive the proceeds. It takes about 4 days to clear cheques in a clearing area. The assets described above represent the claim that the bank has on other banks for items in course of collection. On the Balance Sheet in our example, this item is ₦35.2 million. As cheques are constantly being paid into the accounts of customers, there are always cheques in the course of collection. (The Clearing System will be discussed in detail later in this book.)

8-2.2 Government Securities

These include Treasury Bills, Treasury Certificates and Development Stocks and Bonds. Treasury Bills and Treasury Certificates provide a safe short-term investment avenue for the surplus funds of banks. A reasonable return is normally expected, though it is lower than other more risky investments. They are issued by the CBN weekly for 90-91 days, but they are very liquid as they can be rediscounted with the CBN before their maturity date.

8-2.3 Statutory and Other Deposits with the C.B.N.

These include balances on current account with the Central Bank which do not attract interest, Cash Reserve Deposits, Special Deposits and Letters of Credit deposits, etc.

The balance on current account is a working balance to meet the day-to-day cash requirements of the bank, such as cash withdrawals by branches, foreign exchange allocations, adverse clearing balances and payments for other investments. The Statutory Cash Reserve Deposit ranges from 2-5% of demand deposits, in accordance with the classification of the particular bank. These are deposits which all banks are required to make with the Central Bank and have been fully discussed in an earlier Chapter. Other deposits are self-explanatory.

8-2.4 Investments with Other Banks

These include investments in Call Money, Fixed Deposits and Negotiable Certificates of Deposit with other banks. The investments yield a high return and are reasonably safe.

8-2.5 Loans and Advances

This is by far the largest asset on the Balance Sheet of many banks. It stood at ₦540 million on the Balance Sheet under consideration. All loans and advances are technically repayable on demand, except for term loans. In practice this is not the case. The rates charged on these assets are quite high and are usually fixed by the Central Bank.

8-2.6 Other Assets

Items under other assets include Prepayments, Accrued Interest Receivable, Suspense Resources and Uncapitalised Expenditure.

8-2.7 Fixed Assets

This represents the bank's investment in buildings (premises) equipments and furniture, etc.

8-3 LIABILITIES: SOURCES OF FUNDS

8-3.1 Share Capital

The issued and paid-up Share Capital is represented by the shares held by individuals, institutional investors and governments. Most of the shares issued by Nigerian banks are ordinary shares with ₦1 or 50k nominal value each. One or two banks did, however, issue preference shares during 1981 and 1982.

8-3.2 Statutory Reserves

Every bank in Nigeria is required by law to:

"maintain a reserve fund, and shall, out of its net profits each year and before any dividend is declared —

a) *Transfer to the reserve fund, where the amount of the reserve fund is less than the paid-up share capital, a sum equal to not less than 25% of such profits; or*

b) *Transfer to the reserve fund, where the amount of the reserve fund is equal to or in excess of the paid-up share-capital 12½% of the net profit of the bank, but no transfer under the foregoing provisions of this section shall be made until any past losses have been made good."*[1]

8-3.3 Undistributed Profit, Share Premium Account and General Reserve

These are the profits earned over the years which have not been distributed. Part of the balance on these accounts may eventually be capitalised or used for the purpose it was set aside for. It can also be called Revenue Reserve.

---

[1] Banking Act, 1969, Part II 9 (a) & (b).

A bank may have Capital Reserve on its Balance Sheet as a result of revaluation of fixed assets, especially branch premises purchased and revalued at higher than purchase price at a future date. Another type of Capital Reserve arises when shares are issued at a higher price than the nominal price. The excess is placed on a Share Premium Account. The important difference between Capital Reserve and Revenue Reserve is that the latter can be distributed to the shareholders as dividend, while the former cannot be touched.

The sum of Share Capital, Statutory Reserve, General Reserve and Undistributed Profit, etc. are Shareholders' Funds.

8-3.4 Debenture Stock or Loan Capital

These are medium term loans to a bank at a fixed rate of interest and repayable over a fixed period of time to finance certain capital projects of a bank. In the event of a winding up, the holders shall be paid only after depositors have been fully repaid. Long-term debts are issued either through public underwriting or private placement. Like other liabilities of a bank they provide funds that support the bank's credit expansion and other financial activities or capital expenditure.

8-3.5 Customers' Deposits

As loans form the largest asset of a bank, customers' deposits are the largest liability on a bank's Balance Sheet. The depositors are creditors of the bank whose money, or part of it, must be repaid on demand or notice in accordance with the agreement.

8-3.6 Other Liabilities

These include provision for taxation due to the Board of Inland Revenue and provision for dividend. They also include cash security for Letters of Credit, collection deposits and remittance deposits. These deposits relate to foreign exchange transactions awaiting allocation by the Central Bank. Also included are interest reserves in respect of deposit liabilities, which have been accrued but have not been paid, cashiers/managers' cheques or bank drafts and certified cheques. Mail transfer and telegraphic transfers which require additional information before payment can be effected also form part of the total.

8-3.7 Acceptances, Guarantees and Other Obligations for Account of Customers

These are treated as contra items, appearing on both sides of the Balance Sheet. They comprise mainly outstanding Letters of Credit, acceptances, guarantees and other obligations not yet utilised or concluded.

REVIEW QUESTIONS

8.1 Draw up a typical Balance Sheet for a commercial bank, illustrating the main classes of liabilities and describing the significance of each of them.

CHAPTER NINE

PROFITABILITY AND LIQUIDITY OF BANKS

9-1 INTRODUCTION

At the micro level, the individual commercial bank is viewed as an economic unit whose goal is to maximise profits. Banks hold portfolios of assets and, given the characteristics and distribution of their liabilities, they attempt to structure these in such a manner as to yield the greatest returns, subject to certain constraints.

The assets held by banks may be divided into two broad classes, frequently called *earning assets* and *non-earning assets.*[1] Earning assets are the two groups of Balance Sheet items called Loans and Investments. Non-earning assets consist of fixed assets, the total reserves of the bank, and non-interest earning deposits with the Central Bank.

Profits are generated by earning assets (Loans and Investments); while liquidity is provided partly by earning assets like short-term investments and partly by non-earning assets (e.g. cash balances held in the vault and at the CBN and cash reserves).

9-2 MAINTAINING EQUILIBRIUM BETWEEN PROFITABILITY AND LIQUIDITY

Why must banks make profit? The answer is simply that, like other companies, they incur substantial costs and must earn an income at least sufficient to meet these costs and make an adequate return on their assets. They are also accountable to their shareholders who have invested in them with the aim of good returns in the form of future dividends and growth. From these points of view, banks need assets which produce income substantially higher than their expenditures.

A bank's profit fulfils several other important function which may be summarised as:

i) Profit constitutes a buffer to absorb the shock of unexpected losses, especially losses arising from bad debts. Every bank makes annual provisions in respect of loans considered uncollectible or of

---

[1] Thomas M. Havrilesky and John T. Boorman *Current Perspectives in Banking 2nd Edition* Harlan Davidson, pp. 5-6

such doubtful value that their being shown as active assets of the bank becomes questionable. Such provisions are made from profits.

ii) The strength of a company is usually measured by the size of its capital base which serves as a cushion for unforeseen losses. Hence, well managed companies plough back a sizeable amount of profits into the business. These are called retained earnings or reserves which contribute to the growth of the capital account. Such balances may also be used to write off losses, especially those placed on specific reserves.

iii) In the case of banks with publicly quoted shares, a good record of profitability must be maintained. The ability to attract more capital and the price and terms of any new issue, etc, are influenced by the past profit performance of the bank.

iv) If a bank is to attract money market funds from other banks, financial institutions and large corporations, the profit record and capital position of the bank must be sound. Even the public will lack confidence in a bank with a consistent record of many years of losses.

At the same time, the assets of a bank must be kept reasonably liquid so as to meet possible demands from depositors and to maintain public confidence. This is why the Central Bank prescribes a minimum level of liquidity that a bank must maintain, both as regards cash and as regards other liquid assets which can be turned into cash.

In practice, these two objectives (profitability and liquidity) tend to work in opposite directions. Cash itself produces no income and the relatively liquid assets like Call Money, Treasury Bills and Treasury Certificates usually produce low income, or at least earn less than the less liquid assets. Advances to customers, even though they may be expressed as repayable on demand, are in practice not particularly liquid, but these are the assets on which banks normally earn the highest rate of return. If they did not need to balance profit motives and the maintenance of adequate liquidity, most banks would certainly over-emphasise the pursuit of profitability at the detriment of remaining liquid. This would, however, have disastrous consequences. The precise way in which this harmonious balancing is achieved in Nigeria will be examined in detail later, but Table 9-1 below illustrates this persistent conflict between profitability and liquidity.

Table 9 – 1
Liquidity vs Profitability

Asset	Tenure	Rate (%)	Liquidity	Profitability
Cash	-	-	Very High	Nil
Call Money	1-30 days	6 -7	High	Low
Treasury Bills	91 days	7	High	Average
Treasury Certificates	1-2 years	7½-8	High	Average
Fixed Deposits	1-12 months	7½-9	Average	High
Eligible Govt. Stocks	1-3 years	9-9½	Average	High
Other Govt. Stocks	4-25 years	9 -9½	Low	High
Loans & Advances	Revolving	9½-13	Low	Very High

This table shows that highly liquid assets like cash and Call Money have low yields, as far as profitability is concerned; while relatively illiquid assets like loans and advances are highly profitable due to the higher returns on them. The CBN sets a fixed liquidity ratio of 25% for all banks. If, as a result of an undue pursuit of profit, loans are allowed to grow excessively, then the ratio will not be met. The bank will become illiquid and CBN penalties will be imposed, although it should be stressed that, other things being equal, banks will still probably make good profit.

Central Bank actions such as a change in cash and liquidity ratio requirements or interest rates lead to a portfolio adjustment process on the part of individual banks in order to maintain the desired distribution of assets for the maximisation of profits.

9-3 THE MAJOR FINANCIAL RISKS

9-3.1 Market Risk

One basic aspect to bank asset and liability management is that assets are managed with the explicit recognition of the relationship between risk, rate of return and liquidity. So, in accepting and deploying funds, banks have two overall objectives which they must balance: sustained earnings growth and control of exposure to financial risks. The three major financial risks are: *market risks; credit risks and liquidity risks.*

This reflects the influence of market forces upon the availability of funds which creates liquidity risk or upon movements in foreign exchange rates which create foreign exchange risk. Market forces relate to economic, financial and political developments. Market risks are inherent in virtually all sources and uses of funds. These risks are absent only when sources and uses of funds are matched identically as to maturity, interest rate and currency. For example, market risks can be controlled by:

i) operating actively on the money market, although the Nigerian Money Market is not as mature as it should be yet; and,

ii) diversifying sources of funds, types of instruments and maturities (e.g. inter-bank, customers' deposits, Negotiable Certificates of Deposit, debenture stock and capital).

9-3.2 Credit Risk

This is the risk that credits extended to customers will not be repaid according to the terms and conditions of the loan agreement between the bank and the customer. Credit risk is inherent in all extensions of credit — loans, advances, deposit placements, investments and foreign transactions. These risks are controlled by:

i) Diversifying credits so as to avoid excessive concentration of credit risk among individual debtors or within any geographical area (i.e. extending credit in smaller amounts to a larger number of borrowers).

ii) Maintaining standards and control procedures for the approval of credits.

iii) Maintaining adequate reserves for possible loan losses. The Central Bank of Nigeria, during its periodic inspection of banks, also ensures that adequate reserves for loan losses are maintained.

iv) Requiring that all credits be supported by primary and secondary sources of repayment.

v) Accepting only readily marketable securities as collateral for those credits that are supported by security.

vi) Avoiding term credits with maturities of 5 years or more without substantial amortisation.

vii) Declining non-productive credits (e.g. those that are speculative in nature).

viii) Performing an on-going examination of credits extended. Most banks have Credit Examination Departments or Inspection Departments which evaluate credits periodically and monitor both credit quality and loan portfolio continuously. These Departments have the responsibility for determining the degree of risk inherent in credits. Exceptions include such circumstances as credit deterioration, non-compliance and credit terms, past-due and non-performing loans. Problem loans are classified by Credit Examiners according to criteria established by each bank. However, such criteria should conform to Central Bank guidelines.

9-3.3 Liquidity Risk

This is the risk that funds will not be available to meet deposit withdrawals, loan draw-downs, maturities of borrowings or other cash out-flows. Bank liquidity is managed with the aim of meeting the following criteria:

i) Assuring credit customers that funds are available to meet their borrowing requirements.

ii) Assuring deposit customers that funds are available to provide for their withdrawal of funds upon demand or at maturity.

iii) Maintaining access to liquid resources sufficient to enable the bank to respond to potentially profitable credit or investment opportunities.

iv) Diversifying sources of funds in terms of types of instruments and maturities.

v) Maintaining the statutory liquidity ratio of 25% and also satisfying the CBN as to the bank's ability to meet its commitments under varying economic and financial conditions.

Liquidity is available on both the asset and liability sides of the Balance Sheet. Asset liquidity resides in:

i) the ability to convert assets to cash; and,

ii) the self-liquidation of assets — liquid assets which can be sold to other banks or on open market include marketable securities and certain loans: maturing loans and inter-bank placements provide liquidity as they are repaid.

Liability liquidity resides in the bank's ability to:

i) attract deposits; and,

ii) issue money market liabilities and Negotiable or Non-Negotiable Certificates of Deposits.

Asset liquidity and liability should be regarded as co-equal elements in any liquidity management policy. In terms of very short-term assets and liabilities, however, greater liquidity generally is available on the liability side of the Balance Sheet. Investible funds tend to be fully utilised at any given time, but additional liquidity can be generated through the bank's access to the money market by rolling-over (renewing) or marketing additional liabilities. Potential domestic liability liquidity resides in commercial banks' access to the money market through the issue of Negotiable Certificates of Deposit (NCDs), inter-bank borrowings, Call Money, rediscount arrangements and the issue of commercial paper. The domestic liquidity of banks also resides to a great extent in their retail deposit base (demand, savings and time deposits).

Major liquid assets include Treasury Bills and Treasury Certificates as these can be quickly and easily converted to cash for funding purposes by sale or rediscount arrangement. Liquidity is also provided as these assets mature.

Banks prefer to invest in Treasury Bills in order to earn interest rather than keep idle cash in the vault or large balances at the CBN. Interest on Treasury Bills (which are issued weekly by the CBN) is relatively low when compared with other possible investments, but they are highly liquid assets. The current yield is 7% p.a. This is the most readily realisable form of government paper as the CBN will repurchase it on demand at a penalty rate of 1% p.a.

Treasury Certificates for 1 and 2 years are issued 3 to 4 times a year by the CBN, although they possess the same attributes as Treasury Bills. Federal Government stocks are issued for anything between 1 and 25 years. Those with more than 3 years to maturity do not count for liquidity purposes.

9-4 COMPUTATION OF RESERVE RATIOS

9-4.1 Liquidity Ratio

The minimum specified liquidity ratio that must be maintained by banks is 25%. In computing the liquidity ratio of a bank, the following items qualify:

i) Liquid Assets:

   a) Cash.

   b) Balance held with the CBN less any shortfall on loans for agriculture and residential buildings.

   c) Balance held with internal banks (excluding uncleared effects) less any balance held for internal banks (if net minus add to current liabilities).

   d) Nigerian Treasury Bills.

   e) Nigerian Treasury Certificate.

   f) Money at Call held with other banks less Money at Call held for other banks.

   g) Certificates of Deposit held (of not more than 18 months to maturity).

   h) Government Securities (eligible stocks i.e. of not more than 3 years to maturity).

   i) Bankers' Unit Fund.

ii) Current Liabilities:

   k) Current, savings and time deposit accounts.

l) Certificates of Deposits issued (of *not* more than 18 months to maturity).

m) Excess balances held for internal banks (see c).

n) Excess Money at Call held for other banks.

o) Balance held for external office less any balance held with external offices (if net minus ignored).

$$\text{Liquidity Ratio} = \frac{\text{Total Specified Liquid Assets}}{\text{Total Current Liabilities}} \times 100$$

Deposits made with the Central Bank in respect of shortfalls on loans to agriculture and residential building construction and cash holdings for meeting cash reserves and deposits for Letters of Credit do not count for the purpose of computing the liquidity ratio. Reserve requirements must be met on a monthly average basis, so may be under or over the required level on any one day.

When a bank's reserves exceed legal requirements, it may adjust its position by selling the surplus to another bank in order to earn interest on these funds. Similarly, a bank that has not met its reserves requirements must take steps to cover the deficiency by increasing its deposit base. In the event of a temporary shortage of liquid cash Call Money can be purchased from other banks. These transactions are effected through the Banking Office of the Central Bank by debiting and crediting the respective bank accounts.

Ultimately, a bank with a persistent liquidity problem must curtail its lending activities, as excessive lending is usually the major cause of a shortage of liquidity. If a bank is unable to attract sufficient deposits, but continues to expand its lending activities, this will result in illiquidity.

9-4.2 Cash Ratio

The Central Bank of Nigeria requires banks to maintain a non-interest earning reserve against demand deposits. The cash deposit is expressed as a ratio of each banks's total demand deposit liabilities. For this purpose banks are classified into 4 classes. The classes and the minimum rate of cash to demand deposits in 1982 were:

Class	Total Deposit Liabilities	Ratio of Cash to Demand Deposits
A	₦300 million or more	5%
B	₦100 million or more but less than ₦300 million	4%
C	₦30 million or more but less than ₦100 million	3%
D	Less than ₦30 million	2%

These reserves are carried in form of frozen deposits at the CBN. With effect from June 1979, the CBN assumed the responsibility for calculating the Cash Reserves of all banks. Each bank was debited with the appropriate percentage (i.e. 2 - 5% as stated above) of its total demand deposits which was immediately placed on a non-interest earning Cash Reserve account with the Bank. Thereafter, the calculation is repeated every month and the Reserve is either increased or reduced in accordance with the position of demand deposits at the end of the month.

When there is growth in demand deposits, the bank's current account at CBN is debited and the Reserve Account credited with the difference in order to raise the percentage to the appropriate level and vice-versa when there is a drop in demand deposits. Thus, after the initial deposit, subsequent debits or credits to the Reserve Account are insignificant.

Compounding the problem of liquidity and profitability is the absence of a viable money market in Nigeria. A money market is expected to provide facilities for profitable investment of surplus short-term funds and also provide short-term borrowing facilities to the institutions in need of funds.

With the abolition of the Call Money Scheme in 1974, the Central Bank virtually pulled out of the arrangement and banks were compelled to operate a private call money system. This scheme, as presently operated without CBN participation, has several shortcomings. A bank having temporary liquidity problem has no central point to avail itself of money market funds. It will have to go from bank to bank or make series of telephone calls — when telephones are working! On some bad days it may end up not having a kobo. On another day the same bank may have surplus funds to invest on Call Money and discover that every other bank is liquid. Thus, the funds will remain idle on the current account with the CBN or in the bank's vault. In the days when the CBN operated the scheme such problems would not arise. Surplus balances were automatically invested on a daily basis in short-term securities like Treasury Bills and those in need could always obtain funds. The result is that banks are now compelled to hold higher cash reserves than required.

9-5 CONCLUSION

Banks are compelled to maintain fixed minimum liquidity ratio mainly because of the need to balance the pursuit of profit and the need to remain liquid. Every bank is faced with the choice and it is usually discovered that actions designed to raise liquidity to the stipulated level would generally reduce earnings, while actions designed to increase earnings may reduce liquidity.

However, as illiquidity appears to be an unacceptable option, profit opportunities should be pursued without incurring undue exposure to liquidity risks. Banks face a serious dilemma here, because the quicker an asset can be converted into cash, the lower the rate of interest it earns. Assets that take longer to turn into cash command higher rates of interest and generally the highest rates are charged for the most illiquid of a bank's earning assets (i.e. loans and advances to customers). So, a bank must strike a balance between adequate liquidity and its reducing effect on profits and high profitability with the consequent worsening of the liquidity position. This conflict between liquidity and profitability may be regarded as the central problem in the management of bank assets.

REVIEW QUESTIONS

9.1 What makes a bank's assets liquid?

9.2 Discuss the view that the distribution of a commercial bank's assets is determined by a balance between the needs of liquidity and those of profitability.

9.3 Write short notes on:

i) Cash Ratio.

ii) Liquidity Ratio.

CHAPTER TEN

CAPITAL MANAGEMENT AND CAPITAL ADEQUACY

10-1 INTRODUCTION

Capital, so far as a commercial bank is concerned, is its own funds or resources. It is necessary to measure *capital adequacy* to determine whether a bank's capital is adequate to cushion possible losses resulting from loan losses or disappointing interest margins. Such funds should, therefore, not be subject to fixed interest payments or fixed redemptions.[1] The following are regarded as Shareholders' Funds or resources: paid-up capital, share premium accounts, statutory reserves, undistributed profits, general reserves and (free) general provisions.

However, for certain regulatory measures only paid-up capital and statutory reserves are allowed by the Central Bank as Shareholders' Funds, for the simple reason that the other items enumerated above are transient and can be reduced by a management decision.

Capital management includes the management of long-term debt and equity capital funds of a bank. Long-term debts consist of borrowing instruments issued by a bank with maturities exceeding one year (e.g. debenture stock). Such long-term debts are issued either through public underwriting or private placement. Long-term debts perform the same function as other liabilities of a bank — they provide funds that support the bank's credit expansion and other financial activities or capital expenditure.

Sound capital management in banking requires the maintenance of an adequate base of equity funds, supplemented by long-term debt. It is the policy of banks generally to maintain sound capital growth by balancing earnings allocation between dividend payout and profit retention in order to enhance future assets and earnings and by issuing new equity whenever the need arises.

---

[1] Hugo Coljé: "How Much Capital is Adequate?" *The Banker,* June 1982 p. 55

10-2 MEASUREMENT OF CAPITAL ADEQUACY

The monetary authorities in Nigeria have consistently used three methods for capital control purposes:

i) Fixed minimum capital requirement.

ii) Limitation of lending limit.

iii) Weighted risk/assets ratio.

10-2.1 Fixed Minimum Capital Requirement

Since 1952 when the first Banking Act was promulgated, provisions for minimum capital requirements have been made. The Banking Act, 1969, as amended in 1979, stipulated that the paid-up capital of an indigenous bank should not be less than ₦600,000, while the paid-up capital of banks with a foreign interest was fixed at ₦1,500,000. (Merchant banks must have a minimum paid-up capital of ₦2 million.)

10-2.2 Limitation of Lending Limits (i.e. Limits on Large Loans)

By this method, the Central Bank sets a limit for lending to individual debtors or groups of inter-related debtors. This limit is expressed as a percentage of the banks' own funds. It is otherwise called the *Legal Lending Limit*. As bank capital provides a cushion against risk, the maximum lending limit of a commercial bank is thus statutorily tied to its own funds. In 1982, the maximum loan that any Nigerian bank could grant to a single customer was 33⅓% of the sum of the paid-up capital and statutory reserves of the bank. This was computed as follows:

	₦
Capital (Paid-up)	20,000,000
Statutory Reserve	8,200,000
Total	28,200,000
33⅓% of ₦28,200,000	₦9,400,000

The legal lending limit of this (hypothetical) bank is ₦9.4 million, so it cannot lend more than ₦9.4 million to a single customer.

Table 10-1

Limits on Large Loans

% of a bank's own resources

	%
Canada	75
France	75
Germany	75
Italy	100
Japan	20-40
Netherlands	15-25
Sweden	15
United States	10
Nigeria	33⅓

Source: Hugo Coljé. How Much Capital is Adequate? *The Banker,* June 1982 p. 56

10-2.3 Weighted Risk/Assets Ratio

This method relates Shareholders' Funds to the sum total of risk bearing assets, weighted by the degree of risk involved.[2] For instance an unsecured loan will attract a higher rate of solvency requirement than a secured loan. We shall consider in detail how this method works by considering the Balance Sheet shown overleaf.

To determine the adequacy of the capital of this bank, the assets will be grouped into the following categories and each group will be assigned and allocated a solvency requirement.

The first group comprises of the most liquid of bank assets like cash in the bank's strong rooms (notes and coins), the balance with Central Bank of Nigeria, balances held with other banks — including Call Money, fixed deposits and investment in government securities (e.g. Treasury Bills and Treasury Certificates, Bankers' Unit Fund and Certificates of Deposit of not more than 18 months' maturity and other government stocks with not more than 3 years' maturity). This will

---

[2] Hugo Coljé *Ibid.* p. 55

Table 10.2

Bank Balance Sheet

Uses of Funds (Assets)	1980 ₦'000s	1981 ₦'000s
Cash & short term funds	17,832	22,465
Statutory & other deposits with Central Bank	52,692	19,650
Investments with other banks	8,000	49,000
Government securities	19,597	17,493
Loans & advances	150,889	208,770
Other assets	28,557	24,508
Fixed assets	6,551	20,704
	284,118	362,590

Sources of Funds (Liabilities)		
Share Capital	9,000	10,000
Statutory reserve	5,920	6,734
Undistributed profit	2,625	3,066
Shareholders' Funds	17,545	19,800
Customers' deposits	142,602	261,299
Other liabilities	123,971	73,991
Debenture Stock	—	7,500
	284,118	362,590

cover virtually the whole of the first three items and part of the fourth item on the assets side. These can be regarded as 'riskless' assets and do not, therefore, require capital cover.

The second group of assets to be considered are Certificates of Deposit held whose tenure exceeds 18 months and government stocks of over 3 years' maturity. Loans and advances fully secured by time and/or savings deposit are also included in this group. These are regarded as 'minimum risk assets'. The amount of risk is very minimal and it is believed that this risk can be absorbed by internally-generated current earnings. Hence, as in the first group, the capital requirement is nil.

The third category includes the non-classified loan portfolio and other investments in Nigeria. The risk here is also minimal, so capital backing is not required. (These can be called 'Normal Risk Assets'.)

The fourth category covers loans classified by Central Bank of Nigeria examiners as sub-standard due to the poor financial standing of the customer, insufficiency of security or failure to meet engagements. These are called 'Sub-standard Assets' against which 10% of capital should be provided.

The fifth category also relates to the loan portfolio. Under this category, all debts classified by CBN examiners as doubtful of recovery require 50% cover. These are called 'Doubtful Risk Assets'.

The sixth category includes known losses of the bank and bad debts. Bad debts are debts which have become worthless and uncollectible. 100% capital support is required for this category of assets.

The seventh and final category consists of the fixed assets of the bank. These are bank premises, equipment, furniture and fixtures, etc. These items are expected to be funded by the bank's capital funds and not with depositors' funds. 100% capital support is also required.

The minimum capital required by a bank is the sum of the percentages required for its various assets. Thus, the minimum capital requirement of the bank under consideration is computed as overleaf.

The minimum capital requirement of the bank in 1981 is approximately ₦26.5 million. The bank's adjusted capital as at the date of the Balance Sheet was ₦19.8 million. This is a situation of under-capitalisation. When the position in the previous year (1980) is examined, it is very revealing. In 1980, the bank had an adjusted capital fund of ₦17.5 million. Our computation reveals that the desirable minimum capital requirement of the bank in 1980 was ₦9,795,000 (or ₦10 million approximately) which confirms that the capital of the bank was as at that date quite adequate.

However, during 1981, the bank increased its investments in fixed assets from ₦6,551,000 to ₦20,704,000 without much increase in its capital base. This resulted in the position shown in 1981 when capital requirement was approximately ₦26.5 million and the adjusted capital fund was ₦19.8 million. This would have been a classic case of a bank relying on depositors' funds to finance fixed assets, except that in the

		1980	1981
	%	₦'000	₦'000
Category 1 Assets — cash balance with CBN & other bank	0%	—	—
Category 2 Assets — short-term securities, etc.			
Category 2 Assets — Negotiable Certificates of Deposit, Government Securities	0%	—	—
Category 3 Assets — good loans	0%	—	—
Category 4 Assets — classified debts (Sub-standard Loans)	10%	100	400
Category 5 Assets — classified debts (Doubtful)	50%	1,134	2,894
Category 6 Assets — classified debts (Losses)	100%	2,010	2,534
Category 7 Assets — fixed assets	100%	6,551	20,704
		9,795	26,532

case of this bank, a debenture stock was issued to finance the bulk of the excess capital expenditure.

It is pertinent to mention that this is not a hypothetical example, but a true story of what happened in a Nigerian bank. This bank has since taken corrective measures to increase its capital base by a rights issue to existing shareholders and staff and by public subscription. The bank's capital grew to ₦25 million in 1982 and was further increased to ₦28 million soon after.

10-3 CONCLUSION

To conclude this Chapter, it is pertinent to explain briefly classified debts and their common classifications.

Bank loans are examined periodically and monitored continuously by in-house Credit Examiners of Bank Examiners from the Central Bank of Nigeria to assess the quality of the bank's assets. Loans are examined as to degree of risk and likelihood of orderly repayment of the loan.

This exercise involves a thorough analysis of the loan portfolio. Weaknesses likely to degenerate into serious problems in the future are promptly reported to senior management.

Any of the loans considered to have some inherent weaknesses are regarded as problem (or potential problem) loans and are classified as sub-standard, doubtful or loss, depending on how serious the problem is. Consequent upon the classification of a loan, especially if it is classified as doubtful or loss, adequate provision for losses must be made from the resources of the bank. Generally a provision of 50% for doubtful loans and 100% for losses is considered adequate by the Central Bank. No specific provisions are made for sub-standard classifications, but some banks make a 10% provision.

i) Sub-Standard

Loans classified as sub-standard are loans that are no longer regarded as good assets because of weaknesses that jeopardize the bank's ability to recover the debt.

Such weaknesses include:

a) Past-due loan repayments or a dormant condition of account. Generally, any loan that has been delinquent for six months or more is due for classification.

b) Deteriorating trends in the borrower's financial condition.

c) Persistent excess on the line of credit.

d) Stale financial statements or lack of financial information.

e) Lack of adequate support and security and non-perfection of security.

f) Signals that the borrower's business is grinding to a halt, hence no apparent source of repayment, especially when the loan account is also showing severe delinquency.

ii) Doubtful

A loan is classified as doubtful when the bank expects to lose part of the principal amount of the loan. Doubtful loans have all the weaknesses of sub-standard loans shown above, but in this case the weaknesses are so pronounced that collection or liquidation in full becomes improbable. While there is a probability of total loss, other factors may help in strengthening the deteriorating condition or liquidation of the loan.

iii) Loss

Loans classified as a loss are considered uncollectible and of such little value that the bank must charge it off. However, this does not mean that loans charged off do not possess partial recovery or salvage value.

REVIEW QUESTIONS

10.1 Describe the three methods used for capital control purposes in Nigeria.

10.2 Describe what you understand by classified debts.

CHAPTER ELEVEN
OTHER FINANCIAL INSTITUTIONS

11-1 WHAT IS A MERCHANT BANK?

Merchant banks are financial institutions providing specialist services like acceptance of bills of exchange, corporate finance, portfolio management or equipment leasing. Their principal function is the provision of medium and long-term lending as opposed to short-term lending. The Banking Act, 1969, allows merchant banks to engage in all banking activities except current accounts, although they are still allowed to offer cheque accounts for their large corporate customers.

The major differences between merchant banks and commercial banks can be summarised as:

i) Merchant banks are wholesale bankers accepting deposits only in large blocks with a minimum of ₦50,000, whilst commercial banks act primarily as retail bankers. Thus, while commercial banks do business with individuals and companies, merchant banks concentrate on corporate customers.

ii) Being wholesale bankers merchant banks operate with only a few branches, while commercial banks, as retailers, need a wide network of branches.

iii) Merchant banks provide mainly medium and long-term finance while commercial banks grant short-term loans and advances.

iv) They also differ in their sources and uses of funds. While commercial banks accept deposits from all and sundry, merchant banks depend on public and private corporations. In their lending activities, commercial banks deal with a wide variety of customers, while merchant banks deal mainly in the acceptance and discounting of commercial bills to finance trade.

11-2 HISTORY AND DEVELOPMENT

The first merchant bank in Nigeria was Phillip Hill (Nig.) Limited which started operations in Nigeria in 1960. In July 1969 it merged its activities with that of Nigerian Acceptances Limited to become the only merchant bank in Nigeria until 1973, when a license to carry out merchant banking business was issued to UDT Bank (Nig.) Limited, later restructured and named Nigerian Merchant Bank Limited.

Today, there are six merchant banks in Nigeria; namely, NAL (Merchant Bankers) Ltd.; Nigerian Merchant Bank — formerly UDT Bank (Nig.) Ltd.; ICON Limited — formerly First National Bank of Chicago Ltd.; Chase Merchant Bank Ltd., Nigerian-American Merchant Bank Ltd. and Indo-Nigeria Merchant Bank Ltd.

In April, 1982 three new merchant banks were approved. These are expected to start operations before the end of the year. They are:

i) Merchant Bank of Africa (Nig.) Ltd.

ii) African Banking Consortium Merchant Bank Nigeria Limited.

iii) City Securities Limited.

11-3 FUNCTIONS

11-3.1 Domestic and International Banking Service

The range of services offered by merchant banks has changed constantly. However, merchant banks in Nigeria have always been engaged in providing finance for international trade by means of Acceptance Credits covering both imports and exports and bridging finance for companies needing temporary finance pending the conclusion of funding arrangements. Other services in this area include the establishment of documentary letters of credit on behalf of importers, granting term loans and advances, certificates of deposit and equipment leasing, etc.

11-3.2 Corporate Finance

Corporate finance ranges from the management of the issuance of private and public equity shares to corporate debt securities. Merchant banks provide expertise in the arrangement of syndicated loans for the financing of large-scale industrial projects, general financial and investment advisory services, company floatation, mergers and recon-struction, financial planning and portfolio management.

11-3.3 Issuing House: Debt and Equity Issues

Merchant banks act as Issuing Houses at the Nigerian Stock Exchange. In this role they provide financial services to corporate entities including governments, quasi-government institutions and companies seeking to raise long-term or permanent finance for their operations, by sponsoring their capital issues and the sale of their securities to the public. The Issuing House functions of merchant banks include:

i)   giving advice on the most appropriate capital structure (i.e. capital gearing);

ii) determining the most appropriate time to make an issue;

iii) providing publicity and marketing facilities for the security to be issued; and,

iv) giving backing to an issue in the form of underwriting.

11-3.4 Treasury/Financial Services (Money Market Activities)

As part of their money market activities, deposits are taken from banks, institutions, large corporations and rich individuals at attractive interest rates.

Merchant banks also accept call and time deposits from individuals, partnerships and corporate customers, as well as from other banks and Government Corporations. Being actively engaged in the local money market, they are able to advise customers on up-to-date conditions prevalent in the market. Merchant banks are authorised issuers and dealers of Negotiable Certificates of Deposits. The negotiability of these instruments makes them attractive investments for customers. Merchant banks are also 'Authorised Dealers' in foreign exchange.

11-3.5 Equipment Leasing

Leasing is the hiring of an asset for the duration of its economic life. The asset is initially purchased by the finance company and then leased to the user who has no option to purchase.

The system is suitable for large and costly assets such as computers, aircraft or expensive plant and equipment. Leasing is an alternative to outright purchase of an asset on credit, mortgage finance or term loan. In a leasing agreement, no capital outlay is involved. It requires no cash deposit or down payment; the only disbursement being the fee payable to the merchant bank.

11-3.6 Portfolio Management

Most merchant banks in Nigeria have investment departments set up to manage the portfolios of customers. This includes attending to registrations, rights issue or bonus issues.

They also act as receiving banker for public issues, offers for sale and right issues.

11-4 THE ROLE OF MERCHANT BANKS IN NIGERIA

In Nigeria, the role of merchant banks is not precisely defined, as it has been an uphill task for the monetary authorities to define their role in a developing economy whose capital market is not fully developed. As a result, merchant banks were for a long time performing virtually the same functions as commercial banks. The Central Bank in its annual monetary policy circulars to banks has endeavoured to distinguish merchant banks and carve out specific roles for them. In this context, the current Monetary Policy Circular provides that:

i) A minimum of 40% of total loans and advances shall be of medium and long-term nature with a maturity of not less than three years.

ii) A maximum of 20% of loans and advances shall be of short-term nature (i.e. maturing within twelve months).

iii) A maximum of 15% of total assets shall be in equipment leasing.

The above requirements seek to restrict the activities of merchant banks in the traditional area of commercial banking activities (i.e. short-term lending) and thus avoid unnecessary competition or duplication of functions. At the same time merchant banks are encouraged to do more medium and long-term lending so that commercial banks can concentrate on short-term. They are also required to provide specialist services like equipment leasing and other corporate banking services.

The Central Bank has given official support to the argument in financial circles that merchant banks would make a more tangible contribution to the economic development of the country if they provided more specialist services such as equipment leasing and other corporate services. However, to fulfil the role mapped out for them, merchant banks face the problem of liquidity. The source and nature of funds available to them, outside their own capital and reserves, are essentially short-term deposits repayable within one year. In these circumstances, it is difficult for merchant banks to concentrate on long-term lending, as the resultant effect of using short-term funds to finance long-term projects could be quite disastrous.

11-5 INTRODUCTION TO DEVELOPMENT BANKING

The idea of setting up development banks was mooted soon after the establishment of the Central Bank of Nigeria. It became clear that there was an urgent need for financial institutions capable of providing medium and long-term capital to fill a serious gap in the financial structure. It was recognised that the commercial banks were traditionally providers of short-term finance for working capital purposes, although they did entertain some medium-term financing, but only in exceptional circumstances. Similarly, the Central Bank confined its activities to its normal functions as discussed in Chapter Six — i.e. the financing activities of the Bank ended with granting temporary day-to-day advances to the Federal Government and acting as lender of last resort to the commercial and merchant banks. It was initially thought that merchant banks could fill the gap and provide medium and long-term finance to industry, but it was found that merchant banks were also ill-equipped to fill the gap. Merchant banks are, by tradition, small, although they deal with substantial sums of money and they depend almost solely on short-term funds. Thus, the need for *development banks* devoted primarily to stimulating the private sector of the economy and concerned with the promotion and finance of enterprises by the provision of long-term and medium-term finance was accepted. With the support and encouragement of the International Bank for Reconstruction and Development (World Bank), the first development bank — the Nigerian Industrial Development Bank (N.I.D.B) — was established in 1964. Other development-orientated banks which followed later included the Nigerian Agricultural and Co-operative Bank, the Nigerian Bank for Commerce and Industry and the Federal Mortgage Bank.

11-6 THE NIGERIAN INDUSTRIAL DEVELOPMENT BANK(N.I.D.B.)

This was established in 1964 through the reconstitution of the Investment Corporation of Nigeria which had been in operation since 1959.

The capital structure on establishment comprised equity capital (₦4.5 million) and an interest-free loan from the Nigerian Government of ₦4 million, making a total capital fund of ₦8.5 million. By 1978 the resources available to the N.I.D.B. had risen to ₦76.6m. This was made up of equity (₦7.1 million) and borrowed funds (₦69.5 million). The N.I.D.B is jointly owned by the Federal Government of Nigeria and the Central Bank of Nigeria.

11-6.1 Functions

i) Provision of medium and long-term finance for the public and private sectors.

ii) Identification of investment bottlenecks in the economy, thereby helping to determine investment priorities.

iii) Promotion and development of projects.

iv) Advice and assistance to indigenous enterprises in Nigeria. This includes financial, technical and managerial advice. For example, foreign business organisations coming to establish in Nigeria are free to avail themselves of the bank's expert advice on government policies as regards the nature of the business concern, indigenisation, repatriation of capital and profits.

v) Supervising the implementation of projects financed by it by requesting progress reports and visiting the project sites.

vi) Nominating technical and managerial advisers/partners to industrial organisers.

vii)Fosters the development of the capital market in Nigeria by encouraging prospective borrowers to list their shares in the Lagos Stock Exchange.

viii)Serves as a channel for bringing into Nigeria investible funds from international organisations.

11-6.2 Principles Guiding its Operations

The N.I.D.B. will finance any enterprise which by virtue of its size will make a significant contribution to economic growth and development in Nigeria. However, it will only assist limited liability companies (i.e. it will not assist sole traders and partnerships).

The N.I.D.B. does not give loans or invest any amount less than ₦50,000 or more than 49% of the total capital required in any enterprise. (The promoter's stake must not be less than 25%.) This means that the smallest project that can attract N.I.D.B. participation must be ₦90,000 to ₦120,000. However, after the establishment of a concern financed by the N.I.D.B., it may increase its participation to 60%.

11-6.3 Sources of Funds

The N.I.D.B. does not take deposits from the public. It borrows in bulk from institutional lenders like banks or insurance companies or secures loan capital from the CBN and the Federal Government. Equity participation is by both the Federal Government and the Central Bank.

11-6.4 Problems

The principal problem facing the N.I.D.B. since its inception is the inherent weakness of the Nigerian entrepreneur. He is reluctant to co-operate with financing agencies, especially in matters relating to business intelligence and financial management and he is unreliable. Many Nigerian entrepreneurs divert funds approved for a specific project to other uneconomic ventures. This creates a high rate of loan losses.

11-7 NIGERIAN BANK FOR COMMERCE AND INDUSTRY (N.B.C.I.)

11-7.1 Introduction

N.B.C.I. is a development bank and opened for business on 4 October 1973. It has an authorised share capital of ₦50 million and long-term financial resources from the Federal Government and the Central Bank of Nigeria. It was established with the prime objective of aiding the implementation of the indigenisation of the economy. Thus, it provides medium and long-term finance for the acquisition, expansion and establishment of viable business by Nigerian individuals and corporate bodies. N.B.C.I. is also expected to conduct merchant banking and commercial banking business as deemed appropriate.

11-7.2 Functions

i) Share underwriting.

ii) Provision of facilities for the take-over activities of businesses in Schedule I and Schedule II in form of loans and equity.

iii) The N.B.C.I. will assist indigenous business by the provision of consultancy services in the following areas:

   a) Identification of viable projects.

   b) Preparation of well-articulated feasibility surveys.

   c) Provision of guidance on the appropriate ways of achieving a reasonable return on investments, including advice on relevant technical and managerial matters.

   d) It functions as a member of Lagos Stock Exchange.

11-7.3 Principles Guiding its Operations

i) It will not normally engage in business such as real estate.

ii) It will not invest in infrastructure projects such as schools or roads.

iii) It will not finance the mining business.

iv) It will not consider an application for a loan below ₦20,000.

v) It will be principally interested in applications from Nigeria businesses that have limited liability and fall under Schedule I.

vi) In exceptional cases, it might consider partnerships and other types of business.

vii) It has to ensure that the business it finances has competent managers. The owners' stake must not be less than 30% and they must be credit worthy.

viii) The business must show satisfactory evidence of recovery of loan capital and interest.

11-7.4 Sources of Funds

The N.B.C.I. does not take deposits from the public. It borrows in bulk from institutional lenders like banks or insurance companies and from the Federal Government and the Central Bank. Equity participation is by both the Federal Government and the Central Bank.

11-7.5 Problems

N.B.C.I is faced with the same problems as those of the N.I.D.B.

11-8 THE NIGERIAN AGRICULTURAL & CO-OPERATIVE BANK (N.A.C.B.)

11-8.1 Introduction

The N.A.C.B was established in 1973 by the Federal Government with an initial capital of ₦12 million. The bank was set up in order to improve the level and quality of all aspects of agricultural production, to enhance the availability of storage facilities and to promote the marketing of agricultural products through liberal credit to farmers.

11-8.2 Functions

The three major functions of the Nigerian Agricultural and Co-operative Bank are:

i) To grant loans for agricultural production including horticulture, poultry farming and pig breeding and for the purposes of storage, distribution and marketing connected with such production to any State, group of States or any institution for on-lending to any farmer, group of farmers, or body corporate, subject to the States or State institutions guaranteeing repayment of the loan.

ii) To grant direct loans to individual farmers, co-operative societies or other bodies (corporate and unincorporated) in appropriate cases provided that it is satisfied that the schemes for which the loans are requested are viable and there is adequate security to cover such loans.

iii) To do all such other things as may be deemed incidental or conducive to the attainment of the above objectives.

11-8.3 Principles Guiding its Operations

i) It grants two types of loans: one is to State Governments, other governmental bodies, co-operative societies and co-operative banks against repayment guarantees for on-lending to third parties and the other type is 'direct lending' to individual Nigerian farmers.

ii) Applicants for loans must have a clear title to the land on which the project is located.

iii) It may grant short-term loans for up to 2 years or medium or long-term loans for 5 to 15 years.

11-8.4 Sources of Funds

The N.A.C.B. is funded almost entirely by the Federal Government and the CBN. It has not been feasible to raise funds from the capital market as the bank's preferential lending rates militate against this. The bulk of agricultural loans are given at 8%, whereas the lowest lending rate on the money capital market is 8½%.

11-9 THE AGRICULTURAL CREDIT GUARANTEE SCHEME

Commercial and merchant banks in Nigeria are required to channel a minimum of 8% and 5% respectively of their total loans and advances to the agricultural sector. Stiff penalties are imposed on banks that fail to meet this requirement. As this percentage, even when achieved by banks is not adequate, a study was commissioned by the Federal Government and the Central Bank for the purpose of identifying the problems in agricultural finance in Nigeria. The following problems were identified:

i)   the absence of clear title to land;

ii) the absence of acceptable security;

iii) the high cost of lending to many small farmers and the associated high bad debts provision;

iv) the inherent risks of crop failures; and,

v) the long-term nature of the finance required.

It was recommended that a Credit Guarantee Scheme should be introduced by the Government and the Central Bank to *"underwrite the (often feared) credit risks and to minimise the problem of lack of collateral securities"*.[1] To this end a fund was established by the Federal Government under the Agricultural Credit Guarantee Scheme Fund Act 1977 with an initial capital of ₦100 million subscribed to by the Federal Government (60%) and the Central Bank of Nigeria (40%).

The objective of the Scheme, as stated in the Act, is to provide *"guarantees in respect of loans granted for agricultural purposes by any bank in accordance with the provisions of the Act"* in order to increase bank credit to the agricultural sector.

The Act went on to define agricultural purposes as those projects connected with the establishment or management of plantations for the production of rubber, oil palm and similar crops, the cultivation of cereal crops, animal husbandry including cattle rearing and poultry and fish farming.

To protect banks against diversion of funds, the Act provides that where loans are granted to purchase livestock, farm machinery and

---

[1] Ojo and Adewunmi, *Banking & Finance in Nigeria* Graham Burn, 1982 — p. 287

equipment, the loan should be paid direct to the supplier who must furnish the bank with evidence of delivery.

At present, the maximum liability of the Fund in respect of any guarantee given is 75% of the approved loan. The maximum loan that can be granted is restricted as follows:

i) to individuals — ₦50,000 maximum

ii) to co-operative societies and corporate bodies — ₦1 million maximum.

The Fund is managed by a Board of Directors of six members. Two of the members represent the Central Bank, while the remaining 4 are appointed by the Government — one each from the Federal Ministry of Finance and the Federal Ministry of Agriculture & Water Resources, plus two non-government officials, one of whom is Chairman of the Board.

Between April 1978 when the Scheme came into operation and the middle of 1980, a total of 1,986 agricultural loans amounting to ₦64,640.7 million had been guaranteed by the fund. [2]

The following securities are now acceptable for agricultural loans:

i) a charge on land in which the borrower holds a legal interest or a right to farm or a charge on the crops on such land;

ii) a charge on the movable property of the borrower;

iii) a life insurance policy, a promissory note or other negotiable security;

iv) stocks and shares;

v) a personal guarantee;

vi) any other security acceptable to the bank.

11-10 FEDERAL MORTGAGE BANK

11-10.1 Introduction

The Federal Mortgage Bank was created by Decree No. 7 of 20 January 1977 to take over the assets and liabilities of the Nigerian Building Society (NBS) which had been operating essentially in the mortgage administration industry after Incorporation in 1956. On establishment,

---

[2] Ojo and Adewunmi, *Op. Cit.* p. 288 – 9

the Federal Mortgage Bank had a share capital of ₦20 million. This was, however, increased to ₦150 million in 1979.

11-10.2 Functions

i) The provision of long-term credit facilities to other mortgage institutions in the country at such a rate and upon such terms as may be determined by the Board in accordance with the policy of the Federal Executive Council.

ii) The encouragement and promotion of the development of mortgage institutions at state and national level.

iii) The supervision and control of activities of mortgage institutions in Nigeria.

iv) The provision of long-term credit facilities directly to Nigerian individuals.

v) The provision of loans, with the approval of the Minister, at competitive commercial rates of interest or credit facilities to commercial property developers, estate developers and developers of offices and other specialised types of buildings.

11-10.3 Powers of the Bank

i) To accept deposits and savings from mortgage institutions, trust funds, post offices and private individuals.

ii) To promote the mobilisation of savings from the public.

iii) To invest in companies engaged in the manufacture and production of building materials with a view to stabilising the cost of such materials.

iv) To furnish financial advice and assist in the provision of managerial, technical and administrative services for companies engaged in the building material industry or building construction and development in the country.

v) To guarantee loans from private investment sources for building development.

vi) To provide guarantees including in respect of promissory notes and other bills of exchange issued by licensed banks in the country and to discount such notes or bills.

vii)To issue its own securities including debentures and bonds under Federal Government guarantee and issue promissory notes and other bills of exchange for the purpose of raising funds from financial institutions.

viii)To establish a sinking fund for the redemption of securities issued by it and provide for contribution by it to the sinking fund.

ix) To carry out research aimed at improving housing patterns and standards in both urban and rural areas of Nigeria.

x) To carry out research on mortgage finance activities and the building construction industries in the country.

xi) To organise and operate, in collaboration with reputable insurance companies, a mortgage protection system designed to guarantee liquidity to mortgagors as well as offering liberal premium terms.

11-10.4 Principles Guiding its Operations

Apart from satisfying the usual bank financial parameters and canons of prudent bank lending, a proposed mortgagor must satisfy the following requirements:

i) He must be a Nigerian not less than 21 years old.

ii) The purpose must be for either the construction or the purchase of a residential house, development of property or for alteration/renovation.

iii) The engineering and architectual drawings must have been approved by the town planning authority.

iv) He must hold a certificate of occupancy, the governor's consent and a tax clearance certificate.

v) He must show satisfactory evidence of income and hold a savings account pass book of the mortgage bank with a minimum credit balance of ₦500. The account must show evidence of regular savings.

11-10.5 Types of Loan

The bank at present operates three types of loan:

i) Social Loans. These are for private house owner-occupier buildings which cost not more than ₦30,000. It is also available for residential buildings by a Housing Corporation provided the cost is

143

not more than ₦30,000 per unit. The usual interest rate is between 8% and 9½%, while the duration is between 10 years and 20 years.

ii) Economic Loans. This type of loan is for building construction where the cost is not less than ₦65,000 per unit. The buildings could be available for letting. Mixed housing estate development and building materials project could also attract this loan. The interest rate is between 11% and 11½%, with a usual duration of 15 years.

iii) Commercial Loans. These are available for all commercial ventures in the building and construction industry. It is available for private, State and Federal Government projects. The Interest rate is between 12% and 13%. The duration of the loan is 10 years if the project is residential buildings and 7 years if non-residential.

11-10.6 Sources of Funds

The sources of funds to the bank are:

i)   The Federal Government of Nigeria — through grants, soft loans and capital injections.

ii) The Central Bank of Nigeria — through capital contributions.

iii) The commercial banks — the bank is free to negotiate loans from institutional lenders like banks, insurance companies, etc.

iv) Private individuals — the bank encourages the general public to open time deposit and savings accounts with it. This is a major source of funds.

11-10.7 Problems

The Federal Mortgage Bank is the major financial institution operating on the housing development market. With its limited resources, it has been impossible to cope with demand, so commercial and merchant banks have been forced by government directives to participate. Interest rates on housing loans are generally below market rates, but if the growth of the market is to be fostered, these interest rates must become more competitive, so that other institutional lenders will be more prepared to participate so as to increase the flow of funds to the market.

11-11 THE FEDERAL SAVINGS BANK

11-11.1 Introduction

The Federal Savings Bank was established in 1974, making the former Post Office Savings Bank (established in 1889) independent of the Post and Telegraph Department, with a separate management committee and director. The bank carries out some commercial banking functions, but the objectives of the bank, as stated in the Post Office Savings Act, 1958, were not altered. These are essentially:

i) to provide a ready means for the deposit of savings; and,

ii) to encourage thrift and the mobilisation of savings, especially in rural areas.

11-11.2 Operations

Between 1889 and 1892 (when the first commercial bank was established), the Post Office Savings Bank enjoyed the monopoly of savings. Thereafter, the rate of interest of the commercial banks which were more attractive lured customers away from the Savings Bank, causing a decrease in deposits.

In 1950, the Post Office Savings Bank had 65% of total savings in the banking system, but by 1964 the bank accounted for only 9% of total savings and by 1976 the total savings deposit in the Post Office Savings Bank was less than ½% of total deposits in the banking system.

The bank has three different types of savings schemes:

i) Savings Stamps.

ii) Development Savings Certificates.

iii) National Premium Bond.

These special savings schemes which were designed to mobilise funds for national development had very little to write home about and, indeed, the total deposits mobilised through them has remained below ₦100,000 since 1975.

11-11.3 Source of Funds

Customers' deposits constitute, by definition, the only source of funds for the bank.

11-11.4 Problems

i) Rigidity of the operations. The processes of the operations are cumbersome (e.g. a customer needs guarantees, declarations and recommendations before opening an account).

ii) Stagnant and uncompetitive. The rates were 2½% for a long time and they were sliding (i.e. the more saved, the lower the rate). In 1976, the rate rose 4%, but the commercial banking rate now applies.

iii) Poor and uncompetitive service. Compared to commercial banks and other saving institutions, it has not been adequately competitive. Untrained staff, low morale and the absence of one-stop banking-supermarket facilities have also hindered development.

iv) Poor image. This is partly a reflection of the poor image of the P & T Department (e.g. long queues) and the lack of application of marketing concepts.

It was hoped that most of these problems would be solved after the change of name from Post Office Savings Bank to Federal Savings Bank in 1974 and the appointment of new management to run the affairs of the bank, but so far there has not been any appreciable improvement in the activities of the bank. It is, however, believed that the bank will eventually become an effective channel for the mobilisation of rural and small savings.

11-12 OTHER NON-BANK FINANCIAL INSTITUTIONS

11-12.1 Insurance Companies

Insurance companies are classified into life companies and non-life companies. The non-life companies handle general business such as fire, accident and motor vehicles, etc. The majority of the insurance companies fall into this category. Only a few companies deal in life assurance or combine the two.

A life policy can be either endowment or whole-life assurance. An endowment policy provides life assurance for an agreed term of years and for a fixed amount of money. A whole life assurance differs from endowment in that the assurance company pays the benefits only upon the death of the life assured.

Insurance companies are a major source of finance for industry directly or indirectly through the banks.

11-12.2 Pension Funds

Most large companies operate pension schemes for their staff. Each member of staff contributes a small portion of his salary every month, while the employer also sets aside a certain amount as provision for staff pension expenses. This amount can be invested in the stocks and shares of companies and government. The Pension Fund Act in Nigeria stipulates that pension scheme funds must be invested in the ratio of 50:50 in government and private stocks. Thus, pension funds constitute another reliable source of finance for industry.

11-12.3 National Provident Fund

This was established in 1961 by the Federal Government. Its resources are gathered from industrial and commercial firms which are legally required to make deductions from their staff and deposit the amounts deducted with the Fund. The N.P.F. is the largest single fund in the country. Its funds are invested in government stocks only.

11-12.4 Credit & Co-operative Societies

These are non-profit making lending institutions organised by private individuals. They accept deposits from their members and make loans to needy members rather than to industry.

11-12.5 Investment Corporations

These are state government institutions set up to provide credit for agriculture, small and medium scale industry and housing. Some of them provide both loans and equity finance to industry.

11-12.6 Finance Companies

Finance companies are privately owned investment companies which give assistance to companies which are unable to finance the purchase of assets through borrowing, hire purchase or leasing arrangement. Apart from providing finance, finance companies help companies to establish efficient management structures and controls. They also provide corporate finance services such as capital restructuring and project financing services.

REVIEW QUESTIONS

11.1 What are the main differences between merchant banks and commercial banks?

11.2 How far have the authorities succeeded in carving out specific roles for merchant banks in Nigeria?

11.3 Write short notes on:

i) Equipment leasing.

ii) Issuing Houses.

11.4 How do the functions of a merchant bank differ from the functions of a development bank?

11.5 What are the services offered by:

i) The Nigerian Bank for Commerce and Industry?

ii) Federal Mortgage Bank?

11.6 Write short notes on:

i) The National Provident Fund.

ii) Pension Funds.

11.7 Write brief notes on the Agricultural Credit Guarantee Fund.

CHAPTER TWELVE

BANKING LEGISLATIONS SINCE 1952

12-1 THE BANKING ORDINANCE, 1952

The first banking legislation in Nigeria was enacted in 1952. Prior to this time it was a period of free-for-all banking which culminated in several bank failures and losses to depositors. The need for laws and regulations to control the activities of banks led to the Paton Commission being set up in 1948. The report of the Commission led to the enactment of the first banking legislation — the Banking Ordinance, 1952.

Although this Ordinance has since been repealed, we shall nevertheless briefly examine the main provisions of this historic law to enable us to understand the development of the law of banking in Nigeria.

The Paton Commission defined banking as *'the business of receiving from the public on current account money which is to be repayable on demand by cheque and of making advances to customers'.* [1]

The Ordinance restricted, for the first time, the establishment and practice of banking to companies holding valid licenses. To qualify for a licence, the amount of paid-up capital for indigenous banks was fixed at ₦25,000 (£12,500) and ₦200,000 (£100,000) for expatriate banks. Banks were also required to maintain a reserve fund (Statutory Reserve) into which a minimum of 20% of annual profits had to be paid, until the balance on the reserve account was equal to the paid-up capital. Adequate provision also had to be made for liquidity.

The above stipulations were aimed at strengthening existing banks in order to avoid further failures, and also to stop the proliferation of banks. The Financial Secretary, a Briton, was given wide powers and sole authority to grant banking licenses after all conditions had been fulfilled.

The Ordinance became effective immediately for new banks, while existing banks were given up to three years to comply with its main

---

[1] G.D. Paton *Report on Banks and Banking in Nigeria* Government Printer, 1948.

provisions. About a year after the regulations came into effect six banks (3 expatriate and 3 indigenous) had been registered. These were:

i) Foreign: The British Bank of West Africa.

Barclays Bank (DCO).

The British and French Bank.

ii) Nigerian: The National Bank of Nigeria.

Agbonmagbe Bank.

African Continental Bank.

The Ordinance also introduced for the first time the periodic examination and supervision of all banks by government bank examiners. They were mandated to scrutinise the books of licensed banks and ensure that they complied with the regulations.

While it is generally admitted that the 1952 Banking Ordinance contributed immensely to the development of banking in Nigeria, the following defects were apparent:

i) The Ordinance did not make any provision for assisting banks in need, as there was no Central Bank then to act as 'lender of last resort'.

ii) The investment avenues for the banks' surplus funds were limited, so banks were compelled to keep their liquid resources idle. The indigenous banks were more seriously affected than the foreign banks as the latter had free access to the London Money Market and could also seek assistance from their London Head Offices.

iii) Although the minimum capital requirement clause in the Ordinance helped to reduce the number of banks, dubious practices and other abuses were not all prevented due to the lack of effective supervision by the government bank examiners.

12-2 THE BANKING ORDINANCE, 1958 (as amended in 1962)

The 1958 Ordinance defined banking business as *'the business of receiving money on current account, of paying and collecting cheques drawn by or paid in by customers, and of making advances to customers'*. Except for the slight change in phraseology, this definition was the same as that contained in the 1952 Ordinance.

The necessity for a licence was retained in the new Ordinance. However, the responsibility for the issue of the licence moved to the Minister of Finance or a person acting under his direction, after consultation with the Central Bank of Nigeria after its establishment in July, 1959.

12-2.1 Minimum Paid-Up Capital

The minimum paid-up capital as stipulated in the 1952 Ordinance for indigenous banks (i.e. ₦25,000) was retained in 1958 as it appeared to have curbed proliferation effectively. However, the capital requirement for foreign based banks was raised to ₦400,000 (£200,000). Since it was easier for foreign banks to mobilise capital, the figure was raised to avoid domination of the banking scene by expatriate companies.

12-2.2 Statutory Reserve

The reserve requirement of 1952 was raised by 5% to strengthen the capital base of existing banks. Every licensed bank in Nigeria was required to transfer a minimum of 25% of its net profit before any dividend was declared to a statutory reserve. This transfer had to be made every financial year until the balance on the reserve fund became equal to the paid-up capital of the bank. Where the amount of the reserve fund is equal to or in excess of the paid-up share capital, 12½% of the net profits are to be transferred to the Reserve Fund. No transfers are to be made until any past losses have been made good.

12-2.3 Legal Lending Limit

The maximum lending to one borrower was limited to 20% of the sum of paid-up capital and the statutory reserve, although inter-bank lending, international trade activities and lending to Marketing Boards were all excluded. This was a new provision aimed at ensuring a reasonable spread in the loan portfolios of banks rather than a concentration of loans in a few hands which would make banks vulnerable. The provision was also expected to contribute towards the capital adequacy of banks.

12-2.4 Other Major Provisions in 1958

The following additional restrictions (which was the beginning of tight official control over the activities of commercial banks in Nigeria) were imposed on the activities of banks:

i) The granting of advances or credit facilities against the security of the banks' own shares was prohibited.

ii) The granting of unsecured credit facilities in excess of ₦1,000 (£500) to any of the directors jointly or severally, or to any company or firm in which any directors had an interest, was prohibited.

iii) The granting of unsecured advances to the officials and employees of banks in excess of one year's emoluments was also prohibited.

iv) Banks could not engage in trade, acquire or hold shares in other companies or purchase, acquire or lease real estate except as may be necessary for the purpose of conducting their businesses, housing their staff or held as security.

12-2.5 Minimum Specified Liquid Assets

The 1958 Ordinance listed for the first time, the following as the specified liquid assets of a bank:

i) Notes and coins which are legal tender in Nigeria.

ii) Balances at the Central Bank.

iii) Balances at any other bank in Nigeria and money at call in Nigeria.

iv) Balances at any bank overseas.

v) Treasury Bills issued by the Federal Government.

vi) U.K. Treasury bills maturing within 93 days.

vii) Inland bills of exchange and promissory notes rediscountable at the Central Bank.

viii) Bills of exchange bearing 2 good signatures, drawn and payable in the U.K.

The Ordinance stipulated that every licensed bank should maintain a ratio of specified liquid assets to total demand liabilities as prescribed from time to time by the Central Bank of Nigeria.

12-2.6 Appointment of Examiner

The Ordinance specified the appointment of an examiner by the Minister of Finance or the Central Bank to examine periodically, under conditions of secrecy, the books and affairs of each and every licensed bank. Up to the opening of Central Bank of Nigeria bank examiners were on the staff of the Federal Ministry of Finance.

12-2.7 1962 Amendment

The 1958 Banking Ordinance was amended in 1962 as follows:

i) The paid-up capital of indigenous banks was raised from ₦25,000 (£12,500) to ₦500,000 (£250,000). The aim of the authorities was clearly to restrict the number of new banks, as existing banks were given up to seven years to comply with the new regulation.

ii) Foreign banks were required to keep assets of at least ₦500,000 (£250,000) within Nigeria to help the development of a money market and capital formation.

iii) The composition of specified liquid assets was slightly changed.

iv) Banks were allowed to own real estate for the purpose of future development.

There is no need to provide a detailed discussion and analysis of the 1962 amendment as both the 1958 Ordinance and its amendment in 1962 were repealed in 1969 by the Banking Act of that year which remains the current banking legislation in Nigeria, except for minor amendments in 1970, 1972 and 1979. (We shall examine this important banking legislation — The Banking Act, 1969 — 12-4 below).

12-3 CENTRAL BANK OF NIGERIA ACT, 1958

A review of banking legislations in Nigeria would be incomplete without some comments on the Central Bank of Nigeria Act, 1958. In this brief review we shall examine the main provisions of the Act.

12-3.1 Objects

The principal objects of the bank are stated in section 4 as:

i) Issuing legal tender currency in Nigeria.

ii) Maintaining external reserves and safeguarding the international value of the currency.

iii) Promoting monetary stability and a sound financial structure in Nigeria.

iv) Acting as banker and financial adviser to the Federal Government.

12-3.2 Capital and Reserve

The Bank's authorised capital was fixed at £1.5 million (₦3 million) and was held by the Federal Government. The Bank maintains a general reserve fund. Each year 1/8 of net profits of the Bank for the year was allocated to the fund until it was equal to the paid-up capital. Thereafter 1/16 of the net profits of the year was to be allocated. The remaining profit was appropriated as follows:

i) One half was to be applied to the retirement of any outstanding obligations of the Federal Government to the Bank arising from the financing of the cost of the printing, minting and shipment of the initial stock of the Bank's notes and coins.

ii) The remainder of the net profits was to be paid to the Federal Government.

12-3.3 Board of Directors

The Board consists of a Governor, a Deputy Governor, three Executive Directors and eight part-time Directors. It is responsible for the policy and general administration of the affairs and business of the bank.

The Governor or, in his absence, the Deputy Governor, are in charge of the day-to-day management of the bank and are answerable to the Board for their acts and decisions.

12-3.4 Sole Right to Issue Currency

The Bank has the sole right of issuing notes and coins throughout Nigeria and neither the Federal Government nor any State Government nor any person shall issue currency notes and coins. Notes and coins issued by the Bank are legal tender in Nigeria at their face value for the payment of any amount.

12-3.5 External Reserves

The Bank is authorised to maintain a reserve of external assets consisting of all or any of the following:

i) Gold coin or bullion.

ii) Balances at any bank outside Nigeria with convertible currencies.

iii) Treasury Bills having maturity not exceeding one year by a foreign government with a convertible currency.

iv) Securities of, or guaranteed by, a government of a foreign country whose currency is convertible to sterling or gold.

v) Securities of, or guaranteed by, international financial institutions of which Nigeria is a member, if such securities are expressed in sterling or in a currency which is freely convertible into sterling, dollars or gold and whose maturity does not exceed five years.

vi) Nigeria's gold tranche in the International Monetary Fund.

The value of the reserve of external assets must not be less than 25% of the total demand liabilities of the Bank.

12-3.6 General Powers of the Bank

The main banking functions of the Bank are to:

i) issue demand drafts;

ii) purchase and sell gold coin or bullion;

iii) open accounts for, and accept deposits from the Federal and State Governments or corporations and institutions of such governments, banks and other financial institutions;

iv) purchase, sell, discount and rediscount bills of exchange; and,

v) purchase and sell securities of the Federal Government maturing in not more than 5 years.

12-3.7 Relations with the Federal Government

The Bank is entrusted with the Federal Government's banking and foreign exchange transactions in Nigeria and abroad, including payments to, or in respect of, the International Monetary Fund. However, the Federal Government may maintain accounts in Nigeria with other banks with the approval of the Minister of Finance and the Central Bank. The Bank is also entrusted with the issue and management of Federal Government loans publicly issued in Nigeria.

12-3.8 Relations with Other Banks

The Bank may act as banker to other banks in Nigeria and abroad. The bank is permitted to seek the co-operation of other banks in Nigeria in order to:

i) promote and maintain adequate and reasonable banking services for the public; and,

ii) ensure a high standard of conduct and management throughout the banking system.

The Bank may also regulate advances by prescribing a minimum ratio to be maintained by each bank in respect of total loans, advances and discounts granted to indigenous persons. It can also issue directives in respect of cash reserves and liquidity ratios, etc.

The direct control of banks as a tool of monetary control is used frequently. Details of these measures are contained in the Monetary Policy Circulars issued annually and have already been discussed — see Chapter Three in particular.

12-4 BANKING ACT, 1969 (as amended by Banking (Amendment) Act 1970)

12-4.1 Definition

Banking business is defined in the 1969 Act as *"the business of receiving monies from outside sources as deposits irrespective of the payment of interest, and the granting of money loans and acceptance of credits or the purchase of bills and cheques or the purchase and sale of securities for account of others or the incurring of the obligation to acquire claims in respect of loans prior to their maturity or the assumption of guarantees and other warranties for others or the effecting of transfers and clearings, and such other transactions as the commissioner may, on the recommendation of the Central Bank, by order published in the Federal Gazette designate as banking business".*

A banker means any person who carries on banking business, and includes a commercial bank, an acceptance house, discount house and financial institution, while commercial banking is described as a bank whose business includes the acceptance of deposits, withdrawable by cheque.

Acceptance houses specialise in the granting of acceptance facilities, while discount houses are those whose main business consists of trading in and holding commercial bills of exchange, Treasury Bills and other securities.

Financial institution means those institutions allowed to transact banking business, but which are not a commercial bank, an acceptance house or a discount house.

Upon the enactment of the Banking Act 1969, the Banking Ordinance of 1958 was repealed. For the full text of the Banking Act, 1969 see Appendix 1.

12-4.2 Licensing

As mentioned earlier, banking business in Nigeria is restricted to companies duly incorporated in Nigeria and in possession of a valid licence granted by the Federal Minister of Finance. To apply for a banking licence, the 1969 Act stipulates that an application should be made in writing, through the Central Bank, to the Federal Minister of Finance. The applicant must submit:

i) a copy of the Memorandum and Articles of Association;

ii) a copy of the latest Balance Sheet of the company; and,

iii) any other particulars called for by the CBN.

12-4.3 Requirements as to Minimum Paid-Up Capital

The minimum capital requirement for indigenous banks was increased from ₦500,000 to ₦600,000; while the paid-up capital of a bank directly or indirectly controlled from abroad was raised from its existing level of ₦400,000 to ₦1,500,000 — an increase of 275%. It is believed that the aim was to curb the proliferation of foreign banks.

Discussions about the indigenisation of foreign banks began during this period.

12-4.4 Maintenance of Reserve Fund (Statutory Reserve)

The 1958 provisions regarding statutory reserves discussed earlier were retained without any amendment. The provision in respect of disclosure of interest by directors, as contained in the 1958 Ordinance, was also retained in 1969.

12-4.5 Cash Reserves and Liquidity Ratio

The Act required that the Central Bank shall, from time to time, stipulate minimum holding by licensed banks of cash reserves, specified liquid assets, special deposits and stabilisation securities. Each bank must ensure that its holdings of these items are not less than the amount prescribed by the Central Bank. (These ratios are specified every year in the CBN Monetary Policy Guidelines discussed in Chapter Three.) In 1982, cash reserves range between 2% and 5%, depending on the size of the bank, while the liquidity ratio stands at 25%.

12-4.6 Restriction on Certain Activities of Licensed Banks

The maximum lending to one borrower which was limited to 20% in 1958 was revised upwards to 33⅓% of the sum of the paid-up capital and statutory reserves of the bank. The other restrictions stipulated in 1958 were retained in 1969.

In addition, the 1969 Act provided that no bank should own any subsidiary company which is not carrying on banking business, except a nominee company dealing in stocks and shares for, or on behalf of, the bank's customers or clients.

12-4.7 Books of Accounts

Every licensed bank is required to keep proper books of account with respect to all the transactions of the bank.

12-4.8 Delivery of Returns, etc. to Central Bank

The Act specified all the reports that must be rendered to the Central Bank. These include:

i)   1st Schedule — Monthly Statement of Assets & Liabilites (submitted monthly)

ii) 2nd   ''   — Report on Loans and Advances analysed sector by sector (submitted monthly)

iii) 3rd   ''   — Accounts: Balance Sheet and P & L (submitted annually)

iv) 4th   ''   — Auditor's Report (Annually)

v)   5th   ''   — Auditor's Analysis of Doubtful Advances (Annually)

12-4.9 Powers of the Central Bank

The Act empowered the Central Bank to appoint officers of the Bank as examiners with power to examine periodically, under conditions of secrecy, the books and affairs of each and every licensed bank. The examiners have a right of access at all times to the books and accounts and vouchers of banks. They are also entitled to require from the officers and directors of any bank such information and explanation as they think necessary for the performance of their duties. Apart from the periodic and routine examinations, special examinations can also be conducted. An examination report may lead to reorganisation, control of the operations of the bank by the CBN or revocation of the bank's licence and the winding up of the business.

The provisions of the 1969 Act, particularly with regard to the supervisory powers of the CBN, were aimed at correcting known defects in the banking system and to close all the loopholes in the previous legislations.

12-5 BANKING (AMENDMENT) ACT, 1979

The Act was promulgated on 28 September, 1979 as an amendment to the Banking Act, 1969. There were three principal amendments.

12-5.1 Requirements as to Minimum Paid-Up Capital

i) The minimum capital requirement for indigenous banks should not be less than ₦600,000, while the minimum paid-up capital of banks with foreign interests should not be less than ₦1,500,000. The paid-up capital of a merchant bank should not be less than ₦2,000,000.

ii) The Central Bank was given authority to specify the minimum ratio which licensed banks should maintain between their respective paid-up capital, plus reserves on the one hand and their loans and advances on the other.

iii) The CBN would also specify for merchant banks the ratio of deposits and call money held for other banks to be retained in liquid assets, loans and advances to the bank's total assets and total loans and advances that may be repayable within one year.

iv) A bank which fails to maintain any ratio specified may not increase its loans and advances without the approval of the CBN.

12-5.2 Authorised Lending Limit

The Act restated the authorised lending limit to be 33⅓% of the sum of the paid-up capital and statutory reserves of a commercial bank and, in the case of a merchant bank, not more than the sum of its paid-up capital and statutory reserves. Other statutory restrictions in respect of bank shares as security, loans to directors, loans to staff, remained unchanged.

12-5.3 Merchant Banking

The following new provisions were made in respect of merchant banks.

A merchant bank should not accept any deposit withdrawable by cheque except from its corporate clients nor accept from any depositor total interest-bearing deposits of an amount lower than ₦50,000. Similarly, except with the prior approval of the Central Bank, a merchant bank may not hold for more than 6 months any equity interest acquired in a company while managing an equity issue.

The amendment included merchant banking in the list of banks and financial institutions and defined a merchant banker as *"any person in Nigeria who is engaged in wholesale banking, medium and long-term financing, equipment leasing debt factoring, investment management, issue and acceptance of bills and the management of unit trusts".*

With the above amendments, the Banking Act, 1969 remains the sole operating banking law and legislation in Nigeria.

12-6 DISHONOURED CHEQUES (OFFENCES) ACT, 1977

The Act was designed to protect businessmen and other individuals against the fraudulent use of cheques. The Act renders it an offence for any person in Nigeria to induce the delivery of valuable goods to himself or to any other person or to purport to settle a lawful obligation by means of a cheque which, when presented within a reasonable time, is dishonoured on the grounds that no funds or insufficient funds were standing to the credit of the drawer of the cheque. Such offences are punishable by two years imprisonment (without an option of a fine) in the case of individuals and a ₦5,000 fine in the case of a corporate body. Cheques must be presented within 3 months of the date of issue.

REVIEW QUESTIONS

12.1 Outline the main provisions of the Banking Act, 1969.

12.2 Write short notes on:

    i) Dishonoured cheques (Offences) Act, 1969.

    ii) Banking (Amendment) Act, 1979.

PART III

SERVICES OFFERED
BY BANKS

CHAPTER THIRTEEN

BANKER & CUSTOMER RELATIONSHIP AND RESPONSIBILITIES

13-1 INTRODUCTION

In this opening Chapter of Part III, it is appropriate to examine the relationship which exists between the banker and his customer, concentrating particularly on the duties and responsibilities of the former and the obligations of the latter. We shall also examine the types of customers with which banks usually deal.

The basic relationship between banker and customer is that of debtor and creditor respectively. To constitute a person as a customer an account — current or deposit — must be opened. Normally, the banker is the debtor and the customer the creditor, but when a customer overdraws his account, the roles are reversed (i.e. the banker becomes the creditor, while the customer becomes the debtor). The money which the customer deposits for the credit of his account is not, in Banking Law, held in trust for the customer, but borrowed from him with a promise to repay it or any part of it. The banker is, therefore, obliged to honour the customer's request for repayment addressed to the branch where an account is kept, in writing, during banking hours.

Thus, it can be seen that the banker/customer relationship is governed by the general rules of contract, agency, bailor/bailee, mortgagor/mortgagee and the various rules and conventions of banking practice.

A relationship of principal and agent exists when the banker is acting as collecting banker for cheques paid in by customers. When a customer keeps valuables with his banker for safe custody the bailor/bailee relationship is established. When granting an advance or loan secured by real estate or other tangible assets, such assets are mortgaged to the bank. When a bank takes such a mortgage the relationship of mortgagor/mortgagee is established. Finally, certain rules of banking practice (e.g. taking references before a new current account is opened) have assumed the force of law and a bank which fails to comply with such rules does so at its own peril.

13-2 THE BANKER'S DUTIES

The banker's duties can be summarised as:

i) To receive money, cheques and other instruments for collection and subsequent credit to the customer's current or deposit account.

ii) To pay cheques and other withdrawal authorities properly drawn by the customer, during banking hours at the branch where the account is kept or elsewhere as agreed.

iii) To maintain secrecy concerning the customer's account and other affairs.

iv) To give reasonable notice to a customer before closing his account, especially a credit account.

v) To pay agreed interest on deposits and to ensure that the customer's money is safe.

13-3 THE CUSTOMER'S OBLIGATIONS

The customer is obliged to draw his cheques, etc., in such a manner as not to facilitate fraud and to pay reasonable fees for services rendered by the bank. In Nigeria, these charges are fixed in a Bankers' Tariff issued by the CBN on the recommendation of the Bankers' committee.

13-4 TYPES OF CUSTOMERS

13-4.1 Personal Customers

These are mainly workers whose salaries and wages are paid direct to banks for the credit of their accounts. Other categories of personal customers are pensioners and students who receive cheques for their maintenance.

In order to open a personal account, the bank's application form needs to be completed. The information required on the form includes the full name, address and occupation of the applicant. A column is usually provided for a speciman signature and the name of previous or existing bankers. Most banks require a new current account customer to be introduced by two referees who may be customers of the bank or another bank. The referees are required to attest to the fact that the applicant is considered a suitable person to operate an account. A letter of introduction from the employer of the applicant will, in most cases, be sufficient reference for the opening of an account. This is the only method used by banks to ascertain that a new customer is responsible and reputable.

If a bank takes all the necessary precautions before opening a new account, it will receive full protection of the law, even where a person, who is not the true owner of a cheque, uses it to open an account. The bank must, however, act in good faith and without negligence. Failure to obtain and follow up references and to obtain the name and address of the employer of a new customer would be deemed to be negligence on the part of the bank.

13-4.2 Business Customers

i) The Sole Trader

This is the one-man business. The proprietor provides all the initial capital to start the business. Such businesses are, therefore, generally small as the owner has limited funds or capital. Sole traders are usually shop-keepers, small factory owners, farmers or professionals (doctors, accountants, architects, etc.)

The main advantages and disadvantages of being a sole trader are:

1. Advantages

a) The owner has independence — he can run the business the way he likes without consulting anybody.

b) Customers can receive personal attention and service.

c) Employees are personally known and supervised, thus ensuring effective operations.

d) The business is easy to establish, especially if the owner is using his personal name. However, if a business name is to be used, then the name must be duly registered and a Certificate of Registration issued by the Registrar of Business Names.

2. Disadvantages

a) The owner has unlimited liability for the debts of the business. This means that if the business should become bankrupt, the owner's personal assets may be used to pay its creditors.

b) The owner probably has only a limited amount of capital, so expansion is hampered.

c) Long hours have to be worked and holidays often cannot be taken as this could mean closing the business. Should the owner go sick, the business may slow down or stop operating altogether.

Opening an account for sole trader follows the same procedure as for a private individual. However, if the businessman is using a business name, the bank would normally require sight of the original certificate issued by the Registrar of Business Names and keep a photocopy of the certificate in its records.

Sole traders are not required by law to submit audited annual accounts. However, many sole traders prepare accounts annually to ascertain their tax liability and also the profitability of the business. Indeed, whenever such business require a bank loan, audited accounts are called for by the bank to ascertain how profitable the business has been.

ii) Partnerships

A partnership is a form of business organisation in which two or more persons agree to own and run a business enterprise in common with a view to making profit. The partners have joint responsibility for the risks, profits or losses of the business.

The partnership has some similarity to the sole trader as a business unit, but is often larger because, as there is more than one owner, there is likely to be more capital. The most common types of partnerships are those formed by professionals such as doctors, accountants, lawyers and surveyors. A partnership is usually governed by a written agreement known as the Deed of Partnership, which sets out:

a) the nature of the business;

b) the ways in which the partnership may be ended;

c) the amount of capital to be contributed by each partner; and,

d) the method of sharing of profits and losses, etc.

1. Advantages

a) The capital contributions of each partner increases the pool of capital fund.

b) The special skill of each partner can be tapped at no extra cost to the firm.

c) It is easier to borrow money, because a bank may have greater confidence in a group of people instead of one person.

2. Disadvantages

a) It is not a legal entity.

b) Decisions may take longer as there is more than one owner.

c) There may be disagreements among partners.

d) Liability is unlimited for active partners.

e) The death or resignation of a partner may disrupt the business.

To open an account for a partnership, the bank must ensure that the application is signed jointly by all partners. (Where the members appoint one partner to operate the account without restriction, then whatever he does binds the firm. In such a case, that partner has a right even to arrange an overdraft for the firm.) To open an account for a partnership, instructions are taken as to who is to sign cheques and other authorities and a mandate is taken in respect of this, signed by all partners. This establishes the joint and several liability of each partner for monies lent to the partnership. As some partnerships can have up to 20 partners, banks usually insert a clause in the mandate which states that an act carried out by any partner in connection with the bank account is deemed to be in the ordinary course of business. This means that one partner can negotiate a loan from the bank and all partners would be jointly and severally liable.

iii) Private Limited Liability Companies

The most important advantage that private companies have over the sole trader and partnerships, is that of limited liability. This means that the owners — the shareholders — are liable only for the amount of their share capital, so their personal assets cannot be taken to pay for the debts of the company. Also, the limited liability company has a separate legal entity and can be sued. All companies are required to file their annual accounts and directors' report with the Registrar of Companies.

To open an account for a limited liability company in Nigeria, the bank's prescribed forms must be completed. The bank must obtain a copy of the resolutions of the Board of Directors authorising the opening of the account and that resolution should indicate the signatories to the account. Then, the banker will obtain a copy of the Memorandum and Articles of Association of the company and the Certificate of Incorporation. The borrowing powers of the company must also be ascertained.

iv) Public Limited Companies

This is the largest form of business organisation. Any member of the public can buy shares in a public company. The shares are sold on the Stock Exchange and the daily/weekly prices of shares are published in newspapers. The shareholders of public companies can attend the annual general meeting of the company where the annual report and accounts are presented.

1. Advantages

a) Separate legal entity and limited liability.

b) Ability to raise capital by issuing shares.

c) Ability to borrow money, because of the volume of its assets.

2. Disadvantages

a) It is expensive to form.

b) Shareholders have no real say in the running of the company.

c) Employees do not have enough contact with those in charge.

The *Memorandum of Association* is a document drawn and signed by the founders of a proposed company. It contains the company's name and address, its object, the liability of members, the number of shares and their value and division. It also contains the rules governing the company's relationship with third parties.

The *Articles of Association* contain the rules for the internal conduct and management of the company. They deal with such matters as the issue of shares, meetings of shareholders and how they are to be conducted, appointment of directors, the borrowing powers, voting rights of shareholders and provisions as to audits, accounts and so on.

Registration of a company is effected by forwarding an application accompanied with copies of the Memorandum and Articles of Association (usually printed as a single booklet) to the Registrar of Companies. After ensuring that all legal requirements have been met, the Registrar will issue a Certificate of Incorporation, after which a private company may commence trading. However, a public company is also required to send a copy of its *Prospectus*, which states how the company has raised its capital, to the Registrar of Companies. The Registrar will then issue a trading certificate which authorises it to start business.

As stated above, the Memorandum of Association of a company states the number and value of the proposed share capital and the types of shares. This is the *authorised capital* of the company. Out of the authorised capital, shares are issued from time to time as the need arises until the whole amount becomes exhausted. The amount of the authorised capital issued is the *issued and paid-up capital.* There are three main types of share which are commonly issued by public limited companies.

1. Ordinary Shares

These are the most common types of shares. Ordinary shareholders bear the main risk of business. When good profits are made, they receive high dividends, but when poor profits are made, they receive a small dividend or none at all. In the event of a company going out of business, the ordinary shareholders will be the last to receive any repayment of capital on their shares. In return for the higher risk which ordinary shareholders take, they have the power to control the business through voting at annual general meetings.

2. Preference Shares

These are shares that have a fixed rate of dividend or interest and that fixed rate is paid in preference to the ordinary shareholders. However, the interest is only paid if the company makes profits. In the event of winding up such shareholders will also have preference over ordinary shareholders in the repayment of capital.

There are three types of preference shares. In the case of *cumulative preference shares,* if insufficient profits are made during a certain year to pay a dividend to preference shareholders, the arrears are carried forward each year until it can be paid off. In the case of *non-cumulative preference shares,* any dividends not paid in one year are lost. *Redeemable preference shares* are shares which the company can buy back. *Participating preference shares* can participate in further dividends after the ordinary shareholders have been paid a specified percentage. This means that in a good year when high dividends are paid the preference shareholders will also participate in the company's prosperity.

3. Deferred Ordinary Shares or Founders' Shares

These are now scarcely issued. They used to be issued to the promoters or founders of a company. These shareholders share the remaining profit (if any) after all the shareholders have been paid.

v) Other Customers

1. Clubs and Societies

The procedure to be followed in opening accounts for clubs, societies and other voluntary organisations is similar to those of sole traders and partnerships. A copy of the society's rules and regulations should be examined. It is necessary to see what powers are vested in the Chairman, Secretary and other officials of the society (e.g. have they any borrowing powers?). A copy of the resolution certified by the President and the Secretary authorising the opening of the account and appointing the signatories to the account must be obtained. This will be in the form of extracts from the minutes book certified by the President and the Secretary. In law a club or society cannot be sued, so it is necessary for a member to assume personal responsibility for any loan granted by a bank.

2. Executors, Administrators and Trustees

The person appointed to execute the will of a deceased customer is *the executor.* The executor collects all monies due to the estate and makes distributions to the beneficiaries of the will. Where a person dies without a will (i.e. he dies intestate), his friends or relatives can be appointed as administrators to deal with the estate.

As shown above, executors and administrators hold their appointments for a relatively short time to assemble the assets, pay the relevant tax on them and distribute them accordingly.

A person who looks after another person's property for a long period of time is called *a trustee.* An example is when a large sum of money is provided for in a will to be invested and held in trust for the children of a deceased person until they attain a certain age. Another type of trustee is the trustee in bankruptcy. Here the trustee takes charge of selling the assets of the bankrupt and using the proceeds to pay off his debts. In the case of limited liability companies, this function is performed by liquidators and receivers. The liquidator is appointed by a court in a compulsory winding up or by members of the company in a voluntary winding up.

The executor, administrator or trustee usually assumes control over the relevant bank account which will already be in existence. The appropriate proof for the assumption of such responsibility will naturally be required by the bank.

13-5 A BANKER'S DUTY OF SECRECY

The banker's duty of secrecy is a very important obligation as a breach gives a customer a claim to damages if he takes up the matter in a court of law. As a result, every bank in Nigeria requires its staff to sign a declaration of secrecy as regards the affairs of the customers of the bank. The banker must exercise extreme care in disclosing the balance on customers account, in answering requests for status reports from other banks and in giving other information about customers. When a customer's cheque cannot be paid for lack of sufficient funds on the account only the accepted reason (e.g. 'Refer to Drawer') must be stated. Telephone enquiries must also be handled with great care. Balances should only be given on the telephone when the customer can be reasonably identified.

There are certain circumstances under which a banker is discharged from his duty of secrecy. These include:

i) where disclosure is under compulsion of law;

ii) under a public duty;

iii) where the interests of the bank demand disclosure (e.g. where a bank issues a writ for the repayment of an advance as the amount due is normally stated on the writ); or,

iv) where made by the express or implied consent of the customer.

Even when a customer has closed his account the duty of secrecy does not cease.

REVIEW QUESTIONS

13.1 Explain the relationship between banker and customer. In your answer outline:

    i) the duties owed by a banker to his customer; and,

    ii) the duties owed by a customer to his banker.

13.2 What are the advantages and disadvantages of being in business as a sole trader?

REVIEW QUESTION

CHAPTER FOURTEEN
GENERAL BANKING SERVICES

14-1 SERVICES PROVIDED BY NIGERIAN BANKS

Our discussion of banking services will be restricted to the services provided by commercial banks and merchant banks. Merchant banks in Nigeria are wholesale banks, accepting deposits only in large amounts with a minimum of ₦50,000. They operate with a few branches, so are not equipped to provide some services. On the other hand, commercial banks with their extensive network of branches can be described as retail bankers, providing a wide range of banking services. Merchant banks engage mainly in medium and long-term finance, while commercial banks provide short-term loans and advances. In our discussion of banking services we shall clearly distinguish those services that are provided exclusively by merchant banks.

Before one can benefit from all the numerous services provided by banks one is expected to be a customer of the bank, operating a current account. Those operating only deposit and savings accounts may not be able to take advantage of all the services available. In view of this, before the services are discussed, it is necessary to examine briefly the types of accounts offered by banks.

14-2 TYPES OF ACCOUNT

14-2.1 Current Account

This is the principal and most popular account. They are accounts opened so that cheques can be paid into them and drawn on. Deposits on current accounts are repayable on demand (i.e. no notice is required before money can be withdrawn). Thus, it is also called a *demand deposit.* Before a current account is opened, proper references will be required.

Debit and credit entries are posted to the account on the day of the transactions, with the net balance being shown at the close of business. No interest is payable on credit balances on current account.

The account must always be kept in credit, except in cases where overdraft facilities have been granted. When an overdraft facility is granted, a 'limit' is set, up to which the customer can draw. Security may be required to support the overdraft. The customer is charged interest on such facilities. Apart from this, banks also charge fees for services rendered to current account customers. In cases where customers keep reasonable balances on their current accounts, these charges may be waived.

14-2.2 Deposit Accounts

When a customer wants to earn interest on his money, he can open a *deposit account*. The customer can deposit and withdraw funds at short notice, which is not insisted upon in practice, by using standard deposit and withdrawal forms. No cheque book is required to operate a deposit account and no references are needed to open them, so it is relatively easy to open such an account. It must be mentioned that no overdrafts are allowed on deposit accounts. It is also possible to open a fixed deposit account for 3 months, 6 months, 9 months and 1 year. Such deposits attract higher rates of interest, but they are expected to be kept for the fixed period of time. These are also called time deposits.

14-2.3 Savings Accounts

Savings accounts are similar to deposit accounts in many ways. They attract interest at a fixed rate and funds can be withdrawn at any time without notice. Savings accounts are used mainly by small depositors to save for a 'rainy day'.

14-2.4 Loan Accounts

The loan facility is mainly, but not exclusively, used by sole traders and individuals such as salary earners to help them over a difficult period or supplement the payment of school fees, medical bills and some unforeseen expenses. The amount granted is generally small and it is repayable in the shortest possible time.

When a loan is granted to Mr X, a new account entitled "Mr X Loan Account" is opened in the books of the bank. This will be in addition to his normal current account. First, the amount of the loan will be debited to Mr X's current account either by a cheque drawn by him or by a debit voucher to draw the approved loan in cash. Then the current account will again be credited with the same amount, while the new account "Mr X Loan Account" will be debited with the amount of the loan. Thus, the current account will revert to its old position as it was before the loan was granted, while the new account (i.e. Loan Account) will carry a debit balance being the total loan granted to Mr. X. If repayment is on monthly basis the loan account will be credited with the agreed amount every month; while the current account absorbs the debit. The deductions will continue until the loan is totally liquidated. Repayments will also take into consideration the interest element.

Merchant banks and some foreign banks do not use the system described above.

Operating a current account is not a *sine qua non* for obtaining a loan. A loan can be granted and a Loan Account created without a current account. Cheques will then be required monthly to cover the agreed monthly repayments. Prepayments can be made by sending a cheque covering repayments for 3 months, 6 months or more. Interest charges are paid upon demand.

On some occasions a business customer may have a need for medium to long-term finance for extending the business premises of the company or buying new and more sophisticated machines. In Nigeria, the merchant banks specialise in this area. However, commercial banks are now also undertaking more term lending. In such cases the bank will lend on loan account.

14-2.5 Overdrafts

Commercial banks are usually more interested in short-term lending, so funds advanced on overdraft are in theory repayable on demand, while interest is payable on the outstanding balance on a daily basis.

Overdraft facilities are generally granted to business customers — large corporate bodies and some medium/small-scale enterprises. When a company is granted an overdraft of say ₦500,000 a separate account is not opened as in the case of loan. The facility allows the customer to overdraw his current account up to a limit of ₦500,000 until a specified date or further notice. The faciltiy is generally renewable on an annual basis. An overdraft is intended to fluctuate within the agreed limit, but need not always be utilised (i.e. the account can sometimes be in credit).

14-3 SERVICES TO PERSONAL CUSTOMERS

14-3.1 Open Credits or Cashing Credits

When a customer is travelling to another town to do business which will necessitate his staying there for some days or weeks, he can request his bank to establish an open credit for him. The customer's bank will authorise the branch concerned to honour all cheques drawn by the customer up to a certain limit. The specimen signature of the customer will be sent to the branch concerned. This arrangement can also be made with a branch of another bank where it is not represented.

14-3.2 Services to the Traveller

i) Travellers' Cheques

All commercial banks and merchant banks in Nigeria offer services to travellers by providing them with travellers' cheques and foreign currency. Travellers' cheques are a form of travel currency giving the holder the security of a letter of credit and the convenience of a local currency. They are issued in several denominations of the currency and are encashable at the correspondents of the issuing bank abroad. In practice, they are also usually acceptable at hotels, departmental stores, etc. Travellers' cheques can be denominated in several foreign currencies, but in Nigeria they are generally in dollars or sterling. The holder signs the cheques on their issue. When they are to be cashed the holder countersigns them in the presence of the cashier who checks the signatures before effecting payment.

In the event of loss of travellers' cheques a report should be filed immediately to the issuing bank by letter or cable. Invariably, the holder will be reimbursed fully for the loss in all genuine cases.

ii) Foreign Currency

Foreign currency notes especially pounds sterling and US dollars are available in limited quantities from all banks in Nigeria. These can be obtained to meet minor expenses like taxi or bus fares prior to encashing travellers' cheques, when on a journey. Unused Travellers' cheques and foreign notes can be cashed on return from foreign travel at the issuing bank. Nigeria has stringent foreign exchange regulations which limit the amount of foreign currency and travellers' cheques that can be obtained.

14-3.3 Safe Custody

As bank strongrooms are one of the safest places to keep valuable articles, customers usually sieze the advantage to keep their government stocks, share certificates, life assurance policies, certificates of occupancy (i.e. official title to landed property), deeds of conveyance, wills and jewellery in them for safety. Articles can either be deposited in sealed boxes or envelopes with the contents unknown to the bank officials, or made 'open' when the articles are listed and signed for.

A banker enters into a contract of bailment when safe custody items are received from a customer. If the bank charges for the service he is a paid bailee, and if he does not charge he becomes a gratuitous bailee. In law the paid bailee is expected to show greater care in the handling of the articles.

14-3.4 Status Inquiries

When a customer gives his bank's name to a supplier or to another bank for reference purposes, a request is sent to the customer's bank for brief assessment of the customer's financial standing. This is a reciprocal service among banks. In most cases the reply appears vague to the layman, but it means a great deal to the bank receiving the reply. A typical reply may read "considered good for your figures and purpose" (a favourable reply) or "we cannot speak for your figures" (an unfavourable reply). A suitable tactfully worded unfavourable reply could be put as follows:

"On the figures before us we are unable to answer your enquiry, but we do not think that our customer would enter into any contract which he could not see his way clear to fulfil".

Banks have developed a whole series of stereotyped replies which they can easily interpret. For instance:

i) "Undoubted for your figures" — this indicates considerable strength.

ii) "Considered good for your figures" — satisfactory.

iii) "Should be good for your figures" — this indicates some degree of doubt.

This service is provided in respect of both personal and business customers.

14-4 SERVICES TO BUSINESS CUSTOMERS

14-4.1 Financial Services

i) Loans and Overdrafts

We have already discussed this topic above.

ii) Medium and Long-Term Loans

In Nigeria one of the major differences between commercial banks and merchant banks is the line of demarcation drawn between short-term and medium or long-term financing.

By the nature of the sources of their funds, commercial banks are expected to provide only short-term facilities on loans or overdrafts to their customers which, in theory, are repayable within one year. This means that commercial banks provide mainly short-term facilities for working capital purposes. On the other hand merchant banks provide medium-term finance for expansion and development plans lasting over several years. Facilities are granted for periods between 3 and 7 years.

In recent years most of the leading commercial banks in Nigeria have started to widen the scope of their operations by setting up Corporate Service Offices which specialise in providing short and medium term finance to their corporate customers. Such finances are provided to businesses for factory construction and for the purchase of plant and machinery (i.e. project financing).

iii) Performance Bond

This service is provided to customers in the building and contracting industry where they are required to supply a performance bond before they can tender for contracts. The bond guarantees that the company has adequate financial resources to execute the contract successfully. When a banker gives such a guarantee, it usually takes a counter-indemnity so that he can claim against the customer in a case of default.

iv) Guarantees and Indemnities

An example is when a shareholder has lost his share certificate and has applied that a duplicate certificate be issued to him. Before a company consents to such a request, it will want a banker to add his guarantee to the request to reassure the company of its genuineness. As in the case of performance bond, the banker covers himself against loss by taking a counter-indemnity from his customer.

v) Bankers Drafts

A bank draft is a cheque drawn by a branch of a bank on another branch. It is issued on request to a customer who is compelled to make payment to a payee who wants to make sure that the cheque will not 'bounce'. Bank drafts are requested for when large payments are involved and when the payee has to part with valuable articles due to high incidence of bouncing cheques in this country.

14-4.2 International Trade Services

i) Bills for Collection

Assume that the customer is an exporter and that he is shipping goods to a buyer in New York, USA. The goods are being shipped on a *collection basis*. The exporter draws a bill of exchange payable on a specified date on the importer. The Nigerian exporter then gives the bill to his Nigerian banker to collect the proceeds on his behalf. The bank sends the bill to its correspondent in New York and requests that the bill be presented at the end of the term for payment. When the proceeds are received, the customer's account is credited with the naira equivalent.

In some cases the customer may forward the bill direct to the importer in New York for acceptance. After which the bill is returned to him. He then attaches the necessary documents to the bill when demanded, and passes it to his bankers who will forward it to New York for payment. A bill with documents attached to it is called a *documentary bill*. If no documents are attached, it is a *clean bill*. The customer will give clear instructions to the bank as to whether documents are to be released against acceptance — Documents Against Acceptance (D/A) — or only against payment — Documents Against Payment (D/P).

ii) Bills for Negotiation

If the customer is in dire need of funds and wants the proceeds of the bill immediately he may request his bank to negotiate the bill. This means that he sells the bill to the bank. The bank pays the customer the face value of the bill less a discount. It must be noted, however, that such negotiation is done 'with recourse'. This means that if the acceptor fails to pay the bank, the bank will claim from the customer. In such a situation the bank may ask the customer for security. If it is a documentary bill the documents will form part of the security.

iii) Documentary Credits

Nigeria being a major importer of manufactured goods, plant and machinery, etc. from abroad, we will consider a hypothetical case of a Nigerian importer receiving goods from a British exporter.

As soon as the British exporter sends his goods by sea, he receives a bill of lading from the ship's master. Prior to this he will have prepared an invoice showing details of the goods and their cost. He is also required to insure the goods and after doing this he obtains an insurance certificate. (In the case of an air shipment he obtains air waybill which takes the place of bill of lading.)

The bill of lading, the invoice and insurance certificate form the necessary papers required for a documentary credit. The documents are forwarded to the importer in Nigeria through a correspondent bank, also called the collecting bank, by the quickest possible means, as the Nigerian importer cannot claim the goods without the bill of lading.

This system gives protection to both the importer and the exporter. The exporter retains control of the goods until he is paid, since documents will not be released unless payment is effected. The importer too will be able to scrutinise the documents to make sure the description, cost and quantity of the goods are in conformity with the original contract.

One of the means devised by banks to handle this process is the documentary credit system.

The exporter is expected to indicate how payment is to be effected. If a documentary credit is stipulated, the importer will instruct his bankers to open a letter of credit in favour of the exporter. He will list all the conditions that must be fulfilled and the documents that must be submitted before payment can be made. Usually, the documents are the same as those discussed above.

After the opening of the letter of credit, the importer's bank will send a notification of the opening of letter of credit in favour of the exporter to its correspondent in the city where the exporter resides. The agent bank will then send a copy of the notification to the exporter. Depending on the terms of the credit, the agent bank may add its confirmation to the credit (i.e. its own undertaking to pay if all conditions are fulfilled). Thus, the bill becomes a confirmed credit. The credit may also be revocable or irrevocable. Generally, the terms of the credit cannot be altered without the agreement of all the parties.

Upon receipt of notification that a letter of credit has been opened in his favour, the exporter can rest assured that he will be paid as soon as he fulfils his own side of the bargain. A letter of credit is normally opened for a reasonable period of time.

As soon as the U.K. exporter ships the goods he presents the documents of title to the agent bank in London and receives payment after the documents have been carefully scrutinised and found to be in order.

The agent bank forwards the documents in two separate mails to the importer's bank in Nigeria and debits the importer's bank with the cost plus charges. An extra charge is levied if the agent bank (in U.K.) has itself confirmed the credit. The importer's bank (in Nigeria) checks the documents, and if in order, debits the customer's account with the total cost plus all the charges, including its own.

iv) Open Account

When goods are shipped by an exporter and he sends documents of title direct to the buyer with instructions that payment be effected on or before a certain date, such goods are said to have been shipped on open account basis. In this type of transaction, the credit worthiness of the importer should not be in doubt, so for obvious reasons, it will not be available to an importer who is just developing a trading relationship with an exporter.

14-4.3 Standing Orders

Customers making regular monthly or quarterly payments to an Insurance Company, or to the Federal Mortgage Bank or in respect of subscriptions to clubs, institutes and so on, may give banks standing instructions to effect such payments as and when due. Sufficient funds must be kept in the account to absorb the debit on the due date.

14-4.4 Business Advisory Service

One or two banks in Nigeria have started offering this service to their customers. The aim is to assist small business customers to develop their businesses in such a way that they can attract bank finance. Small scale traders are taught how to introduce simple record keeping and accounting into their operations. Union Bank, the pioneer in the provision of this service, has reported significant success.

14-4.5 Night Safes

A few banks provide this service in Nigeria. It enables customers to make deposits after normal banking hours. The customer is provided with a night safe wallet which can be locked. The customer puts his paying in slip and the cash in the wallet supplied, locks it and 'posts' it in the safe through the exterior wall of the bank.

The wallets are cleared in the morning and the customer's account credited. This service is particularly suitable for shopkeepers wishing to bank the day's takings rather than leave them in the shop overnight or carry large amounts home.

REVIEW QUESTIONS

14.1 A company in Japan sends goods to a customer in Kano. Describe the methods available to the Kano customer through his bank to make payment to the company in Japan. Indicate the relative merits of the methods.

14.2 Write short notes on:

    i) A Status Inquiry/Report.

    ii) Open credits or cashing credits.

14.3 List and describe the special services offered by a commercial bank in Nigeria which are likely to be of greatest use to personal customers.

CHAPTER FIFTEEN

BANK LENDING 1 — BASIC PRINCIPLES

15-1 THE BASIC PRINCIPLES OF LENDING

In the opening Chapters of this Part, we discussed the relationship between the banker and customer and the types of customers and accounts, (e.g. the different types of deposit accounts and loan accounts, including overdraft facilities).

Banks generally provide avenues for savings to those who have surplus funds. The bulk of such funds are then lent out to needy personal and business customers in loans and overdrafts. As lending appears to be one of the most intricate services provided by banks, we shall (in this chapter and the next), examine in some detail both the basic principles of bank lending and the mechanics of safe lending by delving into financial statement analysis and interpretation.

L. C. Mather, a banking author of great renown and an expert in the practical aspects of banking, has advised against following lending rules and regulations rigidly. He compares the principles of lending to economic laws *"in that certain facts and other things being equal a prescribed course should follow. They are neither independent nor unbreakable"*.[1] Thus, the principles must be weighed carefully and with an open mind. The three basic principles behind all bank lending, as recommended by Mather, but which should serve only as a guide, are discussed below.

15-1.1 Safety

The safety of any loan/advance is of paramount importance to the bank. Hence, banks lay great emphasis on the character, integrity and reliability of borrowers. There must be a reasonable certainty that the amount granted can be repaid from profits and cash flow generated from the operations of the company. If the advance is granted to a personal borrower the source of repayment must not be doubtful. In support of the safety requirement, the borrower must be able to provide acceptable security which will serve as something to fall back on if the expected source of repayment should fail.

---

[1] L. C. Mather *The Lending Banker 4th Edition* Waterlow & Sons, 1972. Page 16

15-1.2 Suitability

The banker should also satisfy himself about the suitability of an advance. Even where the requirements of a borrower satisfy all safety and risk considerations, it is absolutely necessary for the banker to ensure that the purpose of the loan is not in conflict with the economic and monetary policies of the Government. In Nigeria bank lending is highly regulated and controlled by the Central Bank. This is done through the issue of annual credit allocation guidelines and the imposition of quantitative and qualitative limitations on bank lending.[2] The guidelines vary from year to year depending on the monetary policy being pursued by the Federal Government. The purpose of the advance and its implications on the economy are, therefore, given due consideration when granting an advance.

Apart from the guidelines, there are certain ventures that are not encouraged by banks. For instance, a banker is not expected to lend to finance gambling, betting and other speculations. Commercial banks would also not usually provide long-term capital or equity.

15-1.3 Profitability

It is a well known fact that banks are businesses established mainly to make profits and not as charitable organisations. Therefore, any facilities granted are expected to yield some profit to the bank. What determines the amount of profit is the rate of interest charged. In Nigeria interest rates on advances are fixed by the Central Bank and are generally higher than the interest paid to depositors. Thus, banks are able to make profits relatively easily.

15-2 CANONS OF LENDING

These three basic principles of lending can be further broken down into other factors which must be considered when granting an advance. These other factors can be described as the *canons* of *lending*. An analysis of these canons follows.

In spite of all the myriad of controls, regulations and guidelines in respect of bank lending in Nigeria, banks have to exercise care and prudence in their lending activities.

[2] See Monetary Policy Circular — Credit Guidelines No. 16 Appendix 3.

When a bank manager or lending officer is approached for a loan or overdraft facilities, he should obtain satisfactory answers to some basic questions which we have described as the canons of lending:

i)   How much does the customer want to borrow?
ii) Why does the customer want bank finance? In other words, what does he want it for?
iii) How long does he want it for?
iv) How does he intend to repay?
v)   Is the customer's business financially strong enough to keep going if his plans suffer a setback?
vi) What security can he offer?
vii) What is your assessment of the customer?

15-2.1 Amount

The customer is expected to be able to determine fairly accurately how much finance he requires. He should, therefore, submit a cash budget. The capital resources of the borrower will also have to be determined. In the case of companies and partnerships, financial statements must be submitted covering a period of years. This will enable the branch manager to build up a picture of the business. He will be looking for trends in the changes of various figures over the years to see whether the business is growing in strength or whether there are signs of financial strain.

It is also necessary to evaluate the adequacy of the amount required. Is the bank being asked to lend too much or too little? There is no point granting a maximum amount which is inadequate to finance the project if the customer cannot contribute the balance from his own resources. The customer's contribution to the project is very important. It must be reasonable, as it is one of the ways the banker can determine the borrower's commitment. The higher his investment the greater will be his determination to succeed and make profits.

15-2.2 Purpose of the Loan

It must be emphasised here that commercial banks specialise in short-term loans. It is only in rare cases that they agree to go into medium and long-term finance. However, the Federal Government has for some years encouraged all banks to provide both short and medium-term finance especially to the manufacturing, agriculture and construction sectors. These are grouped in the preferred sector of the economy. Some other activities like domestic trade, import, personal and professional loans, etc. are not encouraged and classified in the 'less-preferred' sector of the economy. Banks are given the maximum amount of loans that can go to this class.

There are some ventures that are completely banned by the government and are not expected to be touched by any banker. For instance a banker is not expected to lend to finance gambling, betting and speculation. To lend money to a customer in anticipation of winning a gamble is not banking business. On the other hand, it is perfectly in order to lend money to a customer to enable him to acquire stock or shares in the anticipation of a rise in price.

15-2.3 For How Long?

As stated above, commercial banks are basically interested in short-term financing. Most of their deposits are repayable on demand or at short notice, so they cannot afford to lend in the long-term.

In general, requirements for capital outlay are not desirable banking business because they take the form of long-term debts repayable from profits generated from operations over a long period of time. Unless a speedy means of repayment can be seen, the borrower will be advised to seek more permanent finance elsewhere.

Banks are prepared, however, to grant working capital finance repayable on demand or renewable every year. This is generally done by overdraft, whereby a 'limit' is granted up to which the customer can draw. When the need is for medium-term loans, in which merchant banks specialise or lay emphasis, a good customer can be introduced to such a bank, or advised to approach a merchant bank. In some cases, two banks or more can pool their resources in what is called a syndicated loan to finance jointly a large project.

However, it should also be mentioned that in practice most of the leading commercial banks have now set up Corporate Finance Departments (with government encouragement) to make medium-term loans to a wide range of corporate customers.

15-2.4 How Does He Intend to Repay the Bank?

This is a crucial point. Repayment lies at the heart of any proposition before a bank manager or lending officer, as he will be more inclined to lend if the customer can demonstrate how and when repayment is to be made.

The borrower should be able to demonstrate clearly that he has carefully examined and worked out how the additional finance will help profitable growth and how the business can comfortably cope with arrangements for reducing the borrowing steadily. As repayment of every loan or advance is expected from future earnings, a borrowing customer must be able to submit a simple cash budget.

In the case of a personal loan, the manager will ask for details of the customer's earnings now and in the immediate future and his normal monthly expenditure. This statement will also show existing payments on a mortgage, insurance premiums, hire purchase repayments, personal and housekeeping expenses.

In the case of a business customer, loans and advances can only be repaid from future profits generated from operations as long as the business remains a going concern. Therefore, it is necessary to see that by granting bank facilities the company will make more profits. The manager will require a cash budget, projected profit and loss account and projected balance sheet of the company for the forth-coming year. For large corporate customers, a five year business plan and financial projections may be required.

A cash budget gives a monthly estimate of all future cash receipts and payments and shows the estimated closing bank balance at the end of each month for the period for which it is prepared. It, therefore, provides a guide to the maximum overdraft that is likely to be needed. In assessing the proposals, the bank manager examines the cash budget (or *Cash Flow*) and the projected financial statements critically. In considering the cash flow of a business, the manager should remember that although depreciation is treated as a business expense, it does not deplete cash and can be regarded as cash retained in the business.

The expected source of repayment usually signifies to the bank the type of advance required. For instance, if the facility is a bridging loan to cover a temporary deficit, the source and likely date of repayment can be determined with reasonble accuracy. Similarly, reliable borrowers may indulge in capital outlay with bank support pending a capital or debenture issue. Advances to a good borrower to expand his trading activities will usually be repaid from internally generated funds from operations. When a trader borrows to increase stocks, repayment should come from the proceeds from the sale of the goods. So, another very important factor that must be considered is the ability of the customer to manage his business efficiently. If there is any doubt about the ability, efficiency and integrity of the borrower, no facilities should be extended.

15-2.5 Strength of the Business

As discussed above, Balance Sheets and Profit and Loss Accounts for at least three years must be submitted, including the current and projected cash budget. The bank manager should analyse these carefully and compare the statements and figures with the trend shown in the accounts of the customer. Later, a meeting with the customer should be arranged to clear any outstanding questions and doubts. The customer should be prepared at such a meeting to outline details of his financial planning and control systems. After the meeting, the manager will be in a position to determine the inherent strengths and weaknesses of the company and whether the company is strong enough to keep going if the plans suffer a set back.

15-2.6 Security

The ability to produce tangible security is not the most important criterion for granting credit facilities, as the offer of security does not weaken the need for a thorough examination of the proposal. This does not mean that security is unimportant. After the bank manager has thoroughly evaluated the proposal, he is able to assess what risks the bank runs in lending to the customer. It is upon this assessment that he bases his request for security.

Security should never be looked upon as the source of repayment, but only as something to fall back on if the expected source of repayment should fail. It should serve only as a buffer (i.e. as insurance against unforeseen adverse developments). People generally make the mistake of thinking that because they have inherited a house worth ₦50,000 they can walk straight into any bank and take a loan of ₦50,000.

The customer is expected to satisfy all the conditions enumerated above before consideration is given to the question of security. In other words, an advance must be granted on the strength of the feasibility of the purpose for which it is required. However, the best plans may go astray and a real loss may be sustained: security is intended to minimise or eliminate such losses.

It is generally agreed, therefore, that advances are not to be made just because they are secured. As stated above, security is taken only as a form of insurance. The real security for any advance is the character of the borrower. The bulk of bank lending is based on trust and faith in the customer and his business.

15-2.7 The Borrower

As a general rule, the customer to whom facilities are to be extended must pass the test of reliability, personal integrity and honesty. He does not qualify for bank assistance if he lacks any of these qualities — however strong his security. It is, therefore, necessary for a good banker to know his customer very well and be able to judge not only the qualities mentioned above, but also the customer's ability, intelligence, dedication to work, knowledge of the basic operations of his company and business experience generally. This will enable the banker to determine whether or not the borrower will use the facility to advantage and repay it within the agreed period. The past records of the business can also throw some light on the performance of the borrower.

In the case of small companies, the success of the company is the success of the proprietor. The banker should see the profits record of the business and what happens to these profits. Does the proprietor spend all the profits or plough back a reasonable proportion into the business? If he does this, it is a sign of prudent financial management. It is also wise to know about the life style of the director or proprietor. Does he live prudently and modestly? If he is extravagant, this will reflect in his business expenses. To ensure the safety of the bank's money, it is necessary to know something about the health of the borrower and whether he possesses energy and drive. It is also very important that the customer be knowledgeable about his proposed venture. A person who has been a clerical worker all his life is not likely to succeed as a farmer because he lacks the experience. From the foregoing, it can be seen clearly that it is important that a banker assesses his customer's character fairly accurately before he determines his credit-worthiness.

15-3 SECURITIES ACCEPTABLE TO NIGERIAN BANKERS

As stated above, every lending proposition must be so good that the question of security becomes secondary. The branch manager only asks for security or support in case the business plans suffer a set back and the loan goes bad or becomes doubtful of repayment.

The types of securities submitted to banks include stocks and shares, life policies, bills of exchange, promissory notes, guarantees by third parties, title deeds, etc. Whatever class of security is taken, it is necessary for it to be valued professionally. Usually a margin will be deducted to cover the bank against over-valuation and market fluctuations.

There are four ways in which security can be taken:

i) by lien;

ii) by pledge;

iii) by mortgage; or,

iv) by assignment.

In these four cases the banker does not become the absolute owner of the property, but has rights over the property until the debt is repaid in full.

15-3.1 Lien

The borrower remains the owner of the property, but the creditor is in actual or constructive possession of the property. The creditor has no right to sell it, so it is a mere right to retain a thing.

15-3.2 Pledge

The pledgee (creditor) is entitled to the exclusive possession of the property until the debt is repaid. In certain circumstances he can sell. However, the ownership remains with the pledgor subject to the pledgee's rights. Thus, a pledge gives a special property in the thing pledged.

15-3.3 Mortgage

In a legal mortgage a special interest in the property passes conditionally to the mortgagee, who also has a right of sale, but not necessarily the possession of the property, which usually remains with the mortgagor[3]. Under an equitable mortgage the bank only establishes a right on the asset — it cannot sell. While it is advisable to take a legal mortgage, most banks relax the rules in some cases by taking an equitable mortgage, especially on stocks and shares. In such cases, the transfer forms are duly signed in blank which, when completed, becomes a legal mortgage. (A mortgage is the conveyance or transfer of an interest in land or other assets as security for a debt.) .

15-3.4 Assignment

The difference between a mortgage and an assignment is that a mortgage transfers an interest in assets, while an assignment transfers rights under contracts. For example, under a contract of life assurance, the insured or beneficiary has a right to receive a sum of money at maturity or death. It is this right that is assigned to the bank when an assignment is effected.

15-3.5 The Nigerian Context

In Nigeria, every bank has a set of rules and regulations on lending. These rules and regulations when they are made have legal backing. Nigerian Law makes it mandatory to obtain security for loans and advances. The Banking Act, 1969 as amended by the Banking Amendment Act, 1972 provides, *inter alia,* that no manager or other official of a licensed bank shall grant any advance, loan or credit facility to any person unless it is authorised in accordance with the rules and regulations of the bank. The regulations, however, allow banks to grant unsecured advances.

Securities acceptable to a Nigerian banker can be grouped into the following four classes:

i) a mortgage over land (and buildings);

ii) an assignment of a life policy;

---

[3] H. P. Sheldon *Practice and Law of Banking* MacDonald & Evans, 1958 p. 334

iii) a mortgage of stocks and shares; and,

iv) a guarantee.

15-3.6 Land as Security

A person owning land, which includes anything on it like buildings and other developments, must be able to submit proof of ownership. In Nigeria, prior to 1978, the title to land was evidenced by:

i) freehold conveyances and leases;

ii) certificates of occupancy; or,

iii) assignments of freehold conveyances, leases and certificates of occupancy,

So freehold conveyances, leases and assignments effected before March, 1978 are still valid. However, with effect from that date when the Land Use Act came into force, all undeveloped land in each State of the Federation became vested in the Governor of the State. Thus, only the State Governments could have a freehold interest in land. Under this Act, it is now illegal for individuals to prepare freehold conveyances in respect of undeveloped land. Those freehold conveyances effected before March 1978 are, however, still valid and are converted to rights of occupancy and are still acceptable as bank security[4].

As to developed property, leases and assignments effected after the Land Use Act, 1978 are valid provided the consent of the Governor is obtained to the transactions as provided by the Act[5].

The Act defines developed land as meaning land where there exists any physical improvement in the nature of road development services, water, electricity, drainage, building structure or such improvement that may enhance the value of the land for industrial, agricultural and residential purposes.

Since the enactment of the Land Use Act, the Certificate of Occupancy has become the most important title document to land. This certificate can only be issued by a State Governor and only relates to land in urban areas. The title to land in rural areas is called a Right of Occupancy.

---

[4] See Q. A. Adeniji *The Law & Practice of Banking in Nigeria* University of Ife Press. p. 86-94.

[5] *Ibid.*

This is processed by the Local Government, but must be signed and approved by the State Governor. Other valid title documents include a land certificate in parts of Lagos, conveyances registered before March, 1978 and assignments of developed property. It is, however, pertinent to mention that the Certificate of Occupancy is superior to any other title document. A Certificate of Occupancy must be registered within 6 months.

15-3.7 Valuation

A professional firm of Estate Surveyors and Valuers is usually engaged to value any property to be mortgaged to a bank. The customer pays the cost of the valuation, but the appointment of the valuer may be made by the bank which will only utilise the services of a reliable and reputable firm.

15-3.8 Perfecting the Security

A lawyer is usually appointed to determine the ownership of the property. Searches are conducted at the Land Registry and the Ministry of Lands and Surveys. After ascertaining the genuiness of the title documents, then the bank's charge forms must be duly completed. Thereafter, the customer should seek the consent of the Governor to mortgage or assign the property to the bank as required by law.

Following the execution of the charge forms and the grant of the Governor's consent, they must be stamped within 30 days. The stamp duty, payable to the Commissioner for Stamp Duty, is at the rate of 75k for every ₦200 in the case of legal mortgages and 35k for every ₦200 in the case of equitable mortgages. After stamping, registration must also be effected within 30 days at the Land Registry of the State where the property is located.

15-3.9 Assignment of a Life Policy

Assignment of a life policy is another security acceptable to Nigerian banks. In accepting the insurance certificate as security for bank loans, the banker must ascertain that:

i) The insurance company is registered under the Insurance Act, 1976.

ii) The insurance company is reputable and honours its obligations.

iii) The policy has acquired a surrender value. A policy does not acquire a surrender value until premiums have been paid for three years. The surrender value can be ascertained on a yearly basis from the insurance company of the assured.

iv) The age of the assured has been admitted. Before a life policy is taken, evidence of age is required. Usually a birth certificate or a sworn declaration of age is acceptable. Where this has not been submitted the insurance company may still go ahead to issue the policy and state that age is not admitted. Since the premium is based on age and lower premiums are payable by younger people, insurance companies usually reserve the right to adjust the sum assured before paying upon the policy on which age has been incorrectly stated. A bank taking a policy as security must, therefore, ensure that age has been admitted. If not, the assured should be requested to produce his birth certificate or sworn declaration of age which should be passed to the insurance company for the necessary admission of age.

v) The instalment premium payments have not fallen into arrears, as to be able to claim on a policy payments of premium must be regular.

vi) The policy holder has an insurable interest in the assured. An insurable interest is presumed in the following cases:

— individual on his own life;
— man on the life of his wife; and,
— woman on the life of her husband.

In other cases, the interest must be proved. For instance, a parent has no insurable interest in the life of a child and vice versa.

vii) Upon accepting a life policy as security, the beneficiary clause of the policy should be amended to cover assignment of the policy to the bank.

15-3.10 Stocks and Shares as Security

Stocks and shares of companies listed on the Nigerian Stock Exchange are generally acceptable as security for a bank loan. The prices of shares in public companies are published every week in the Business Times and other national papers. The prices can also be obtained from the Stock Exchange.

The mortgage of stocks and shares can be either legal or equitable. A legal mortgage is effected by taking steps to transfer the shares to be registered in the name of the bank or the bank's nominee. (Nigerian banks do not transfer shares into their names and they seldom use nominee companies.) In the case of an equitable mortgage, the share or stock certificates are deposited, with or without delivery of a blank transfer form to the lender[6]. Most banks in Nigeria take equitable mortgage by asking the borrower to surrender the share certificate and signing a transfer form. A bank cannot accept its own shares as security for its loan.

15-3.11 Guarantees as Security

In a contract of guarantee, the guarantor or surety agrees to be liable for the debts of another person (i.e. the customer of the bank), if he fails to pay the bank. Thus, the liability of the guarantor is secondary, since he cannot be called upon to pay unless the debtor defaults. Directors of a limited company are usually asked to guarantee the debts of the company. Officers of a club or society may also be requested to guarantee a loan or advance to the club.

In taking a guarantee as security, the guarantor will complete the necessary forms. When a limited company is guaranteeing an individual or another company, the banker must ensure that:

i) the Memorandum and Articles of Association of the company permit the company to issue guarantees;

ii) the Board resolution authorising the issue of guarantee is submitted; and,

iii) there is a Resolution authorising the guaranteed company to borrow from the bank[7].

Guarantees must be dated and stamped with a 15k stamp at the time of execution. The guarantor(s) should sign across the affixed stamp and

---

[6] See O.A. Adeniji — *The Law & Practice of Banking in Nigeria* p. 117

[7] *Ibid*

this should be witnessed by a bank official. A guarantee under seal must also be dated and stamped within 30 days with ₦3.00 stamp, usually affixed by the Commissioner for Stamp Duty[8].

15-3.12 Other Securities

i) Vehicles/Chattels

A bank can create a lien or bill of sale on vehicles or chattels. The invoices and other title documents are deposited with the bank. Thereafter, charge forms are prepared.

ii) Fixed and Floating Charge

This is created when all the assets of a limited company - plant, machinery, stocks, debtors, etc. (fixed and floating assets) — are charged to the bank for a bank loan by the creation of debenture. There are two kinds of debentures:

a) A charge on the company's fixed and floating assets, covering both present and future assets.

b) A charge on the company's fixed and floating assets incorporating a mortgage on factory buildings. This is called a mortgage debenture and is now generally more favoured by banks.

A limited liability company cannot create a debenture or borrow from a bank unless the Articles and Memorandum of Association of the Company empowers the Board of Directors to do so. The banker must, therefore, take the following steps before a debenture is created:

1. Ascertain from the Articles and Memorandum of Association that the Board is empowered to borrow and to charge the assets of the company.

2. Obtain a board Resolution to borrow from the bank and to create a fixed and floating charge in favour of the bank.

3. Obtain a current Tax Clearance Certificate covering three years from the company to facilitate the perfection of the security.

---

[8]Ibid

4. In the case of landed property, ensure that:

   a) the Governor's consent to mortgage has been granted, and,

   b) a seperate legal mortgage distinct from the debenture is created on the building.

5. Ensure that all legal documents are signed by authorised signatories.

6. Seek legal assistance as and when necessary.

208

REVIEW QUESTIONS

15.1 i) What are the basic requirements of any security?

ii) Describe the methods by which security can be taken.

15.2 i) What is the difference between a second mortgage and a sub mortgage?

ii) Describe how land as security can be perfected in Nigeria.

15.3 Apart from bringing an action against a mortgagor for the amount owed, what other remedies are available to a mortgagee when his mortgagor has defaulted?

CHAPTER SIXTEEN

BANK LENDING II — FINANCIAL STATEMENT ANALYSIS AND INTERPRETATION

16-1 INTRODUCTION

In this Chapter we shall concentrate more on the analysis of Balance Sheets of customers. However, as the title indicates, we shall also examine other financial statements which must be produced before a Balance Sheet can be constructed. These include Manufacturing Accounts, Trading Accounts, Profit and Loss Accounts and Appropriation Accounts.

It is necessary for a commercial bank to analyse the financial statements of customers seeking credit facilities in order to assess their credit worthiness and to ascertain that, when a facility is extended, it will be fully repaid. By studying and thoroughly analysing his customer's financial statements the branch manager can properly assess the degree of risk he is taking by approving a loan. Balance Sheet analysis complements other considerations like the future prospects of the company and the ability and experience of the proprietor.

16-2 ANALYTICAL DOCUMENTS

For a commercial enterprise the following final accounts are usually prepared at the end of the trading year: Trading Account, Profit and Loss Account, Appropriation Account and Balance Sheet. A manufacturing company also prepares a Manufacturing Account. We shall briefly examine these documents.

16-2.1 Manufacturing Account

This shows the direct cost of the production of the goods which includes the cost of raw materials and transportation to the factory, plus other direct costs like fuel, electricity and wages. Depreciation of plant and machinery is also taken into consideration:

Manufacturing Account
A.B.C Ltd
for the year ended 30 September 19X2.

	₦		₦
Materials (opening)	2,600	Finished stock:	
Purchases	90,000	To Trading Account	110,000
Carriage Inwards	280		
Fuel, Electricity etc	1,220		
Wages	23,000		
Depreciation of plant	900	Materials (closing)	8,000
	118,000		118,000

16-2.2 Trading Account

This shows the value of goods purchased or transferred from the Manufacturing Account plus the opening stock, less closing stock, compared with the value of sales. The difference is the gross profit for the year:

Trading Account
A.B.C Ltd.
for the year ended 30 September 19X2.

	₦		₦
Opening stock	24,000	Sales	250,000
Add: Purchases or from manufacturing account	110,000		
	134,000		
Less: Closing stock	21,000		
Cost of goods sold	113,000		
Gross Profit, transferred to Profit and Loss Account.	137,000		
	250,000		250,000

16-2.3 Profit and Loss Account

This account shows all the operating expenses for the year. The expenses are deducted from the gross profit transferred from the Trading Account to give the net profit for the year. While the Trading and Manufacturing Accounts deal with the purchase and production of goods, the Profit and Loss Account is concerned with the distribution of the goods. Expenses shown in the Profit and Loss Account include all overhead and administrative costs:

Profit and Loss Account
A.B.C. Ltd.
for the year ended 30 September 19X2.

	₦		₦
Salaries	51,000	Transfer from	
		Trading Account	137,000
Rent & Rates	1,900	Discounts Received	2,400
Insurance	750		
Printing & Stationery	520		
General Office			
Expenses	5,200		
Provision for			
Depreciation	830		
Provision for Bad			
Debts	250		
Discounts Allowed	990		
Net Profit	77,960		
	139,400		139,400

16-2.4 Appropriation Account

The net profit realised by a sole trader belongs to him and is transferred to his capital account to increase his investment in the business. This may also be done in a partnership.

In the case of a limited liability company, the net profit is transferred to an Appropriation Account. This account shows how the net profit has been *appropriated,* or divided:

Appropriation Account
A.B.C Ltd.
for year ended 30 September 19X2

	₦		₦
Proposed Dividend	8,000	Balance brought forward from previous year	5,000
Tax	35,100		
Reserve	24,860	Net Profit for the year	77,960
Balance carried forward	15,000		
	82,960		82,960

16-2.5 Balance Sheet

The Balance Sheet is not an 'account', but a statement showing the assets and liabilities of a company or trader at a given time. Assets are what the business *owns,* while liabilities are what it *owes*.

Liabilities (which are listed on the left-hand side of the Balance Sheet) show the sources of the company's funds, while the assets (listed on the right hand side) show the uses of the funds (see opposite).

A.B.C Ltd

Balance Sheet

as at

30 September 19X2

	₦		₦
Capital		**Fictitious or Intangible Assets**	
50,000 ordinary shares at ₦ each	50,000	Goodwill	10,000
Reserve	24,860		
Profit and Loss A/C	15,000	**Fixed Assets**	
	89,860	Factory Buildings	45,000
		Plant & Machinery	27,000
Long-Term Liabilities		Motor vehicles	13,000
Debenture	10,000		
Directors' Loans	5,000		
	15,000	**Current Assets**	
		Stock	29,000
Current Liabilities		Debtor	26,500
Tax	35,100	Cash	5,500
Creditors	6,040		61,000
Bank Loan	10,000		
	51,140		
	156,000		156,000

215

A Balance Sheet may also be given in column form:

A.B.C Ltd.
Balance Sheet
as at 30 September 19X2

Assets	₦	₦	₦
Goodwill			10,000
Fixed Assets			
Factory Buildings			45,000
Plant & Machinery			27,000
Motor vehicles			13,000
			95,000
Current Assets			
Stock	9,000		
Debtors	26,500		
Cash	5,500		
		61,000	
Less Current Liabilities			
Tax	35,000		
Creditors	6,040		
Bank Loan	10,000	51,140	
Working capital			9,860
			104,860
Authorised Share Capital			
75,000 ordinary shares at ₦1 each			75,000
Issued Share Capital			
50,000 ordinary shares at ₦1 each			50,000
Reserves	24,860		
Profit & Loss A/C	15,000		
			39,860
Long-Term Liabilities			
Debenture	10,000		
Directors Loan	5,000		
			15,000
			104,860

16-3 EXPLANATION OF MAIN BALANCE SHEET ITEMS

The following are some of the important items shown on company Balance Sheets:

i) Capital

The Issued Share Capital is the amount invested in the business by the owners or shareholders. Limited liability companies can issue various types of shares (see Chapter Thirteen).

ii) Revenue Reserves

These are the profits earned over the years which have not been distributed. Part of, or the bulk of, these reserves may eventually be capitalised or distributed. Some companies have capital reserves which, unlike revenue reserves, cannot be distributed as dividends. The sum of capital, reserves and balance on Profit and Loss Account represents the shareholders' stake in the business and is also called shareholders funds.

iii) Long-Term Liabilities

These are medium-term loans to a company at a fixed rate of interest and repayable over a fixed period of time and are usually used to finance specific capital projects (e.g. Debenture Stock).

iv) Current Liabilities

These are short-term debts incurred in the normal course of business repayable within one year. They include taxes due but not yet paid, trade creditors, bank balances (debit) and the amount of any proposed dividend.

v) Fictitious and Intangible Assets

Intangible assets are assets such as patents, trademarks or goodwill, while fictitious assets are those relating to preliminary expenses incurred in the course of forming a new company. Intangible assets may turn out to be very valuable assets. Fictitious assets, however, have no value and are usually written off.

vi) Fixed Assets

These are assets acquired for production purposes and not for resale. They are used in the business permanently until they become obsolete. They are usually depreciated over a period of time. The depreciation charge is debited to the Profit and Loss Account as an expense.

vii) Current Assets

These are also called circulating or floating assets. They include stock, debtors and cash-in-hand and at bank. They are acquired purposely either to be resold or so that they may pass through manufacturing processes before they are sold for cash.

16-4 ANALYTICAL METHODS

16-4.1 Introduction

Statement analysis must be done in a very logical and systematic way. Every calculation or ratio must provide useful information, otherwise there will be no point presenting it.

The technique employed in statement analysis is usually known as *ratio analysis.* A ratio is simply one number expressed in terms of another number to show the relationship between the two numbers. For example, the relationship between 12 and 3 is 12/3 indicating that the former figure is four times as great as the latter figure. An alternative way of stating this relationship would be to omit stating the base of 1 and merely to give the ratio as 4 (the word 'times' being understood). If the number order is reversed to 3 and 12, the ratio is 3/12 or 0.25:1 (or 25 times). A variation is to use a base of 100. This is termed a percentage. Using the figures 3 and 12, the percentages is $3/12 \times 100/1 = 25\%$.

It can be seen, therefore, that ratios, by using a common base of 1 or 100, afford a means of comparing figures prepared on different bases.

In financial statement analysis, it is recognised that there are certain important relationships (expressed by means of ratios) between items within the Trading Account, within the Profit and Loss Account and within the Balance Sheet.

There are also equally, if not more, important relationships between items in the Trading Account and the Profit and Loss Account, between items in the Trading Account and in the Balance Sheet and between items in the Profit and Loss Account and the Balance Sheet.

Calculation of the ratios is a relatively easy and straightforward task. However, the real skill in financial analysis is in the selection of those ratios most appropriate under specific circumstances and subsequently in the interpretation of the position which these reveal.

In order to interpret company financial statements effectively most banks use a system called *statement spreading*. This is a system of transferring the figures in the company's financial statements to the bank's comparative spread sheet — see overleaf.

The main features of statement spreading are:

i) It makes it easier to analyse statements by reducing the number of items to be considered. Some items are reclassified, combined and rearranged logically; while others are completely eliminated·to facilitate meaningful analysis.

ii) It makes the figures from the most recent statements easier to compare with those from previous years' statements.

These features are clearly manifested in our example. It will be observed that the number of items on the borrower's financial statements has been reduced. The figures have been listed more logically and in a single column for easy comparison with figures from a previous set of statements. Spreading is not done arbitrarily. The spreader is expected to interpret, adjust or reclassify the items on the borrower's financial statements in line with his bank's policy to facilitate meaningful ratio analysis.

16-4.2 Ratios

After the statements have been carefully spread, it is easier to calculate the ratios. Ratios can be designed to illustrate the various facets of a business which fall into the following broad categories:

i) Long-Term Solvency and Stability.

ii) Short-Term Solvency and Liquidity.

iii) Efficiency and Profitability.

iv) Potential and Actual Growth.

We shall now examine each of these categories.

i) Long-Term Solvency and Stability

The ratios which measure this are:

Table 16-1

'Spreading' of Financial Statements

Tight-Rite Canning Company
Balance Sheet, December 31, 19X6

ASSETS

Cash on Hand		1,486	
Cash in Banks		6,383,078	6,384,564
Accounts Receivable			
Trade (less allowance for cash discounts)	1,636,798		
Employees	954		
Other	460,796	2,098,548	
Less allowance for doubtful accounts		113,102	1,985,446
Inventories at average cost			
Finished goods		18,894,594	
Work in process		1,258,466	
Manufacturing supplies, etc		1,643,882	21,726,942
Merchandise and/or cash with salesmen		129,998	
Total Current Assets		30,296,950	
Fixed Assets at cost			
Land		161,430	
Buildings	1,678,450		
Machinery and equipment	2,658,658		
Furniture and fixtures	120,428		
Autos and trucks	294,534	4,752,070	
Less depreciation		2,422,060	2,330,010
Total Fixed Assets			2,491,440
Prepaid Expenses and Deferred Charges			
Insurance		177,354	
Advertising		45,618	
Prepaid and renewal supplies, etc.		236,492	
Interest		59,192	
Other items		34,238	
Total Miscellaneous Assets		552,894	
Brands and trademarks, at cost		689,994	
Total Assets		34,031,278	

LIABILITIES

Notes Payable			
To Banks		13,830,000	
To Others		2,365,984	16,195,984
Accounts Payable			
Trade		191,064	
Employees		13,942	
Other		35,534	240,540
Dividends Payable			40,794
Accrued Liabilities			
Salaries and wages		71,662	
Taxes, other than on income		51,932	123,594
Provision for contingencies			20,038
Accrued Federal and State Taxes, estimated			376,664
Total Current Liabilities			16,997,614
Preferred capital stock	2,719,600		
Class B common stock	2,841,600	5,561,200	
Earned surplus		11,472,464	17,033,664
Total			34,031,278

Statement of Income
For the Year Ended December 31, 19X6

Sales, less returns	43,367,270
Cost of Sales	36,102,732
Gross Profit	7,264,538
Selling, Administrative, and General Expenses	7,025,146
Profit from operations	239,392
Other income, less other expenses	383,798
Profit before taxes	623,190
Federal and State Income Taxes	333,401
Net Profit	289,789

Source: American Bankers Association — *Statement Analysis.* Part 1, p. 2

16 - BANK LENDING II – FINANCIAL STATEMENT ANALYSIS AND INTERPRETATION

Tite-Rite Canning Company	December 31, 19X5 (000's omitted)	December 31, 19X6 (000's omitted)
Cash	7,394	6,385
Accounts Receivable — Trade (Net)	987	1,524
Inventory	19,248	20,153
TOTAL CURRENT ASSETS	27,629	28,062
FIXED ASSETS (NET)	2,387	2,491
Accounts Receivable — Employees	120	1
Accounts Receivable — Other	508	461
Manufacturing Supplies, etc.	1,504	1,644
Mdse. and/or Cash with Salesmen	125	130
Prepaid Exp. and Deferred Chgs.	460	553
Intangibles	690	690
TOTAL ASSETS	33,423	34,032
Notes Due Banks	12,000	13,830
Notes Due Others	3,722	2,366
Accounts Payable	228	241
Dividends Payable	41	41
Accruals	120	124
Provision for Contingencies	10	20
Accrued Taxes	351	377
TOTAL CURRENT LIABILITIES	16,472	16,999
Capital Stock	5,561	5,561
Retained Earnings	11,390	11,472
TOTAL	33,423	34,032
Tangible Net Worth	16,261	16,343
Net Working Capital	11,157	11,063
Net Sales	41,246	43,367
Gross Profit	6,283	7,265
Operating Profit	212	239
Other Income	345	384
Federal and State Taxes	315	333
Net Profit	242	290

a) Fixed Interest Cover

$$\frac{\text{Net Profit*}}{\text{Fixed Interest}}$$

*Before fixed interest and taxation.

This ratio indicates the number of times fixed interest is covered by profit. The inability of a company to meet its fixed interest commitment (e.g. secured debenture interest) can lead to the necessity to wind up the concern.

b) Fixed Dividend Cover

$$\frac{\text{Net Profit After Tax}}{\text{Fixed Dividends}}$$

This indicates the number of times fixed dividends are covered by taxed profit.

c) Total Debt to Shareholders' Funds (or Debt/Equity Ratio)

$$\frac{\text{Total External Liabilities*}}{\text{Shareholders' Funds**}}$$

* Short and Long-term Debit.
**Net Worth.

This indicates whether the business is solvent and the extent of 'cover' for the external liabilities. It is, therefore, a test of financial stability.

d) Long-Term Debt to Shareholders' Funds

$$\frac{\text{Fixed External Liabilities*}}{\text{Shareholders' Funds}}$$

*Long-term debts only.

This indicates the extent of 'cover' for fixed liabilities (e.g. loans, debentures).

e) Proprietary Ratio

$$\frac{\text{Shareholders' Funds}}{\text{Total Assets (tangible)}}$$

This indicates the degree to which unsecured creditors are protected in the event of liquidation.

f) Gearing or Leverage or Debt/Worth Ratio

$$\frac{\text{Fixed Interest Loans plus Preference Share Capital}}{\text{Ordinary Share Capital}}$$

This indicates the degree of vulnerability of earnings available to ordinary shareholders.

There are various alternatives to the formula given. Some companies use ordinary shareholders' funds as the denominator (i.e. ordinary share capital plus reserves), some use the book value of loans and shares, whilst others include them at their market values. Textbooks usually state that a gearing greater than 1:1 is high and less than 1:1 is low. In practice, however, greater than 0.6:1 is regarded as high and less than 0.2:1 is low, with the range between these extremes being regarded as relatively low. There is no optimum gearing as such.

ii) Short Term Solvency and Liquidity

The ratios which measure this include:

a) Stock Turnover

$$\frac{\text{Cost of Sales}}{\text{Average Stock}}$$

This indicates the velocity, in number of times per period, at which the average figure of trading stock is being 'turned over' (i.e. sold). This is best converted to a time period (i.e. '20 times a year' or 'every 18 days').

b) Current or Working Capital Ratio

$$\frac{\text{Current Assets}}{\text{Current Liabilities}}$$

A current ratio of 2:1 is usually regarded as satisfactory. This indicates the ability of a business to meet its immediate obligations from short-term assets. Working capital is the difference between current assets and current liabilities.

c) Liquidity (or Acid Test or Quick Assets) Ratio

$$\frac{\text{Current Assets (excluding inventories)}}{\text{Current Liabilities}}$$

This indicates the relative amount of assets in cash (or those which can be converted into cash quickly) available to meet short-term liabilities. Liquid assets consist of cash and bank balances, debtors and marketable securities. This ratio will clearly indicate whether or not the company has enough cash to pay creditors.

d) Debtor Collection

Turnover:
$$\frac{\text{Credit Sales}}{\text{Trade Debtors}}$$

This indicates the number of times trade debtors have been turned over during the period.

Collection Period:
$$\frac{\text{Trade debtors}}{\text{Credit Sales}} \times \frac{12}{1} \text{ (or } \frac{52}{1} \text{ or } \frac{365}{1})$$

This indicates the average period for which debtors remain uncollected.

e) Creditor Payment Period

$$\frac{\text{Trade Creditors}}{\text{Credit Purchases}} \times \frac{12}{1} \text{ or } \frac{52}{1} \text{ or } \frac{365}{1}$$

This indicates the average period for which creditors remain unpaid.

iii) Efficiency and Profitability

The ratios which measure this include:

a) Gross profit as % of turnover (sales).

b) Individual expenses as % of total expenses or turnover.

c) Net profit as % of sales.

d) Sales as % of total assets.

e) Sales as % of capital employed.

f) Net profit as % of capital employed:

$$\text{Percentage Return} = \frac{\text{Net Profit} \times 100}{\text{Equity} + \text{Long Term Loans}}$$

A fall in the % from year to year indicates that the business is not using its capital effectively.

The others are basically self-explanatory, but a word of warning is that one should try to get some idea of a trend in the business being examined, as well as comparing it with similar businesses or industrial averages, etc; otherwise the resultant figures may become meaningless.

iv) Potential and Actual Growth

The ratios which measure this include:

a) Net Book Value of Ordinary Shares

$$\frac{\text{Net Book Value of Ordinary Shares}}{\text{Number of Ordinary Shares}}$$

This indicates the historical cost base to which the price per ordinary share relates. Net book value consists of fixed assets plus working capital less debenture and preference share capital. An alternative way of arriving at the same figure is to deduct preference share capital from shareholders' funds.

b) Earnings per share

$$\frac{\text{Total Earnings (in kobo)}}{\text{Number of Ordinary Shares}}$$

The earnings figure is the net profit after tax, but before extra-ordinary items, *less* minority interests and preference dividends.

c) Dividend per Share

$$\frac{\text{Total Dividend (in kobo)}}{\text{Number of Ordinary Shares}}$$

This indicates the dividend and retention policy of the company when used in conjunction with earnings per share.

d) Price/Earnings Ratio

$$\frac{\text{Market Price per Ordinary Share}}{\text{Earnings per Share}}$$

This indicates the number of years' purchase of the earnings and is regarded internationally as an indicator of future performance. In other words, the P/E ratio indicates the number of years the investor must wait before his investment is repaid in dividend.

e) Earnings Yield

$$\frac{\text{Earnings per Share}}{\text{Market Price per Ordinary Share}} \times \frac{100}{1}$$

This indicates the potential return on the investment. Like the P/E ratio of which it is the inverse expressed as a percentage, it highlights the amount earned on the shares relative to their market price.

f) Dividend Yield

$$\frac{\text{Dividend per Share}}{\text{Market Price per Share}}$$

This indicates the current return on investment. The ratio is commonly used by Central Bank Examiners.

16-5 BASIC INTERPRETATION OF FINANCIAL STATEMENTS BY THE LENDING BANKER

When a banker is faced with the mass of figures which are usually contained in the Balance Sheet and other statements submitted by a customer, he should 'spread' the statements, as already discussed.

This will facilitate the exercise of extracting the relevant figures and information from the accounts. The calculation of the ratios is a

relatively easy and straightforward task. However, the real skill in
financial analysis is the ability to select those ratios which are most
appropriate under specific circumstances and then to interpret the
position which they reveal.

A lending banker will normally examine the following major areas
when analysing a set of accounts submitted by a customer:

16-5.1 Shareholder's Stake and the Percentage Return on Capital Employed

This percentage measures the efficiency and profitability of the
company. A fall in the percentage from year to year shows that the
business is not using its capital efficiently and effectively. The
calculation is made as follows:

$$\frac{\text{Net Profit Before Tax}}{\text{Shareholder's Stake \& Long-Term Loans (if any)}} \times \frac{100}{1} \%$$

16-5.2 Long-Term Loans

The bank should probe into these items whenever they are shown on a
customer's Balance Sheet. When are they due for repayment? Are they
secured on the company's assets and, if so, which assets? If the loans
are from the company's directors, are they prepared to sign a
subordination agreement with the bank? This means that the loans will
rank after any facility granted by the bank and cannot be repaid until
the bank loans have been fully liquidated.

16-5.3 Working Capital

For any company to continue operating as a going concern it must
maintain a reasonable level of working capital. Sufficient working
capital ensures that the business is able to pay its creditors without
undue delay, maintain reasonable stocks and allow debtors some time
for payment.

The amount of working capital may be calculated as follows:

Working capital = Current Assets - Current Liabilities

However, the working capital ratio (or current ratio) is calculated as
follows:

$$\text{Current Ratio} = \frac{\text{Current Assets}}{\text{Current Liabilities}}$$

A current ratio of 2:1 is usually regarded as satisfactory. This indicates
the ability of a business to meet its immediate obligations from short-
term assets, since for every ₦100 of current liabilities there are ₦200
of current assets.

16-5.4 Liquidity

This indicates the relative amount of assets in cash, or which can be
quickly converted into cash, available to meet short-term liabilities.
Liquid assets consist of cash and bank balances, debtors and
marketable securities. Stock is not usually regarded as a liquid asset,
because it has to be converted into debtors before it becomes cash.
Therefore, if the bulk of the current assets are in the form of slow
moving stock, which are generally sold on credit, the company will
most probably have liquidity problems. Future liquidity should also be
given some attention in order to determine the ability of the company
to service its debts.

This ratio is calculated as follows:

$$\frac{\text{Current Assets (excluding inventories or stocks)}}{\text{Current Liabilities}}$$

A liquidity ratio of 1:1 is regarded as reasonable. It means that the
business, without selling its stocks, could cover its current liabilities. A
ratio of 1.5:1 is even better, but if it is higher it may be an indication
that too much is tied up in debtors and the bank (i.e. it is idle money
that is not working for the business.[1])

16-5.5 Gearing or Leverage or Debt/Worth Ratio

The lending banker must also test the gearing or leverage of the
company, as it indicates the degree of vulnerability of earnings for
ordinary shareholders and also compares the shareholders' stake in
the business with the amount of external finance.

---

[1] Cox, David *Success in Elements of Banking* John Murray, 1979, p.241.

It is generally believed that a gearing greater than 1:1 is high, while less than 1:1 is low. In practice, however, greater than 0.6:1 is regarded as high and less than 0.2:1 is low, with the range between these extremes being regarded as relatively high or relatively low. There is no optimum gearing as such.

16-5.6 Trading Figures

These should also be critically evaluated. The figures for a number of years (say, 3 years) should be compared and large fluctuations noted.

The debtors' accounts should be carefully scrutinised. Are there just a few hard-core debtors or are they spread over a fairly large number of small debtors? Are the stocks moving fast enough? Is there obsolete stock? Has an excessive amount of stock been consigned to customers? Is stock turnover in line with turnover for other businesses in the same industry? Or is money being tied up too long in stocks? Are they unsaleable items? Are creditors waiting too long for their money? Probing further into debtors: Are there indications that some of the debtors have already been pledged to another creditor? What is the turnover of debtors? Have adequate reserves been set up to cover doubtful accounts?

The following calculations will be helpful:-

i) How many times have trade debtors been turned over during the period? i.e. $\dfrac{\text{Credit Sales}}{\text{Trade Debtors}}$

ii) How long have creditors remained uncollected? i.e.

$$\frac{\text{Trade Debtors}}{\text{Credit Purchases}} \times \frac{365}{1}$$

iii) How long have creditors remained unpaid? i.e.

$$\frac{\text{Trade Creditors}}{\text{Credit Purchases}} \times \frac{365}{1}$$

The following percentages should also be calculated to determine efficiency and profitability:

$$\text{Gross Profit percentage} = \frac{\text{Gross Profit}}{\text{Sales}} \times \frac{100}{1}$$

$$\text{Net Profit Percentage} = \frac{\text{Net Profit}}{\text{Sales}} \times \frac{100}{1}$$

16-5.7 Other Items

Finally, the banker must always use his initiative to bring out any other salient points in his customer's accounts. Any significant changes from one year to the other must be closely examined.

The ratios specifically mentioned above are only a guide. Any other ratios or percentages may be used if useful information can be derived from the results.

16-6 BASIC FORECASTING

The normal end of year financial statements submitted by bank customers cover the activities of prior years. Consequently, these statements provide a historical trend which enables the analyst to ascertain the progress made to date and to determine what is likely to happen in the future.

However, to assist in determining the future needs of the company, banks usually request that a *cash budget* is submitted so that the company's future needs can be properly assessed. The amount of money that a company needs to borrow depends on the purpose for which the funds are needed. It is relatively easy to calculate the amount required for business expansion — factory construction and the acquisition of plant and equipment. Term loans or equity capital are usually required to cover such expenditure. In these instances, therefore, specific cost estimates should be provided by the suppliers of the equipment or the architects and builders.

On the other hand, the amount of *working capital* required by a business depends on its particular activity. In this case, a detailed projection of the sources and uses of funds over a period of time — usually 12 months — should be prepared and submitted to the bank. The budget should be based on the recent operating experience of the company plus its own assessment of its probable performance during the period covered by the projection. A good cash forecast comprises a detailed estimate of the cash receipts and disbursements during the period and should include, at a minimum, the items shown in the format overleaf.

Item 4 shows the total cash receipts month by month, while item 13 gives the total cash payments. Item 14 shows the expected cash balance at the beginning of each month and item 16 shows the month end balances. The desired working cash balances are given in item 17. The difference between items 17 and 16 (if the former is larger) represents the amount or level of short-term loans which are required by the company. If item 16 is larger than item 17, then there is a surplus of funds available for use on capital expenditure, short-term investments or dividend payments. Item 22 shows the amount of long-term funds required.

16-7 'GOING-CONCERN' AND 'GONE -CONCERN' APPROACH[2]

Balance Sheets generally cover the activities of prior years and are, therefore, basically historical records. Most Balance Sheets are prepared on the basis that business activities will continue and that the business will remain a *going-concern*. Invariably, therefore, the company's assets are shown on the Balance Sheet at a value which reflects their actual worth to the company.

However, bankers know from experience that the best plans can go wrong and that even a company with good prospects can collapse due to factors over which the management has little or no direct control. In view of this possibility, bankers usually use the *gone-concern* approach so that lending risks can be realistically assessed. This method involves a critical examination of the company's assets as shown in the Balance Sheet and reducing them by different percentages or amounts in order to determine their 'forced sale' value.

A few examples will illustrate the type of treatment required when the gone-concern basis of assessment is used:

---

[2] This section is based on *Success in the Elements of Banking* David Cox, John Murray, 1979, pp. 244 – 245 and the author acknowledges his debt thereto.

16 - BANK LENDING II – FINANCIAL STATEMENT ANALYSIS AND INTERPRETATION

Cash Budget
for 6 months ending 30 June 1983

	Jan.	Feb.	Mar.	Apr.	May	June
Expected Cash Receipts:						
1. Cash Sales						
2. Collections from debtors						
3. Other income						
4. Total cash receipts						
Expected Cash Payments:						
5. Raw materials						
6. Payroll						
7. Other factory expenses						
8. Advertising						
9. Selling expenses						
10. Administrative expenses						
11. New plant & equipment						
12. Other payments — tax, loan repayments, interest, etc.						
13. Total cash payments						
14. Expected cash balance at beginning of month						
15. Cash + or − (Item 4 minus 13)						
16. Expected cash balance at month end (Item 14 plus 15)						
17. Desired working cash balance						
18. Short-term loans needed (Item 17 minus 16, if 17 larger)						
19. Cash available for cap. exp., inv. or divs. (if 16 is larger)						
Capital Cash:						
20. Cash available (Item 19 less divs.)						
21. Desired capital cash (Item 11)						
22. Long-term loans needed (Item 21 minus 20)						

i) Land and Buildings

In Nigeria, if the land is freehold or leasehold of 30 years or more, located in an urban area and developed and if the bank holds a perfected legal mortgage with a professional valuation of at least the amount of the loan, then 100% value is given. This may be reduced by up to 50% if the security is not yet perfected or if any other defect is found.

ii) Plant & Machinery, Fixtures & Fittings and Office Equipment

These items usually have little or no resale value, so a banker will have to use his experience and judgment to determine what value to place on them. In practice, a small percentage of 10% to 25% of the Balance Sheet figure may be used.

iii) Motor Vehicles

The depreciation policy of the company should be verified. If adequate provision for depreciation has been made over the preceding years, then these assets may realise an amount very close to the amount shown on the Balance Sheet. Consequently, 75% of the Balance Sheet value can be used with safety.

iv) Stock, Work-in-Progress and Raw Materials

If a company is in difficulties, one of the reasons may be that it is unable to sell its stocks. In such an instance, if the stock is to have any resale value, the price may have to be reduced drastically. So, a reduction of some 50% of the Balance Sheet value is recommended. Work-in-progress should, however, be treated as a valueless asset, although raw materials may realise a reasonable amount if they are not too specialised. The banker will have to use his judgment here.

v) Debtors

Debtors should be critically examined and reduced by the amount owed by 'hardcore' debtors. Furthermore, long overdue accounts should be written off.

vi) Creditors

The bank will have to 'line up' with other creditors and prove its debt
for that portion of its lending which is unsecured or where, after
realisation of all securities, its lendings have not been fully repaid.

REVIEW QUESTIONS

16.1 **Final Accounts of Gama Ltd as at 31 December**

Profit and Loss Account

	1983 ₦	1982 ₦
Sales Revenue	525,000	425,000
Trading Profit	53,500	41,000
Debenture Interest	3,500	3,500
Net Profit Before Tax	50,000	37,500
Taxation	20,000	15,000
Net Profit After Tax	30,000	22,500
Dividends	15,000	10,000
	15,000	12,500

Balance Sheet

	1983 ₦	1983 ₦	1982 ₦	1982 ₦
₦1 ordinary shares		100,000		50,000
Share premium account		90,000		35,000
Revenue reserves		135,000		120,000
7% Debentures		325,000		205,000
		50,000		50,000
		375,000		255,000
Fixed assets:				
Premises		125,000		75,000
Plant		130,000		70,000
		255,000		145,000
Current assets:				
Stocks	120,000		100,000	
Debtors	80,000		60,000	
	200,000		160,000	
Less: Current Liabilities:				
Creditors	45,000		30,000	
Overdraft	15,000		5,000	
Taxation	20,000		15,000	
	80,000		50,000	
Working capital		120,000		110,000
		375,000		255,000

Additional information:

	1983 ₦	1982 ₦
Cost of Sales	446,000	361,000
Opening Stocks	—	90,000
Credit Sales	500,000	400,000
Credit Purchases	400,000	320,000

235

Required:

i) Computation of the following ratios for both years:

a) Gross profit as % of sales.

b) Net profit as % of sales.

c) Working capital ratio.

d) Quick asset ratio.

e) Average stock turnover period.

f) Average debtors' collection period.

g) Average creditors' payment period.

h) Gearing ratio or leverage.

Comment on any significant findings.

ii) "The working capital ratio should be 2:1." Discuss in the context of business solvency.

16-2 Write short notes on:

i) Intangible and fictitious assets.

ii) Floating assets.

16-3 As a lending banker what would you be looking for in your borrowing customer's Balance Sheet and Trading Accounts?

16-4 Anulupo Ltd. own a number of shops in and around Lagos. They have always followed an expansion programme, buying suitable premises and altering the layouts of their existing shops to enable a greater range of stock to be displayed. In the past they have had overdraft facilities which have been satisfactorily cleared. The company bank account is currently in credit. The latest Balance Sheet shows the following position:

Anulupo Ltd.
Balance Sheet
as at 31 December 1982

	₦		₦
Issued share capital:		Fixed assets:	
100,000 ₦1 ordin- ary shares, fully paid	100,000	Freehold premises (net)	90,000
		Leashold prem- ises (net)	55,000
Reserves		Shop fixtures fitt-	
Profit and Loss a/c	60,000	ings (net)	5,000
		Delivery vans (net)	6,000
			156,000
Long-term liabilities:			
Loans from direc- tors	10,000		

	₦		₦
Current liabilities:		Current assets:	
Creditors 8,000		Stock	23,000
Corporation		Debtors	3,000
Tax 7,000		Bank	2,500
	15,000	Cash	500
			29,000
	185,000		185,000

Relevant figures from the trading and profit and loss accounts for
the year:

Sales	₦143,000
Purchases	₦100,000
Gross profit	₦ 46,000
Net profit before tax	₦ 20,000

237

The company came to you in February 1983 seeking an overdraft facility of ₦10,000 for six months to enable them to carry out extensions at one shop at a cost of ₦3,000 and to allow them to build up their stocks in readiness for May when there is always a big increase in demand for products.

How would you treat their request?

16.5 Your customer Modyse Boyode Designs Ltd. has been trading for 2 years. The directors are Modyse Boyode, who holds a majority shareholding and her husband Femi, who owns the remaining shares. The company sells handmade dresses to small shops, most of the manufacturing and selling being carried out by Modyse herself, assisted in production by a few outworkers. The Balance Sheet for the third year of trading is as follows:

Modyse Boyode Designs Ltd.
Balance Sheet
as at 31 December 1982

	₦		₦
Issued share capital:		Fixed assets:	
1,000 ₦1 ordinary shares, fully paid	1,000	Machinery (net of depreciation)	500
Long-term liabilities:		Delivery van (net of depreciation)	750
Loans from directors	1,000		

Current Liabilities:	₦			Current assets:		
Creditors	3,000			Stocks:	₦	
Bank	350			Raw materials	200	
		3,350		Work-in-progress	900	
				Finished goods	500	
				Debtors	1,500	
						3,100
				Fictitious assets:		
				Profit and Loss a/c		1,000
		5,350				5,350

Relevant figures from the trading and profit and loss accounts for the year:

Sales	₦10,000
Purchases of raw materials	₦ 8,000
Gross profit	₦ 1,000
Net loss	₦ 500

Although there is no official overdraft limit on the account, cheques have recently been paid to meet pressing creditors. Despite the loss that was made last year, Modyse Boyode is convinced that if she can organise production properly, she can make profits and she comes to you with the following proposition. She requires an overdraft limit of ₦10,000 to pay a year's advance rental of ₦3,500 on vacant factory premises on the local industrial estate, to buy new machinery and fixtures for ₦2,500, to carry out alterations to the new premises at a cost of ₦2,000 and to provide additional working capital of ₦2,000.

How would you treat this request and what suggestions would you make to the directors?

CHAPTER SEVENTEEN
BILLS OF EXCHANGE & CHEQUES

17-1 BILLS OF EXCHANGE

17-1.1 Introduction

Bills of exchange and cheques are credit instruments used in the discharge of both internal and external debts. Bills of exchange, as used internationally, may be either bank bills or trade bills. Bank bills have greater security and are much more attractive for international trade payments. Trade bills are those drawn by one company or individual upon another. They do not bear the acceptance of a bank, but are sometimes held and collected by the bank which may also purchase them from the original owners.

In Nigeria, bills of exchange are handled by merchant banks and commercial banks; whereas cheques are restricted to commercial banks. Since these payment systems cannot operate without banks, they may be considered as special services offered by banks. In the light of the above, we shall examine bills of exchange and cheques — the next Chapter discusses the cheque clearing system in some detail.

There are no specific laws governing the operations of bills of exchange and cheques in Nigeria with the exception of the Dishonoured Cheques (Offences) Act, of 1977 (see Chapter Twelve) and the Bills of Exchange Act, 1964 which is a carbon copy of the British Cheques Act, 1957. The British Bills of Exchange Act, 1882 has also been fully adopted for use in Nigeria (see 17-3 below).

17-1.2 Definition of Bills of Exchange

The Bills of Exchange Act, 1882 defines a bill of exchange as:

An unconditional order in writing addressed by one person to another, signed by the person giving it, requiring the person to whom it is addressed to pay on demand, or at a fixed or determinable future time. a sum certain in money to or to the order of a specified person or bearer.

241

The above definition of a bill of exchange can be explained by using the specimen bill:

A Specimen of a Bill of Exchange

EXCHANGE FOR ₦10,000   —   Lagos 15th March, 1982

6 months after date
At .... pay this – Bill of Exchange to the order of

Ourselves
....

the sum of ten thousand naira.

For and on behalf of FEMI ADE
& Co. Limited.

Jinmi & Co. Ltd.   Femi   Amoke

To: ....

Accra, Ghana   Director   Director

---

i) It must be an 'unconditional order (i.e. no conditions must be stipulated before payment). Our specimen bill gives a clear, unconditional order to 'pay'.

ii) It must be in writing, whether typewritten or in ink, print or pencil, on paper or any other writing material.

iii) It must be 'addressed by one person to another'. In our specimen it is addressed by Femi Ade & Co. Ltd. to Jinmi & Co. Ltd.

iv) It must be 'signed by the person giving it'. In our example it is signed on behalf of Femi Ade & Co. Ltd. by two directors.

v) It must require 'the person to whom it is addressed to pay'. In the specimen it is addressed to Jinmi & Co. Ltd. who are required to pay.

vi) It must be payable 'on demand, or at a fixed or determinable future time'. Our specimen bill is payable six months after date which is a determinable future time (i.e. 15th September, 1982).

vii) The amount payable must be 'a sum certain in money', which is ₦10,000 as stated on our bill.

viii) The payment must be 'to or to the order of a specified person or bearer'. Our specimen bill is made payable 'to the order of ourselves'.

To satisfy the 'valuable consideration' requirements in the law of contract, bills of exchange usually contain the words 'value received' after the amount in words.

17-1.3 Parties to a Bill

The three original parties to a bill are the drawer (who has drawn the bill), the drawee (on whom the bill is drawn and who has to make payment) and the payee (to whom the payment will be made). In our specimen bill Femi Ade & Co. is the drawer and payee, while Jinmi & Co. Ltd, is the drawee. In some cases, the payee is different from the drawer.

Our specimen bill is a term bill, because it is drawn for a certain term and must be sent to the drawee for acceptance. In our example, the bill will be sent to Jinmi & Co. who will sign the bill as indication of their acceptance, after which they become the acceptors. Sight bills (i.e. bills payable at sight) do not require acceptance.

A bill that has been accepted or endorsed by a reputable firm is usually regarded as a better bill than one endorsed by an unknown small-scale trader. This was how the business of merchant banking started in Britain. Wealthy merchants lent their names to a bill for a fee — these merchants eventually became generally known as Acceptance Houses (or Merchant Banks).

A holder of an accepted bill of exchange becomes the rightful owner of the bill and can rediscount the bill to his bank. He can also negotiate the bill by asking his bank for a loan against the bill. The bill is, thus, pledged as security. The loan is automatically repaid when the bank collects the proceeds at maturity. If the holder has no liquidity problems, he can hold the bill until maturity and collect the proceeds.

17-1.4 Presentment for Acceptance

The drawer of a bill should present it for acceptance without delay, because until the drawee has accepted it, he is not liable to the holder. This is particularly necessary in respect of tenor bills (i.e. bills not payable at sight), because the due date is usually calculated from the date of acceptance. The law stipulates that the drawer or the holder must either present it for acceptance or negotiate it within a reasonable time. If he does not do so "the drawer and all prior endorsers are discharged". Also, where it is expressly stated that a bill must be presented for acceptance, it is important to comply with this requirement. Bills payable at sight may not be presented for acceptance.

17-1.5 Discharge of a Bill

The main grounds of discharge of a bill are payment, merger, waiver, cancellation and alteration.

i) Payment

A bill is discharged by payment in due course by, or on behalf of, the drawee or acceptor. *"Payment in due course means payment made at, or after, the maturity of the bill to the holder thereof in good faith and without notice that his title to the bill is defective"*.[1]

Payment to a person who holds the bill after a forged endorsement is not payment to the holder and will not operate as a discharge. However, if a banker pays to a person claiming through a forged endorsement, a cheque drawn upon himself in good faith and in the ordinary course of business, he is protected.

ii) Merger

An example of discharge by merger is where the acceptor becomes the holder of a bill at or after maturity in his own right — that is he becomes the owner of the bill on which he is liable.

iii) Waiver

A bill is discharged when the holder at or after maturity renounces his rights against the acceptor unconditionally. The renunciation must be in writing, unless the bill is surrendered to the acceptor.

iv) Cancellation

Where a bill is cancelled by the holder or his agent, and the cancellation is apparent thereon, the bill is discharged. An unintentional, mistaken or unauthorised cancellation is inoperative.

---

[1] *Practice & Law of Banking* Sheldon H.P. (MacDonald & Evans) 1958. p. 126

v) Alteration

Where a material alteration has been made to a bill, (e.g. change of the date or the amount payable) without the assent of all parties liable on the bill, then all parties prior to the alteration are discharged, but not those liable by negotiation after the alteration.

17-1.6 Dishonour of a Bill

A bill of exchange may be dishonoured by non-acceptance or non-payment. A bill is dishonoured by non-acceptance when acceptance is refused or cannot be obtained. When a bill is thus dishonoured, the holder has immediate legal right of recourse against the drawer and endorsers, provided due notice of dishonour has been given, and also against the acceptor, to whom notice need not be sent. Similarly, failure by the acceptor to pay on the due date is a dishonour by non-payment.

In the case of foreign bills the holder must take certain steps to protect himself. These steps are known as *noting* and *protest.* A bill is noted in order to obtain official evidence that it has been dishonoured. The noting is handled by a notary public, usually a legal practitioner. The process of noting requires the notary public to present the bill to the drawee or acceptor again and, if he still refuses to pay, necessary documentation is prepared. Thereafter, a formal document called a 'protest' is issued attesting that the bill has been dishonoured. A protest is accepted in the courts of most countries as evidence of dishonour.

17-2 CHEQUES

17-2.1 Definition

Section 73 of the Bills of Exchange Act defines a cheque as *"a bill of exchange drawn on a banker payable on demand".* From this brief definition of a cheque, a cheque was defined by Dr. Hart, as *"an unconditional order in writing drawn on a banker signed by the drawer, requiring the banker to pay on demand a sum certain in money to, or to the order of, a specified person or to bearer, and which does not order any act to be done in addition to the payment of money."*[2]

---

[2] Dr. Hart "Law of Banking" 4th Edition, P. 327

This definition shows that there are three parties to a cheque:

i) the drawer of the cheque;

ii) the drawee (i.e. the party authorised to pay out the money — the banker); and,

iii) the payee, to whom or to whose order the money is to be paid — the beneficiary.

All the other conditions are the same as those of a Bill of Exchange which have been fully covered in Section 17-1 above. However, unlike a Bill of Exchange, the holder of a cheque normally has no rights against the drawee banker. A cheque does not need to be accepted prior to payment as all cheques are payable on demand and no notice of dishonour for non-payment is required. A banker would not pay a cheque if the drawer has countermanded payment. A cheque would also be returned unpaid if the drawer does not have sufficient funds to cover the payment or for some other technical reasons which will be discussed later.

The Bills of Exchange Act gives valuable protection to bankers against loss by theft or fraud. If a banker pays a cheque bearing a forged endorsement *"in good faith and in the ordinary course of business"* the banker will not be liable to the customer for the amount, provided it is an order cheque payable on demand and drawn on the banker.

17-2.2 Crossed Cheques

"(1) Where a cheque bears across its face an addition of:

> *(a) The words 'and company' or any abbreviation thereof between two parallel transverse lines, either with or without the words "not negotiable" or*
>
> *(b) Two parallel transverse lines simply, either with or without the words 'not negotiable', that addition constitutes a crossing and that cheque is crossed generally.*

(2) Where a cheque bears across its face an addition of the name of a banker, either with or without the words 'not negotiable", that addition constitutes a crossing, and the cheque is crossed specially to that banker."

A crossed cheque cannot be cashed at a bank, but must be paid in for the credit of an account. Thus, crossed cheques are safer to handle than open cheques. A thief who has stolen a crossed cheque cannot cash it; he is compelled to pass the cheque through an account. As a result, it will usually be easy to trace him. In some exceptional cases a crossed cheque can be opened by the drawers of the cheque.

Crossings, thus, can be classified into two main groups — a general crossing and a special crossing as quoted above from the Bills of Exchange Act. Examples of the two types of crossings are shown below:

General Crossing

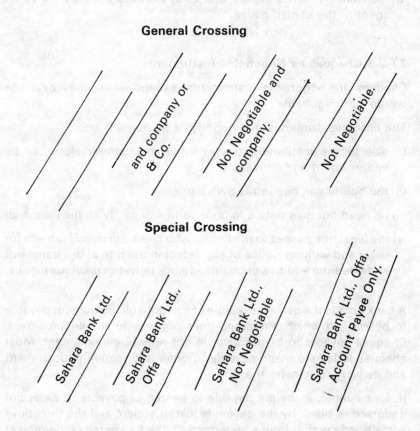

Special Crossing

A cheque is specially crossed when, with or without the addition of two parallel lines, it bears across its face the addition of a banker's name: the cheque is then said to be crossed specially to that banker.

The effect of a special crossing is that the cheques can only be paid into an account with the specified bank and, if indicated on the crossing, the specified branch. It is the practice of all banks to stamp cheques paid in by their customers with the name of the bank, thus crossing the cheques specially to themselves. The effect is that even when the cheques are lost in transit they cannot be credited to any other account in another bank.

The crossing 'Account Payee' has no satutory significance. However, by convention, banks ensure that such cheques are credited to the account of the named payee.

17-2.3 Cheques as Negotiable Instruments

Cheques are negotiable instruments, except where they bear the words 'not negotiable'.

The essential attributes of a negotiable instrument are:

i) title to the instrument passes either by delivery alone, or by endorsement and delivery;

ii) the holder can sue in his own name;

iii) he need not give notice to prior parties to establish his title; and,

iv) the legal title passes to the holder who takes it in good faith and for value and without notice of any defect in the title of the transferor and free from equities or counter-claims between previous parties.

A bank note is the perfect example of a negotiable instrument payable to bearer and which, therefore, does not require any endorsement. Cheques payable to bearer also do not require endorsement. Most cheques today are made payable to order and require endorsement and delivery to transfer the title.

If, for example, a cheque payable to bearer, or payable to order but endorsed in blank by the payee, is lost or stolen, and the thief buys some goods with it from a supermarket, the transferee (supermarket owner) has a legal right to the value of the cheque and all previous parties would be liable. To avoid such a liability the drawer of a cheque should cross it 'not negotiable'. However, it must be understood that this does not mean such a cheque cannot be transferred from one person to the other. It only warns that a person taking such a cheque cannot have or give a better title than that of the transferor. Even an innocent person cannot acquire any better rights than those of the person from whom he received it.

17-2.4 Holder and Holder for Value

A 'holder' is the payee or endorsee of a bill or cheque who is in possession of it, or the bearer of a bearer bill. A 'holder for value' is the holder of a bill for which value has at sometime been given. A holder for value can enforce the bill against all parties prior to the time value was given.

17-2.5 Holder in Due Course

A 'holder in due course' is the holder who has taken a bill, complete and regular on the face of it, before it was overdue, without notice of previous dishonour, in good faith and for value, and finally without notice of any defect in the transferor's title. There can be no holder in due course where a bill is marked 'Not Transferable', or made payable only to a specific name, or bears the forgery of an essential signature.

Thus, the original payee of a cheque or bill is not a 'holder in due course'. Before a person can be a holder in due course, the bill or cheque must have been negotiated to him — the original delivery of the instrument is not such a negotiation. The original payee or subsequent holder in due course is the 'true owner'.

17-2.6 Endorsement

The specimen bill in 17-1 above is payable to order. It may, therefore, be transferred to another person on the 'orders of' the payee by endorsement and delivery, which is generally called *negotiation*. There are three types of endorsements:

i) A blank endorsement which specifies no endorsee, thus making the bill or cheque become payable to bearer.

ii) A special endorsement which specifies the endorsee. For example:

> Pay K.G. Enterprises or Order.
> For and on behalf of
> Femi Ade & Co. Ltd.

> F.A.A.   M.A.A   (Signed)
>   Directors

A blank endorsement may be converted by any holder into a special endorsement by adding the words 'pay...'.

iii) A restrictive endorsement prevents further endorsement of the bill:

> Pay K.G. Enterprises only.
> For and on behalf of Femi Ade & Co. Ltd.
> F.A.A.   M.A.A   (Signed)
>   Directors

17-2.7 Negotiation

The Bills of Exchange Act of 1882 describes negotiation of a bill as:

> *"its transfer from one person to another in such a manner as to constitute the transferee the holder of the bill. A bill payable to bearer is negotiable by delivery, if to order by endorsement and delivery".*

Every person who signs a bill as endorser guarantees to a subsequent holder that the bill will be paid when presented for payment on the due date. Thus, the holder of a bill that is not paid on the due date has the right to sue any or all previous parties to the bill.

17-3 THE NIGERIAN BILLS OF EXCHANGE ACT, 1964

As mentioned in the introduction, this Act is a carbon copy of the British Cheques Act, 1957. The Act came into force on 1 June, 1964. It brought some important changes in the law and practice relating to the endorsement of cheques in Nigeira. The main objective of the Act was to dispense with the necessity for the endorsement of instruments which are paid into a bank *for the credit of the account of the payee.* For instance, endorsement is *not* required in the following cases:

i) Instruments paid in for the credit of the account of the payee. Where an instrument is paid into a bank for the credit of the account of the payee, endorsement will not be required. This rule applies irrespective of whether the account is kept at the branch at which the cheque is paid in or at another branch of that bank or at another bank.

ii) Instruments paid in for the credit of a joint or partnership account. Instruments payable to an individual will normally be accepted without endorsement for the credit of a joint or partnership account *provided that the payee is one of the account holders.*

However, endorsement is required in the following cases:

i) Instruments cashed or exchanged across the counter.

ii) Negotiated instruments (i.e. instruments tendered for the credit of an account other than that of the ostensible payee). In such cases the endorsement of the payee and any subsequent endorsee, including that of the customer for whose account the cheque is collected, will be required.

iii) Cheques payable to joint payees. These will require endorsement if tendered for the credit of an account to which all are not parties.

iv) Bills of Exchange (other than cheques) and Promissory Notes.

Similarly the following continue to require endorsement:

i) Drafts drawn on or payable by any of the Accountants-General of the Federation or States, drafts and other instruments drawn on the Post Office or payable at a Post Office and Inland Revenue Warrants.

ii) Travellers' cheques.

iii) Instruments payable by banks abroad.

A bold outline letter "R" on the face of an instrument is an indication to the payee that there is a receipt which he is required to complete. The letter "R" must be at least half an inch high and must be as close to the "₦" sign in the "amount" box as practicable. However, the issue and endorsement of receipts are usually unnecessary as the Act provides in section 1(2) that *"A prescribed instrument which is unendorsed but appears to have been paid by the banker on whom it is drawn is evidence of the receipt by the payee of the sum mentioned in the instrument".*

It is to be noted that in an endorsement, where the name of the payee is mis-spelt or the payee is otherwise incorrectly designated, the instrument will normally be accepted or collected only if the instrument is endorsed as mis-spelt or mis-designated.

REVIEW QUESTIONS

17.1 Distinguish clearly between a 'bearer' cheque and an 'order' cheque. What is the significance of 'not negotiable' on a 'crossed order' cheque?

17.2 D drew a bill upon T, payable to P on demand. D delivered it to P who presented it to T for payment. T refused payment. What, if any, are P's rights on this bill?

17.3 Define the term 'holder in due course'.

17.4 Explain the various ways in which a bill of exchange may be discharged.

17.5 In the context of a bill of exchange distinguish between:

i) A holder and a wrongful possessor.

ii) A holder for value and a holder in due course.

17.6 You have just opened a current account for Mrs. Adama. She asks if she should use crossed or open cheques. Advise her.

CHAPTER EIGHTEEN

THE CHEQUES CLEARING SYSTEM

18-1 THE CLEARING HOUSE OPERATIONS

The Clearing House is where banks exchange cheques. Each commercial bank sends a representative to the clearing house to deliver cheques drawn on other banks and to receive the cheques drawn on it. If the drawer and payee of a cheque have accounts in the same branch of a bank or even at different branches of the same bank, there is no Clearing House involvement in the clearing of their cheques. To explain how the clearing system works, when the drawer and payee of a cheque belong to different banks, we shall monitor the movement of cheques drawn on other banks and paid in by customers of the branch. I will use my bank as an example.

Apapa Branch of Savannah Bank of Nigeria Limited is one of our busiest branches. At the close of business, all cheques paid in by customers which are drawn on other banks are assembled by the branch's Clearing or Remittance Department. On a typical day these cheques number up to a total of 1,000. The clearing clerk lists the cheques according to the banks on which they are drawn. A copy of the machine list and the cheques are immediately sent off by hand to Centralised Accounting Department at Savannah Bank Headquarters in Lagos. All other branches of the bank within the Lagos clearing area also deliver their cheques at about the same time to Centralised Accounting Department of Head Office.

At the Head Office, the cheques delivered by the branches are consolidated, bank by bank. Machine lists of all cheques to be presented on each bank are then prepared for individual banks. The grand total of all the banks is agreed with the grand total of all cheques received. The totals are then entered bank by bank on the credit side of the Central Bank Presentation Form. The Presentation Form and the cheques are taken to the Clearing House at the CBN the following morning where they are presented to the representatives of the respective banks.

Clearing House sessions start at 10 a.m. daily and take about an hour. At the same time, cheques drawn on Savannah Bank branches within the Lagos clearing area are presented to our representative by the other banks. These are later entered on the debit (left) side of the Presentation Form bank by bank.

When presentations are completed each representative works out the net position of his bank on his Presentation Form which is normally completed in duplicate. The original copy is submitted to the Clearing House Superintendent, who is a senior official of the Central Bank. He presides as the Chairman of the daily clearing house sessions.

Upon receipt of the completed Presentation Forms from all banks, the Clearing House Superintendent balances the day's work by entering the net balances of the banks on a *Clearing Settlement Form.* The Settlement Form is later balanced and used as the authority by CBN to debit or credit individual banks in their books, depending on whether a bank has a favourable (credit) or adverse (debit) balance.

At the end of the clearing session, the Savannah Bank representative brings back all cheques drawn on our Lagos area branches which were presented on us by other banks. The cheques are handed over to the officer in charge of clearing in the Centralised Accounting Department. The cheques are then sorted out into branches and a machine list prepared for each branch. Later in the day, these cheques are picked up by accredited representatives of these branches for further processing and posting to customers accounts. Dishonoured cheques must be returned immediately as cheques not returned within four working days are deemed to have been paid.

Apart from the Lagos Clearing House, there are Clearing Houses in Ibadan, Kaduna, Kano, Jos, Maiduguri, Sokoto, Port Harcourt, Enugu, Calabar, Ilorin and Benin (i.e. in all the state capitals where the CBN has a branch).

The system of clearing cheques described above is the same in all Clearing Houses in Nigeria. Each Clearing House is managed by a Clearing House Committee comprising a Chairman appointed by the Central Bank (usually the Director of Domestic Operations or his representative in the case of Lagos Clearing House, or the Branch Controller or his representative in the case of up-country Clearing Houses) and representatives of all member banks.

Table 18-1
How Cheques are Cleared

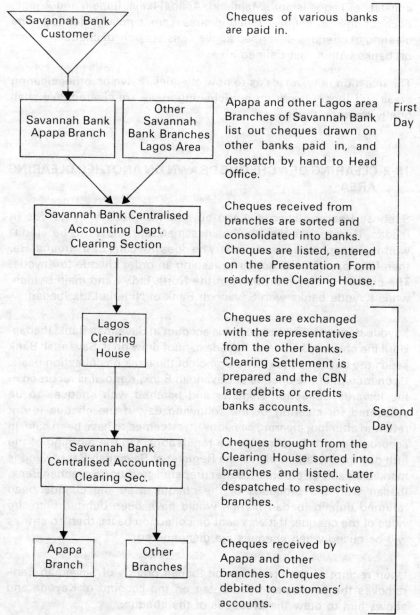

Savannah Bank Customer	Cheques of various banks are paid in.
Savannah Bank Apapa Branch / **Other Savannah Bank Branches Lagos Area**	Apapa and other Lagos area Branches of Savannah Bank list out cheques drawn on other banks paid in, and despatch by hand to Head Office.
Savannah Bank Centralised Accounting Dept. Clearing Section	Cheques received from branches are sorted and consolidated into banks. Cheques are listed, entered on the Presentation Form ready for the Clearing House.
Lagos Clearing House	Cheques are exchanged with the representatives from the other banks. Clearing Settlement is prepared and the CBN later debits or credits banks accounts.
Savannah Bank Centralised Accounting Clearing Sec.	Cheques brought from the Clearing House sorted into branches and listed. Later despatched to respective branches.
Apapa Branch / **Other Branches**	Cheques received by Apapa and other branches. Cheques debited to customers' accounts.

First Day

Second Day

Each clearing area is defined in the rules and regulations governing it. The Lagos clearing area as defined in the rules and regulations consists of Lagos Island, Mainland, Apapa, Ikeja, Ilupeju and Agege. Each of the up-country clearing areas are similarly defined. The clearing of cheques described above consists only of cheques drawn on banks within that defined area.

The question now, arises as to how cheques drawn on other clearing areas and those drawn on non-clearing areas are cleared. We shall briefly examine these.

18-2 CLEARING OF A CHEQUE DRAWN ON ANOTHER CLEARING AREA

Suppose Hassan, living in Kano buys some goods from Kayode in Ibadan. Hassan is a wealthy businessman and known to be credit-worthy. To avoid the risk of robbery he does not carry cash around. He, therefore, pays for the goods by issuing an order cheque to Kayode. The cheque is drawn on Bank of the North Ltd., Kano main branch, while Kayode banks with Savannah Bank of Nigeria Ltd., Ibadan.

Kayode deposits the cheque in his account at Savannah Bank, Ibadan. Until the cheque is cleared, Kayode cannot draw on it. Savannah Bank sends the cheque to the Kano Branch of the bank on collection basis. Upon receipt of the cheque at Savannah Bank, Kano, it is recorded in the Inwards Collection Register and batched with cheques to be presented for clearing on the following day. If the cheque is not returned after four clearing sessions, it is deemed to have been paid, in accordance with Clearing House regulations. On the morning of the fifth day the Inwards Collections Register at Savannah Bank, Kano is marked off and a Settlement Letter prepared crediting Savannah Bank, Ibadan with the proceeds of the cheque. Had the cheque been returned unpaid Ibadan branch would have been debited with the value of the cheque. If it was sent on collection basis, then no entries will be raised when cheques are dishonoured.

Upon receipt of the credit advice Ibadan branch of Savannah Bank removes the 'uncleared effects' tag on the account of Kayode and allows him to draw the proceeds of the cheque.

18-3 CLEARING A CHEQUE DRAWN ON A NON-CLEARING AREA

Suleiman, a pharmacist living in Bauchi issues a cheque to pay for drugs purchased from Alpha Pharmaceutical Company Ltd., Lagos. Suleiman banks with Union Bank Branch, while Alpha Pharmaceutical Company banks with Wema Bank Limited, Lagos.

The cheque is credited to Alpha's account as an uncleared effect item which means the proceeds cannot be withdrawn until the fate of the cheque is known. The cheque is sent to Union Bank, Bauchi, direct by post, on collection basis. On receipt of the cheque, Union Bank ensures that the cheque is drawn in accordance with the mandate given by Suleiman, bears a genuine signature and that the account is in funds. Thereafter, the cheque is debited to the account of Suleiman and a Union Bank draft payable in Lagos is prepared and despatched to Wema Bank Limited, Lagos. Upon receipt of the draft the uncleared effect tag is removed, so Alpha Pharmaceutical Company Ltd. can withdraw the amount. The Union Bank draft is presented for payment by Wema Bank through the Lagos Clearing House system described earlier.

18-4 PAYMENT OF CHEQUES

After cheques have passed through the clearing system and they get to the branch on which they are drawn, the next step is the payment of the cheques. The branch must ensure that the cheques are properly drawn and that the branch has authority to debit the customers' accounts. The branch must make sure that the customers have not stopped payment of any of the cheques and that the accounts are in funds. The signatures on the cheques must be critically examined to ensure that they are genuine and that the cheques are signed in accordance with the mandate given to the bank. For instance, if two signatories are required to sign, the bank must ensure that this is complied with. The cheque itself must be scrutinised to ensure it is properly endorsed and that is is not post-dated, stale, mutilated or altered.

The following are the list of approved reasons for returning cheques in Nigeria, as reviewed by the Clearing House Committee.

i)   Refer to drawer.
ii)   Refer to drawer — present again.
iii)   Amounts in words and figures differ.

iv) Amount in words required.

v) Material alteration requires drawer's confirmation.

vi) Payment stopped, payment countermanded or orders not to pay.

vii) Account closed.

viii) No account.

ix) Account attached.

x) Crossed to two bankers.

xi) Requires banker's crossing

xii) Out of date or stale.

xiii) Post-dated.

xiv) Date incomplete.

xv) Effects uncleared.

xvi) Effects uncleared — present again.

xvii) Endorsement irregular.

xviii) Endorsement required.

xix) Endorsement requires banker's confirmation.

xx) Payee's endorsement required (1st or 2nd).

xxi) Signature differs.

xxii) Second/further signature(s) required.

xxiii) Drawer's signature required.

xxiv) Cheque drawn in foreign currency — please present specially.

xxv) Cheque mutilated.

xxvi) Drawer deceased.

xxvii) Receipt stamp required.

xxviii) Wrong delivery.

xxix) Cheque incompletely drawn.

The reason for returning a cheque must be written in full and boldly on the face of the cheque and must be the true reasons why the cheque is being returned unpaid.

18-5 SPECIAL CLEARING

If a customer is in urgent need of funds and wants the proceeds of a cheque to be credited to his account on the same day or wants to know the fate of a cheque on the same day, he can ask his bank to send the cheque for special clearing or to arrange special presentation. In this case, the branch sends the cheque direct to the drawee bank's branch through a messenger or clerk for payment. If the cheque is in order and paid the drawee bank will debit its customer's account immediately and send a banker's payment to the presenting bank. Upon receipt of the banker's payment, the account of the payee is credited with the proceeds of the cheque the same day. A fee is normally charged for this service, but as stated above, it enables the customer to know the fate of a cheque on the same day and to have immediate use of funds when in need.

REVIEW QUESTIONS

18.1 Ahmed, the drawer of a crossed order cheque, sends it through the post to Shade, the payee, who also has a bank account. Trace the course of the cheque until it is finally paid.

18.2 Describe how a cheque drawn on a Lagos branch of another bank and credited to an account in one of your Lagos area branches can be cleared.

18.3 Describe what you understand by special clearing.

18.4 Cheques may be returned unpaid for a number of reasons. Identify 10 of these reasons and indicate what precautions you would take to preserve the customer's interests.

CHAPTER NINETEEN

EXCHANGE CONTROL AND FOREIGN EXCHANGE SERVICES [1]

19-1 INTRODUCTION

In Chapter Fourteen, whilst discussing general banking services, we touched upon international trade services like bills for collection, bills for negotiation, documentary credits and other foreign exchange transactions. In this Chapter we shall delve into the mechanics of exchange control and foreign exchange regulations in Nigeria and all its ramifications. Merchant and commercial banks in Nigeria play a very significant role in the implementation of these regulations. Virtually all exchange control transactions are processed through commercial and merchant banks and may, therefore, be considered as special bank services.

Nigeria has a very stringent Exchange Control Law. The Exchange Control Act, 1962, as amended in 1966 and 1969, is the principal legislation governing foreign exchange transactions in Nigeria. The main objective of the Act is to prevent the outflow of funds from the country and to conserve the country's reserves of gold and foreign currencies.

The Act vests overall authority with the Minister of Finance, with power to delegate. The Minister has in turn appointed the Central Bank of Nigeria as the principal agent to administer Exchange Control Regulations in the country. The Bank is responsible for the day-to-day administration of the law, but the Minister is still responsible for the determination of certain applications relating to specific purposes directly relevant to overall policy.

All licensed banks in the country have also been appointed by the Minister to act as *Authorised Dealers.* These Authorised Dealers are required to carry out their duties in accordance with Central Bank instructions, with limited authority to approve a certain category of applications like Basic Travel Allowance and other minor sundry payments, although all Exchange Control transactions are first handled

---

[1] The author is indebted to the Exchange Control Department of the Central Bank of Nigeria for their assistance in the preparation of this Chapter.

and processed through an Authorised Dealer. Selected Hotels are also empowered to buy foreign currencies from travellers to Nigeria for surrender to Authorised Dealers. These approved hotels are called Authorised Buyers. In pursuit of government policy on Exchange Control, the Central Bank issues a series of instructions called E.C Memoranda (E.C Memo) to all Authorised Dealers.

These instructions are amended from time to time. By June 1982, the Central Bank had issued 22 E.C Memoranda covering a wide range of Exchange Control subjects. In this Chapter we shall examine these subjects in some detail.

19-2 DESIGNATION OF EXCHANGE CONTROL RESPONSIBILITIES:

Responsibilities for the determination of applications for exchange control approvals are designated to:

i)   the Federal Ministry of Finance.

ii) the Central Bank of Nigeria.

iii) Authorised Dealers — licensed commercial and merchant banks.

iv) Authorised Buyers — standard hotels in the country.

There is a clear demarcation of authority for final approval of applications depending on the sensitivity and importance of the request. For example, all applications relating to:

i)   repatriation of capital, profits and dividends to any country outside Nigeria;

ii) raising of external loans including repayments of such loans;

iii) granting of "Approved Status" for non-resident capital investment in Nigeria;

iv) payment for copyrights, patents and royalties; or

v) any dealings in foreign securities, etc.

must be referred to the Federal Ministry of Finance for determination. Applications relating to payment for imports, commission and brokerages, insurance, business travel, leave and medical tours (private), training, leave payments, final remittances and miscellaneous payments, etc., are determined by the Central Bank of Nigeria. Consequently, banks (Authorised Dealers) have very limited approving authority, confined to basic travel allowances, student education, monthly home remittances by foreign nationals (up to three months), sundry payments and pre-import processing of form M for the value of not more than ₦5,000 (C. & F).

19-3 EXTERNAL TRANSACTIONS

Under the Exchange Control Act, 1962 residents of Nigeria are required to obtain approval from the appropriate authorities before effecting the following foreign exchange transactions:

i) Payment to, or for, the credit of a person resident outside Nigeria.

ii) Payment to, or for, the credit of a person resident in Nigeria by order of, or on behalf of, a person resident outside Nigeria, where such a transaction would involve a compensating payment by the Nigerian resident.

iii) Placing any sum to the credit of a person resident outside Nigeria.

iv) Borrowing any foreign currency from, or lending any foreign currency to, any person other than an Authorised Dealer. Any residents who own foreign currency are required to offer it for sale to an Authorised Dealer.

Requests for all payments in Nigerian currency or any foreign currency to or for the credit of any non-resident must be made on the appropriate Exchange Control forms supported by documentary evidence, including tax clearance certificates for the preceding three years, and be duly approved by the Central Bank.

19-4 SPECIFIED CURRENCIES

Below is a list of approved specified currencies which can be officially dealt in:

Austrian Schillings	French Francs
Belgian Francs	Italian Lire
Canadian Dollars	Japanese Yen
Danish Kroner	Netherlands Guilders
Deutschemarks	Norwegian Kroner

Portuguese Escudos	Swiss Francs
Spanish Peseta	U.K. Sterling
Swedish Kroner	U.S. Dollars

It is clearly stipulated that any of the above currencies acquired in respect of export and non-export proceeds by Nigerians must be surrendered to the Central Bank through Authorised Dealers.

19-5 EXCHANGE CONTROL FORMS

A comprehensive list of all forms in use for exchange control purposes is given below. Authorised Dealers are expected to keep an adequate stock of the forms for the use of applicants.

Exchange Control Forms

	Title and Description of Form	Colour
Form A	Application to purchase foreign currency (not for imports)	White
Form D	Application to establish a banker's credit.	White
Form E	Export Certificate for currency notes, gold, securities of foreign currency	White
Form F	Declaration of foreign currency holdings	White
Form M	Application to purchase foreign currency (for imports only)	Pink
Form N	Returns of Naira notes and coins collected on board plane/ship	White
Form NCD 3	For non-commercial exports	Blue
Form NCD 3 (A)	Exports from Nigeria (for commercial exports)	Blue
Form PHR	Particulars for home remittances	Blue
Form SAC	Students' Advisory Committee Form (students' recommendation)	White

Form T	Returns on B.T.A. Allocation	White
Form X	Application to purchase prepaid travel advices and air-tickets. (The form is not valid for the purchase of foreign currency)	Green
Forms 1 & 2	For the use of Authorised Buyers	White

Source: Central Bank of Nigeria Exchange Control Department

19-6 DEALINGS IN FOREIGN CURRENCIES (excluding notes and coins)

The rates of exchange for foreign currencies are fixed by the Central Bank and circulated to banks from time to time. Both spot and forward transactions are allowed, provided that an approved Form A or M is held by the Authorised Dealer in respect of the sales. The presentation of tax clearance certificates covering 3 years is mandatory.

19-7 DEALINGS IN FOREIGN NOTES AND COINS

Authorised Dealers may buy foreign notes and coins without limit and also sell against an approved Form A from residents and non-residents (other than visitors to Nigeria). In the case of non-residents, Authorised Dealers may draw from, or collect through, banking correspondents outside Nigeria, notes and coins of the country or monetary area concerned where it is possible to do so.

They may also purchase foreign notes and coins from non-resident visitors to Nigeria and provide them in return with Nigerian currency notes or with travellers' cheques, letters of credit, etc., if other conditions relating to payments for imports have been fulfilled. Dealers must also keep abreast of currency regulations in force in the countries of issue and limit transactions accordingly.

Authorised Buyers (i.e. approved hotels) are also authorised to purchase foreign currency from travellers to Nigeria and must turn the proceeds over to Authorised Dealers within 48 hours.

19-8 IMPORT AND EXPORT OF FOREIGN NOTES, BILLS OF EXCHANGE, ASSURANCE POLICIES, ANNUITIES, ETC.

Foreign currency notes, bills of exchange, promissory notes, drafts, travellers' cheques and letters of credit may be imported into Nigeria without restriction and without limit as to their value. However, there is a limit to the amount of foreign currency that may be exported by travellers from Nigeria. The maximum amount allowed with effect from April, 1982 is ₦500 per adult person in any fiscal year. Visitors leaving the country may be allowed to take out with them up to the amount which they brought in (less expenses) on completion of Form E for approval by the CBN, where the amount exceeds the ₦500 limit set.

Banks are permitted to export assurance policies and annuities owned by non-residents to any country outside Nigeria where such non-residents have no resident accounts and foreign currency assurance policies and annuities owned by residents for collection at maturity or for endorsement and return to Nigeria. Those owned by residents should be referred to the Central Bank.

19-9 IMPORTATION AND EXPORTATION OF NIGERIAN NOTES AND COINS

Travellers to and from Nigeria are allowed to hold a maximum of ₦50 in Nigerian notes and coins. Collections of foreign airlines and shipping companies will be converted to foreign exchange on application to the CBN, supported with the passenger manifest. The Central Bank will not exchange Naira for non-resident holders such as foreign banks.

19-10 TRAVEL

The Nigerian Exchange Control regulations permit Authorised Dealers to approve applications for Basic Travel Allowances for Nigerian residents (excluding merchant seamen, civil airline officials resident in Nigeria and emigrants) up to a maximum of ₦500 per adult person during any fiscal year. (In 1982, the allowance for children under the age of sixteen years was suspended.) Pilgrims are allowed up to ₦800. The allowances are applicable to 1982 fiscal year and are subject to change thereafter depending upon the external reserve position of the country.

A Nigerian resident wishing to travel abroad is required to take the following steps in order to obtain foreign exchange for his personal travel expenditure abroad. (Foreign Exchange will usually be provided in the form of travellers' cheques or foreign currency notes.)

The following documents must be submitted before an application can be approved:

i) Completed Form 'A' in duplicate.

ii) Valid Passport.

iii) Travel ticket or evidence of travel.

iv) Tax Clearance Certificate for the preceeding three years or Form H2 — issued by the applicant's employer.

The amounts obtained in respect of foreign nationals constitute part of their 50% permissible Home Remittances. The amount must also be marked on the passport of the traveller by the Authorised Dealer providing the facility. Travellers must return the foreign exchange if travel arrangements are cancelled for any reason. To ensure that this requirement is enforced airline and shipping companies have been instructed not to refund money paid in respect of tickets issued for journeys subsequently cancelled without reference to the Central Bank.

19-10.1 Medical Travel

Where evidence is produced that surgery or serious medical care is required, up to ₦2,000 may be approved by the Central Bank or any of its branches for medical attention. Otherwise, the traveller is expected to utilise his Basic Travel Allowance. To support an application, a letter of reference from a specialist (not a general practitioner) must be obtained. Any bill in excess of ₦2,000 must be supported by a letter or a bill from the overseas hospital authorities.

19-10.2 Business Travel

Application for foreign exchange facilities for business travels should be submitted on Form A in duplicate to the Central Bank through an Authorised Dealer.

The following information and supporting documents are required:

i)   The amount required.

ii) The countries to be visited.

iii) The duration of the travel and commencement date.

iv) The purpose of the business trip.

v)   Documentary evidence in support of i)-iv) (e.g. letter of invitation from a foreign business associate).

vi) Certificate of Registration or Incorporation of the company as applicable.

vii) Tax Clearance Certificate for the preceding three years certified and signed by the authorised signatory of the Internal Inland Revenue Office.

The maximum amount of foreign exchange allowance for business travel in 1982 was ₦2,500 per annum (i.e. ₦100 per day for a maximum of 25 days per year). No individual trip is allowed to extend beyond 15 days.

19-10.3 Transfer of Air Ticket Sales

Foreign airlines operating in Nigeria may be granted permission to remit to their parent companies outside Nigeria the proceeds of air ticket sales. Form A must be completed to which the following documents must be attached:

i)   Details of all tickets and prepaid travel allowances (PTA's). PTA's relate to journeys commencing outside Nigeria. PTA applications require prior approval by CBN before commencement of the journey.

ii) Statements of sales, refunds, expenses and PTA's issued during the period must be specified.

iii) Tax Clearance Certificate.

iv) An External Auditor's Statement certifying the correctness of the statements.

19-11 PAYMENTS FOR IMPORTS INTO NIGERIA

19-11.1 Comprehensive Import Supervision

All applications in respect of payments for imports into Nigeria must be supported with a Form M, irrespective of the value. A system of comprehensive import supervision or pre-shipment inspection of imports into Nigeria was introduced in 1978 to curb abuses in international trade transactions. The objective was to ensure that imports into Nigeria are of the correct quality, price and quantity. In pursuit of this objective, the Central Bank of Nigeria appointed Societe Generale de Surveillance S.A., (S.G.S.) Geneva, Switzerland as its agent. Since January, 1979 imports into Nigeria have been subject to compulsory quality and quantity inspection and price comparison by S.G.S. *before shipment is effected.* Before shipment of the goods, sellers are required to give at least 14 days notice to S.G.S. indicating the place where the goods may be inspected and the expected time of despatch.

Upon completion of inspection, S.G.S. issues a report of findings which may be:

i) A Clean Report of Findings if the inspection yields a satisfactory result. S.G.S. does not issue this report until the Inspection Order copy of Form M has been received and the seller has submitted a copy of the final invoice covering the goods.

ii) A Non-Negotiable Report of Findings if the inspection reveals discrepancies.

No payment can be effected against a letter of credit, bill for collection, or any other form of claim unless the documents presented for payment include a Clean Report of Findings.

19-11.2 The Use of Form M

The above scheme gave birth to the Form M procedure which was introduced in January, 1979. All imports of goods into Nigeria, shipped from any port whether under letters of credit or bills for collection or any other form of payment became subject to Pre-Import Processing by the Exchange Control Department of the Central Bank of Nigeria.

This means that prior approval of Form M by the CBN is a precondition for the importation of goods into the country. A processed Form M by the CBN serves as authority to open a letter of credit. The Central Bank gives full details of the S.G.S. contact office in the country of the seller on the approved Form M. However, all goods whose value are below ₦5,000 (C & F) are exempted from the pre-shipment inspection exercise.

19-12 EXPORTS FROM NIGERIA

For all shipments of goods from Nigeria, an Exchange Control Form N.C.D. 3 (non-commercial) or N.C.D. 3 (A) for commercial exports must be completed. An export licence must be obtained.

The exporter or his agent should submit the completed form N.C.D. 3 or N.C.D. 3 (A) with the export licence to the Customs and Excise at the time the goods are entered for export, while page 5 of the N.C.D. 3 (A) form is lodged with the Central Bank through an Authorised Dealer. Customs and Excise forwards these forms to the Central Bank which in the case of commercial exports retains pages 1 and 2 while page 3 is despatched to the Authorised Dealer named on the form for certification. The form N.C.D. 3 covering non-commercial exports is retained by the Central Bank of Nigeria for record purposes.

Eventually when payment is received by the Authorised Dealer, the forms are certified as to the amount of foreign currency received and sent to the Central Bank.

The Exchange Control Act Section 18 empowers the Minister of Finance to make orders prescribing the manner in which payment shall be received for goods exported to any destination outside Nigeria.

Exported goods must be paid for immediately or within 3 months from the date of export or such other periods as the Minister may direct.

19-13 CREDITS AND GUARANTEES

The term "credits" includes facilities providing for the payment of drafts drawn for usance and payments by banks against documents. (It does not include travellers' letters of credit.)

Credits in favour of residents of Nigeria in respect of exports from Nigeria may be paid for by payment against documents or by drafts, accompanied by documents drawn for usances.

For credits in favour of residents outside Nigeria in respect of imports into Nigeria, it is necessary to comply with the requirements of the regulations relating to imports. Where a specific import licence is required, the validity of the credit does not exceed the expiry date of the licence. A processed Form M must be submitted in respect of all payments made under credits opened in favour of residents outside Nigeria.

CBN approval must be obtained for dealings in any guarantee or similar undertaking, the implementation of which would involve a payment to a resident outside Nigeria or a payment in any foreign currency, as well as for dealings in any guarantee to a resident in Nigeria on behalf of, or for the account of, a resident outside Nigeria. However, licensed banks are permitted to give guarantees on behalf of their customers in the ordinary course of business covering missing documents, the authenticity of signatures, the release of goods under trust receipts, etc.

19-14 INSURANCE PAYMENTS

19-14.1 Non-Trade

Nigerian residents are barred from taking out life or endowment policies or purchase annuities payable in any foreign currency, except with the permission of the Central Bank.

19-14.2 Trade

All imports of goods into Nigeria must be effected only on cost and freight (C & F) basis. The insurance must be taken out with a registered insurance company in Nigeria. Applications for permission to import goods into the country must be supported by documentary evidence of insurance in Nigeria.

For any insurance company in Nigeria to make payments to beneficiaries outside Nigeria for any insurance business such as premiums in respect of insurance and reinsurance which cannot be undertaken locally, Central Bank approval is required.

19-15 FISHING, SHIPPING & AIR TRANSPORT PAYMENTS

All contracts for the charter of aircraft, shipping and fishing vessels involving foreign exchange should receive the approval of the Central Bank of Nigeria.

19-16 SUNDRY AND MISCELLANEOUS PAYMENTS

Authorised Dealers may approve applications by residents on Form A to make payments to beneficiaries outside Nigeria for the following items: correspondence courses, examination fees, subscription to clubs, societies and professional bodies, single copies of magazines, books, etc.

Applications in respect of subscriptions to trade organisations, educational and training tours covering allowances for staff on training courses, seminars, etc., should be forwarded to the Central Bank through an Authorised Dealer for determination.

Any amount approved for sundry payments for the benefit of resident foreign nationals constitutes part of the overall limit of 50% net income allowed.

Applications for management fees, royalties, technical service fees, commissions, patents and trade marks payable outside Nigeria are determined by the Minister for Finance. These remittances are now limited to 3% of the *net* profit. Management Agreement Fees are not entertained from existing well-established companies. The proportion of consultancy fees remittable abroad to foreign associates is fixed at 30% of the total fees, while the maximum fee payable to a non-resident director of a Nigerian Company is ₦4,000 per annum.

The Minister, through the CBN, may grant approval to purchase foreign exchange to make payments outside Nigeria in respect of the above services. The following documents are required in support of such applications:

i) Form 'A' duly completed.

ii) Copy of the contract agreement.

iii) A demand note from the beneficiary.

iv) Documentary evidence that the contract has been performed.

v) Certified copy of resolution in respect of Directors' Fees for the year.

19-17 CASH GIFTS

Cash gifts are remittances by individuals and organisations resident in Nigeria on compassionate grounds which represent *gifts* as opposed to the *settlement of liabilities.*

Applications on Form A should be forwarded to the Central Bank through Authorised Dealers. Donations not exceeding the equivalent of ₦500 and ₦150 may be made to charitable organisations and individuals respectively during any fiscal year. Individual applications exceeding this amount would be treated on their merits.

19-18 RESIDENT, NON-RESIDENT AND EXTERNAL ACCOUNTS

19-18.1 Resident Accounts

A foreign national must have been resident, or show that it is his intention to be a resident, for at least six months before he can operate a 'resident' account. A 'resident' account is an account operated by a Nigerian National or foreigner permanently resident in Nigeria. Applications from foreign organisations/companies to open 'resident' accounts must be referred to the Central Bank of Nigeria for determination.

19-18.2 External/Non-Resident Accounts

'External' accounts refer to all those accounts opened in favour of non-residents, but which are fed with funds derived from external sources. Central Bank approval must be obtained before the account is opened.

'Non-Resident' accounts refer to accounts opened in favour of non-residents, but which are funded from local sources.

Members of foreign diplomatic corps who are career or established members of staff are treated as non-residents for exchange control purposes.

All applications to open resident, non-resident and external accounts should be submitted under a covering letter from the proposed bankers on behalf of customers to the Exchange Control Department, Central Bank of Nigeria, Lagos.

19-18.3 Change of Residential Status

When a foreign national is leaving the country finally, he may apply to transfer his savings and other balances to his home country or to where he is emigrating. Applications should be submitted through an Authorised Dealer to the Central Bank (see 19-19.2 below).

19-19 FOREIGN NATIONALS' REMITTANCES

19-19.1 Remittances by Foreign Nationals

Foreign nationals resident in Nigeria are allowed to remit 50% of their net income outside Nigeria for family maintenance. Female foreign nationals married to Nigerians and naturalised aliens are only allowed 25% of the net annual income in any fiscal year for the maintenance of their parents outside Nigeria upon request.

The following documents must be attached to each application:

i) Tax deduction card or tax assessment notice and tax receipt for the relevant period, certified and signed by the authorised signatory of the Inland Revenue Office.

ii) A duly completed P.H.R. Form (Particulars for Home Remittance).

iii) Details of total remittances made outside Nigeria since 1 January of the current or previous financial year, certified by the applicant's bankers, in respect of self-employed persons.

iv) Photocopy of resident permit.

19-19.2 Transfer on Final Departure from Nigeria

When a foreign national is leaving Nigeria finally, he will be allowed to transfer the net balance on his account to his home country.

The following documentary evidences are required:

i) A certificate from the applicant's banker confirming total remittances made during the last four years.

ii) A banker's certificate of the balance on applicant's account as at the date of application.

iii) An employer's confirmation that the applicant will not be returning to Nigeria.

iv) A signed statement of assets in Nigeria.

v) Tax clearance for the past four years and one for the current year certified and signed by the authorised signatory of the Inland Revenue Office.

vi) P.H.R. form duly completed.

vii)Where payment of a gratuity is involved, a statement from the applicant's employer confirming the payment, together with a tax clearance certificate or tax receipt.

viii)Documentary evidence of sale of assets (if any).

ix) An employer's confirmation of fringe benefits (if any) and their value.

19-20 SECURITIES

Residents of Nigeria may not, except with the permission of the Federal Ministry of Finance, buy from or sell to, non-residents of Nigeria, any shares, stocks, bonds, debenture stocks, etc., payable in Nigerian currency.

Similarly, residents of Nigeria may not buy or sell any security denominated in foreign currency without the permission of the Federal Ministry of Finance.

Only residents are permitted to issue securities. Non-residents can only do so with the permission of the Federal Ministry of Finance.

19-21 DIRECT CAPITAL INVESTMENT IN NIGERIA

Non-residents who wish to invest capital directly in Nigeria can apply to the Federal Ministry of Finance for 'Approved Status'. The granting of 'Approved Status' means that future requests for repatriation of capital directly invested in Nigeria to the extent of any distributions of a capital nature arising in respect of the realisation thereof will receive sympathetic consideration.

The following guidelines apply to repatriation of proceeds of the sale of shares under the Nigerian Enterprises Promotion Act, 1977:

i) Repatriation will be on instalment basis at the following rates:

   a) amounts not exceeding ₦300,000 shall on approval be transferred in a single transfer; and,

   b) the excess over ₦300,000 shall be transferred at the rate of ₦300,000 every six months.

ii) To qualify for repatriation as above, applications should be supported by documentary evidence of 'Approved Status' or evidence of capital importation.

iii) On re-investment in Nigeria, enterprises already enjoying 'Approved Status' will have 'Approved Status' conferred on their new investments.

iv) All enterprises that cannot produce evidence of 'Approved Status' would, on reinvesting not less than 50% of the proceeds of the sale of their shares in new enterprises in the Nigerian economy, qualify for the transfer of dividends for both their old and new investment, thus rationalising their position.

The concession in respect of 'Approved Status' will not apply to the purchase of shares on any Stock Exchange which may be established in Nigeria unless this forms an integral part of the approved investment project. Applications should be submitted to the Federal Ministry of Finance by letter containing full information of the proposed investment.

19-22 LOANS AND OVERDRAFTS

19-22.1 Borrowing in Nigeria

The permission of the Federal Ministry of Finance is required for the granting of any loan in Nigeria to any non-resident individual, firm or company and any company registered in Nigeria (other than a bank) which is controlled, whether directly or indirectly, by non-residents.

Authorised Dealers may approve applications by foreign-controlled companies for overdrafts in Nigeria to finance imports into and exports from Nigeria without prior approval of the Ministry of Finance.

19-22.2 Borrowing Outside Nigeria

The permission of the Federal Ministry of Finance is required for any individual, firm or company resident in Nigeria to borrow outside Nigeria for any purpose. Applications for permission to enter into such commitments should be submitted by letter through an Authorised Dealer giving the following particulars:

i) the amount, duration and purpose of the loan;

ii) the rate of interest payable; and,

iii) the proposed arrangement for repayment.

Existing loans of this nature should be reported to the Federal Ministry of Finance, but may not be renewed without its permission.

19-23 EDUCATION OUTSIDE NIGERIA

Nigerian students attending approved colleges and universities outside Nigeria may be granted foreign exchange facilities to meet their educational expenses. However, for undergraduate students still in Nigeria, their applications must first be approved by the Student Advisory Committee.

For undergraduate students the following additional documents are required:

i) Evidence of admission to an overseas institution.

ii) Detailed student particulars (e.g. course of study, duration of course).

iii) Student Advisory Committee recommendation or letter from the Nigerian Embassy/High Commission in respect of students who are already in foreign institutions confirming that it is a recognised educational institution.

No recommendation will be required in respect of students on partial or full scholarships.

For post-graduate students, the following documents are required:

i)   Letter of admission issued by the Registrar or Bursar or Principal of the college, stating the fees payable per annum plus maintenance — an estimate of maintenance expenses from Embassies or High Commissions may be requested.

ii) Particulars of the course showing its duration.

iii) Evidence of a scholarship (if any).

iv) Passport (to be sighted).

Except for the maintenance allowance, payments are made direct to the institutions concerned.

For correspondence courses and examination fees, post offices are permitted to approve up to ₦50.00.

REVIEW QUESTIONS

19.1 Describe how payments for imports can be effected in Nigeria.

19.2 Write short notes in relation to Nigerian foreign exchange regulations on:

i) Basic Travel Allowance (B.T.A.)

ii) Cash Gifts.

19.3 Describe the exchange control regulations relating to exports from Nigeria.

19.4 Explain briefly exchange control regulations relating to:

i) Remittances by foreign nationals.

ii) Direct capital investment in Nigeria.

PART IV
MONEY & CAPITAL MARKETS

CHAPTER TWENTY

THE NIGERIAN MONEY MARKET

20-1 INTRODUCTION

Money, like any other commodity, is bought and sold in a market which is called the *money market.*[1] The Nigerian Money Market started to function in 1959 after the establishment of the Central Bank. The market brings together those financial institutions with surplus funds which they wish to lend on a short-term basis and those wishing to borrow. Unlike the capital market which has fixed a place for transacting business, the money market is not located in any one building. It operates by means of the telephone and personal contact between those who operate in the market.

However, after a deal is struck the transaction is finally concluded at the Central Bank. The participants in the market are commercial banks, merchant banks, the Central Bank and other financial institutions.

20-2 DEVELOPMENT

To aid the development of the market, the CBN introduced Treasury Bills in 1960 and Treasury Certificates in 1968. These are short-term government debt instruments. They created an avenue for commercial and merchant banks and other financial institutions to invest their surplus funds in Nigeria instead of London. Treasury Bills have a tenure of 91 days, while Treasury Certificates are issued for 1 – 2 years.

The Call Money Scheme was also introduced to provide banks with an outlet for the temporary or overnight investment of their surplus funds. This Scheme was initially managed by the CBN, but due to the shortage of government short-term debt instruments during the post war year of excess liquidity, the Scheme was abandoned in 1974.

20-3 CALL MONEY SYSTEM

Presently, the banks still operate a private call money system, whereby surplus funds of Bank A are placed on call with Bank B which is temporarily in need of liquid funds. Bank A can ask for repayment at any time the need arises. On the other hand, Bank B is free to repay the debt as soon as its funding position improves. Thus, those funds are invested on a day-to-day basis. The actual movement of the funds from

---

[1] G. O. Nwankwo *The Nigerian Financial System* Macmillan 1980 p. 123

Bank A to Bank B and vice versa upon repayment is concluded at the Central Bank, acting on the instructions of the paying bank.

The following are examples of call money transaction instructions to the Central Bank of Nigeria.

i) Bank Investing in Call Money

The Banking Manager
Central Bank of Nigeria
Lagos.

Dear Sir,

Before the close of business today, please transfer the sum of ₦... from our account number... to the account of... Bank Nig. Ltd., with you.

This represents money placed on call with them at 8½% p.a.

Yours faithfully,

Authorised Signatory

Authorised Signatory
cc: ... Bank of Nig. Ltd.

ii) Bank Repaying Call Money

The Banking Manager
Central Bank of Nigeria
Lagos.

Dear Sir,

Before close of business today, please transfer the sum of ₦ ... from our account number ... to the account of ... Bank Nig. Ltd., with you.

This represents the principal amount plus interest on money placed with us.

Yours faithfully,

Authorised Signatory

Authorised Signatory
cc: ... Bank of Nig. Ltd.

20-4 OTHER MONEY MARKET INSTRUMENTS

20-4.1 Commercial Bill Finance Scheme

Other instruments of the Money Market included Commodity Boards Bills in respect of export produce which are rediscountable with the CBN and other trade bills or commercial bills. Through this scheme, Marketing Boards (now Commodity Boards) issue 90 day bills (supported by sales contracts on the Nigerian Produce Marketing Company) to producers who could discount the bills with commercial or merchant banks. They, in turn, could also rediscount with the CBN. Three Marketing Boards — Northern Nigeria Marketing Board, Western Nigeria Marketing Board and the Mid-Western Nigeria Marketing Board — used the scheme and most of the commercial banks participated as a consortium. The Scheme was abandoned in 1968, because Marketing Boards were unable to produce sales contracts which formed the basis on which bills were drawn. Consequently the banks became unwilling to grant advances. Eventually, the CBN assumed the responsibility of granting direct credit to the Commodity/ Marketing Boards.

20-4.2 Certificates of Deposits

Negotiable (NCD) or *Non-Negotiable (NNCD)* Deposits are inter-bank debt instruments designed mainly to channel commercial banks' surplus funds into the merchant banks. NCD's are rediscountable with the CBN and those with not more than 18 months tenure are eligible as liquid assets in computing a bank's liquidity ratio. These attributes make the instrument attractive to banks.

20-4.3 The Bankers' Unit Fund and Stabilisation Securities

These were introduced to mop up excess liquidity in the economy in 1975 and 1976 respectively. The need for these additional money market instruments arose because of the excess liquidity in the economy following the oil boom and the Government's reluctance to increase its borrowings through the issue of Treasury Bills and Treasury Certificates.

20-4.5 Treasury Bills, Treasury Certificates and Eligible Development Stocks

Treasury Bills are short-term debt instruments (91 day maturity) issued by the CBN to raise finance for the Federal Government. Treasury Certificates are issued for the same purpose with a maturity of one year or two years . Development stocks maturing within three years are also eligible money market instruments.

20-5 GENERAL COMMENTS

The Nigerian Money Market is still evolving and is not presently performing its functions effectively. However, its principal functions are:

i)   The provision of facilities for profitable investment of surplus short-term funds and the provision of short-term borrowing facilities to the institutions in need of funds.

With the abolition of the Call Money Scheme in 1974, the Central Bank virtually pulled out of the arrangement and banks were compelled to operate the private call money system. The scheme as presently operated without CBN participation has several shortcomings. A bank which has a temporary liquidity problem has no central point to avail itself of money market funds. It will have to go from bank to bank or make a series of telephone calls — when the telephones are working! On some bad days it may end up not having a kobo. On another day the same bank may have surplus funds to invest on call money and discover that every other bank is liquid. Thus, the funds will remain idle on current account with the CBN. In the days when the CBN operated the Call Money Scheme such problems would not arise. Surplus funds were automatically invested on a daily basis on short-term securities such as Treasury Bills, etc., and those in need could always obtain funds. The result is that banks are now compelled to hold higher cash reserves.

ii) The second major function of a money market is the provision of market facilities for Treasury Bills, Treasury Certificates and Bills of Exchange. The Treasury Bill and Treasury Certificate and other short-dated government stocks are sources of short-term borrowing for the Government. They also provide an avenue for the investment of banks' and other financial institutions' surplus funds. The

Treasury Bill/Certificate markets have now become active again after the slowdown in 1976. However, the abolition of the bill market scheme in 1968 remains the most serious blow to the development of the money market in Nigeria. It is hoped that both the call money and the bill market schemes will be reactivated in the not-too-distant future by the Central Bank.

iii) A well-developed money market can also be used as an effective instrument of monetary control, through the provision of a channel for injection or withdrawal of liquidity from the economy by Open Market Operations, or through the proper use of the Bank Rate and Rediscount Rate. As discussed in Chapter Six, these instruments cannot be used unless there is a well-developed money market.

REVIEW QUESTIONS

20.1 Write short notes on:

    i)   Treasury Bills.

    ii) Treasury Certificates.

20.2 Describe the structure and functions of the Lagos money market.

CHAPTER TWENTY ONE

THE NIGERIAN CAPITAL MARKET

21-1 INTRODUCTION

A Stock Exchange is a market where buyers and sellers of stocks and shares transact business. However, members of the public or investors have no direct access to the market. The buying and selling can only be done by stockbrokers acting on their behalf.

The market also provides facilities for governments (Federal and State), large corporations and companies to raise new or additional capital.

21-2 THE NIGERIAN STOCK EXCHANGE

The Lagos Stock Exchange started operations in 1961. It is a non-profit making organisation and a private company limited by guarantee. Some years after the establishment of the Lagos Stock Exchange, the Government decided to establish branches outside Lagos. In 1977, the Nigerian Stock Exchange took over the activities of the Lagos Stock Exchange and branches were opened at Kaduna and Port Harcourt.

21-2.1 Membership

There are three categories of membership:

i) Foundation members, comprising three companies and three individuals who subscribed to the original shares of the institution.

ii) Ordinary members, comprising those admitted to membership after the establishment of the Exchange in 1961 by subscription to the shares. Thus, ordinary members are shareholders.

iii) Dealing members comprise the individuals, firms or corporate bodies *"Licensed by the Council of the Exchange to deal in stocks, shares and all securities for the time being granted quotation on the Exchange"*.[1]

---

[1] G. O. Nwankwo *The Nigerian Financial System* Macmillan 1980 p. 133

Dealing members are people who buy and sell securities on behalf of investors for a commission called "brokerage". They are mainly firms of stockbrokers. As the Exchange is not fully developed yet, all dealings are handled by brokers. They deal both directly with the public and also operate on the market, unlike in the London Stock Exchange where the broker can only operate on the market through a jobber, who cannot also deal directly with the public. A jobber buys and sells securities from or to stockbrokers and makes profits on them. Such gains are called "the jobber's turn".

On the London Stock Exchange, an investor must first approach a broker who, in turn, will contact several jobbers to compare prices before striking a deal on behalf of his principal (the investor). As stated earlier, there are no jobbers on the Nogerian Stock Exchange and all transactions are handled by brokers.

Issuing Houses also operate as members of the Stock Exchange, as they help to prepare prospectuses and to sell the shares offered to the public by companies and government. Almost all the Issuing Houses in Nigeria are merchant banks.

21-2.2 The Functions of the Stock Exchange

The main functions of the Nigerian Stock Exchange are:

i) To act as a central meeting place for members to buy and sell existing stocks and shares and for granting quotations to new issues through the provisions of opportunities for raising new or fresh capital.

ii) To provide machinery through stocks and shares for mobilising private and public savings and making these available for productive investment.

iii) To facilitate the purchase and sale of securities, thereby reducing the risk of illiquidity. Ideally, this should encourage more investment in stocks and shares since investors will be confident that they can realise their investments easily.

iv) To act as a channel for implementing the indigenisation programme by providing facilities to foreign businesses to offer their shares to the Nigerian public for subscription.

v) To provide opportunities for the continued operation and attraction of foreign capital for Nigeria's development.

vi) To facilitate dealings in Government securities"[2]

21-3 GENERAL COMMENTS

The main financial institutions operating on the capital market in Nigeria are the CBN, development banks, commercial banks, insurance companies, the Federal Mortgage Bank, the Federal Savings Banks, the stockbroking firms and other investment corporations.

The Central Bank of Nigeria has always encouraged the growth of the Stock Exchange by giving it subventions and by acting as "Buyer of Last Resort" of government stocks not absorbed by the capital market. The Exchange is an independent organisation controlled by the Stock Exchange Council (Board). However, like other financial institutions, its activities are reported periodically to the Nigerian Securities and Exchange Commission. (See Chapter Twenty Two). These reports enable the authorities to monitor the activities of the Exchange.

Instruments listed on the Nigerian Stock Exchange are:

i) Federal Government Development Stocks.

ii) State Government Bonds or Stock.

iii) Commercial and industrial loan stocks and debentures.

iv) Company shares or stocks.

---

[2] G. O. Nwankwo — *The Nigerian Financial System* Macmillan 1980, p. 134

REVIEW QUESTIONS

21.1 What are the functions of the Nigerian Stock Exchange?

21.2 Describe briefly the roles of brokers and jobbers, with particular reference to the Nigerian Stock Exchange.

CHAPTER TWENTY TWO

THE NIGERIAN SECURITIES AND EXCHANGE COMMISSION

22-1 INTRODUCTION

The forerunner of the Nigerian Securities and Exchange Commission was the Capital Issues Committee which came into existence in July 1962. It was essentially an ad hoc committee which handled about twenty issues between 1962 and 1973. Although its decisions were accepted by Investment Houses, it lacked any legal backing to enforce its decisions.

An Act was, therefore, promulgated in March, 1973, establishing the Capital Issues Commission to supersede the ad hoc Capital Issues Committee. The Act empowered the Commssion to determine:

i)   the price at which the shares or debentures of a company are to be sold;

ii) the timing and the amount of sale; and,

iii) in the case of a company whose securities have been quoted on any recognised stock exchange, the price, timing and amount of any supplementary offers for sale.

One of the main objectives of the Commission was to complement the activities of the Nigerian Enterprises Promotion Board to ensure that the correct proportion of shares in foreign companies were transferred to Nigerians, in accordance with Schedules I, II and III of the Enterprises Promotion Act.

In April, 1978, following the recommendation of the Committee on the Nigerian Financial System, the Capital Issues Commission was replaced by the Nigerian Securities and Exchange Commission, as the apex institution of the Nigerian Capital Market.

The Board membership of the Commission is made up of:

i)   A representative of the CBN as Chairman.

ii) One representative of the Nigerian Stock Exchange.

iii) One representative of the Nigerian Enterprises Promotion Board.

iv) On representative each of:

    a) Federal Ministry of Finance.

b) Federal Ministry of Trade.

c) Federal Ministry of Industries.

v) The Executive Director of the Commission.

vi) Five private members appointed by the Federal Government who hold office for a period of 5 years and are eligible for re-appointment.

The Commission functioned in the same way as the Capital Issues Commission until the Securities and Exchange Commission Act became law in September, 1979. Up to that date, the Commission was run as a department or arm of the Central Bank of Nigeria.

The Commission took steps to put into force the autonomy conferred on it by the Act. To ensure a smooth take-off, the Commission and the Central Bank of Nigeria agreed that all the staff of the Commission (who were regular staff of the Bank) be seconded to the Commission. Hence, the Commission became fully autonomous with effect from 1 January, 1980 with its own vote and budget.

22-2 FUNCTIONS OF THE COMMISSION

The Commission is charged with the responsibility of:

i) Determining the amount of, and time at which, securities of a company are to be sold to the public either through offer for sale or subscription.

ii) Registering all securities proposed to be offered for sale to, or for subscription by, the public or to be offered privately with the intention that the securities shall be held ultimately other than by those to whom the offers were made.

iii) Maintaining surveillance over the securities market to ensure orderly, fair and equitable dealings in securities.

iv) Registering stock exchanges or branches, registrars, investment advisers, securities dealers and their agents and controlling and supervising their activities with a view to maintaining proper standards of conduct and professionalism in the securities business.

v) Protecting the integrity of the securities market against any abuses arising from the practice of inside trading.

vi) Acting as the regulatory apex organisation for the Nigerian Stock Exchange and its branches to which it would be at liberty to delegate powers.

vii) Creating the necessary atmosphere for the orderly growth and development of the capital market.

viii) Undertaking such other activities as are necessary or expedient for giving full effect to the provisions of the Act.

The approval of the Commission is required before an offer of shares and debentures for sale by companies can be made. The Commission has similar powers to its predecessor, but, in addition, can determine whether the initial or subsequent issue or sale of the securities issued by an enterprise shall be restricted or made public and when such an enterprise shall seek a quotation of the Stock Exchange.

The Act also stipulates that the commission must ensure that any shares issued by a bank, otherwise than by capitalisation out of reserves of the bank, shall be by way of public offer.

REVIEW QUESTIONS

22.1 What are the main functions of Nigerian Securities and Exchange
Commission?

Commission?

PART V
INTERNATIONAL
BANKING

CHAPTER TWENTY THREE

INTERNATIONAL FINANCIAL SYSTEM

23-1 THE WORLD BANK GROUP

The World Bank is a group of three institutions: the International Bank for Reconstruction and Development (I.B.R.D.), the International Development Association (I.D.A.) and the International Finance Corporation (I.F.C.).

The common objective of these institutions is to help raise standards of living in developing countries by channelling financial resources from developed countries to the developing world. More specifically, they have two principal objectives:

i) to make or guarantee loans for development projects in less-developed countries either from their own capital or with borrowed funds; and,

ii) to provide technical assistance to the less-developed countries which in most cases have no experts available in the field of investment projects.

23-1.1 The World Bank

The oldest of these three institutions is the International Bank for Reconstruction and Development (I.B.R.D.), popularly known as the World Bank. The Bank came into existence in 1945, following the deliberations of the representatives of the 44 nations assembled at Bretton Woods, New Hampshire, U.S.A. in 1944. The participants at the Bretton Woods Conference realised that at the end of the war, there would be a pressing need for international capital to finance the reconstruction of productive facilities destroyed by the war and to increase productivity and living standards of the under-developed areas of the world. It was felt that private capital alone could not cope with the enormous problems faced in the post-war era. It recommended, therefore, the creation of a new type of international investment institution which would be authorised to make or guarantee loans for productive reconstruction and development projects, both with its own capital funds and through the mobilisation of private capital.

As at July 1981 the World Bank had 139 member countries subscribing to its share capital. The Bank finances its lending operations primarily from its own borrowings in the world capital markets. In addition, substantial contributions to the Bank's resources come from its retained earnings and the flow of repayments on its loans.

The Bank's loans generally have a grace period of five years and are repayable over 20 years or less. The loans currently carry an interest rate of 11.6% which is far cheaper than other commercial Euromarket loans.

The operational structure of the Bank consists mainly of six Regional Offices at the Bank's headquarters for Eastern Africa, Western Africa, Asia, Europe, the Middle East and North Africa and Latin Amercia and the Caribbean. Each office is responsible for planning and supervising the execution of the Bank's development assistance programme within its assigned countries. The Bank's charter details certain basic rules that govern its operations. It must lend only for productive purposes and must stimulate economic growth in the developing countries where it lends. Each loan is made to a government or must be guaranteed by the government concerned.

In functional terms World Bank investments are mainly for agriculture, transportation, water supply, telecommunication, power generation industry, education, urban development, development finance and technical assistance etc.

23-1.2 The International Development Association

The International Development Association (I.D.A.) is an affiliate of the World Bank and was established in 1960. The World Bank had become aware of the urgent need for an institution that could provide development finance on terms more lenient and bearing less heavily on the balance of payments of developing countries than its own loans.

Also, the debt-servicing problem in many low-income countries had become so severe in the early 1960's that it was difficult for these countries to finance their development with conventional loans from the I.B.R.D. In order to raise or maintain their rate of economic growth, these poorer countries needed external financial assistance on concessionary terms. The I.D.A., therefore, provided a welcome supplement to the Bank's own development lending activities. The

I.D.A.'s assistance is, therefore, concentrated on the very poor countries — mainly those with an annual per capita gross national product of less than $681. More than 70 countries are currently eligible under this criterion.

Membership in the I.D.A. is open to all members of the World Bank and presently there are 125 of them. The funds used by the I.D.A. — usually called 'Credits' — come mostly in the form of subscriptions, general replenishments from the I.D.A.'s more industrialised members and special contributions and transfers from the net earnings of the World Bank. The terms of I.D.A. credits, which are made to governments only, are a 10-year grace period, 50 year maturities and no interest. However, an annual service fee of 0.75% is charged on the disbursed portion of each credit. Although legally and financially distinct from the Bank, the I.D.A. is administered by the same staff.

In 1981 total bank loans and I.D.A. credits to the different countries and sectors stood at $92.2 billion (or ₦62.4 billion at current rates). Out of this amount, Nigeria has secured about ₦1.18 billion (or $1.74 billion). Most of the loans went to agriculture, port development, power transmission, railways and roads. Since 1958, Nigeria has lent a total of about ₦289.6 million (or $428 million) to the Bank.

23-1.3 International Finance Corporation

The International Finance Corporation (I.F.C.), established in 1956, is the member of the World Bank group that encourages the growth of productive private enterprise in the developing countries.

Membership in the I.F.C. is open to all governments which are members of the World Bank. The purpose of the I.F.C. is to further economic development in its less developed member countries by investing directly in private enterprises in association with private investors.

I.F.C. assistance goes mainly to the private sector and in Nigeria it has invested, for instance, in the Arewa Textile Mill, Kaduna, the Nigerian Industrial Development Bank (N.I.D.B.) and the Funtua Cottonseed Crushing Plant.

23-2 INTERNATIONAL MONETARY FUND

The International Monetary Fund (I.M.F.) and the World Bank are two complementary (or sister) institutions that came into existence after the Bretton Woods Conference in 1944. While the Bank was assigned the responsibility of reconstructing and developing post-war Europe and developing countries respectively, the I.M.F. was assigned the responsibility of restoring monetary confidence in the international scene.

The most important objectives of the I.M.F. were to:

i) promote international monetary co-operation;

ii) establish a code of conduct in international payment practices;

iii) provide financial resources to member countries to enable them to support the foreign exchange value of their currencies during temporary balance of payments difficulties; and,

iv) provide for the orderly growth of international liquidity through the Special Drawing Rights Scheme (SDR's).

The membership of the Fund consists of all the member countries of the World Bank. The Fund is run by a Board of Governors made up of the Finance Ministers or Central Bank Governors of the member countries. Subscriptions to its capital stock are based on each member's quota in the I.M.F. which is designed to reflect the country's relative economic strength, especially in such areas as the volume of a country's international trade, fluctuations in its balance of payments and the level of its international reserves. The quota was originally made up of 25% in gold and 75% in a country's own currency. From the pool of currencies the I.M.F. lends to countries in balance of payments difficulties. The size of the quota determines the extent to which a country can draw currencies from the pool held by the I.M.F. for purposes of settling its international debts.

The problem of international liquidity (i.e. ultimate means of settlement of debts between countries) led the I.M.F. to introduce other forms of reserve assets — the Special Drawing Rights (SDR's) as a means of settlement among its members.

SDR's are essentially a book-keeping transaction which created additional reserve assets for the use of member states. Created in

1970, SDR's are allotted to members in proportion to their quotas in the Fund. Rather than use currencies or gold for settlement of debts, countries now use their allocation of SDR's (which are mere book-entries), when they face balance of payments or reserve problems.

Previously, the value of an SDR was defined in terms of gold, but since 1974 it has been defined in terms of basket of 16 national currencies — the weights in the basket being determined by the share of issuing countries in world trade. The currencies in the basket can be changed from time to time and their weights altered, simply to reflect changes in the economic importance of the countries concerned. For example, as at 1 July, 1978, the percentage weight of the U.S. dollar in the basket of currencies was 33%, while that of the deutschemark and pound sterling were 12½% and 7½% respectively[1].

A country which has suffered severe balance of payments problems and is in dire need of external assets to restore the balance of payments, can also make use of its SDR's to buy convertible currency from other participants in exchange. However, there are certain constraints in the use of SDR's as a means of international settlements. For example, a country's holdings of SDR's should not fall below 30% (now 15%) of the quantity it has been allotted, as an average over a 5-year period. Also, an interest charge is levied on countries which have made use of SDR's and this is credited to countries which hold more than their cumulative allocation.

---

[1] Andrew Crocket *Money: Theory, Policy and Institutions* Thomas Nelson & Sons Ltd., 1979 p. 233

REVIEW QUESTIONS

23.1 Write a short account of the International Bank for Reconstruction & Development.

23.2 Write brief notes on Special Drawing Rights.

CHAPTER TWENTY FOUR

INTERNATIONAL FINANCIAL MARKETS

24-1 INTRODUCTION

The international financial markets provide a ready source of short- and long-term capital to multinational companies. In countries where these companies operate subsidiaries or affiliates, they also have access to domestic long-term capital markets. However, the most important international financial markets are the eurocurrency and eurobond markets which we shall examine in some detail in this Chapter.

The eurocurrency and eurobond markets constitute the most successful external money and capital markets, because the market instruments are freely transferable by holders. Secondly, the markets enjoy significant cost advantages over the purely domestic market, in view of the absence of government interference. The markets are exempt from taxes, reserve requirements, deposit insurance premiums, interest rate regulations and government policies to influence credit allocation. Another important factor is that the market is a 'wholesale' market where the sums involved are very large. Eurodollar transactions are usually $500,000 or more. Finally, there is a strong demand from non-bank institutions to hold or use eurodollars for payments. Thus, all the basic conditions necessary for a successful external money or capital market are fulfilled by eurocurrency and eurobond markets.

24-2 EXTERNAL MARKETS

The world's most important international financial markets are London and New York, although since the mid-1960's other locations like Paris, Zurich, Amsterdam and Tokyo have also become prominent. Before an international financial centre can be created, there must be a pool of domestic investors of depositors supplying the funds. Investors supply funds by purchasing securities such as bonds, commercial paper or shares; while depositors supply their funds to banks, insurance companies and other financial intermediaries whose function is to pool such deposits and make loans or equity investments from the pool. When such domestic funds are supplied to foreign users, or when foreign funds are supplied to domestic users, an international financial centre is created. In some cases even foreign funds are supplied to foreign users in what is known as the 'offshore' financial centres, which exist by providing a service for non-residents. They usually keep their international business separate from their domestic business. The best-known offshore financial centres are Luxembourg, Singapore, Hong Kong, the Bahamas, the Netherlands, Antilles, Bahrain, Kuwait and Panama. Some offshore financial centres facilitate both investment and intermediary activities, while others limit themselves just to intermediary activities through commercial banks. The major requirements for success as an offshore banking centre are:

i) Economic and political stability, which gives confidence to non-residents that funds movements will not be restricted.

ii) An efficient and experienced financial community able to carry out the necessary technical operations with skill.

iii) Good communication and support services, so that market information can be quickly and efficiently transmitted to participants.

iv) A regulatory climate that protects investors and depositors but is not unduly restrictive to financial institutions.[1]

24-3 EURODOLLARS AND OTHER EUROCURRENCIES

A eurodollar is a U.S. dollar deposited in a bank outside the United States. The bank receiving the deposit may be a foreign bank or the overseas branch of a U.S. bank. The deposit itself must be of a large amount of money, at least $500,000, and usually in the form of a time deposit or a certificate of deposit. Eurodollar time deposit maturities range from call money and overnight funds to upwards of five years. Certificates of deposits are usually for three months or more. Eurodollar deposits are not demand deposits and are, therefore, not withdrawable or transferrable by cheque. They are usually transferred by cable or telegraphic transfer.

Any convertible currency can exist in 'euro' form. Thus, there are euromarks (Deutsche marks deposited in banks outside Germany), eurosterling (British pounds deposited in banks outside the United Kingdom) and euroyen (Japanese yen deposited outside Japan), as

---

[1] Gunter Dufey & Ian Giddy, *The International Money Market* Prentice Hall, 1978, p. 39

well as eurodollars. From fairly simple operations, the eurocurrency market has grown to become virtually a complete financial system in its own right and many countries of the world now benefit from the services offered by these markets. The main use made of the short-term eurocurrency facility is the financing of international trade. In addition, governments have borrowed from the eurocurrency markets for purposes of financing investment projects when internal resources are inadequate. For example, the Nigerian government benefited from the eurocurrency market by borrowing from the market in 1978 when bilateral arrangements failed. Thus, the system helps in harnessing excess corporate liquidity to serve as a major source of short-term bank loans to finance corporate working capital needs, including the financing of imports and exports. The market is also useful for arbitrage deals.

The banks in which eurocurrencies are deposited are called 'eurobanks'. A eurobank is defined as *"a financial intermediary that simultaneously bids for time deposits and makes loans in a currency, or currencies, other than that of the country in which it is located".*[2] Eurobanks are major world banks that combine eurobusiness with their domestic banking business. Thus, invariably the eurocurrency operation is a department of a large commercial bank and not a separate bank as the name indicates. The prefix 'euro' does not mean that the bank must be in Europe. It may be London, Amsterdam, Paris,Nassau (the Bahamas), Hong Kong, Singapore (Asiadollars) or Tokyo.

24-4 HOW EURODOLLARS ARE CREATED

Let us illustrate the process by which eurocurrencies are created with dollars. Eurodollars are created when a dollar deposit is transferred from a bank within the U.S. to a bank in, say, Europe or Japan, or someone in these countries acquires dollars, either through a commercial transaction or a purchase in the foreign exchange market, and deposits those dollars in a bank outside the U.S.

To illustrate further, assume that a British multinational company acquires $1 million on demand deposit in a New York bank. Now the British company decides to convert its dollar demand deposit into an

---

[2] *Ibid,* p. 10

interest-earning asset. The company, therefore, instructs the New York bank to invest the funds ($1 million) in money market instruments like Treasury Bills or time certificates of deposit. However, for reasons of higher yield, the British company may decide to deposit the funds in a dollar-denominated time deposit at a London or Paris bank. By this decision, a eurodollar (i.e. a U.S. dollar deposit liability of a foreign bank) has been created. Although there are more intricate transactions relating to the creation of eurocurrency, the above example represents the basic manner in which eurocurrency is created.

24-5 EURODOLLAR BANK LOANS AND DEPOSITS

European banks receiving eurodollars as deposits may either redeposit the funds in another European bank, including branches of U.S. banks in Europe or make a loan to a non-bank user such as a multinational company. The borrower can use the dollars to settle its own dollar obligation or exchange them for local currency. Thirdly, a eurodollar deposit in Europe can be transferred to a U.S. branch bank in Europe (if the initial bank deposit was not a U.S. branch) and then be loaned to the U.S. Head Office of the bank to help the bank's liquidity during a tight money period in the U.S.

Eurodollar deposits are either term deposits or negotiable certificates of deposit (CDs). About 90% of eurodollar deposits are in the form of a specific term deposit with a fixed rate of interest. Presently, over 100 banks issue negotiable CDs, thus creating a strong CD market for the remaining 10%. There is a London CD market called 'Euro-CD'. This is a negotiable receipt for a U.S. dollar deposit with a London bank, issued in bearer form. It is a negotiable instrument which can be sold at any time in the secondary market. There are two types of CDs — the *tap* CD and *tranche* CD. A tap CD (which is more common) is available for maturities of less than 1 year in multiples of $1,000, with a minimum purchase of $25,000. The tranche CD is not a single certificate, but a series of identical 'tranches', each with a smaller denomination such as $10,000 or $25,000, but with identical yields, interest payment dates and maturities. Tranche issues may range from $10 million to $25 million in a public offering intended to be widely distributed in the financial world. Individual parts of a tranche can be paid off.

Upon the introduction of the 5-currency based SDR in 1980, seven London banks began to issue CDs denominated in SDR's. These are now sold to institutional investors in minimum denominations of one million SDR's.

24-6 INTERNATIONAL BOND MARKET & EUROBOND MARKET

An international bond is sold outside the country of the borrower. A Federal Government of Nigeria bond sold in London, underwritten by British banks, is a foreign bond. International bonds are either eurobonds or foreign bonds.

A eurobond is normally underwritten by an international syndicate of banks and is principally sold in countries other than the country of the currency in which the issue is denominated. On the other hand, a foreign bond is floated by a foreign borrower and underwritten by a syndicate composed of banks from a single country, sold principally in that country and denominated in that country's currency, like the Nigerian example above. Eurobonds are bonds of leading multinational companies or governments or government corporations which are sold simultaneously in several international capital markets, except the capital market of the country in whose currency the bond is denominated. They are mostly in bearer forms. As mentioned above, they are usually managed by a syndicate of major international banks.

The following three main factors are responsible for the growth and success of the eurobond market:

i) Governments generally impose less stringent regulations on securities denominated in foreign currencies, but sold locally to holders of foreign currencies.

ii) The market has less stringent disclosure requirements than those of, say, the Securities and Exchange Commission for security transactions within the U.S. and similar regulatory bodies in other countries.

iii) The market offers tax flexibility. The bonds are usually in bearer form, thus the identity of the holder is not disclosed. Moreover, interest paid on them is generally exempt from withholding tax. In the U.S., for instance, all bonds, whether by foreign or domestic issuer, are subject to a 30% withholding tax. To circumvent this, a eurobond in the U.S. is usually issued by a wholly-owned offshore finance subsidiary that does not have to withhold taxes on interest paid.

24-7 CONCLUSION

References to the eurodollar and eurocurrency markets are to one and the same market. As mentioned above, the market began in early 1960 with dollar deposits in London and it was then rightly called the eurodollar market. A few years later, other markets like europound, euromark, eurofranc, euroyen, etc., were created. Then the name appropriately changed to eurocurrency. However, the original name (eurodollar) was not completely dropped and is used interchangeably up to the time of writing.

REVIEW QUESTIONS

24.1 Write brief notes on the eurocurrency markets.

CHAPTER TWENTY FIVE

THE AFRICAN DEVELOPMENT BANK AND OTHER AFRICAN REGIONAL/SUB REGIONAL GROUPINGS

25-1 THE AFRICAN DEVELOPMENT BANK GROUP

25-1.1 Historical Background

In Chapter Twenty Three we discussed the World Bank Group and its role in the economic development of the poorer countries. However, it must be recognised that third world countries have only a minority voice in the manner in which economic assistance is being provided and used. This factor provides the political reality behind the emergence of regional/area development banks, especially the *African Development Bank* (ADB). Additional rationale for the establishment of ADB included the desire:

i) to exercise more control over the receipts of financial assistance;

ii) to devise and implement the development process most relevant to the problems of Africa; and,

iii) to forge closer regional co-operation and economic unity.

The ADB was established by the Articles of Agreement signed in Khartoum, Sudan, by 30 independent African countries on 4 August, 1963. It commenced business at its headquarters in Abidjan, Ivory Coast, in July 1966 with representative offices in London and Nairobi. Its authorised share capital was initially fixed at 250 million units of account (U.A.).

However, the authorised capital stock as at 30 June, 1981 stood at UA2,385 million (one unit of account is equivalent to U.S. $1.15060) and membership had risen to 50. Membership is presently restricted to independent African countries, although in May, 1978 the Board of Governors passed a resolution to open the membership to non-African countries on the condition that the President of the Bank should always be an African, that the Bank should confine its loan activities to Africa, that African countries should always have at least two-thirds of the number of votes and that policy decisions should always require a majority of 51% of the votes.

The current 50 member countries are: Algeria, Angola, Benin, Botswana, Burundi, Cameroon, Cape Verde, Central African Republic, Comoros, Congo, Ivory Coast, Djibouti, Egypt, Ethiopia, Gabon, Gambia,

25 - THE AFRICAN DEVELOPMENT BANK AND OTHER AFRICAN REGIONAL/ SUB REGIONAL GROUPINGS

Ghana, Guinea, Guinea-Bissau, Equatorial Guinea, Upper Volta, Kenya, Lesotho, Liberia, Madagascar, Malawi, Mali, Morocco, Mauritius, Mauritania, Mozambique, Niger, Nigeria, Uganda, Rwanda, Sao Tome & Principe, Senegal, Seychelles, Sierra Leone, Somalia, Sudan, Swaziland, Tanzania, Chad, Togo, Tunisia, Zaire, Zambia and Zimbabwe.

25-1.2 Functions

The main functions of the Bank are:

i) To use the resources at its disposal to finance projects and specific investment programmes which enhance the economic and social development of its member countries. Priority is given as much as possible to projects and programmes which foster regional co-operation and integrated development within the member countries, especially those designed to make the economies of its members increasingly complementary and to bring about an orderly expansion of their foreign trade.

ii) To undertake or participate in the selection, study and preparation of projects, enterprises and activities contributing to such development.

iii) To mobilise and increase in Africa, and outside Africa, resources for the financing of such investment projects and programmes.

iv) To promote generally investment in Africa of public and private capital in projects or programmes designed to contribute to the economic development or social progress of its members.

v) To provide such technical assistance as may be needed in Africa for the study, preparation, financing and execution of development projects or programmes.

vi) To undertake such other activities and provide such other services as may advance its purpose.

In addition to governments, other enterprises can also obtain loans from the bank provided their government guarantees the loan. The bank grants lines of credit to national and sub-regional development banks for on-lending in their respective countries. The bank may operate independently or jointly with other finance institutions.

25-1.3 Sources of Funds

The bank's main sources of funds are:

i) Capital subscribed by member states.

ii) Funds raised through borrowing by the bank.

iii) Funds received in repayment of past loans.

iv) Funds received as income from loans made by the bank.

Other special resources available to the Bank which are meant to make the terms of lending more flexible are:

i) Resources initially contributed to any special fund established by the bank or entrusted to it.

ii) Funds borrowed for the purpose of any special fund.

iii) Funds borrowed by the bank from any member in its currency for financing expenditure in the lending country in respect of goods or services needed to carry out a project in the territory of another member.

iv) Funds repaid in respect of loans or guarantees financed from the resources of any special fund.

v) Income derived from operations undertaken by using or committing any of the special resources.

vi) Any other resources at the disposal of any special fund.[1]

The capital stock is by far the most important source of funds for the bank.

25-1.4 African Development Fund and Nigerian Trust Fund

The African Development Bank has two subsidiaries: the African Development Fund (ADF) and the Nigerian Trust Fund (NTF). The ADF was established in 1972 to provide development finance on concessionary terms in independent Africa. It has a membership comprising of the African Development Bank and 24 non-African

---

[1] E.A. Ajayi *African Development Bank Domestic & Int'l Banking Services* Nigerian Institute of Bankers Annual Seminar, 1980, p. 142-143

capital exporting countries and its total lending amounted to U.S. $1,048 million for the period 1974 to the end of 1980.

The Nigerian Trust Fund (NTF) was established by the Nigerian Government in 1976 to assist the development effort of the poorer ADB members. The ADB administers the NTF in consultation with the Nigerian Government. The initial capital was about U.S. $80 million. The cumulative commitments of the NTF as at end of 1980 amounted to U.S. $83 million to projects in member countries. The loans are granted for up to 25 years with a moratorium of up to 5 years, subject to 4% interest per annum on outstanding balances plus a commitment fee of 0.75% per annum on the undisbursed amount to be charged after 120 days of the execution of the loan. The loan may be utilised for up to 60% of the project cost or a maximum of ₦5 million, whichever is lower.

25-2 THE WEST AFRICAN MONETARY UNION (W.A.M.U)

On 1 November, 1962 the West African Monetary Union (W.A.M.U) was born. The Union, established among francophone countries in West Africa, comprises the following countries. Peoples Republic of Benin, The Republic of Ivory Coast, The Republic of Upper Volta, The Republic of Niger, The Republic of Senegal and the Republic of Togo. It has since developed into a perfect example of monetary integration and the first of its kind that has survived in Africa. It is similar to the defunct West African Currency Board which was dissolved on the independence of the countries.

The six member states recognise a common currency unit, the Franc of the Communaute Financiere Africaine (C.F.A. Franc) which is issued by a common central bank — the Central Bank of the West African States (B.C.E.A.O). The Head Office of the Bank is located in Dakar, Senegal.

In 1972, after ten years of existence, the Union was given a new impetus to enable it to contribute more actively and effectively to the economic development and integration of the member countries. This led to the signing of a reform treaty in November 1973. As part of the reform measures, the West African Development Bank (W.A.D.B), a common institution for financing regional economic development, was set up. The objective of the bank is to promote the economic development and integration of the member countries of the West

African Monetary Union. The Bank's Head Office is located in Lome, Republic of Togo.

25-3 THE ASSOCIATION OF AFRICAN CENTRAL BANKS

The Association of African Central Banks (A.A.C.B) was established in December 1969 by the Governors of African Central Banks to:

i) promote co-operation in the monetary, banking and financial sphere in the African region;

ii) assist in the formulation of guidelines along which agreements among African countries in the monetary and financial fields shall proceed;

iii) help strengthen all efforts aimed at bringing about and maintaining monetary and financial stability in the African region;

iv) examine the effectiveness of international economic and financial institutions in which African countries have an interest and suggest ways of possible improvement.

The main functions of the Association aimed at achieving the objectives enumerated above can be summarised as:

i) to provide an avenue for regular meetings of Governors of African Central Banks;

ii) to promote the exchange of ideas and experiences on monetary and banking matters and on questions of monetary, banking and financial co-operation in Africa;

iii) to facilitate the collection, pooling and dissemination of information on monetary, banking, financial and other economic matters of interest to its members;

iv) to undertake the study of monetary and financial problems in the African region;

v) to organise seminars, courses and other training programmes for the personnel of banking and financial institutions in the African region; and,

vi) to provide technical advice and assistance which serve its purposes and come within its functions.

The Association is governed by an Assembly of Governors, comprising Governors of Central Banks or heads of similar institutions in the region. There is an Executive Committee and a number of Sub-Regional Committees. There are four sub-regions: North, West, Central and East. The Assembly of Governors meet once in two years, while the Sub-Regional Committee consisting of the Chairman, Vice Chairman of the Association and the Chairman of each of the Sub-Regional Committees meet once a year. Nigeria has served as Chairman of the Association and of the West African Sub-Regional Committee.

In 1978 the A.A.C.B established the African Centre for Monetary Studies to promote the economic development of Africa. The centre is charged with the responsibility of studying *"on a continuous basis monetary problems of Africa arising from the impact of international monetary developments on African economics".*[2]

The A.A.C.B has also made a tangible contribution to international monetary reform and has helped African Countries to formulate a common policy that is considered to bring greater advantage to African countries.

25-4 THE WEST AFRICAN CLEARING HOUSE

The West African Clearing House was established in 1976 with the following aims and objectives:

i)   to promote the use of the currencies of the members of the Clearing House for sub-regional trade and other transactions;

ii) to bring about economies in the use of foreign exchange of the members of the Clearing House;

iii) to encourage the members of the Clearing House to liberalise trade among their respective countries; and,

---

[2] *Twenty Years of Central Banking in Nigeria, 1959-79.* CBN Research Dept. p.200

iv) to promote monetary co-operation and consultation among members of the Clearing House.[3]

The West African Clearing House was established on the recommendation of the Governors of the West African Sub-Regional Committee of the Association of African Central Banks to reduce delays and facilitate inter-regional payments. It was a first step towards the introduction of a clearing system for the continent.

25-5 THE WEST AFRICAN BANKERS ASSOCIATION

This is a new Association made up of commercial merchant banks in Ecowas countries. The decision to establish this Association was taken at a meeting of West African bankers in Bamako, Mali, in 1978. The Association's draft constitution was adopted in November 1980 at a meeting of bankers in the sub-region held in Freetown, Sierra Leone.

The main objectives of the Association are:

i)   to exchange information on commercial bank practices and to enhance the promotion and strengthening of links among commercial banks in the sub-region;

ii) to provide a forum for resolving mutual problems which may arise through correspondent relationships;

iii) to act as a liaison point between the commercial banks and the Association of African Central Banks; and,

iv) to investigate ways in which the Association can help promote trade, industry and agriculture within the sub-region.

It is hoped that when the Association finally takes off, it will actively promote co-operation in banking transactions and thus facilitate inter-bank transfers and the clearing of bank instruments within the Ecowas region. Nigerian banks are represented by the Bankers' Committee.

---

[3] Article 2, Clearing House Articles of Agreement.

REVIEW QUESTIONS

25.1 Discuss briefly the objectives and organisation of the Association of African Central Banks.

28.1 Discuss briefly the objectives and organisation of the Association of African Central Banks.

PART VI
CONCLUSION

CHAPTER TWENTY SIX

SUMMARY AND BANKING EDUCATION IN NIGERIA

26-1 SUMMARY

Throughout this book, emphasis has been placed consistently on the Nigerian banking system.

In Part I, an attempt is made to introduce the reader to the theory of money and the monetary system in general. This is followed by a discussion of monetary policy in Nigeria since 1959 and the evolution of the money system.

In Part II, we examine banking in general with particular reference to the Nigeria banking system. We cover banking in all its ramifications, including development banking. This part is rounded off with a review of the major legislation relating to banking since 1952. This ended the mainly theoretical part of the book.

Part III deals exhaustively with the services offered by Nigerian banks to their customers, both personal and corporate and to governments. Apart from discussing the general banking services, this part also deals with the practical aspects of bank lending including financial statement analysis and interpretation. Other special services like the use of bills of exchange and cheques and exchange control/foreign exchange services are also discussed in detail.

Part IV is devoted to money and capital markets and a brief review of the activities of the Nigerian Securities and Exchange Commission.

In Part V, the international financial system and financial markets are reviewed, with the last chapter devoted to the African Development Bank and African regional and sub-regional groupings.

It is hoped that, for the general reader, who has no previous knowledge of banking, but wants to find out what it is all about, the book will prove useful. For the young student or bank worker, trying to make up his mind about pursuing a career in banking, the book gives a broad insight into the basic requirement of a general banking education.

This is so, because *Elements of Banking,* as the name indicates, is a subject which touches upon almost all aspects of banking, ranging from monetary theory to bank lending. It introduces the student to general banking studies prior to specialisation and detailed work later in his career. Therefore, to help the prospective student or worker, the final conclusion of this book is devoted entirely to professional training and banking education generally.

26-2 THE NIGERIAN INSTITUTE OF BANKERS

26-2.1 Objects and Structure

The history of the Institute of Bankers in Nigeria can be traced to the founding in 1963 of the Lagos Local Centre of the Institute of Bankers, London. The Lagos Local Centre is the nucleus of the Nigerian Institute of Bankers which was granted full autonomy in November, 1977 with the following major aims and objectives:

i) To help promote banking education in the country with a view to helping staff employed in the banking industry to acquire modern banking techniques and prepare them for higher responsibilities in their various institutions.

ii) To facilitate the consideration and discussion of matters of interest to bankers and to keep members in touch with the latest developments in banking and business generally.

iii) To take any measures which may be desirable to further the interest of banking.

iv) To hold and further help secure the observance of professional ethics and traditions in the banking system.

v) To hold lectures, seminars and conferences on banking, finance and other kindred subjects.

vi) to hold and conduct examinations in banking.

vii) To issue certificates to those who satisfy the conditions for its awards from time to time.

viii) To promote the general advancement of the theory and practice of banking in any or all of its branches to facilitate the exchange of information and ideas relating to banking amongst the members of the Institute.

ix) To pursue actively research into banking theory and practice with particular reference to local conditions and to study and tackle the professional problems confronting its members.

x) To do all or any such lawful things as are incidental or conducive to the attainment of the objects and generally to further the profession of banking in Nigeria as well as enhance the status of banking in Nigeria.

The Institute has an elected Council comprising 19 members which decides the policy of the Institute. The 19 council members comprise 8 elected members plus the immediate past president, 5 representatives of the Bankers' Committee and 5 representatives of branches.

26-2.2 Membership

Membership of the Institute is open only to those employed in banks or students on full time courses in approved colleges who have satisfied the entry requirements for the prescribed examinations. There are six grades of membership.

i) Ordinary Membership is open to all persons excluding service staff, who although not professionally qualified, work in a bank in Nigeria and perform functions relating to the disposition of depositor's funds in the form of loans and advances, etc.

ii) Student Members are those who have not yet passed their Associateship examination, but are in possession of the minimum examination requirements. They must either be engaged in full time work with a bank or attending a banking course or pursuing a course in banking in any technical college/polytechnic or university approved by the Council. Bank staff who are 21 years of age and above, with a minimum of 5 years banking experience may be allowed to take the Institute's examinations as mature candidates, even though they may not have satisfied the prescribed minimum entry requirements for student mambership.

iii) Licentiate Membership is open to persons who have passed all the parts of the examinations prescribed by the Council, but need to fulfil other conditions before they can become Associates.

iv) Associate Membership. A person is not eligible for enrolment as an Associate member unless:

   i) he has attained the age of 25;

   ii) he has passed all the parts of the examinations prescribed by the

Council followed by a minimum of two years post-qualification experience; or

iii) has had a minimum of 5 years continuous working experience in a bank as a banker.

He will then be entitled to use the letters A.I.B. (Associate of the Institute of Bankers) after his name.

v) Fellows of the Institute of Bankers (FIB) are elected by the Council from Associates who have achieved Senior Professional status and have performed services on behalf of the Institute. A person is not eligible for enrolment as a Fellow unless he has had at least 10 years post-graduate experience.

vi) Honorary Fellows. The Council of the Institute has the power to elect as Honorary Fellows men of distinction in the practice or literature of banking, political economy, management and other kindred subjects.

26-2.3 Examinations

The Nigerian Institute still maintains some ties with the Institute of Bankers, London. At present the Part I examinations are conducted locally by the Institute, but the examinations in Part II are still handled by the London Institute. The Nigerian Institute is expected to become fully autonomous and start conducting all examinations as from 1984.

i) Syllabus Structure

Part I — Non-Professional Examinations

Section I:

    (1) Economics 1
    (2) Accounting 1
    (3) Elements of Banking
    (4) General Principles of Law

Section II:

    (1) Statistics
    (2) Economics 2
    (3) Accounting 2
    (4) English Language

Candidates are required to pass all subjects of each section at a sitting. Referrals may be allowed in two subjects, but the candidate must pass the subjects within the following twelve months, otherwise he will be required to resit all the subjects in the section in subsequent examinations.

Part II — The Professional Examination

Section I: (1)   Accountancy
              (2)   Applied Economics
              (3)   Law relating to Banking

Section II: (1)   Investment
              (2)   Nature of management
              (3)   Finance of International Trade

Section III: (1)   Practice of Banking I
              (2)   Practice of Banking II

Candidates will be required to satisfy the examiners in all subjects of each section at the same sitting. Candidates who fail marginally in one of the subjects may be referred and will be given one further opportunity to pass that subject within the following twelve months.

The completion of all sections of Part II will qualify a candidate for the award of the A.I.B., provided the candidate has had at least five years banking experience and has been a member of the Institute for the same period.

The A.I.B. qualification is generally equated to a good honours degree and is accepted for post-graduate degree courses leading to M.Sc., M.B.A. or Ph.D in leading universities in Nigeria and the United Kingdom.

ii) The Financial Studies Diploma

This is quite separate from the professional examinations. It is a higher diploma comparable to a post-graduate qualification in banking and management subjects for those who are expected to reach senior management levels. The entry requirements are the A.I.B. or a recognised degree or professional qualification. Where a person is allowed direct entry as a result of possessing a degree or professional qualification other than A.I.B., he is required to sit and pass two introductory papers before being allowed to take the Diploma Course. The introductory papers are:

i) Financial Institutions and Monetary System.

ii) Practice of Banking.

The Diploma course is in two sections and the subjects in each are:

Section I: (1)   Practice of Banking III
                  (2)   Human Aspects of Management
                  (3)   Business Planning and Control

Section II: (1)   Marketing of Financial Services
                  (2)   Practice of Banking IV
                  (3)   Practice of Banking V

The Financial Studies Diploma is presently conducted exclusively by the Institute of Bankers, London and is awarded to candidates who have successfully completed both sections in a period of not more than five years, have at least three years' banking experience and have been members of the Institute for at least three years.

26-3 THE FINANCIAL INSTITUTIONS TRAINING CENTRE

26-3.1 Introduction

The Bankers' Committee in a recent survey highlighted the manpower problems in the banks as a result of the expansion in business activities following the oil boom and the Central Bank Rural Banking Scheme. It was agreed that the banking industry would require a greater workforce in the 1980's and, more importantly, the workforce must be given the necessary training to make them efficient and effective. To this effect a sub-committee was established at the 124th meeting of the Bankers' Committee held on 10 April, 1979 with the following terms of reference:

i) To examine the broad issues raised in a memorandum submitted by the Central Bank on training programmes for financial institutions.

ii) To propose a specific procedure for the accomplishment of the objective of accelerating training to meet the needs of the banking industry in particular and the entire banking sector in general.

iii) To make further recommendations to facilitate the pooling together of all training resources in banking institutions and possibly other institutions of learning for the benefit of accelerated and mass training to combat the shortage in manpower now existing in these institutions.

The Union Bank of Nigeria Ltd. served on this sub-committee as Chairman, whilst the Savannah Bank of Nigeria Ltd. served as Secretary.

The result of the recommedations of the sub-committee was implemented with the establishment of the Financial Institutions Training Centre towards the end of 1981, as a non-profit making body. It is in the process of being formally incorporated as a company limited by guarantee.

26-3.2 Objectives and Functions

The main aims and objectives of the Centre are:

i) To carry on the business of training and education of personnel employed or to be employed by banks and other financial institutions.

ii) To protect, promote and advance the knowledge and practice of banking and finance throughout Nigeria by the organisation of seminars, lectures, workshops and other practical and theoretical courses.

iii) To collect and disseminate statistical and other information relating to banking, finance, commerce, trade and other related disciplines.

iv) To co-operate with the Nigerian Institute of Bankers.

v) To print and publish any newspapers, periodicals, bulletins, books or leaflets that the Institution may think desirable for the promotion of its objects.

vi) To engage in consultancy and advisory services in its area of competence.

26-3.3 Composition of Board of Governors

The Centre is managed by a Board of Governors composed of:

i) The Executive Director of the Centre.

ii) Representatives of 5 member banks representing the Bankers' Committee. The following banks are presently represented on the Board — Central Bank of Nigeria (permanent member and Chairman of the Board), UBA, IBWA, NAL Merchant Bank and National Bank of Nigeria Ltd.

iii) One representative of the Centre for Management Development.

iv) One representative of the Nigerian Chamber of Commerce.

26-3.4 Funding and General Comments

The Centre is financed by the annual subscriptions of member banks and through contributions to the budget. The CBN contributes 50% to the budget of the Institute, while all the other members of the Bankers' Committee contribute the remaining 50%. Another source of funds is the receipt of course fees paid by banks in respect of their participating staff. Courses are run on a break-even basis.

In 1982, the Centre ran the following courses:

1. Bank Lending & Credit Administration.
2. Effective Bank Audit.
3. Management.
4. Advanced Finance & Accounting.
5. Corporate Banking.
6. Effective Branch Administration.
7. Corporate Planning & Assessment of Bank Performance.

The Centre can be described as an Institute for continuing professional education in banking. Its role can thus be clearly distinguished from that of the Nigerian Institute of Bankers. While the Centre will concentrate on providing a range of courses and seminars designed to meet the needs of qualified professional bankers, the Institute of Bankers mainly provides facilities for pre-qualification professional training.

26-4 BANKERS' COMMITTEE

As the Bankers' Committee has featured prominently in this Chapter, we shall briefly examine its composition, functions and its role in the regulation of banking in Nigeria.

26-4.1 Composition

The Committee is composed of representatives of all licensed commercial and merchant banks in Nigeria and the Central Bank of Nigeria. Each bank is officially represented on the committee by one representative, usually the Managing Director or General Manager of the bank or his accredited representative. Most banks send two representatives to committee meetings — one official representative and one in attendance. Committee meetings are held at the offices of the Central Bank of Nigeria. The Deputy Governor of the Central Bank of Nigeria is the Chairman of the Committee, while a senior official of the Bank acts as Secretary to the Committee

26-4.2 Functions

i) The Committee being a recognised body representing all licensed banks in the country serves as an effective channel of communication between banks and the Federal Government or its regulatory agencies in the financial sector like the Federal Ministry of Finance and the Central Bank of Nigeria.

ii) The Committee makes proposals and suggestions every year to the Federal Government in the areas of banking, finance and the Nigerian economy for consideration by the authorities and possible inclusion in the budget plans.

iii) As banking has grown and diversified both nationally and internationally, the changes and developments in banking techniques and the expansion of financial services all demand thorough training and a professional approach. It has been discovered that the normal in-house training facilities provided by individual banks are becoming inadequate for their needs.

In the light of the above, the Bankers' Committee has taken positive steps to spearhead the development of high level manpower in banking by founding, supporting and funding the Financial Institutions Training Centre and by giving moral and financial support in the form of donations to the Nigerian Institute of Bankers through its member banks.

iv) Another major function of the Committee is the preparation and periodical review of the Bankers' Tariff. The Bankers' Tariff is a list containing approved bank charges and commissions. Banks are not allowed to charge fees in excess of the amounts listed in the tariff.

v) Any major issue affecting banks must be examined by the Committee before a final decision is taken. The Committee's recommendations are normally taken into consideration by the monetary authorities when considering any issue that can affect the operations of banks.

26-5 IN-HOUSE TRAINING IN BANKS

26-5.1 Introduction

As banking business expanded in the late 1950's and as the struggle for independence intensified, foreign banks in Nigeria, which constitute the "big three" today (First Bank, Union Bank and U.B.A) were forced to recruit many Nigerians in their clerical and supervisory grades. They had to do this, because the business was booming, and they had no intention to leave the lucrative scene. Hence, if they were to continue to be efficient, they would have to train the local staff as well, rather than concentrate their training efforts on their expatriate staff. Initially, the practice was to select some bright Nigerians for training in the United Kingdom, in the home offices of the British banks or in France in the case of U.B.A. No attempt was made to establish a training centre in Nigeria. At the same time the banks' requirements for capable Nigerians continued to increase because of expansion in banking business. The foreign banks mentioned above soon realised that it was too expensive to send a handful of trainees overseas and even then the number of trained hands produced was no longer adequate to meet demands. In the light of the above, the need to establish local training centres to run short courses for Nigerian staff became more pressing.

26-5.2 The Beginning of Staff Training in Nigeria

The first bank to establish a local training centre in Nigeria was Barclays Bank D.C.O (now Union Bank of Nigeria Ltd) in 1955. The training centre was located at 19/21, Balogun Square in Lagos.

The Centre offered courses in routine banking services, as well as skilled courses for cashiers, foreign exchange, bills and credit clerks. In 1970, the Centre moved from Balogun Square to a more spacious apartment at 2 Onike Road, Yaba from where it is still operating. The number of courses have increased over the years and both clerks and officers go for training at the Centre, including a one week Management Development Programme for officers to enhance their managerial effectiveness. Another pioneer in the field of training within the banking industry was the Standard Bank of West Africa Ltd (now First Bank of Nigeria Ltd).

26-5.3 Present Training Efforts in the Banking Industry

Today, most banks have their own Training Centres and each of them organise courses that will help in the career development of their staff. Union Bank, apart from having a Training Centre in Lagos, operate branches of the Training Centre in Jos and Port Harcourt. This arrangement has reduced the travelling distance of staff from the Northern and Eastern areas and increased the number of staff benefitting from training courses. First Bank of Nigeria operate a similar system. Apart from the Training Centre located at Murtala Mohammed Way, Ebute Metta, Lagos, there are now branches at Kano and Benin. The arrangement in First Bank is slightly different because trainees from the Lagos Area may be sent to Kano or Benin and vice versa. In any case, the number of staff benefitting from training programmes is greater than having all courses at a single centre.

U.B.A., A.C.B, National Bank, I.B.W.A, Savannah Bank, Wema Bank, Societe Generale and Bank of the North have all established Training Centres for the training of their staff. The Central Bank of Nigeria has also established its own Training School offering courses for both junior and intermediate staff in Banking Operations and Management.

The banks without established Training Centres at the moment usually patronise those with established training centres, notably Union Bank. Another interesting point about Union Bank is the fact that most of the training centres of the other banks were established by ex-staff of the Bank. Thus, it can be said that Union Bank has made and continues to make a great contribution in the development of human resources in the banking industry in Nigeria.

26-5.4 Conclusion

There is no better way to end this section on in-house training in banks than by quoting the recent remarks of Mr. J. A. Adeniji, Manager Savannah Bank Training Centre, in a recent talk on "Development of Staff Training within the Banking Industry in Nigeria" to participants on the Instructor's Course 1/82 at the Union Bank Training Centre, Yaba:

"My assessment of the training efforts in the Banking Industry in Nigeria today is that appreciable progress has been made by the big banks and some of the smaller banks in the training of their staff in the clerical staff category. Whilst some have intensified their efforts in the training of officers, a lot of improvement is still required in this respect. I consider, too, that overseas exposure will only yield the desired results if it is properly co-ordinated. In some banks, arrangement for staff to attend Overseas Seminars/ Courses is done by Executives without the recommendation of their Training Centres. Such practice is fraught with danger in that it may deprive the banks the opportunity to seize the maximum advantage of well-thought and carefully co-ordinated programmes. Of course, the importance of exposing trainers to the most up-to-date techniques and practices cannot be over-emphasised. Banking itself is becoming more and more soph-isticated and any bank that wishes to survive in this age of keen competition and technological changes must also be prepared to expose its trainers. No doubt, such arrangements will have a multiplier effect for the banks as the trainers will then be able to transfer their acquired knowledge and skills to other staff.

Training is an important management tool; it has to be systematic if it is to give the desired results. It is costly but if you feel that way try no training and be prepared for the disastrous con-sequences!"

REVIEW QUESTIONS

26.1 What are the main functions of the Bankers' Committee?

26.2 What are the aims and objectives of:

    i) the Nigerian Institute of Bankers; and,

    ii) Financial Institutions Training Centre?

ANSWERS TO REVIEW QUESTIONS

CHAPTER ONE

THE BASIC CONCEPTS OF MONEY

Answer 1.1

Any commodity can serve as money, provided it is widely acceptable within the given community. This means that people must have confidence in the 'thing' to be used as money. This confidence (which leads to general acceptability) is enhanced if the money possesses some other specific qualities. Before the abolition of the gold standard, it was necessary for money to have an intrinsic value equal (or similar) to its monetary value. As many countries had limited stocks of gold, this system was abandoned. The advent of fractional reserves (fiduciary issue) and the use of book and paper money greatly economised on scarce gold reserves. Most money today consists of bank deposits, bank notes and coin without a specific gold content.

Another quality that money must have is relative scarcity. To be generally acceptable, the supply of any thing being used as money must be restricted. It must neither be too scarce nor too plentiful.

Nowadays, when paper money and token coinage is the order of the day, the control of notes and coin issue is exercised by the Central Bank. The Central Bank also restricts the ability of banks to create money through the 'credit creation' process.

The following qualities are also desirable:

i) Durability. For anything to serve as money it must be durable. It must not be a living thing that can die easily or a thing that can break easily. It must be a thing that will last for a long time. This is why precious metals like gold and silver have remained one of the best forms of money.

ii) Divisibility. It must be possible to sub-divide money into smaller units.

iii) Portability. Good money must be easy and convenient to carry about. Precious metals lack this quality, while bank notes and deposits possess it in abundance.

iv) Homogeneity. This means that one unit of money is identical to another unit of the same value and that one can be exchanged for the other. For instance, a ₦1 note or a 10k coin are the same anywhere in Nigeria and they are instantly recognisable.

Answer 1.2

It is generally agreed by banking experts that banks create money. The process by which the banking system creates money is through the granting of loans and overdrafts. This can be illustrated with a simple example. Every loan and overdraft approved by a bank creates money. Upon the granting of a bank facility the customer draws a cheque on his account in favour of a third party. Usually, the cheque will be paid into an account with another bank. After the cheque has been cleared, there is an increase in the total deposits in the banking system as a new deposit has been created.

In Nigeria banks generally lend up to a maximum of 70% of their total deposits. The remaining 30% is held in liquid assets to meet demands for cash by depositors.

Assume that Ade deposits ₦1,430 in his current account at Jos Bank Ltd. Jos Bank Ltd. later granted a ₦1,000 overdraft (approx. 70% of the original deposit) to its customer Boyode to enable him to pay ₦1,000 to Ahmed and Sons, who pay the cheque into their current account with Sokoto Bank Ltd. Sokoto Bank keeps 30% of this new deposit of ₦1,000 (i.e. ₦300) as reserves and proceeds to give out 70% (i.e. ₦700) as a loan to its customer Abedayo. He issues his own cheque for ₦700 to Akin Garages to pay for the cost of a car. Akin Garages pay the cheque into their current account with Benue Bank Ltd. Benue Bank Ltd. also lends 70% of the deposit (i.e. ₦490) to Bayo. This process goes on and on and can be measured by the credit creation multiplier which is calculated as follows:

Total Amount of New Deposits Created

Amount of Original Advance

In our example the original deposit of ₦1,430 can be expanded to about ₦4,719 — a multiplier of 3.3 times. For the system to work, the following assumptions are made:

i) There are many banks in the system.

ii) There is a legal reserve ratio of 30%.

iii) All banks have given out a maximum of 70% of their deposits.

iv) A member of the banking system initially receives ₦1,430 in cash.

v) There is no drain on the system and the public is willing to borrow as much as banks are able and willing to lend.

The major factor limiting the ability of banks to create money is the limitation imposed by the legal reserve requirements. If there had been no cash and liquidity ratio requirements and all transactions were settled by cheque, there would be no limit to credit creation. Secondly, an increase in the currency requirement of the community means a reduction in cash in the banking system and its potential to create more credit. Finally, as a member of a banking system, a bank cannot expand credit more rapidly than other members of the system. If it did, it would lose much of its reserves to other banks through the clearing house. In the final analysis such a bank will experience serious liquidity problems.

Answer 1.3

Barter is the system of exchanging goods for goods or exchanging service for service. The four major shortcomings of the system are:

i) Lack of a common unit of measure. An inventory of many kinds or qualities of various goods could only be ascertained by listing the different commodities that made up the inventory. Instead of recording the monetary value of goods and services, one is compelled to list them as the number of yams, goats, tables, etc.

ii) Double coincidence of wants. A man wanting to exchange goats for yams must find someone who has yams which he does not want and at the same time happens to want goats. Money is the only common factor that can solve this problem. In a money economy, the seller of goats can sell his goats for money and keep the proceeds until such a time he wants yams.

iii) In a barter system future contracts could not be negotiated. Problems would also be encountered with the payment of wages, salaries, interest, rents, etc.

iv) There was no means of storing wealth or value since neither was ascertainable. Even where wealth was designated in a particular commodity, the problem of storage facilities would arise, whilst the goods would also be subject to spoilage and the risks of being stolen.

ANSWERS - 1

Answer 1.4

The four major functions of money are:

i) A unit of value. Every country has evolved its own unit of account or currency which circulates within the national boundary. In Nigeria, we have our naira and kobo, in Ghana they have the Cedi and Pesewa, in America they have dollars and cents, while pounds and pence are used in the U.K. The existence of a unit of account makes it easy to ascertain the value of commodities in any market and to compare the prices of different commodities. It also enables us to keep accounting records, such as bank statements, invoices and other books of accounts.

ii) Money as a medium of exchange. Anything that is generally accepted by people in exchange for goods and services is regarded as a medium of exchange. The 'thing' may be salt, cowries, manilla, gold, copper or book entries by banks. The essential requirement of this object is the general willingness of people to accept it in exchange for goods and services. By accepting this commodity in exchange for other goods and services, this payment mechanism saves time and encourages further specialisation and production. The shoemaker can now concentrate on his shoemaking with the hope of selling the shoes and obtaining other commodities he needs without having to search for somebody who wants shoes in exchange. This eliminates the problem of double coincidence of wants.

iii) Money as a standard of deferred payments. Money acts as a measure of deferred future payments like instalment repayments of bank loans. Contracts of deferred payments also include pensions, wages, payment of interest and other debts, dividends, hire purchase, etc. and these contracts may range from one month to several years.

Money as a standard of deferred payment cannot function well if it does not maintain a fairly constant purchasing power. The instability in the purchasing power of money has certain implications and affects different interest groups. A rise in the value of money favours lenders, pensioners and wage earners, while a fall in the purchasing power of money, otherwise called inflation, injures those who have agreed to receive fixed amounts and lightens the burden of payers. For example, wage earners, pensioners and lenders, etc. will lose, while manufacturers, who borrow money to start off a business, will gain.

iv) Money as a store of value. Ideally, money should have a reasonably stable value so that whatever is set aside as savings will retain its value. Therefore, money can only serve as a good store of value if its value remains stable over a fairly long period. During a time of inflation the value of money falls in real terms, although the money value will still be the same. Thus, in times of inflation, money does not perform this function very well.

Answer 1.5

i) Near money (or quasi money) may be defined as financial assets that function more as a store of value than as a medium of exchange. These include time and savings deposits with banks and non-bank financial intermediaries, investments in Treasury Bills, stocks and shares, postal and money orders, etc. These assets adequately fulfil the function of a store of value. Deposit and savings accounts are held more with a view to earning interest (a store of value) than as a medium of exchange; the opposite is true of a current account. The definition of near money is generally restricted to the liabilities of the banking system because of the ability of the banks to 'create' more money as a result of the credit-creation multiplier.

ii) Legal tender is money of such description that the person to whom it is tendered will put himself in the wrong if he refuses to accept it. Legal tender requires that the exact sum of the debt must be tendered, without necessitating any change. It may therefore be defined as the notes and coins which must be accepted when offered in payment.

iii) The Fiduciary Issue is that part of the note issue of the Central Bank which is authorised to be made against securities as opposed to being backed by gold.

CHAPTER TWO

THEORIES OF MONEY

Answer 2.1

There are three major motives for holding money — the transaction, precautionary and speculative motives.

Everybody is constantly engaged in spending money for immediate purposes, so they need to hold some money for this purpose. According to the Cambridge School, the demand for money would be proportional to the level of income for each individual and hence for the aggregate economy as well. Keynes reaffirmed that the level of transactions undertaken by an individual and society as a whole had a stable relationship to the level of income. Consequently, he also postulated that the transaction demand for money was proportional to the level of income (i.e. the higher the level of income the larger the amount of money held for transaction purposes).

People also realise that they may at any time be faced with some unforeseen expenditures — these include classes of payments that can not be regarded as regular and planned (e.g. payment of unexpected bills, making purchases at an unexpectedly favourable price, meeting other emergencies that are caused by accidents, ill-health or death). For this purpose most people would consider it necessary to have some cash balances because other assets are not instantly usable as money. As in the transaction motive, the precautionary motive also depends upon the level of income — the higher the level of income the larger the amount held for precautionary purposes.

Finally, another major factor why people hold cash balances, according to Keynes, is the speculative motive. Comparatively rich people and financial institutions may switch into and out of money according to what they think is likely to be the most profitable disposition of their resources. If they think prices are about to fall, they may sell some assets at the current price and hold money while the latter is increasing in purchasing power. They may do the same if they think interest rates are going to rise which would usually be associated with a fall in the value of financial assets like bonds. On the other hand, if the price of bonds is very high in relation to what people think is the normal price (i.e. the rate of interest is thought to be low), people will tend to sell bonds now and postpone intended purchases until prices have come down. In such a situation large quantities of money may be held in anticipation of a more favourable chance to purchase bonds in future. This is the speculative motive.

From the foregoing, we can see that while the transaction and precautionary motives focus on money's role as a medium of exchange, the speculative motive emphasises its role as a store of wealth.

Answer 2.2

The supply of money at any moment is the sum of all the money holdings of all members of the society. Put in another form, money supply can be defined as the stock or quantity of money the society wishes to hold at any time. In Nigeria this could be either M1 or M2.

M1 defines money as the notes and coins issued by the Central Bank plus bank deposits held on current accounts and transferable by cheque. This is the narrow definition of money supply in Nigeria.

M2 (the broader definition of money) defines money as M1 plus time and savings deposits with banks and non-bank financial institutions such as the Federal Mortgage Bank, the Federal Savings Bank, finance houses, etc., plus investments in other financial assets such as Treasury Bills/Certificates, stocks and savings bonds. While M1 focusses attention on the medium of exchange function, M2 focusses attention on the store of value function.

It has long been thought that the supply of money was a factor affecting the economy of a country. At first, inflation was not seen as a dynamic process involving the level of employment, so early theories related the money supply directly to prices.

The first quantity theory of money was expressed as:

$$MV = PT$$

where | M | represented the supply of money
| V | its velocity of circulation
| P | the level of prices and
| T | the number of transactions in a given period

Thus, an increase in the supply of money would be likely to lead to an increase in prices if V and T remained constant. However, it was realised that the additional money might not be fully used, so that V might fall. At the same time, a change in economic activity might lead to a change in T. PT together correspond to the money value of total output.

The Keynesian theory was concerned with the flow of money — as represented by incomes — rather than with the quantity of it outstanding. This was a concept somewhat like MV in the old quantity theory, but it brought in changes in the level of economic activity as an additional factor, maintaining that a rising trend of prices tended to go with a rising level of activity. Little attention was directed to the money supply as such.

In recent years, this view has been challenged by the Chicago School which is based on the monetarist approach. This relates total output at current prices directly to the supply of money, though possibly with a time lag involved. Thus, an increase in the supply of money will lead to an increase in the money value of output, but it is less clear how much of the growth will be real and how much will be an increase in prices. However, if the rate of rise in the money supply is in excess of any conceivable real growth of the economy, as in Nigeria today, then the monetarist would argue that inflation must follow.

Official monetary policy in Nigeria has recently swung over towards the monetarist approach complemented by fiscal measures in an attempt to stabilise the economy more effectively.

Answer 2.3

The value of money is its purchasing power (i.e. what money can buy) and this is indicated by the general level of prices. it is determined, as with other values, by supply and demand. Thus, a significant increase in the supply of money will tend to lead to a fall in its value, other things being equal.

The amount of money in circulation (i.e. its supply) is strictly controlled by the Central Bank deposits are also indirectly controlled through monetary policy.

The demand for money is the demand to hold money balances as an alternative to economic goods in order to satisfy the transaction, precautionary and speculative motives.

It must be noted that the velocity of circulation of money is not constant. It may change. An upsurge in demand may not necessarily lead to an increase in supply, as with most economic goods. In this case, however, the unchanged supply would tend to circulate more rapidly, thus having much the same effect as an increase in supply.

Answer 2.4

The main difference between the 'narrow' and 'broad' definitions of money supply is that one relates to immediate means of payment, while the other includes all deposits in banks and non-bank financial institutions.

Thus, M1 (the narrow definition) comprises of all notes and coins issued by the Central Bank of Nigeria plus bank deposits held on current accounts and transferable by cheque.

M2 (the broad definition of money) defines money as M1 plus time and savings deposits with banks and non-bank financial institutions like the Federal Mortgage Bank, Federal Savings Bank, finance houses, etc, plus investments in other financial assets such as government securities (e.g. Treasury Bills and Treasury Certificates), stocks and savings bonds. While M1 focusses attention on the medium of exchange function, M2 lays emphasis on the store of value function.

Answer 2.5

Money is defined as anything which is generally acceptable in settlement of debts. Money performs a number of functions of which the primary ones are as a store of value and a means of payment. Anything which fulfils these requirements ranks as money — particularly the function of a means of payment. Commercial bank deposits, particularly demand deposits on current account, but also time deposits, fulfil these requirements since these can be easily converted to cash. Demand deposits form part of money supply even when the narrow definition of money (M1) is used, mainly because they can be transferred by means of cheques without ever having to be withdrawn. Although most small payments are made in cash, virtually all large payments are made by cheque. As a result, bank deposits constitute a large proportion of the money supply in Nigeria.

By examining the Balance Sheet of a commercial bank, it will be seen that such deposits are its largest liabilities. Other financial institutions like the Federal Mortgage Bank, the Federal Savings Bank and finance houses, also take deposits from their customers. These deposits can be fairly easily withdrawn, but they cannot be directly transferred by means of a cheque, so cannot be regarded as a means of payment.

It must, however, be mentioned that in the broad definition of money the deposits of these financial institutions in Nigeria form part of the money supply.

CHAPTER THREE

MONETARY POLICY IN NIGERIA

Answer 3.1

Monetary policy can be described as the various ways by which the Federal Government and the Central Bank seek to influence the supply of money and credit as well as their price as indicated by interest rates in order to achieve stated or desired economic goals. The instruments used to achieve this objective include open market operations, variable rediscount rate, moral suasion, reserve requirements, direct credit control (aggregate and selective) and direct regulation of interest rates.

Open market operations relate to the buying and selling of securities in the money and capital markets by the Central Bank. The authorities can influence the level of cash and liquid assets in banks through such operations. Purchases and sales also affect the level of interest rates. The authorities may feel obliged to support the market at times, in order to prevent a rise in interest rates, even though this action increases bank liquidity. Thus, these operations help the authorities to influence rates and/or maintain stability on the market. A well developed money and capital market is a precondition for the successful application of this instrument of monetary policy. We do not presently have this in Nigeria. In practice, therefore, the CBN cannot effectively use this instrument.

In Nigeria, interest rates movements are strictly controlled by the monetary authorities. As a result, they are hardly responsive to market forces. However, the rates are varied from time to time depending on the prevailing economic policy being pursued. The CBN fixes a discount rate to which all interest rates are pegged, but the discount rate policy has not been sufficiently effective in Nigeria. Consequently, the interest rate structure in Nigeria is directly controlled and managed by the Central Bank. Every year the CBN fixes the ranges within which both the deposit and the lending rates are to be maintained.

An effective instrument of control used by the Central Bank is moral suasion. The Governor of the Bank tries in a friendly manner to persuade banks to reduce their lending activities when there is need for such restraint. This instrument has increasingly been used in recent years.

Banks are also required to maintain two reserve ratios — a cash ratio and a liquidity ratio. Cash ratios range from 2% to 5%, while the liquidity ratio is fixed at 25%. The CBN has the power to alter the required liquidity and cash ratios and their composition thereby directly affecting the ability of banks to create credit. An increase in the ratio will compel the banks to reduce lending and transfer funds to reserve assets, while a decrease in the ratio will have the opposite effect. This has been one of the most effective instruments of monetary policy.

Another effective means of influencing bank liquidity is calling for special deposits. Such deposits are usually frozen and do not form part of eligible liquid assets. Similarly, the CBN can also issue stabilisation securities to banks to mop up excess liquidity. This category of monetary control instrument has proved to be quite effective in a developing economy like Nigeria.

Over the years the CBN has discovered that the most effective control instrument is the direct control of credit granting activities by the use of annual credit guidelines. These cover a very wide area, including sectoral distribution of loans and advances, loans to indigenous businesses, loans to rural areas, reserve requirements and interest rate structure. The Central Bank of Nigeria issues a Monetary Policy Circular at the beginning of every fiscal year containing details of the government's new monetary policy.

Answer 3.2

Monetary policy means the various ways by which the Federal Government and the Central Bank seek to influence the supply of money and credit and interest rates in order to achieve stated or desired economic goals. In recent years, monetary policy has been directed towards the control of inflation. Other objectives of monetary policy include a high and stable level of employment, steady economic growth, reasonable stability of the internal purchasing power of money and a balance or surplus on the current balance of payments.

There is usually a conflict between these objectives. For instance, full employment and growth require a high level of monetary demand, but this creates conditions in which costs and prices tend to rise. It also leads to a balance of payments deficit by encouraging imports and discouraging exports. In order to correct this anomaly, demand must be reduced in order to improve the balance of payments and curb rise in prices, but such actions may cause unemployment and may also slow down the rate of growth of the economy.

Answer 3.3

Nigeria pursued a moderate monetary restraint policy during the period 1976 to 1981 and stringent monetary restraint policy from December 1981 to date.

The policy during the first period was aimed at reducing the excess liquidity of the banks. A combination of instruments were used; namely, direct credit ceilings, cash reserve requirements, stabilisation securities, the exclusion of deposits against letters of credit from eligible liquid assets and interest rate changes. The use of the yearly credit guidelines continued to be the major instrument of monetary control by the CBN during this period. The current policy is geared towards conservation of our foreign reserves. Measures taken to slow down the amount of foreign exchange disbursements include the re-introduction of preshipment inspection of raw materials and spare parts, re-introduction of pre-import deposits ranging from 10% to 250%, an outright ban on a variety of commodities and an increase in import duties on others as well as reductions of travel allowances, etc. In addition, interest rates were raised by 2% across the board in April 1982, although they were reduced by 1% in November 1982. There has been noticeable recession in the economy and banks are compelled to curb credit expansion due to tight liquidity.

CHAPTER FOUR

THE EVOLUTION OF THE MONEY SYSTEM IN NIGERIA

Answer 4.1

Before the arrival of Arab and Portuguese traders in the 18th century trade was carried on by barter. Items like coral beads, ivory and cowries were later introduced. Cowries and manilla were popularised by the Portuguese in their trading activities in the ancient Kingdom of Benin. The Portuguese monopoly of trade in Nigeria was broken by the British two arrived in Lagos a few years later.

The extension of British rule into Nigeria encouraged the use of currency which greatly facilitated exchange and diminished the use of barter. This process was further accelerated by the introduction of banking with the opening of the African Banking Corporation in 1892. The African Banking Corporation was later taken over by the Bank of British West Africa in 1894. The process of monetising the economy was carried a stage further by the unification of the currency system in 1912. The West African Currency Board introduced the West African Pound to replace the varieties of circulating media of exchange in 1910 and to augment the British silver coins which had been in circulation since 1886 in Nigeria. The notes and coins were tied to the pound sterling and were easily convertible. In 1913 special silver coins in the denominations of 3 pence, 6 pence, one shilling and two shillings were introduced.

The first Nigerian currency was issued on 1 July 1959 (the day the Central Bank was officially opened) to replace the currencies of the West African Currency Board. The issue of the first Nigerian currency led to the withdrawal from circulation of the West African Currency Board notes. When Nigeria became a republic in 1963, it was decided that the existing Federation of Nigeria notes be replaced. A total of ₦137m was redeemed between 1 July 1965 and June, 1966.

The Nigerian currency was again changed in 1968 during the period of the Nigerian Civil War. The Central Bank (Currency Conversion) Act, 1967 was designed to:

i) ensure the success of the trade embargo on the secessionist States;

ii) forestall the use of mint notes stolen from CBN vaults at Enugu, Port Harcourt and Benin; and,

iii) frustrate the illegal trafficking in the Nigerian currency which was going on in some foreign countries.

The decision to adopt the decimal currency system resulted in another currency exchange in January 1973. New notes and coins were issued in the following denominations:

1 kobo; 5 kobo; 10 kobo; 25 kobo (coins)

50 kobo; ₦1; ₦5; ₦10 (notes)

In February 1976, the largest denomination of note (₦20) was issued.

Answer 4.2

i) The establishment of the West African Currency Board was recommended by the Emmott Committee, which was set up to report on the desirability of introducing a West African silver coinage and a joint issue of the currency in British West African countries (i.e. Nigeria, Ghana (gold Coast), Sierra Leone and Gambia).

The committee's recommendation gave birth in 1912 to the West African Currency Board (W.A.C.B.). In 1913 the Board issued special silver coins in the denominations of 3 pence, 6 pence, one shilling and two shillings. Thus the W.A.C.B. provided a unified currency system that commanded confidence. It relieved the Colonial Government of the problem of currency management and eliminated the danger of locally created inflation or foreign exchange crises.

However the W.A.C.B. suffered from the following shortcomings:

a) It did not provide the flexibility and elasticity required of a currency that could serve developing countries.

b) It was not designed to train indigenes in the art of money management.

c) The idea of 100% sterling backing turned the W.A.C.B. into a mere cloakroom where output was always equal to input.

d) The issue of the same currency for 4 different countries was self-defeating as the countries moved steadily towards self-government.

ii) The word 'seigniorage' is commonly used to describe the profit which the government makes on the manufacture of cupro-nickel and bronze coins. These coins are token money and the value which is affixed to them by law is greater than the value of the metal of which they are composed. It is from that difference that the profit is obtained.

The West African Currency Board received a share of seigniorage (a form of royalty or profit on behalf of West African Governments) for the issue of British coins to West African territories.

Answer 4.3

The West African Currency Board (W.A.C.B.) was not a monetary authority as it was not designed to exercise discretionary control over the money stock. Its essence was the convertibility of West African currency on demand ito sterling. The currency it issued was only in exchange for the pound sterling.

Thus, the W.A.C.B. was, at best, only a passive money exchanger. The issue and redemption was automatic, so the reduction or increase of the money supply was strictly determined by the balance of payments. The W.A.C.B. was not initially allowed to hold government securities, but later was allowed to do so. The Board kept a reserve fund which was always at a level greater than the currency in circulation.

On the other hand, the Central Bank was established for the following principal objectives:

i) To issue legal tender currency in Nigeria. The Central Bank of Nigeria is the only bank that is authorised to issue currency in Nigeria. The Bank does not rely on London or any foreign country before performing this function.

ii) To maintain external reserves and to safeguard the international value of Nigeria's currency. (The currency issued by the W.A.C.B. was fully convertible to the pound sterling and was tied to that currency, so it had no seperate international value. The Central Bank also performs exchange control functions in order to conserve our reserves.

iii) To promote monetary stability and a sound financial structure in Nigeria. To perform this function effectively, the Central Bank of Nigeria has been given wide powers to regulate the activities of all banks and other financial institutions. The West African Currency Board did not have such powers.

CHAPTER FIVE

CENTRAL BANKING

Answer 5.1

The controversy as to whether it was advisable to establish a Central Bank in Nigeria started in the early 1950's. There were two opposing camps. The nationalists who were of the view that a Central Bank was needed and the Colonial Government camp who believed that it was premature to establish a Central Bank in a country where there was no financial system. To resolve the opposing view, a total of three studies were commissioned: J. L. Fisher's Report 1953, I.B.R.D. Mission Report 1955 and J. B. Loyne's Report 1957.

Fisher based his study on orthodox banking principles and reported that it was not feasible to establish a Central Bank on the grounds that the financial environment did not exist and that it would be impossible to find the local staff to man it. He also contended that the Currency Board (W.A.C.B.) was equal to the task of promoting savings and capital formation. He recommended the following three step programme leading to the establishment of a Central Bank:

i) Transfer of the operation of W.A.C.B. to Africa, so that its management would eventually be indigenised.

ii) Establishment of a Nigerian Currency Board and a separate Nigerian Currency to take over Nigeria's share of W.A.C.B. assets.

iii) Establishment of a Bank of Issue as the embryo of a future Central Bank.

Fisher's recommendations were upheld in 1955 by the World Bank mission. The I.B.R.D. mission, however, recommended a State Bank of Nigeria to take over the banking control functions of the Financial Secretary.

Contrary to the above two reports, that of J. B. Loynes in 1957 favoured the establishment of a Central Bank in Nigeria. Thus, by 17 March 1958 the CBN Ordinance was promulgated and it became fully operational on 1 July, 1959.

Answer 5.2

There are very few similarities between a commercial bank and a Central Bank. It is true that a study of their respective Balance Sheets will reveal that their liabilities are almost entirely to customers, either on deposits or on notes, and their assets are nearly all financial in character (i.e. both are essentially banks), but here the similarities end. A country will normally have only one Central Bank (most probably publicly owned); while it will have a number of commercial banks operating in competition with one another. They are normally privately owned, except in Nigeria and other developing countries where governments have majority shares in almost all banks.

The main differences between the Central Bank of Nigeria and a commercial bank can be summarised as:

i)   While maximisation of profits is one of the main objectives of a commercial bank, the making of profits is only incidental to the Central Bank's operations.

ii) Commercial banks serve as bankers to their customers, while the Central Bank serves as banker to the commercial banks, acting as 'lender of last resort' to the banking system and banker to the Government.

iii) Apart from serving as banker to commercial banks, the Central Bank has a supervisory role over the commercial banks and other financial institutions.

iv) The Central Bank controls the activities of banks and other financial institutions, particularly with regard to lending.

v)   The control and issue of currency notes and coins is vested in the Central Bank alone, thus giving it the power to regulate the supply of money.

vi) In view of its privileged position the Central Bank does not normally compete for business with the commercial banks, apart from the Federal and most State Government accounts which are usually maintained by them. However, the Central Bank of Nigeria does not provide services for personal and commercial customers which is the main business of commercial and merchant banks.

Answer 5.3

i)   In Nigeria banks are required to maintain two reserve ratios: a cash ratio and a liquidity ratio. Banks maintain non-interest earning cash reserves against demand deposits. The cash deposit is expressed as a ratio of each bank's total demand deposit liabilities. For this purpose banks are classified into four groups as follows:

Cash	Total Deposit Liabilities	Ratio of Cash to Demand Deposits
A	₦300 million or more	5%
B	₦100 million to ₦299.9 million	4%
C	₦30 million to ₦99.9 million	3%
D	Less than ₦30 million	2%

Cash reserves are carried in the form of frozen deposits at the CBN.

Banks are also required to maintain a liquidity ratio of 25%. The main reserve assets are cash balances with the Central Bank (other than special deposits, deposits to meet the cash ratio and shortfalls on loans to agriculture and residential buildings); balances held with local banks (excluding uncleared effects), less balances held for local banks, Nigerian Treasury Bills/Certificates, money at call (net), certificates of deposits held (of not more than 18 months to maturity); government securities — eligible stocks (i.e. of not more than 3 years to maturity) and Bankers' Unit Fund.

The eligible liabilities consist of current, savings and time deposit accounts, certificates of deposits issued (of not more than 18 months to maturity); excess balances held for local banks, on call money and balances held for foreign banks (net) — if they represent a net minus, they are ignored.

The formula for computing the liquidity ratio is:

$$\frac{\text{Total Specified Liquid Assets}}{\text{Total Current Liabilities.}} \times 100$$

ii) One of the major functions of any Central Bank is to act as lender of last resort to banks. The rate at which the Central Bank lends is known as the Bank Rate or Discount Rate. Generally the Bank lends against the security of 'eligible paper' — this being high-quality short-term paper which it has agreed to accept for this purpose. This arrangement assists the stability of the banking system by ensuring that cash will be available to the banks, even when they may have a sudden and exceptional need for it. Thus, it enables the asset structures of the banks to be kept in a less liquid form than would otherwise be necessary.

Answer 5.4

The Central Bank, being the custodian of the country's foreign reserves, shows the total amount of our external reserves on its Balance Sheet. The items comprising the total external reserves include gold, convertible currencies, foreign government securities and balances with foreign banks, the I.M.F. Gold Tranche and Special Drawing Rights — which shows Nigeria's contribution in convertible currencies to the I.M.F. The Nigerian banking regulations do not permit commercial banks to maintain foreign reserves. They are only allocated working balances by the Central Bank to meet their commitments in international trade transactions.

On the assets side of the Central Bank Balance Sheet a huge balance is shown under Federal Government securities. Government securities are of two categories: short-dated securities like Treasury Bills, Treasury Certificates and stocks maturing within three years and long-dated securities like government stocks with maturities ranging from 4 years to 25 years. The holdings of the Central Bank include those securities purchased as 'buyer of last resort' of stocks not absorbed by the capital market. Commercial banks also have this item on their Balance Sheets as government securities. The bulk of these comprise of highly liquid securities like Treasury Bills/Certificates which they can rediscount for cash at the Central Bank.

By far the largest asset on the Balance Sheet of commercial banks is 'loans and advances'. The Central Bank does not grant loans and advances to individuals and private/public companies. However, the Bank does grant temporary loans to the Federal Government as 'ways and means' advances and also rediscounts bills and securities for banks and Commodity Boards and discount houses in its role as 'lender of the last resort'. Therefore, the equivalent of commercial bank 'loans and advances' is the Central Bank's 'rediscounts and advances'.

On the liabilities side both banks have capital and reserves on their Balance Sheets. Both are expected to increase their reserve funds from year to year. As the Central Bank issues the nation's currency, the total value of notes and coins in circulation is shown on the liabilities side of the Bank's Balance Sheet. There is no item in the Balance Sheet of a commercial bank that can be equated to this.

Both the Central Bank and the commercial banks receive deposits and this is reflected on their Balance Sheets. However, while the Central Bank receives deposits from Federal and State Governments, Government Corporations, parastatals and banks, the commercial banks' deposits are held by individuals, firms, and companies — both private and public.

Answer 5.5

In the United States of America, central banking functions are performed by the Federal Reserve System, which consists of the Board of Governors, twelve Federal Reserve Banks and the Open Market Committee. In Nigeria, central banking functions are performed by one single bank called the Central Bank of Nigeria.

The activities of the Federal Reserve Banks in the U.S.A. include the supervision of banks — a function also performed by the Central Bank of Nigeria . Both in Nigeria and in the U.S.A. the Central Bank acts as banker to the Government and handles the borrowing activities of the Government by acting as registrar for government stocks and bonds.

Both the Central Bank of Nigeria and the Federal Reserve System in the U.S.A. are the sole authority for the issue of notes and coins in their respective countries. They also act as banker to commercial banks, although in the U.S.A. not all the commercial banks are members of the Federal Reserve System. Those banks registered under Federal Law which are known as national banks are compelled to be members, but banks registered under State laws (known as the state banks) have the option to choose whether to be members or not. As a result, all the large banks in the country belong to the System and they control over 75% of the total bank deposits. In Nigeria all banks are under the umbrella of the Central Bank and there is no distinction between state banks and national banks. Both systems provide avenues for collection and clearing of cheques and other instruments.

Unlike the Central Bank of Nigeria which is nationalised (and, therefore, publicly owned), the Federal Reserve System is not •

nationalised, though it operates under Federal statute law and is accountable to Congress and the Federal Government.

While the capital of the Central Bank of Nigeria was fully subscribed by the Federal Government, those of the 12 Federal Reserve Banks are subscribed by the member banks in the area which they serve. The majority of the directors of each Federal Reserve Bank are appointed locally from its area of operations, while the directors of the Central Bank of Nigeria are appointed from all parts of the country to reflect national character.

The U.S.A. has 12 Federal Reserve Banks because of its enormous size and the large number of individual banks — there are over 14,000 commercial banks in the U.S.A. Each of the 12 Reserve Banks operates independently, although policy guidelines are established by the Board which is located in Washington. The Board comprises 7 Governors, appointed by the President of the U.S.A. who also nominates the Chairman and Vice-Chairman. Thus, the Board is the nominal head of the system, but decisions relating to day-to-day operations are taken by the Open Market Committee which consists of the Board together with the heads of 5 of the 12 Reserve Banks which must always include the New York Federal Reserve Bank. On the other hand, the Central Bank of Nigeria is the only central banking authority in the country. It is governed by a Board of Governors comprising the Governor of the Bank as Chairman of the Board, a Deputy Governor, three full-time executive directors and eight part-time directors, all of whom are appointed by the Federal Government for 5 years in the case of the Governor, his Deputy and the 3 executive directors and three years for the other directors.

CHAPTER SIX

THE FUNCTIONS OF THE CENTRAL BANK

Answer 6.1

A Central Bank stands at the apex of the banking system of every country. It is the representative of the Government in the banking sector and acts mainly as banker to the Government. It has a very close association with both the Government and the banking sector of the economy, advising the Government on monetary policy and implementing the policy on its behalf. The Central Bank of Nigeria is the sole authority for issue of notes and coins in the country.

As banker to the Government, the Central Bank keeps the current accounts of government departments. It also handles the Government's borrowing transactions, including acting as registrar for government stocks and bonds.

The Bank also acts as banker to the commercial banks. It keeps accounts for each of them which they use to settle inter-bank transactions. The Central Bank also acts as 'lender of the last resort' to banks. This means that when they are unable to borrow funds elsewhere, they may borrow from the Central Bank or discount specified forms of asset with it.

Another important function of the Bank is to operate the monetary policy of the Federal Government. As regards the domestic monetary system, the Central Bank uses a number of policy instruments to stabilise the economy. These include open market operations, interest rate structure, reserve requirements, special deposits and moral suasion.

The Central Bank is also responsible for the conservation of the country's foreign reserves and for the stability of the exchange rate of the naira through exchange controls.

Answer 6.2

Central Bank Credit Guidelines are issued in the form of a Circular at the beginning of the fiscal year, soon after the presentation of the budget by Mr. President. The Circular is normally addressed to all banks and provides details of the monetary policy to be pursued by the Government in the new fiscal year. The monetary authorities have confirmed that this is certainly the most effective control instrument and most compatible to the economic goals and aspirations of the nation and the attainment of government objectives.

The Circular covers the distribution of loans and advances by commercial and merchant banks, the ratio of loans that must be allocated to indigenous borrowers, loans to rural areas, reserve requirements, interest rate structure, several prudential ratios and regulations for international trade and foreign exchange. Quantitative ceilings on the overall and/or sectoral distribution of credit are also usually imposed.

We shall examine in more detail the most important areas usually covered by the Credit Guidelines:

i) Aggregate Credit. Banks are restricted to a certain growth rate per annum in loans and advances. For example, in 1982 the aggregate loans and advances of banks were not to rise by more than 30%, except in the case of new banks and small banks with total loans and advances not exceeding ₦100 million as at 31 December 1981, which were permitted to grow by up to 40% or 70% of their total deposit liabilities (excluding government deposits maturing earlier than 6 months) whichever was the higher.

ii) Sectoral distribution of loans and advances. For this purpose, the economy is classified into two major sectors — the preferred and the less preferred sectors. The preferred sector consists mainly of those activities which are on the priority list of the Government for development and are, therefore, to be encouraged. These include manufacturing to promote industrialisation, agriculture, housing, public utilities, transportation, communication, exports and de-velopment finance institutions. The less preferred sector consists mainly of credit extended to finance general commerce (imports and domestic trade) and personal loans, etc. The aim is to shift the emphasis from the usual buy-and-sell activities to the development orientated. Each item is allocated a percentage share — a minimum in the case of the preferred sector and maxima in the case of the less preferred sector. The total for the preferred sector should not be less than 75%, while that of the less preferred sector should not exceed 25% of the total loans and advances. In other words, banks may exceed the targets for the preferred sectors within the overall ceiling.

iii) Loans to indigenous borrowers. The guidelines also allocate the minimum credit that must be extended to indigenous borrowers. In the year 1982 this was increased from 70% to 80% of total loans and advances. 16% of the 80% was supposed to go to small scale enterprises wholly owned by Nigerians.

iv) Loans to rural areas. In pursuit of the Government's policy on rural banking, banks are required to lend not less than 30% of the total deposits collected in the rural areas to borrowers in those areas. This policy is intended to accelerate the economic growth of the rural areas and to spread the banking habit and development in the country.

Answer 6.3

i) A bank in Nigeria cannot lend, on the aggregate, more than 10 times its adjusted capital fund or 70% of its total deposit liabilities (i.e. time deposits, savings and demand deposits). Adjusted capital funds are computed as follows:

> Issued and fully-paid up capital
> plus statutory reserves
>   " undivided profit or general reserve
>   " profit & loss account balance
>   " reserve for possible loan losses (as per the bank's books)
> less Reserves for possible loan losses (as recommended by CBN examiners).

ii) Not more than 33⅓% of the sum of the paid-up capital and statutory reserves of a bank shall be lent to an individual borrower. This ceiling is of particular importance when the bank is dealing with a company or firm, with subsidiaries or associates, maintaining accounts in one or more branches.

This regulation is aimed at ensuring that banks diversify credits so as to avoid an excessive concentration of credit risk among individual debtors or within any geographical area. Thus, banks are encouraged to extend credit in smaller amounts to a larger number of borrowers.

Answer 6.4

Open Market Operations are the buying or selling of government securities by the Central Bank on the money and capital markets. In this way the Central Bank absorbs money from, or provides money to, the public who draw it from, or pay it into, their bank accounts. This affects the cash holdings of the banks and hence their liquidity position. A change in their liquidity position will make them reconsider their lending policy.

A well-developed money/capital market with a substantial volume of government securities in existence and an efficient market in them is a pre-condition for the successful application of this instrument of control. Presently, we do not have this in Nigeria, and so Open Market Operations cannot be used effectively.

CHAPTER SEVEN

COMMERCIAL BANKING

Answer 7.1

The structure of commercial banking in Nigeria is tailored toward that of the United Kingdom. Other countries in the Commonwealth, and indeed most countries of the Western World have the same structure which can be described as the branch banking system. This is characterised by a few large banks with a wide network of branches extending to every part of the country. Nigeria has 22 commercial banks (1982) with over 900 branches. The United States of America has a unique banking system called unit banking. The Federal nature of the U.S.A. constitution, means that banks are also subject to State laws which may vary considerably. For instance, in California branch banking is permitted and Bank of America alone has about 1,200 branches in the State. At the other extreme, banks in Chicago may operate from only one office. Other States have regulations between these two extremes. As a consequence, there are about 14,000 separate banks in the United States of America — about 5,000 being registered under Federal laws and 9,000 under State laws.

The branch banking system has many advantages in terms of efficiency, but many of the disadvantages of the U.S.A. structure are ameliorated by the correspondent bank system, whereby large banks act as bankers for small banks in various ways. Even so, the U.S.A. system is comparatively inefficient in terms of time and cost of many operations.

The types of business conducted by the banks in Nigeria and the U.S.A. are broadly similar, as is the structure of their assets and liabilities. A notable difference, however, is that banks in the U.S.A. lend almost entirely on loans, whereas Nigerian banks, like their counterparts in the U.K., lend mainly on overdraft.

Answer 7.2

The primary functions of commercial banks in Nigeria are:

i)   Acceptance and safe-keeping of deposits.

ii) Granting loans and advances to customers.

iii) Transferring of funds on the instructions of their customers.

iv) Management of customers' investments.

v) Providing facilities for safe-keeping of important documents and title deeds.

vi) Providing foreign exchange facilities to travellers.

vii) Advising customers on insurance.

viii) Providing services to the importer and exporter — documentary credits, bills for collection, bills for negotiation, etc.

ix) Providing night safe facilities.

x) Buying and selling of stocks and shares on behalf of their customers.

xi) Providing business status reports and references.

xii) Providing cashing credit facilities to customers.

xiii) Providing standing order facilities to customers.

xiv) Providing a business advisory service to customers.

Answer 7.3

i) At the apex of the banking sector of the economy stands the Central Bank of Nigeria which carries out the full range of central banking activities, using some of the traditional instruments. The main activities of the bank include:

a) Issuance of legal tender currency in Nigeria.

b) Maintenance of external reserves in order to safeguard the internal value of the currency.

c) Promotion of monetary stability and a sound financial structure.

d) Acting as banker to the government and to other banks in Nigeria and abroad.

ii) The commercial banks have a widespread branch network and are generally known as retail bankers as they handle most of the ordinary banking business in Nigeria. Commercial banks are mainly concerned with short-term borrowing and lending, though they have increasingly in recent years been extending medium-term credit and also engaging in various wholesale market activities and international trade financing. They offer a number of other services including the transfer of funds.

iii) Merchant banks are financial institutions providing specialist services such as the acceptance of bills of exchange, corporate finance, portfolio management and equipment leasing. They also engage mainly in medium and long-term lending as opposed to short-term.

iv) There are a number of development banks:

Nigerian Industrial Development Bank (N.I.D.B.)

This bank was established in 1964 as a private concern including foreign investors, with the CBN as the major share holder. The N.I.D.B. specialises in the provision of finance for industry either by way of loans or by taking up equity shares. Presently the Federal Government and the CBN jointly own 94.2% of the Bank's equity capital.

Nigerian Bank for Commerce & Industry (N.B.C.I.)

This was established in 1973 with a paid-up capital of ₦10m, subscribed by the CBN and the Federal Government. The bank's main functions are to provide equity capital and loans for long and medium-term investments to indigenous persons and bodies engaged in industry and commerce. The bank also grants loans to Nigerians to enable them to buy up alien enterprises affected by the Government's indigenisation policy.

Nigerian Agricultural and Co-operative Bank (N.A.C.B.)

This was also established in 1973 by the Federal Government with an initial capital of ₦12 million. The bank was set up in order to improve the level and quality of all aspects of agricultural production, enhance the availability of storage facilities and promote the marketing of agricultural products through more liberal credit to farmers.

The Federal Mortgage Bank of Nigeria (F.M.B.N.)

Formerly known as the Nigerian Building Society, it was established originally in 1957 to expand and co-ordinate mortgage lending in Nigeria.

Federal Savings Bank

This was started as the Post Office Savings Bank and was renamed in 1974 when it was separated from the Post Office and came under the direct control of a Board of Directors appointed by the Federal

Government. However, it is still operated through post offices, so enjoys the advantage of a wide network of branches for effective deposit mobilisation. Depositors' funds are invested in government securities and on the money and capital markets.

Answer 7.4

The first commercial bank — the African Banking Corporation — opened its first branch in Lagos in 1892. The bank experienced some initial difficulties which made it transfer its assets to Elder Dempster & Co. in 1893. This led to the formation of a new bank known as the British Bank of West Africa in 1893 with £10,000 capital, later increased to £100,000 during the same year. It started operations in Lagos in 1894 and later opened branches in Accra, Freetown and Bathurst.

Another bank called Anglo-African Bank was established in 1899 in old Calabar. The bank later changed its name to Bank of Nigeria and established branches in Burutu, Lokoja and Jebba. The bank could not withstand the fierce competition from the B.B.W.A. which later bought it out. Thus B.B.W.A. became the first surviving bank in Nigeria Limited.

Barclays Bank D.C.O. opened its first Lagos office in 1917. The bank is now known as the Union Bank of Nigeria Ltd. The Nigerian banking scene was dominated by these two British banks — B.B.W.A. Ltd. and Barclays Bank D.C.O. between 1894 and 1933. The third expatriate bank — British and French Bank, now called United Bank for Africa Ltd. — was established in 1949.

During this period several abortive attempts were made to set up indigenous banks. In 1933 the National Bank was launched by some patriotic Nigerians and it turned out to be the first indigenous bank to survive. In 1945, Agbonmagbe Bank (now called Wema Bank) was established. Between 1945 and 1947 a number of indigenous banks were established, but they all collapsed under the weight of mismanagement. In 1947 another successful indigenous bank known as the African Continental Bank was founded by Dr Nnamdi Azikiwe. This was a period of free-for-all banking. It is recorded that between 1947 and 1952 a total of 185 banks were registered. It is understood that most of these banks merely registered without actually commencing operations.

The need for legislation for the control of banking in Nigeria became very apparent if only to protect depositors. The Colonial Government, therefore, set up a commission of inquiry — the Paton Commission. Consequent upon the report of the Commission, the first banking legislation was passed in 1952.

CHAPTER EIGHT

STRUCTURE OF A BANK BALANCE SHEET

Answer 8.1

Balance Sheet as at 30 September 1981

Employment of Funds	1981 N'000	1980 N'000
Cash & short term funds	28,924	15,717
Statutory & other deposits with CBN	35,148	18,495
Government securities	13,120	11,600
Investment with other banks	25,000	11,000
Loans & advances	270,161	193,569
Other assets	12,331	38,531
Fixed assets	21,664	19,484
	406,348	308,396
Financed by:		
Share capital	10,000	9,000
Statutory reserve	6,734	5,920
Undistributed profit	5,730	4,030
Shareholders' funds	22,464	18,950
Customers' deposit	244,520	175,843
Other liabilities	131,864	113,603
Debenture stock	7,500	—
	406,348	308,396

The main liabilities of a bank comprise share capital, reserves, undistributed profit, debenture stock or any other loan capital and customers' deposits.

i) Share Capital

The issued and paid-up share capital are shares held by individuals, institutional investors and governments. Most of the shares issued by Nigerian banks are ordinary shares with ₦1 of 50k nominal value each. One or two banks have recently issued preference shares.

ii) Statutory Reserves

Every bank in Nigeria is required by law to maintain a reserve fund and, out of its net profits each year and before any dividend is declared:

a) transfer to the reserve fund a sum equal to not less than 25% of such profits where the amount of the reserve fund is less than the paid-up share capital; or,

b) transfer to the reserve fund, where the amount of the reserve fund is equal to or in excess of the paid-up share capital, 12½% of the net profit of the bank.

However, a transfer need not be made until any past losses have been made good.

iii) Undistributed Profit or General Reserve

These are profits earned over the years which have not been distributed. Part or the bulk of the balance on this account may eventually be capitalised or used for the purpose it was set aside for. It is also called Revenue Reserve.

A bank may also have a Capital Reserve on its Balance Sheet as a result of a revaluation of fixed assets especially branch premises which have been revalued at higher than purchase price. The excess is placed on a Share Premium Account. The important difference between Capital Reserve and Revenue Reserve is that the former can be distributed to the shareholders as dividend while the latter cannot be touched.

iv) Debenture Stock or Loan Capital

These are medium-term loans at fixed rate of interest and repayable over a fixed period of time to finance specific capital projects. In the event of a winding-up, the holders are paid only after depositors have been fully repaid.

v) Customers' Deposits

As loans form the largest asset of a bank, customers' deposits are the largest liability on a bank's Balance Sheet. The depositors are creditors of the bank, whose money, or part of it, must be repaid on demand or notice in accordance with the agreement.

CHAPTER NINE

BANKS' PROFITABILITY AND LIQUIDITY

Answer 9.1

A bank asset is regarded as liquid if it can be turned into cash quickly and without any appreciable loss. Short-dated government securities like Treasury Bills can be turned into cash quickly by re-discounting them with the Central Bank, so they are regarded as liquid assets. Other assets, such as loans and advances, may be realised without loss, but cannot be called in quickly, so are not regarded as liquid.

The assets approved by the Central Bank as liquid are cash balances held with the CBN less any shortfall on loans in respect of agriculture and residential buildings, balances held with local banks (excluding uncleared effects) less balances held for local banks, Nigerian Treasury Bills, Nigerian Treasury Certificates, money at call held with other banks (net), Certificates of Deposit (maturing within 18 months), government securities (maturing within 3 years) and Bankers' Unit Fund.

An individual bank may be able to restore its cash position by disposing of some of its liquid assets at the expense of the liquidity of other banks. For the banks as a whole, liquid assets can only be turned into cash to the extent that the Central Bank — the sole issuer of currency — is willing to take them over. Thus, virtually all liquid assets consist of, or are backed by, assets which may be rediscounted at the Central Bank.

Answer 9.2

A large proportion of the liabilities of a bank are to its depositors and are repayable on demand or at short notice. In the light of this, the assets of a bank must be kept reasonably liquid, so as to meet possible demands from depositors. At the same time, banks, like other companies, incur substantial costs and must earn an income at least sufficient to meet these costs. They are accountable to their share-holders who have invested in them with the aim of good returns in form of future dividends and growth. Therefore, in order to make profits, banks need assets which produce income substantially higher than that paid on deposits and incurred as expenses.

In practice, these two objectives (making profits and remaining liquid) tend to work in opposite directions. Cash itself produces no income and the relatively liquid assets like call money, Treasury Bills and Treasury Certificates produce a relatively low income, or at least earn less than the less liquid assets. Advances to customers, even though they may be expressed as repayable on demand, are in practice not particularly liquid, but these are the assets on which banks normally earn the highest rate of return. Thus, the distribution of a commercial bank's assets is determined by a balance between the needs of liquidity and profitability.

In Nigeria this is achieved by the maintenance of reserve ratios. Banks maintain a ratio of cash to demand deposits of 2% – 5%, depending on the size of the bank; and at least another 25% in liquid assets such as money at call, Treasury Bills and Certificates. If as a result of an undue pursuit of profit, loans are allowed to grow excessively, then the ratio will not be met. The bank will become illiquid and CBN penalties will be imposed.

Answer 9.3

i) The cash ratio is the ratio between non-interest earning cash reserves and the demand deposits which all banks must maintain. The cash deposit is expressed as a ratio of each bank's total demand deposit liabilities. For this purpose banks are classified into four groups:

Class	Total Deposit Liabilities	Ratio of Cash to Demand Deposits
A	₦300 million or more	5%
B	₦100 million or more, but less than ₦300m	4%
C	₦30 million or more, but less than ₦100m	3%
D	Less than ₦30 million	2%

These reserves are carried in the form of frozen deposits at the CBN.

ii) The liquidity ratio is the ratio of reserve assets to eligible liabilities. The minimum specified liquidity ratio that must be maintained by banks is 25%. The main reserve assets are cash, balances with the Central Bank (other than special deposits), balances held with local banks (excluding uncleared effects), less balances held for local banks, Nigerian Treasury Bills/Certificate, money at call (net), Certificates of Deposit (of not more than 18 months to maturity), other government securities (of not more than 3 years to maturity) and Bankers' Unit Fund.

The eligible liabilities consist of current, savings and time deposit accounts, Certificates of Deposit issued (not more than 18 months to maturity); excess balances held for local banks, on call money and balances held for foreign banks (net), although if a net minus, the latter is ignored. The formula for computing the liquidity ratio is as follows:

$$\frac{\text{Total Specified Liquid Assets}}{\text{Total Current Liabilities}} \times 100$$

CHAPTER TEN

BANK CAPITAL MANAGEMENT AND CAPITAL ADEQUACY

Answer 10.1

The three methods used for capital control purposes in Nigeria are:

i) Fixed minimum capital requirement.

ii) Limitation of lending limit.

iii) Weighted risk — assets ratio.

i) Fixed minimum capital requirement.

Since 1952 when the first Banking Act was promulgated attempts have been made to establish the minimum capital for banks. The 1969 Banking Act, as amended in 1979, stipulated that the paid-up capital of an indigenous bank should not be less than ₦600,000; while that of banks with foreign interests was fixed at ₦1.5 million; and ₦2 million for merchant banks.

ii) Limitation of Lending Limit

By this method, the CBN set a limit to lending to individual debtors or groups of inter-related debtors. This limit is expressed as a percentage of the bank's own funds. It is otherwise called the Legal Lending Limit. As bank capital provides a cushion against risk, the maximum lending limit of a commercial bank is thus statutorily tied to its own funds. At present (1982) the maximum loan that any Nigerian bank can grant to a single customer is 33⅓% of the sum of the paid-up capital and statutory reserves of the bank.

iii) Weighted Risk — Assets Ratio

This method relates shareholders' funds to the sum total of risk-bearing assets, weighted by the degree of risk involved. For instance, an unsecured loan will attract a higher rate of solvency capital requirement than a secured loan.

To determine capital adequacy by this method, the assets of the bank are divided into different categories, mainly determined by their safety and risk. Each category is then allocated an appropriate capital cover. Assets like cash and balances with the CBN, short-term securities, Certificates of Deposit, government stocks and high-rated loans, do not require capital support. Loans which have been classified sub-standard, require 10% capital cover or provision. Some banks do not make any provision for this category of classified debts. Loans classified as doubtful require 50% provision; while loans classified as bad or loss require 100% provision. Fixed assets must also be covered 100% as they are expected to be funded by the bank's capital funds and not by depositors' funds.

The minimum capital requirement of the bank is the sum of the percentages required for its various assets.

Answer 10.2

Bank loans and advances are examined periodically and monitored continuously by in-house credit examiners or bank examiners from the Central Bank of Nigeria in order to assess the quality of the bank's assets. This exercise involves a thorough analysis of the loan portfolio. Weaknesses likely to degenerate into serious problems in the future should be promptly reported to senior management. Loans are examined as to the degree of risk and the likelihood of orderly repayment of the loan. Any of the loans considered to have developed some weaknesses are regarded as problem (or potential problem) loans and are classified as sub-standard, doubtful or loss, depending on the seriousness of the problem.

Consequent upon the classification of the loan, especially if it is classified as doubtful or loss, adequate provision for losses must be made from the resources of the bank. A general provision of 50% for doubtful loans and 100% for losses is considered adequate by the Central Bank of Nigeria. No specific provisions are stipulated by the CBN for 'sub-standard' classifications, but some banks make a 10% provision.

CHAPTER ELEVEN

OTHER FINANCIAL INSTITUTIONS

Answer 11.1

The main distinguishing features between merchant banks and commercial banks can be outlined as follows:

Merchant Banks	Commercial Banks
Wholesale Banking — mobilise deposits and lend in large amounts mainly from/to institutional investors and firms. Deal with a relatively small number of large accounts.	Retail Banking — mobilise deposits and lend in both small and large amounts from/to individuals and firms. Deal with a relatively large number of small accounts.
Deposits — usually fixed and interest bearing.	Deposits — may be fixed or on demand, with or without interest.
Loans — less of overdraft type. More of term loan on long-term basis.	Loans — more of overdraft type or on short-term basis.
Cash Reserves — less need to be concerned about liquidity, because of 'matching' principle application.	Cash Reserves — greater need for cash and liquidity: little application of 'matching' principle, as rely more on 'law of large numbers'.
Branch Network — less need as concentration is on industrial/financial centres.	Branch Network — greater need as presence needed everywhere.
Customers — special and concentrated.	Customers — of various types, widespread.
Services — of specialised nature to special customers, mainly in the international banking and finance areas.	Services — of more varied nature to different types of customers, mainly in the domestic banking and finance areas.
General Operation — relatively more flexible and dynamic.	General Operation — relatively more conservative and less dynamic.

In contrast with commercial banks, therefore, merchant banks remain small organisations, offering wholesale banking, concentrating on

---

[1] The author is indebted to Ojo & Adewunmi *Banking & Finance in Nigeria,* Graham Burn, 1982 p. 75 for this answer.

business involving large sums and the use of expertise, leaving the small transactions, retail banking and the subsequent routine clerical work involved to the commercial banks.

Answer 11.2

In Nigeria, the role of merchant banks is not well defined. It has been an uphill task for the monetary authorities to define their role in a developing economy whose capital market is not fully developed. As a result, merchant banks were for a long time performing virtually the same functions as commercial banks. The Central Bank in its annual Monetary Policy Circulars to banks, has endeavoured to distinguish merchant banks and carve out specific roles for them. In this context, the 1982 Monetary Policy Circular provides as follows:

i) A minimum of 40% of total loans and advances shall be of medium and long-term nature with maturity of not less than three years.

ii) A maximum of 20% of loans and advances shall be of a short-term nature (i.e. maturing within twelve months).

iii) A maximum of 15% of total assets shall be in equipment leasing.

The above requirements seek to restrict the activities of merchant banks in the traditional area of commercial banking activities (i.e. short-term lending), thus avoiding unnecessary competition or duplication of functions. At the same time merchant banks are encouraged to do more medium and long-term lending so that commercial banks can concentrate on short-term.

The Central Bank has also given official support for the argument in financial circles that merchant banks would make a more tangible contribution to the economic development of this country if they provide more specialist services such as equipment leasing and other corporate banking services. However, to fulfil the role mapped out for them, merchant banks face the problem of liquidity. The source and nature of funds available to them outside their capital and reserves are essentially short-term deposits repayable within one year. In these circumstances, it is difficult for merchant banks to concentrate on long-term lending, as the resultant effect of using short-term funds to finance long-term projects could be quite disastrous.

Answer 11.3

i) Leasing is the hiring of an asset for the duration of its economic life. The asset is initially purchased by the finance company and then leased to the user who has no option to purchase.

The system is suitable for large and costly assets such as computers, aircraft, expensive plant and equipment. Leasing is an alternative to outright purchase of an asset on credit, mortgage finance or term loan. In a leasing agreement, no capital outlay is involved. It requires no cash deposit or down payment; the only disbursement being the fee payable to the merchant bank or finance house.

ii) Merchant banks in Nigeria act as Issuing Houses at the Nigerian Stock Exchange. In this role, they provide financial services to corporate entities including governments, quasi-government institutions and companies seeking to raise long-term or permanent finance for their operations, by sponsoring their capital issues and the sale of their securities to the public. Specifically, their functions include:

a) giving advice on the most appropriate capital structure (i.e. capital gearing);

b) determining the most appropriate time to make an issue;

c) providing publicity and marketing facilities for the security to be issued; and,

d) giving backing to an issue in the form of underwriting.

Merchant banks do not, however, trade on the Stock Exchange as stockbrokers.

Answer 11.4

While there are a few similarities in the functions of merchant and development banks, the distinguishing features are many.

Most development banks do not take deposits from the public. They borrow from institutional lenders like banks and insurance companies. They also rely on loan capital from the Central Bank of Nigeria and the Federal Government and equity participation by both the Federal Government and the Central Bank. Similarly, merchant banks accept deposits from commercial banks, insurance companies, oil companies and other institutional depositors, but they also accept large deposits — minimum of ₦50,000 — from individuals and companies. Merchant banks also provide short-term facilities for financing international trade. They do not receive any loans from the Government. However, with the acquisition of shares in some merchant banks, one can say that merchant banks also obtain loan capital from the Federal Government.

One of the reasons for setting up development banks is to foster the promotion and development of industrial projects. In this regard, they serve as a channel for bringing into Nigeria investible funds from international organisations. Development banks provide long and medium-term finance for the public and private sectors.
While merchant banks also provide medium and long-term finance for commerce and industry, their decisions are based almost entirely on viability of projects, while development banks take into serious consideration the economic goals and aspirations of the country.
Therefore, while N.I.D.B. or N.B.C.I. may finance an enterprise which by virtue of its size would make a significant contribution to economic growth and development of Nigeria, a merchant bank may reject such a venture.

Answer 11.5

i) The Nigerian Bank for Commerce and Industry was set up to provide medium and long-term finance for the acquisition, expansion and establishment of viable business by Nigerian businessmen. One of the original objectives of the bank was to assist Nigerians by providing credit facilities for the take-over of businesses in schedule I and schedule II in the form of loan and equity participation, in accordance with the Nigerian Enterprises Promotion Act, 1977.

The Bank also assists indigenous businesses by providing consultancy services in the following areas:

a) Identification of viable projects.

b) Preparation of well-articulated feasibility surveys.

c) Provision of guidance on the appropriate ways of achieving a reasonable return on investment, including advice on relevant technical and managerial matters.

d) The Bank also provides full merchant banking services and functions as a member of the Lagos Stock Exchange.

ii) The services provided by the Federal Mortgage Bank are:

a) Long-term credit facilities to other mortgage institutions in the country at such a rate and upon such terms as may be determined by the Board.

b) Promoting the development of mortgage institutions at state and national level and supervising the activities of such institutions.

c) Providing credit facilities to commercial property developers, estate developers, etc.

d) Providing loans to Nigerians for either the construction or purchase of residential house, development or property or for alteration/renovation. The Bank operates three types of loans:

1. Social loans — for private house owner-occupier buildings costing not more than ₦30,000.

2. Economic loans — for building construction where the cost is not less than ₦65,000 per unit.

3. Commercial loans — are available for all commercial ventures in the building and construction industry.

Answer 11.6

i) The National Provident Fund was established in 1961 by the Federal Government. Its resources are gathered from industrial and commercial companies which are legally required to make deductions from their staff and deposit the amounts deducted with the fund. The N.P.F. is the largest single fund in the country. The contributions received from employers are invested in government stocks.

ii) Most large companies operate pension schemes for their staff. Each member of staff contributes a small portion of his/her salary every month, while the employer also sets aside a certain amount as provision for staff pension expenses. The Pension Fund Act in Nigeria stipulates that pension scheme funds must be invested in the ratio of 50:50 in government and private stocks. Thus, pension funds constitute another reliable source of finance for industry.

Answer 11.7

Commercial and merchant banks in Nigeria are required to channel a minimum of 8% and 5% respectively of their total loans and advances to the agricultural sector. Stiff penalties are imposed on banks that fail to meet this requirement. As this percentage even when achieved by banks is not adequate, a study was commissioned by the Federal Government and the Central Bank for the purpose of identifying the problems in agricultural finance in Nigeria.

The following problems were identified:

i)   The absence of clear title to land.

ii) The absence of acceptable security.

iii) The high cost of lending to many small farmers and the associated high bad debts provision.

iv) The inherent risks of crop failures.

v)   The long-term nature of the finance required.

It was recommended that a Credit Guarantee scheme should be introduced by the Government and the Central Bank to under-write the (often-feared) credit risks and to minimise the problem of lack of collateral securities. To this end a Fund was established by the Federal Government under the Agricultural Credit Guarantee Scheme Fund Act, 1977 with initial capital of ₦100 million subscribed to by the Federal Government (60%) and the Central Bank of Nigeria (40%).

The objective of the Scheme as stated in the Act, is to provide *"guarantees in respect of loans granted for agricultural purposes by any bank in accordance with the provisions of the Act"* in order to increase bank credit to the agricultural sector. The Act went on to define agricultural purposes as those projects connected with the establishment or management of plantations for the production of rubber, oil palm and similar crops, the cultivation of cereal crops, animal husbandry, including cattle rearing and poultry and fish farming.

To protect banks against diversion of funds, the Act provides that where loans are granted to purchase livestock, farm machinery and equipment, the loan should be paid direct to the supplier who must furnish the bank with evidence of delivery.

At present, the maximum liability of the Fund in respect of any guarantee given is 75% of the approved loan. The maximum loan that can be granted is restricted as follows:

i) to individuals: ₦50,000 maximum; and,

ii) to co-operative societies and corporate bodies: ₦1 million maximum.

The Fund is managed by a Board of Directors of six members. Two of the members represent the Central Bank, while the remaining 4 are appointed by the Government — one each from the Federal Ministry of Finance and the Federal Ministry of Agriculture & Water Resources, plus two non-government officials, one of whom is Chairman of the Board.

CHAPTER TWELVE

BANKING LEGISLATION SINCE 1952

Answer 12.1

Licensing. The licensing of banks which was first introduced in 1952 was continued in 1969. Only companies holding valid licences granted by the Federal Minister of Finance can operate as banks in Nigeria. Applications in writing, with copies of the company's Memorandum and Articles of Association, together with a copy of the start-up **Balance Sheet** of the company must be filed at the Central Bank of Nigeria for processing and onward transmission to the Federal Minister of Finance.

Minimum Paid-Up Capital. The minimum paid-up capital was fixed at ₦600,000 for wholly owned Nigerian banks and ₦1,500,000 for banks with foreign interests. The aim was to curb the proliferation of both foreign and indigenous banks.

Statutory Reserve. The 1958 provisions regarding statutory reserves were retained in 1969. They provide that every licensed bank in Nigeria must maintain a reserve fund by transferring a minimum of 25% of its net profit before any dividend is declared to its statutory reserve. This transfer must be effected every financial year until the balance on the reserve fund becomes equal to the paid-up capital of the bank. Where the amount of the reserve fund is equal to or in excess of the paid-up share capital, 12½% of the net profits are to be transferred. However, no transfers are to be made until any past losses have been made good.

Cash Reserves and Liquidity Ratio. The Act states that the Central Bank shall from time to time stipulate the minimum holding by licensed banks of cash reserves, specified liquid assets, special deposits, and stabilisation securities. These ratios are specified every year in the Central Bank Monetary Policy Guidelines. In 1982, cash reserves ranged between 2% – 5%, depending on the size of the bank, while liquidity ratio stood at 25%.

Others. The Act also restricts the activities of banks in the following areas:

i) Authorised lending limit. The maximum lending to one borrower was fixed at 33⅓% of the sum of the paid-up capital and statutory reserves of the bank.

ii) A bank must not grant any advances, loans or credit facilities against the security of its own shares.

iii) A bank must not engage in wholesale or retail trade, except in the course of the satisfaction of a debt.

iv) No bank should own any subsidiary company which is not carrying on banking business, except a nominee company dealing in stocks and shares for, or on behalf of, the bank's customers or clients.

Answer 12.2

i) The Dishonoured Cheques (Offences) Act, 1977 was designed to protect businessmen and other individuals against the fraudulent use of cheques. The Act makes it an offence for any person anywhere in Nigeria to induce the delivery of valuable goods to himself or to pay any other person, or to purport to settle a lawful obligation by means of a cheque which, when presented within a reasonable time, is dishonoured on the grounds that no funds or insufficient funds were standing to the credit of the drawer of the cheque. Such offences are punishable by two years' imprisonment (without option of fine) in the case of individuals and a ₦5,000 fine in the case of a corporate body. Cheques must be presented within 3 months of the date of issue.

ii) The Banking (Amendment) Act, 1979 retained the capital requirement stipulated in 1969 (i.e. ₦600,000 for indigenous banks and ₦1,500,000 for banks with foreign interest). For the first time a minimum paid-up capital of ₦2,000,000 was stipulated for merchant banks.

The Central Bank was given authority to specify the minimum ratio which licensed banks should maintain between their respective paid-up capital plus reserves on the one hand and their loans and advances on the other.

For merchant banks the Central Bank also now has powers to specify the ratios of deposits and call money held for other banks to be retained in liquid assets and loans and advances to the bank's total assets as well as the total loans and advances that may be repayable within one year.

The Act stipulated that, except with the prior approval of the Central Bank, a bank which fails to maintain any ratio specified may not increase its loans and advances.

The Act restated the authorised lending limit of a commercial bank to be 33⅓% of the sum of the paid-up capital and statutory reserves and, in the case of a merchant bank, not more than the sum of its paid-up capital and statutory reserves.

On merchant banking, the following new restrictions were made in the Act. A merchant bank should not accept any deposits withdrawable by cheque except from its corporate clients nor accept from any depositor total interest-bearing deposits of an amount lower than ₦50,000. Furthermore, except with the prior approval of the Central Bank, a merchant bank may not hold for more than 6 months any equity interest acquired in a company while managing an equity issue.

CHAPTER THIRTEEN

BANKER/CUSTOMER RELATIONSHIP & RESPONSIBILITIES

Answer 13.1

The relationship between banker and customer is primarily that of debtor and creditor. For a person to become a customer, an account — current or deposit — must be opened with the bank. Normally, the banker is the debtor and the customer the creditor, but when a customer overdraws his account the roles are reversed (i.e. the banker becomes creditor, while the customer becomes the debtor).

A relationship of principal and agent exists when the banker is acting as a collecting bank in respect of cheques paid in by customers. There are other relationships like bailor/bailee, mortgagor/mortgagee, etc.

There are many duties owed by a banker to his customer. These include paying out money when cheques are presented up to the limit of the balance or any borrowing arrangement and to collect cheques for the customer's account as well as receiving cash paid in.

The banker's duty of secrecy is a very important obligation, as a breach gives a customer a claim to damages if he takes up the matter in a court of law. The banker must exercise extreme care in disclosing the balance on a customer's account, in answering requests for status reports from other banks and in giving other information about customers.

For his part, the customer is under a duty to exercise reasonable care when drawing his cheques so that the documents are not ambiguous or are drawn in such a way that facilitates unauthorised alteration by a third party.

Answer 13.2

The sole trader is a one-man business. The proprietor provides all the initial capital to start the business. Such businesses are, therefore, generally small as the owner has limited funds or capital.

The main advantages and disadvantages of this type of business are:

i) Advantages:

a) The owner has independence — he can run the business the way he likes without consulting anybody.

b) Customers can receive personal attention and good service.

c) Employees are personally known and supervised, thus ensuring effective operations.

d) The business is easy to establish, especially if the owner is using his personal name. However, if a business name is to be used, then the name must be duly registered and a Certificate of Registration issued by the Registrar of Business Names.

ii) Disadvantages

a) The owner has unlimited liability for the debts of the business. This means that if the business should become bankrupt, the owner's personal assets may be used to pay his creditors.

b) The owner has only a limited amount of capital, so expansion may be hampered.

c) Long hours have to be worked and holidays often cannot be taken as this could mean closing the business. Similarly, should the owner go sick, the business may slow down or stop operations altogether.

CHAPTER FOURTEEN

GENERAL BANKING SERVICES

Answer 14.1

There are three methods of payment available to the customer in Kano, an importer of goods from Japan. The type of method adopted will depend on the arrangement made with the exporter who normally dictates the mode of payment acceptable to him.

The three methods commonly used are:

i) Open Account.

ii) Bill for Collection.

iii) Documentary Credit or Letter of Credit.

These methods will now be examined in more detail.

i) Open Account

This is an arrangement between the exporter (seller) and the importer (buyer) which allows the buyer to settle his debts with the seller at a pre-determined future date, say a month or two months, after each shipment. In the meantime, the goods and shipping documents are despatched directly to the buyer (importer), so that he can take delivery of the goods and sell them.

Certain risks are inherent in this method of payment. These include buyer's default, the possibility of that the Federal Government of Nigeria will impose regulations deferring or blocking the transfer of funds and the lack of control over the documents and the goods by the Japanese exporter (seller). In the light of these inherent risks, it is most unlikely that the Japanese exporter will agree to ship on open account.

In this type of transaction, the credit worthiness of the importer (the Kano customer) must not be in doubt and, for the above reasons, this method of payment is unlikely to be available to an importer who is just developing a trading relationship with an exporter.

ii) Bills for Collection

The Japanese exporter will draw a bill of exchange on the importer (the Kano customer) with or without documents attached and give these to his banker in Tokyo with appropriate collection instructions. The Tokyo bank will use the services of a correspondent bank in Kano or Lagos to call upon the Kano importer to make payment on the due

413

date. When the importer pays, the funds are transferred to the Toyko bank which then credits its customer's account. In this transaction it is assumed that all exchange control regulations of Nigeria have been observed.

In some cases the Japanese exporter may forward the bill of exchange direct to the buyer in Kano for acceptance. After which the accepted bill is returned to the seller. The seller then attaches the necessary documents to the bill and submits them to his bankers to forward to Kano for payment.

This method of payment provides protection to the seller and is less risky than the open account method.

iii) Documentary Credit or Letter of Credit

This is by far the most acceptable mode of payment in international trade. Assuming that the Japanese company has asked for a documentary credit, the Kano importer will instruct his bankers to open a letter of credit in favour of the Japanese exporter. He will list all the conditions that must be fulfilled and the documents that must be submitted before payment can be made. Usually, the documents called for are the bill of lading, certificates of value and origin, commercial invoices and the insurance certificate. (In Nigeria, insurance must be effected locally, so insurance certificates are not required.)

After the opening of the letter of credit, the exporter's bank in Tokyo or our correspondent bank is advised. The exporter is then advised of the terms of the credit. The Japanese exporter would prefer to see that a bank in Japan adds its confirmation to the credit (i.e. its own undertaking to pay if all conditions are fulfilled).

As soon as the Japanese exporter ships the goods, he can present the documents to the bank in Tokyo and will receive payment. The documents are then forwarded to Nigeria (Kano) for payment.

Answer 14.2

i) Status Inquiry/Report

Frequently customers give their banker's name as a reference. This consists of a short report on a customer's financial standing and is given mainly to another bank or to the Federal or State Governments in respect of contractors. On the face of it, bank replies appear meaningless to the layman, but they mean a great deal to the bank receiving the report. A typical reply may read 'considered good for your figures and purpose' (a favourable reply) or 'we cannot speak for your figures' (an unfavourable reply).

ii) Open Credits/Cashing Credits

This service is provided by a few commercial banks in Nigeria. When customer is travelling to another town to do business which will necessitate his staying there for some time, he can request his bank to provide a cashing facility for him at the new town. The bank authorises its branch there to honour all cheques by the customer up to a specified limit. The specimen signature of the customer is sent to the branch concerned. The arrangement can also be made with a branch of another bank.

Answer 14.3.

Special services provided by commercial banks in Nigeria which are likely to be of interest to personal customers include open/cashing credits, services to the traveller, safe custody and status inquiries. These are in addition to the normal banking services provided by all banks which include facilities for current accounts, savings and deposit accounts, loan accounts and overdrafts. Open/cashing credits and status inquiries were discussed in Answer 14.2 above. The other special services are discussed below.

i) Services to the traveller

a) Travellers cheques. All banks in Nigeria offer this service. Travellers cheques are a form of travel currency giving the holder the security of a letter of credit and the convenience of a local currency. They are issued in several denominations of the currency and are encashable at banks abroad. They are also generally acceptable in hotels and departmental stores etc. They can be denominated in several foreign currencies, but in Nigeria they are generally in dollars or pounds sterling. The holder signs the cheque on issue; when they are to be cashed he countersigns them in the presence of the cashier who compares the signatures before effecting payment.

b) Foreign Currency. Foreign currency notes, especially pounds sterling and dollars, are available in limited quantities from all banks in Nigeria. It must, however, be noted that Nigeria has stringent exchange control regulations which limit the amount of foreign currency and travellers' cheques that can be obtained. Also applications must be submitted and approved prior to the purchase.

ii) Safe Custody

Customers may also keep their valuable articles in the strongrooms of banks for safety reasons. Articles and documents that may be kept in bank strongrooms include government stocks and company share certificates, life assurance policies, certificates of occupancy (i.e official title to landed property), deeds of conveyance, wills and jewellery. Articles can either be deposited in sealed boxes or envelopes with the contents unknown to bank officials or made 'open' when the articles are listed and signed for.

CHAPTER FIFTEEN

BANK LENDING I — BASIC PRINCIPLES

Answer 15.1

i) The three main requirements of any security in order to make it acceptable to a lending banker are:

a) It must be easy to value.

b) Transfer of title must be easy.

c) It must be readily realisable or marketable.

Security may be either direct or collateral. When a customer secures his loan with his own assets, he has given direct security, but when the loan is secured by another person it is called collateral security.

ii) There are four ways in which security can be taken:

a) By lien.

b) By pledge.

c) By mortgage.

d) By assignment.

a) Lien. The borrower remains the owner of the property, but the creditor is in actual or constructive possession of the property. The creditor has no right to sell it, but only a right to retain it.

b) Pledge. The pledgee (creditor) is entitled to the exclusive possession of the property until the debt is repaid. In certain circumstances he can sell. However, the ownership remains with the pledgor subject to the pledgee's rights. Thus, a pledge gives a special property in the thing pledged.

c) Mortgage. In a legal mortgage a special interest in the property passes conditionally to the mortgagee who also has a right of sale, but not necessarily the possession of the property, which usually remains with the mortgagor. Under an equitable mortgage, the bank only establishes a right on the asset, but cannot sell it.

While it is advisable to take a legal mortgage, most banks relax the rules in some cases by taking an equitable mortgage, especially on stocks and shares. In such cases, the transfer forms are duly signed in blank which, when completed, become a legal mortgage.

417

Briefly, a mortgage is the conveyance or transfer of an interest in land or other assets as security for a debt.

d) Assignment. The difference between a mortgage and an assignment transfers rights under contracts. For example, under a

contract of life assurance, the insured or beneficiary has a right to receive a sum of money at maturity or death. It is this right that is assigned to the bank when an assignment is effected.

Answer 15.2

i) A second mortgage is a mortgage of a property already once charged by way of security. This means that a property already mortgaged is again mortgaged to a new lender who ranks after the first mortgagee in respect of any proceeds of sale. In the case of a second mortgage, the original borrower borrows from a new lender.

A sub-mortgage is a mortgage by a lender who is himself a mortgagee. To secure his borrowing, he charges the loan he has made and security he has taken to a third party from whom he borrows. This is otherwise called a mortgage of a mortgage. Thus, the original lender has become a borrower.

ii) Banks usually appoint outside attorneys (lawyers) to determine the ownership of the property. Searches are conducted at the Land Registry and the Ministry of Lands and Surveys. After ascertaining the genuines of the title documents, then the customer is asked to complete the bank's forms of charge. Thereafter, the customer should seek the consent of the Governor of the State where the property is located to mortgage or assign the property to the bank as required by law.

Following the execution of the charge forms and the grant of the Governor's consent, the forms must be stamped within 30 days. The stamp duty is at the rate of 75k for every ₦200 in the case of legal mortgages and 35k for every ₦200 in the case of equitable mortgages, payable to the Commissioner for Stamp Duty. After stamping, registration must also be effected within 30 days at the Land Registry of the State where the property is located.

Answer 15.3

Normally there are four remedies available to a mortgagee of land. These are:

i) The sale of the property.

ii) The appointment of a receiver to collect rents on behalf of the mortgagee.

iii) Foreclosure which means the mortgagee becomes the absolute owner of the property.

iv) Taking possession of the property.

Out of these four remedies, the two most frequently used are the sale of the property and the appointment of a receiver.

CHAPTER SIXTEEN

BANK LENDING II - FINANCIAL STATEMENT ANALYSIS AND INTERPRETATION

Answer 16.1

i)

	1982	1983
a)	9.7%	10.2%
b)	5.3%	5.7%
c)	3.2:1	2.5:1
d)	1.2:1	1:1
e)	3.6 times	3.7 times
f)	54.7 days	58.4 days
g)	35 days	41 days
h)	1.1:1	0.7:1

Comments

The above ratios and percentages reveal that Gama Ltd. (our hypo-thetical company) is an efficiently managed and profitable venture, with a healthy growth in sales and profits during the two years under consideration.

It had a current or working capital ratio of 3.2:1 in 1982 and 2.5:1 in 1983. This indicates the ability of the company to meet its immediate obligations from short-term assets.

The company's liquidity position is also adequate with a ratio of 1.2:1 in 1982 and 1:1 in 1983. These ratios indicate that the company has enough liquid assets/cash to pay its creditors.

Similarly, there is a reasonable turnover of stock. The collection period for credit sales and the period for which the company's creditors remain unpaid appear reasonable. Finally, the leverage is relatively low.

Therefore, based on these figures, Gama Ltd. appears to be in a healthy state and a request for credit facilities should receive favourable consideration if other conditions are met.

ii) Every company must maintain a reasonable working capital in order to operate efficiently. This is the only way the company is able to pay its creditors, hold sufficient stocks for its day-to-day operations and allow sufficient time for payment. When a company expands, its need for working capital increases. A working capital ratio of 2:1 is generally regarded as satisfactory. This indicates the ability of a business to meet its immediate obligations from short term assets and proves that the company is solvent.

Working capital is the difference between current assets and current liabilities. The working capital ratio is calculated as follows:

$$\frac{\text{Current Assets}}{\text{Current Liabilities}} = \text{Working Capital}$$

Answer 16.2

i) Intangible assets are assets like patents, trade marks or goodwill; while fictitious assets are those relating to preliminary expenses incurred in the course of forming a new company. Intangible assets may turn out to be very valuable assets. Fictitious assets, however, have no value and are usually written off.

ii) Floating assets are the current assets of a company. They are also called 'circulating' assets. They include stock (inventory), debtors (receivables) and cash at bank and in hand. These assets are called floating or circulating, because they are changing and are being turned over from day-to-day. They are acquired purposely either to be resold or so that they may pass through manufacturing processes before they are sold for cash.

Answer 16.3

When a banker is faced with a mass of figures as usually contained in a Balance Sheet and other statements submitted by a customer, he should 'spread' the statements. This will facilitate the exercise of extracting relevant figures and information from the accounts. Calculation of the ratios is a relatively easy and straightforward task, but the real skill in financial analysis is in the ability to select ratios most appropriate under certain circumstances and subsequently in the interpretation of the position which they reveal.

A lending banker will normally examine the following major areas when analysing a set of accounts submitted by a customer:

i) Shareholders' stake and the percentage return on capital employed. This percentage measures the efficiency and profitability of the company. A fall in the percentage from year to year shows that the business is not using its capital efficiently and effectively. The calculation is made as follows:

$$\frac{\text{Net Profit Before Tax}}{\text{Shareholders' stake \& Long-term Loans (if any)}} \times \frac{100}{1}\,\%$$

ii) Long-term Loans. The bank should probe into these items whenever they are shown on a customer's Balance Sheet. When are they due for repayment? Are they secured on the company's assets and, if so, which assets? If the loans are from the company's directors, are they prepared to sign a subordination agreement with the bank? This means that the loans will rank after any facility granted by the bank and cannot be repaid until the bank loans have been fully liquidated.

iii) Working Capital. For any company to continue operating as a going concern, it must maintain reasonable working capital. Sufficient working capital ensures that the business is able to pay its creditors without strain, maintains reasonable stocks and allow its debtors some time for payment.

The amount of working capital may be calculated as follows:

Working capital = Current Assets — Current Liabilities

However the working capital ratio or current ratio is calculated as follows:

$$\text{Current Ratio} = \frac{\text{Current Assets}}{\text{Current Liabilities}}$$

A current ratio of 2:1 is usually regarded as satisfactory. This indicates the ability of a business to meet its immediate obligations from short-term assets, since for every ₦100 of current liabilities there are ₦200 of current assets.

iv) Liquidity. This indicates the relative amount of assets in cash or which can be quickly converted into cash which would be available to meet short-term liabilities. Liquid assets consist of cash, bank balances, debtors and marketable securities. Stock is not usually regarded as a liquid asset, because it has to be converted into debtors before it becomes cash. So, if the bulk of the current assets are in the form of slow moving stock which is generally sold on credit, the company will most probably have liquidity problems. Future liquidity should also be given some attention in order to determine the ability of the company to service its debts.

This ratio is calculated as follows:

$$\frac{\text{Current Assets (excluding inventories or stocks)}}{\text{Current Liabilities.}}$$

A liquid ratio of 1:1 is regarded as reasonable. it ramains that the business, without selling its stocks, could cover its current liabilities. A ratio of 1.5:1 is even better, but if it is higher it may be an indication that too much is tied up in debtors and the bank (i.e. idle money that is not working for the business).

v) Gearing or Leverage or Debt/Worth Ratio. The lending banker must also test the gearing or leverage of the company, as it indicates the degree of vulnerability of earnings for ordinary shareholders and also compares the shareholders' stake in the business with the amount of external finance.

It is believed that a gearing greater than 1:1 is high, while less than 1:1 is low. In practice, however, greater than 0.6:1 is regarded as high and less than 0.2:1 is low, with the range between these extremes being regarded as relatively high or relatively low. There is no optimum gearing as such.

vi) Trading Figures. These should also be critically evaluated. The figures for a number of years (say, 3 years) should be compared and large fluctuations noted. The debtors' accounts should be carefully scrutinised. Are there just a few hard-core debtors or are they spread over a fairly large number of small debtors? Are the stocks moving fast enough? Is there any obsolete stock? Has an excessive amount of stock been consigned to customers? Is stock turnover in line with turnover for other businesses in the same industry? Or is money being tied up too long in stocks? Are creditors waiting too long for their money? Probing further into debtors: Are there indications that some of the debtors have already been pledged to another creditor? What is the turnover of debtors? Have adequate reserves been set up to cover doubtful accounts?

The following calculations will be helpful:

a) How many times have trade debtors been turned over during the period?

b) How long have debts remained uncollected?

c) How long have creditors remained unpaid? The following percentages should also be calculated to determine efficiency and profitability:

$$\text{Gross Profit percentage} = \frac{\text{Gross Profit}}{\text{Sales}} \times \frac{100}{1}$$

$$\text{Net Profit percentage} = \frac{\text{Net Profit}}{\text{Sales}} \times \frac{100}{1}$$

vii) Other Items. Finally, the banker must always use his initiative to bring out any other salient points in his customer accounts. Any significant changes from one year to the other must be closely examined.

The ratios specifically mentioned above are only a guide. Any other ratios or percentage may be used if useful information can be derived from the results.

Answer 16.4

This seems to be a highly successful and profitable business. As overdraft facilities have been granted in the past, it is likely that the bank has copies of earlier sets of accounts so that comparisons may be made.

i) Shareholders' stake. The balance of the Profit and Loss Account tells us that profits are being retained in the business. The shareholders' stake is ₦160,000 out of total assets of ₦185,000, so the shareholders are financing 86% of the total assets — a very healthy position from the point of view of the lending banker. The return on capital employed is:

$$\frac{₦20,000}{₦160,000 + ₦10,000 \text{ (long-term loans)}} \times \frac{100}{1} = 11.76\%$$

This seems generally satisfactory and could be compared with the return calculated from previous sets of accounts.

ii) Long-term loans. These are from directors and, as liabilities are low in comparison with assets, it hardly seems appropriate to ask for a subordination agreement.

iii) Working capital. The working capital is ₦14,000 (₦29,000 − ₦15,000) and, as a ratio, is 1.93:1 which seems satisfactory. If the overdraft facility of ₦10,000 was granted the total of current liabilities would increase but, equally, there would be an increase in stocks to compensate, although £3,000 of the advance would be spent on extensions to one shop and this will be reflected in an increase in the fixed assets. Overall there would be a reduction in the current ratio, but it would not be too severe.

iv) Liquidity. The liquid capital (working capital less stocks), is *minus* ₦9,000. As a ratio, this is 0.4:1. This is not such a good position and could indicate that the company would have difficulty in paying its way if a major creditor demanded repayment. A low current ratio is not unusual for the retail trade where most sales are made on a cash basis (confirmed by the low figure for debtors) and with sales of ₦143,000 per year or ₦2,750 each week, it would not take long to raise the money through sales to pay creditors.

v) Trading figures. The credit period being taken by the company is just over four weeks ((₦8,000 ÷ ₦100,000) x 52). This seems quite a short period of time and indicates that the business pays its bills promptly.

Without knowing the amount of credit sales made by the company during the year, the period of credit being allowed to debtors cannot be calculated.

To calculate the stock turnover requires the figure for cost of goods sold, which may be found by deducting the gross profit from sales. This gives ₦97,000. The closing stock is ₦23,000 and the opening stock for the year is ₦20,000 (found by constructing a trading account). Thus, the average stock is ₦21,500 and, therefore, the stock turnover is approximately 4.5 times per year, which means that the stock remains in the shops for just over eleven weeks before being sold and replaced. For the type of business, this seems to be perfectly satisfactory.

The gross profit percentage is 32% which seems satisfactory for the trade. The net profit percentage is 14%.

The figures calculated in this section can be compared with those for previous years and any major changes could be taken up with the directors.

vi) Other items. Inevitably, before making the decision about granting the facilities, the manager will consider the previous conduct of the account (we are told that previous overdrafts have been satisfactorily cleared) and the ability of the directors. From the information given, they seem to be hard-working and prepared to plough profits back into the business.

A further point is the consideration of security (if required) by the bank: the shop premises appear to provide an ideal form of security.

In conclusion, this would seem to be a good lending proposition and the facilities should be granted.

Answer 16.5

The company so far has been unprofitable in both years of trading. There is a net loss of ₦500 in the second year and, as the balance of the Profit and Loss Account of ₦1,000 is shown as a fictitious asset, there must also have been a net loss of ₦500 in year 1.

i) Shareholders' stake. Although there is the issued share capital of ₦1,000, this is cancelled out by the debit balance on the Profit and Loss Account, so the shareholders' stake is nil. As the company has made a loss for the year there is no return on capital employed.

ii) Long-term loans. The assets of the business are partly financed by loans from directors. If any lending is to be considered a subordination agreement would be essential.

iii) Working capital. There is a deficit of working capital of ₦250 and the current ratio is 0.92:1 — hardly a satisfactory position. Granting the proposed overdraft would make the matter even worse.

iv) Liquidity. If there is a lack of working capital, there is an even greater lack of liquid capital — a deficit of ₦1,850 — and a liquid ratio of 0.45. The ratio might not be too bad if there was a substantial element of cash sales but, in selling to shops and boutiques, the company has to allow credit and there will be a time lag between making the sale and receiving the cash.

v) Trading figures. The credit period being taken by the company is nearly twenty weeks.

Debtors, on the other hand, pay their accounts in just under eight weeks; this seems to be a satisfactory figure.

As this is a manufacturing business stock turnover is difficult to calculate on the information given; in order to reach a figure we would need to know the details of the costs of manufacture, such as the wages paid to outworkers.

The gross profit percentage is 10% and there is a net loss of 5% of sales. The percentage gross profit figure is rather low and a suggestion might be made that the selling prices could be increased without jeopardising sales.

vi) Other items. If the bank lent the money as proposed, the company's Balance Sheet would be in an even worse state than it is now. There would also be the additional costs of bank interest which, depending on interest rates and the amount the facility is used, would probably amount to approximately ₦1,000 per year. There is no source of repayment apart from possible future trading profits and there is no security, apart from the possibility of taking directors' personal guarantees.

This is probably the type of business that could be made profitable if it operates in a small way and puts up its selling prices, but to consider expanding by renting a factory would seem to be foolhardy. The request should be turned down and steps taken to get the bank account into credit as soon as possible.

CHAPTER SEVENTEEN

BILLS OF EXCHANGE & CHEQUES

Answer 17.1

The Bills of Exchange Act 1882 defines the 'bearer' as the person in possession of a cheque which is payable to bearer. A cheque is payable to bearer which is expressed to be so payable, or on which the only or last endorsement is an endorsement in blank. A cheque payable to bearer need not be endorsed. Any holder may alter a bearer cheque to an order cheque by striking out the word 'bearer'. He may or may not substitute the word 'order'. This is not treated as a material alteration and need not be initialled or signed.

A cheque is payable to order which is expressed to be so payable, or which is expressed to be payable to a particular person and does not contain words prohibiting transfer or indicating an intention that it should not be transferable. A cheque payable to order should be endorsed by the person to whom it is payable.

A 'not negotiable' crossing deprives a cheque of its negotiability, but not its transferability. A person taking such a cheque shall not have, and shall not be capable of, giving a better title to the cheque than that which the transferor had. For example, if an accounts clerk took a signed blank cheque from his employer which was already crossed 'not negotiable' and fraudulently made it payable to Tana, the employer will successfully recover the value of the cheque from Tana, since the clerk had no title to the cheque and Tana would get no better title because of the crossing.

Answer 17.2

By drawing the bill, D undertakes that it will be paid on presentation, provided that notice and other formalities consequent upon dishonour are observed. However, since T has not signed the bill he is not liable to the holder P. Therefore, P can sue D, the drawer, who is liable to the holder P.

Answer 17.3

A holder in due course is a holder who has taken a bill, complete and regular on the face of it, under the following conditions:

i)   That he became the holder of it before it was overdue and without notice that it had been previously dishonoured, if such was the fact; or,

ii) That he took the bill in good faith and for value, and that at the time the bill was negotiated to him he had no notice of any defect in the title of the person who negotiated it.

Answer 17.4

The main grounds of discharge of a bill are payment, merger, waiver, cancellation and alteration.

i) Payment

A bill is discharged by payment in due course by, or on behalf of, the drawee or acceptor. Payment in due course means payment made at or after the maturity of the bill to the holder in good faith and without notice that his title to the bill is defective.

ii) Merger.

An example of discharge by merger is where the acceptor becomes the holder of a bill at or after maturity in his own right (i.e. he becomes the owner of a bill on which he is liable).

iii) Waiver

A bill is discharged by waiver when the holder at or after maturity renounces his rights against the acceptor unconditionally. The renunciation must be in writing unless the bill is surrendered to the acceptor.

iv) Cancellation

Where a bill is cancelled by the holder or his agent and the cancellation is apparent thereon, the bill is discharged. An unintentional, mistaken or unauthorised cancellation is inoperative.

v) Alteration

Where a material alteration has been made to a bill (e.g. change of the date, or the amount payable) without the assent of all parties liable on the bill, then all parties prior to the alteration are discharged, but not those liable by negotiation after the alteration.

Answer 17.5

i) The holder is the payee or endorsee of a bill or note who is in possession of it, or the bearer. A wrongful possessor is someone who holds under a forgery or as a result of his obtaining it by fraud.

ii) Section 27 of the Bills of Exchange Act provides that a 'holder for value' is one who holds a bill for which value has at any time been given (i.e. by the holder or by some other person). Where the holder of a bill has a lien on it, he is deemed to be a holder for value to the extent of the sum for which he has a lien.

Section 29 (1) provides that a 'holder in due course' is a holder who has taken a bill complete and regular on the face of it, under the following conditions:

a) That he became the holder of it before it was overdue and without notice that it had been previously dishonoured, if such was the fact; and,

b) that he took the bill in good faith and for value and that, at the time the bill was negotiated to him, he had no notice of any defect in the title of the person who negotiated it.

Answer 17.6

Mrs Adama will be advised to use crossed cheques for the following reasons.

A crossed cheque cannot be cashed at a bank, but must be paid in for the credit of an account. Thus, crossed cheques are safer to handle than open cheques. A thief who has stolen a crossed cheque cannot cash it. He will be compelled to pass the cheque through his account. As a result it will be easy to trace him. Even where the thief had endorsed the cheque fraudulently to a third party, the cheque must still pass through the account of the endorsee who should, therefore, be able to locate the thief. (In some exceptional cases a crossed cheque can be opened by the drawers of the cheque.)

There are two types of crossings: a general crossing and a special crossing. A cheque is specially crossed when, with or without the addition of two parallel lines, it bears across its face the addition of a banker's name. The cheque is then said to be crossed specially to that banker. Such cheques can only be paid into an account with the specified bank and, if indicated on the crossing, the specified branch.

Mrs Adama will be warned of the danger of using open cheques. Open cheques can be easily forged and cashed on the counter. The thief may never be traced. If made payable to bearer, no endorsements are required, so they can be easily converted.

CHAPTER EIGHTEEN

THE CHEQUES CLEARING SYSTEM

Answer 18.1

Let us assume that Ahmed, the drawer of the crossed order cheque is resident at Kano and banks with Bank of the North Ltd, Kano. Shade lives in Ibadan and banks with Savannah Bank of Nigeria Ltd, Ibadan. Ahmed sends the cheque by past to Shade at Ibadan. It took about one week for the cheque to get to Ibadan. Upon receipt of the cheque Shade went straight to her bankers — Savannah Bank, Ring Road Ibadan — to deposit the cheque in her account. Until the cheque is cleared, Shade cannot draw on it. Savannah Bank Ibadan would send the cheque to their Kano branch by post or courier service on a collection basis. Upon receipt of the cheque at Savannah Bank Kano, it is recorded in the Inwards Collections register and batched with cheques to be presented for clearing on the following day against Bank of North. If the cheque is not returned after four clearing sessions (four working days), it is deemed to have been paid, in accordance with Clearing House regulations. On the morning of the fifth day Inwards Collections Register at Savannah Bank Kano is marked off and a Settlement Letter prepared crediting Savannah Bank Ibadan with the proceeds of the cheque. If it was sent on a collection basis, then no entries will be raised when cheques are dishonoured. However, the dishonoured cheque will be returned with a covering memo.

Upon receipt of the credit advice, Ibadan branch of Savannah Bank removes the uncleared effects' tag on the account of Shade and allows her to draw the proceeds of the cheque.

Answer 18.2

The cheque will be listed with other cheques drawn on the bank. The cheque, along with other cheques and copies of machine lists, are later despatched to the Centralised Clearing Section at the bank's headquarters. Here, the cheques are consolidated and entered on presentation forms and taken to the Clearing House the following morning for presentation and collection of cheques drawn on Savannah Bank.

In accordance with Clearing House regulations, dishonoured cheques must be returned within four working days. On the morning of the fifth working day the cheque is deemed to have been paid, if notice of dishonour had not been received.

Answer 18.3

If a customer is in urgent need of funds and wants the proceeds of a cheque to be credited to his account on the same day or wants to know the fate of a cheque on the same day, he can ask his bank to send the cheque for special clearing or to arrange special presentation. In this case the branch sends the cheque direct to the drawee bank's branch through a messenger or clerk for payment. If the cheque is in order and paid, the drawee bank will debit its customer's account immediately and send a banker's payment to the presenting bank. Upon receipt of the banker's payment the account of the payee is credited with the proceeds of the cheque the same day. A fee is normally charged for this service, but as stated above, it enables the customer to know the fate of a cheque on the same day and to have immediate use of funds when in need.

Answer 18.4

There are 29 principal reasons for returning cheques unpaid, 10 of which are discussed below:

i) Refer to drawer. This is the accepted reason for returning cheques when there are insufficient funds on a customer's account. The customer should be fully protected by not disclosing any further details about the account and the meaning of 'refer to drawer' to the payee or holder of the cheque.

ii) Amounts in words and figures differ. Here, the customer's intention is not clear. In a case of this nature, a bank will be justified in taking the amount in words as the correct amount. It is, however, advisable that cheques drawn in such an irregular manner should not be paid. This is the only way the customer's interest can be protected.

iii) Amount in words required. As a protective measure, such cheques should not be paid in order to draw the customer's attention to this important omission.

iv) Material alteration requires drawer's confirmation. The customer should be fully protected here. Alterations in date or amounts are regarded as material alterations and must receive the drawer's confirmation.

v) Payment stopped. Countermand of payment can only be effectively made by the drawer, so that when a banker is informed by a holder that he has lost a cheque, he should request the holder at once to communicate with the drawer and obtain the latter's written instructions.

vi) Cheque mutilated. When a cheque is badly mutilated that may be a clear signal that the drawer intends to cancel it. Therefore, as a measure of protection of the drawer, such a cheque should not be paid until it is confirmed by the drawer or a replacement cheque issued.

vii) Drawer's signature required. If the drawer of a cheque has not signed it, then the cheque is not complete and regular on the face of it. A banker should not, under any circumstances, honour such an instrument.

viii) Signature differs. If the signature on a cheque differs from the specimen given by the customer, the cheque should not be paid as it may be a forgery.

ix) Second signature required. The omission of the second signature may not be a genuine mistake. It may be the result of a misunderstanding or dispute between the signatories. Until the mandate is changed, such a cheque must not be honoured.

x) Effects uncleared — present again. This serves mainly as a means of protection for the banker. If a customer is allowed to draw on 'uncleared effects', this may create an unauthorised overdraft on the account of the customer should the cheques represented by the 'uncleared effects' be returned unpaid.

CHAPTER NINETEEN

EXCHANGE CONTROL AND FOREIGN EXCHANGE SERVICES

Answer 19.1

All applications in respect of payments for imports into Nigeria must be supported with a Form M, irrespective of the value. A system of comprehensive import supervision or pre-shipment inspection of imports into Nigeria was introduced in 1978 to curb abuses in international trade transactions and to conserve the country's foreign exchange resources. The aim is to ensure that imports into Nigeria are of the correct quality and quantity as stipulated in contracts and that the prices are reasonable.

In pursuit of this objective the CBN appointed Societe Generale de Surveillance S. A (S.G.S) Geneva, Switzerland as its agent. Imports into Nigeria are subject to compulsory quality and quantity inspection and price comparison by S.G.S. before shipment can be effected from the country of origin.

Upon completion of inspection, S.G.S. issues a Report of Findings, which may be either:

i) a Clean Report of Findings, if the inspection yields a satisfactory

   result, or

ii) a Non-Negotiable Report of Findings, if the inspection reveals discrepancies.

No payment can be effected against a letter of credit, bills for collection, or any other form of claim unless the documents presented for payment include a Clean Report of Findings.

The use of Form M became effective in January 1979, when all importation of goods into Nigeria whether under letters of credit, bills for collection or any other form of payment became subject to Pre-Import Processing by the Exchange Control Department of the CBN. This means that the CBN's prior approval of Form M is a precondition for the importation of goods into the country.

A processed Form M by the CBN serves as authority to open a letter of credit. All goods whose value are below ₦5,000 (C & F) are exempted from the pre-shipment inspection.

Answer 19.2

i) A Nigerian resident wishing to travel abroad is entitled to Basic Travel Allowance of ₦500 (1982) once a year. In 1982 the allowance for children under the age of 16 was suspended. Pilgrims are allowed ₦800.

The traveller may apply to an Authorised Dealer (a commercial or merchant bank) for the amount to be converted to foreign exchange by completing Form A in duplicate. Foreign exchange will usually be provided in the form of travellers' cheques or foreign currency notes.

The Nigerian Exchange Control regulations permit Authorised Dealers to approve applications for Basic Travel Allowance for all residents, excluding merchant seamen, civil airline officials resident in Nigeria and emigrants.

The following documents must be submitted before an application can be approved:

a) Completed Form A in duplicate.

b) Valid passport.

c) Travel ticket or evidence of travel.

d) Tax Clearance Certificate for the preceding three years or Form H2 (issued by the applicant's employer).

The amounts obtained by foreign nationals constitute part of their 50% permissible home remittances. The amount is usually marked on the passport of the traveller to curb abuse.

ii) Cash gifts are remittances by individuals and organisations resident in Nigeria on compassionate grounds to a foreign country. This must represent gifts as opposed to the settlement of liabilities.

Applications on Form A should be forwarded to the Central Bank through Authorised Dealers. Donations not exceeding the equivalent of ₦500 and ₦150 may be made to charitable organisations and individuals respectively during any fiscal year. Individual applications exceeding this amount would be treated on their merit.

Answer 19.3

For all shipments of goods from Nigeria Froms N.C.D 3 (non-commercial or N.C.D 3 (A) (commercial) must be completed. An export licence must be obtained. The completed form with the export license must be submitted to the Customs & Excise at the time the goods are entered for export. Page 5 of the N.C.D 3 (A) form is eventually forwarded to the Central Bank through an Authorised Dealer. Customs & Excise also forward the remaining forms to the Central Bank which, in the case of commercial exports, retains pages 1 and 2 while page 3 is despatched to the Authorised Dealer named in the form for certification. The form N.C.D 3 covering non-commercial exports is retained by the Central Bank of Nigeria for record purposes.

Eventually when payment is received by the Authorised Dealer, the forms are certified as to the amount of foreign currency received and sent to the Central Bank.

Exported goods must be paid for immediately or within 3 months from the date of export or such other periods as the Federal Minister of Finance may direct.

Answer 19.4

i) Foreign nationals resident in Nigeria are allowed to remit 50% of their net income outside Nigeria for family maintenance. Female foreign nationals married to Nigerians and naturalised alliens may be allowed only 25% of the net annual income in any fiscal year for the maintenance of their parents upon request.

The following documents must be attached to an application:

a) Tax deduction card or tax assessment notice and tax receipt for the relevant period, certified and signed by an authorised signatory of the Inland Revenue office.

b) A duly completed P.H.R Form (Particulars for Home Remittance Form).

c) Details of total remittance made outside Nigeria since January of the current or previous financial year, certified by the applicant's bankers, in respect of self-employed persons.

d) Photocopy of resident permit.

ii) Non-residents who wish to invest capital directly in Nigeria can apply to the Federal Ministry of Finance for 'Approved Status'. The granting of 'Approved Status' means that future requests for repatriation of capital directly invested in Nigeria to the extent of any distributions of a capital nature arising in respect of realisation thereof will receive sympathetic consideration.

The following guidelines apply to repatriation of proceeds of sale of shares under the Nigerian Enterprises Promotion Act, 1977:

a) Repatriation will be on an instalment basis, at the following rates:

1) amounts not exceeding ₦300,000 shall on approval be transferred once; while,

2) the excess over ₦300,000 shall be transferred at the rate of ₦300,000 every six months.

b) To qualify for repatriation as above, an application should be supported by documentary evidence of 'Approved Status' or evidence of capital importation.

c) On re-investment in Nigeria, enterprises already enjoying 'Approved Status' will have 'Approved Status' also conferred on their new investments.

d) All enterprises that cannot produce evidence of 'Approved Status' would, on reinvesting not less than 50% of the proceeds of the sale of their shares in new enterprises, qualify for the transfer of dividends for both their old and new investment, thus rationalising their position.

The concession in respect of 'Approved Status' will not apply to the purchases of shares in any Stock Exchange which may be established in Nigeria unless this forms an integral part of the approved investment project. Applications should be submitted to the Federal ministry of Finance by letter containing full information of the proposed investment.

CHAPTER TWENTY

THE NIGERIAN MONEY MARKET

Answer 20.1

i) Treasury Bills are government securities which were first issued by the Central Bank of Nigeria in 1960. They were issued by tender in multiples of ₦1,000 on a monthly basis, until 1963 when weekly issues were introduced. The Bills are still issued in multiples of ₦1,000 every week, with 90-91 days maturity, at a fixed rate of discount. In 1982 the discount rate ranged between 6% and 8%. In November 1982 it stood at 7%.

Advertisements are inserted every week in local newspapers requesting prospective investors to send their applications through licensed commercial or merchant banks to CBN branches by the following Monday. Allotments are made on Thursdays. The Bills are mostly held by banks and other financial institutions mainly because they meet all the requirements of liquid assets, even though the returns on them are relatively low.

ii) Treasury Certificates are another money market instrument which was introduced by Central Bank in 1968. Their maturity ranges from 1 year to 2 years. They have the same attribute of liquidity as Treasury Bills and were introduced mainly to widen the range of maturities of short-term securities and to increase the amount of funds available to the Federal Government.

Answer 20.2

The Lagos Money Market provides the means by which the supply and demand for short-term funds are matched with one another. The main operators on the market are the Central Bank, commercial banks, merchant banks and other financial institutions.

The Lagos Money Market started to function in 1959 after the establishment of the Central Bank. It brings together those financial institutions with surplus funds which they wish to lend on short-term basis and those wishing to borrow. It has no fixed place for transacting business like the capital market, but operates by means of telephone or personal contact, although the Central Bank serves as the central point where transactions are effected after a deal is struck.

To aid the development of the market, the Central Bank introduced Treasury Bills in 1960 and Treasury Certificates in 1968. These are short-term government debt instruments in which banks can invest their surplus funds. Treasury Bills have a tenure of 91 days while Treasury Certificates are issued for 1 - 2 years. Other money market instruments apart from Treasury Bills and Certificates include development stocks maturing within three years, commercial bills, Certificates of Deposit maturing within 18 months, Bankers' Unit Fund and stabilisation securities.

The Call Money Scheme was also introduced in the early 1960's to provide banks with an outlet for the temporary or overnight investment of their surplus funds. This Scheme was initially managed by Central Bank, but due to shortage of government short-term debt instruments during the post Civil War era (1971-1974) of excess liquidity, the Scheme was abandoned in 1974. The commercial banks now operate a private call money scheme.

The Lagos Money Market is still in its embryo stage of development, so it is presently not fulfilling its role effectively.

CHAPTER TWENTY ONE

THE NIGERIAN CAPITAL MARKET

Answer 21.1

The main functions of the Nigerian Stock Exchange can be summarised as:

i) To provide a central meeting place for members to buy and sell existing stocks and shares and for granting quotations to new ones.

ii) To provide opportunities for raising new or fresh capital.

iii) To provide machinery for mobilising private and public savings and making these available for productive investment through stocks and shares.

iv) By facilitating the purchase and sale of securities to help reduce the risk of illiquidity. Ideally, this should encourage more investment in stocks and shares since investors are sure that in case of need they can realise their investments easily and in many cases at a profit in the Stock Exchange.

v) To act as a channel for implementing the indigenisation programme by providing facilities to foreign businesses to offer their shares to the Nigerian public for subscription.

vi) To provide opportunities for the continued operation and attraction of foreign capital for Nigeria's development.

vii)To facilitate dealings in government securities.

Answer 21.2

Dealing members on the Nigerian Stock Exchange are called stock-brokers in Nigeria. All dealings on the Exchange are handled by them. They deal directly with the public and also operate on the market, unlike in the London Stock Exchange where the broker can only operate on the market through a jobber who also cannot deal directly with the public.

Thus, a person who buys and sells securities on behalf of investors for a commission (i.e. a 'brokerage') is called a stockbroker. A jobber also buys and sells securities and makes profits on them; such gains are called "the jobber's turn".

On the London Stock Exchange, an investor must first approach a broker, who in turn will contact several jobbers to compare prices before striking a deal on behalf of his principal (the investor). As stated earlier on, there are no jobbers on the Nigerian Stock Exchange and all transactions are handled by brokers.

CHAPTER TWENTY TWO

THE NIGERIAN SECURITIES AND EXCHANGE COMMISSION

Answer 22.1

The Nigerian Securities and Exchange Commission is charged with the following responsibilities:

i) To register all securities which are to be offered for sale to, or for subscription by, the public or offered privately with the intention that they would be held ultimately other than by those to whom the offers were made.

ii) To maintain surveillance over the securities market so as to forestall, or take steps to reprimand or otherwise punish, anyone responsible for the creation or emergence of a false market in securities.

iii) To register Stock Exchange dealers, other dealers in securities and the agents of the latter with a view to maintaining proper standards of conduct and professionalism in the securities business.

iv) To act as the regulatory 'apex' organisation for the nation's Stock Exchanges to which it is at liberty to delegate a wide range of powers comparable to those delegated to, and the prerogative conferred on, any recognised Stock Exchange under the provisions of the Companies Act, 1968.

Other specific functions of the commission are to:

i) determine the amount of, and time at which, securities of a company are to be sold to the public either through offer for sale or subscription;

ii) protect the integrity of the securities market against any abuses arising from the practice of inside trading;

iii) create the necessary atmosphere for the orderly growth and development of the capital market; and,

iv) undertake such other activities as are necessary or expedient.

CHAPTER TWENTY THREE

INTERNATIONAL FINANCIAL SYSTEM

Answer 23.1

The International Bank for Reconstruction and Development, otherwise called The World Bank, has two affiliates — the International Development Association and the International Finance Corporation. The common objective of these institutions is to help raise the standards of living in developing countries by channelling financial resources from developed countries to the developing world. The main objectives of the Bank can be summarised as follows:

i) To make or guarantee loans for development projects in less developed countries either from its own capital or with borrowed funds on commercial terms.

ii) To provide technical assistance to the less-developed countries, which in most cases have no experts available in the field of investment projects.

The oldest of these three institutions is the International Bank for Reconstruction and Development (I.B.R.D.) popularly known as the World Bank. It came into existence in 1945 shortly after the War, mainly to encourage and assist in post-war reconstruction and the development of member countries. The Bank makes medium or long-term loans for this purpose and also promotes private foreign investment either by providing a guarantee or by providing part of the funds. The bulk of the assistance given by the World Bank went to the under-developed countries of the world for projects like dams, transport, electricity, water supply, irrigation and other agricultural developments.

The aim is to make these countries self-sufficient in food and to raise the standard of living of the people by providing them with essential amenities and the necessary infrastructure facilities for development.

Loans by the World Bank are closely tied to specific development projects which are carefully appraised by the Bank's technical experts. It lends mainly to governments or official government agencies. It may lend to private business enterprises if the Government of the country concerned guarantees the loan. The Bank's loans are made to finance only the foreign exchange costs of the projects and generally have a grace period of 5 years and are repayable over 20 years or less.

The Bank's sources of funds include capital contributions from member countries and income from the sale of its bonds on various national capital markets, particularly those of Britain and America.

The two affiliates mentioned earlier on — the International Finance Corporation (I.F.C.) and the International Development Association (I.D.A.) — were formed in order to expand the activities of the Bank. The I.F.C. invests in productive private enterprises in various ways, including equity participation and loan capital. The I.D.A. only makes loans, but it does so on easier terms where it is found that the country concerned cannot meet the commercial terms offered by the Bank. Thus, these two affiliates have less restrictive terms of reference than the World Bank itself and are able to render even more assistance to less-developed countries.

Answer 23.2

Special Drawing Rights are essentially a book-keeping transaction which create additional reserve assets for the use of member states of the International Monetary Fund. They were introduced in 1970 and are allotted to members in proportion to their quotas in the Fund. Rather than use currencies or gold for the settlement of debts, countries use their allocation of SDR's when they face balance of payments or reserve problems.

The value of an SDR used to be defined in terms of gold, but since 1974 it has been defined in terms of a basket of 16 national currencies, the weights in the basket being determined by the share of issuing countries in the world trade. The currencies in the basket can be changed from time to time and their weights altered, to reflect changes in the economic importance of the countries concerned. A country which has suffered severe balance of payments problems and is in urgent need of external assets to restore its balance of payments, can make use of SDR's to buy convertible currency from other participants in exchange. However, a country must maintain at least 15% of the amount of SDR's allotted to it as an average over a 5-year period. Also, an interest charge is levied on countries which have made use of SDR's and this is credited to countries which hold more than their cumulative allocation.

CHAPTER TWENTY FOUR

INTERNATIONAL FINANCIAL MARKETS

Answer 24.1

Euro-currency deposits are deposits with banks denominated in currencies other than that of the country in which the bank is located. For example, dollar balances deposited with commercial banks outside the U.S.A. (say, in London) and not exchanged into sterling, but remaining denominated in dollars, are called euro-dollar balances. The euro-currency market which began in early 1960 with dollar deposits in London has spread to other financial centres of the world like Singapore, the Caribbean, Tokyo and Bonn.

From fairly simple operations, the euro-currency market has grown to become virtually a complete financial system in its own right and many countries of the world now benefit from the services offered by these markets.

The euro-currency market deals with large balances (minimum one million dollars) deposited or lent for periods ranging from overnight to upwards of five years. The main use made of these short-term euro-dollar or euro-currency loans is the financing of international trade. In addition to financing of trade, governments have borrowed from the euro-currency markets for purposes of financing investment projects when internal resources are insufficient. For example, the Nigerian Government has benefitted from the euro-currency market by borrowing from the market in 1978 when bilateral arrangements failed.

Answer 24.1

Euro-currency deposits are deposits with banks denominated in currencies other than that of the country in which the bank is located. For example, dollar balances deposited with commercial banks outside the U.S.A. (say, in London) and not exchanged into sterling, but remaining denominated in dollars, are called euro-dollar balances. The euro-currency market which began in early 1960 with dollar deposits in London has spread to other financial centres of the world like Singapore, the Caribbean, Tokyo and Bonn.

From fairly simple operations, the euro-currency market has grown to become virtually a complete financial system in its own right and many countries of the world now benefit from the services offered by these markets.

The euro-currency market deals with large balances (minimum one million dollars) deposited or lent for periods ranging from overnight to upwards of five years. The main use made of these short-term euro-dollar or euro-currency loans is the financing of international trade. In addition to financing of trade, governments have borrowed from the euro-currency markets for purposes of financing investment projects when internal resources are insufficient. For example, the Nigerian Government has benefited from the euro-currency market by borrowing from the market in 1978 when bilateral arrangements failed.

CHAPTER TWENTY FIVE

THE AFRICAN DEVELOPMENT BANK AND OTHER AFRICAN REGIONAL/SUB REGIONAL GROUPINGS

Answer 25.1

The Association was established in December 1969 by the Governors of African Central Banks with the following objectives:

a) promotion of co-operation in the monetary, banking and financial sphere in the African region;

b) assisting in the formulation of guidelines along which agreements among African countries in the monetary and financial fields shall proceed; and,

c) helping to strengthen all efforts aimed at bringing about and maintaining monetary and financial stability in the region.

To achieve these objectives the Association aims to:

a) provide an avenue for regular meetings of Governors of African Central Banks, where ideas can be exchanged on monetary and banking matters;

b) facilitate the collection, pooling and dissemination of information on monetary, banking, financial and economic matters of interest to its members;

c) undertake the study of monetary and financial problems in the African Region; and,

d) organise seminars, courses and other training programmes for personnel of banking and financial institutions in the region.

The Association is now governed by an Assembly of Governors, comprising the Governors of Central Banks. There is an Executive Committee and a number of Sub-Regional Committees. There are four sub-regions — North, West, Central and East. The Assembly of Governors meet once in two years while the main Sub-Regional Committee consisting of the Chairman and Vice Chairman of the Association and the Chairman of each of the Sub-Regional Committees meet once a year.

Answer 25.7

The Association was established in December 1982 by the Governors of African Central Banks with the following objectives:

a) promotion of co-operation in the monetary banking and financial sphere in the African region.

b) assisting in the formulation of guidelines along which agreements among African countries in the monetary and financial fields shall proceed; and

c) helping to strengthen all efforts aimed at bringing about and maintaining monetary and financial stability in the region.

To achieve these objectives the Association aims to

a) provide an avenue for regular meetings of Governors of African Central Banks, where ideas can be exchanged on monetary and banking matters;

b) facilitate the collection, pooling and dissemination of information on monetary banking, financial and economic matters of interest to its members;

c) undertake the study of monetary and financial problems in the African Region; and

d) organise seminars, courses and other training programmes for personnel of banking and financial institutions in the region.

The Association is now governed by an Assembly of Governors comprising the Governors of Central Banks. There is an Executive Committee and a number of Sub-Regional Committees. There are four sub-regions — North, West, Central and East. The Assembly of Governors meet once in two years while the main Sub-Regional Committee consisting of the Chairman and Vice Chairman of the Association and the Chairman of each of the Sub-Regional Committees meet once a year.

CHAPTER TWENTY SIX

BANKING EDUCATION IN NIGERIA

Answer 26.1

The main functions of the Banker's Committee are:

i) The Committee being a recognised body representing all licensed banks in the country serves as an effective channel of communication between banks and the Federal Government or its regulatory agencies in the financial sector like the Federal Ministry of Finance and the Central Bank of Nigeria.

ii) The Committee makes proposals and suggestions every year to the Federal Government in the areas of banking, finance and the Nigerian economy for consideration by the authorities and possible inclusion in the budget plans.

iii) As banking has grown and diversified both nationally and internationally, the changes and developments in banking techniques, and the expansion of financial services all demand thorough training and professional approach. It has been discovered that the normal in-house training facilities provided by individual banks are becoming inadequate for their needs.

In the light of the above the Bankers' Committee has taken positive steps to spearhead the development of high level manpower in banking by founding, supporting and funding the Financial Institutions Training Centre and by giving moral and financial support in the form of donations to the Nigerian Institute of Bankers through its member banks.

iv) Another major function of the Committee is the preparation and periodical review of the Bankers' Tariff. This is a list containing approved bank charges and commissions. Banks are not allowed to charge fees in excess of the amounts listed in the tariff.

v) Any major issue affecting banks must be examined by the Committee before a final decision is taken. The Committee's recommendations are normally taken into consideration by the monetary authorities when considering any issue that can affect the operations of banks.

Answer 26.2

i) The main objectives of the Nigerian Institute of Bankers are:
   a) To help promote banking education in the country in order to

help staff employed in the banking industry to acquire modern banking techniques and prepare them for higher responsibilities in their various institutions.

b) To facilitate the consideration and discussion of matters of interest to bankers and to keep members in touch with the latest developments in banking and business generally.

c) To take any measures which may be desirable to further the interests of banking.

d) To hold, and help to secure, the observance of professional ethics and traditions in the banking system.

e) To hold lectures, seminars and conferences on banking, finance and other kindred subjects.

f) To hold and conduct examinations in banking

g) To issue certificates to those who satisfy the conditions for its awards from time to time.

h) To promote the general advancement of the theory and practice of banking in any or all of its branches and to facilitate the exchange of infomation and ideas relating to banking amongst the members of the Institute.

i) To pursue actively research into banking theory and practice with particular reference to local conditions and to study and tackle the professional problems confronting its members.

ii) The main aims and objectives of the Financial Institutions Training Centre are:

a) To carry on the business of training and education of personnel employed, or to be employed, by banks and other financial institutions.

b) To protect, promote and advance the knowledge and practice of banking and finance throughout Nigeria by the organisation of seminars, lectures, workshops and other practical and theoretical courses.

c) To collect and disseminate statistical and other information relating to banking, finance, commerce, trade and other related disciplines.

d) To co-operate with the Nigerian Institute of Bankers.

e) To print and publish any newspaper, periodicals, bulletins, books or leaflets that the Institution may think desirable for the promotion of its objects.

f) To engage in consultancy and advisory services in its area of competence.

APPENDIX 1

THE BANKING ACT, 1969

(formerly The Banking Decree, 1969)

Reprinted from the original

THE FEDERAL MILITARY GOVERNMENT hereby decrees as follows:

PART I
LICENSING OF BANKS

General

1. (1) No banking business shall be transacted in Nigeria except by a company duly incorporated in Nigeria which is in possession of a valid licence granted by the Commissioner authorising it to do so.

Banking business by licensed banks.

(2) The foregoing subsection (1) shall not apply—

(*a*) in relation to a bank (not being a bank to which paragraph (*b*) of this subsection refers), which was duly incorporated in Nigeria prior to the commencement of the Companies Decree 1968, and which holds a valid licence granted under the Act repealed by this Decree;

(*b*) in relation to a bank which was not, prior to the commencement of the Companies Decree 1968, incorporated in Nigeria, and which at the commencement of this Decree holds a valid licence, if—

(*i*) the Nigerian branch or branches of the said bank shall, on or before 18th February, 1969 become incorporated in Nigeria under the Companies Decree 1968 for the purposes of transacting banking business; and

(*ii*) the said bank has before that date applied to the Commissioner through the Governor of the Central Bank for a licence and such application has not been rejected by the said Commissioner.

(3) Any person who transacts banking business without a valid licence contrary to subsection (1) above shall be guilty of an offence and liable to a fine of £50 for each day during which the offence continues.

459

2. (1) Any company which desires to carry on banking business in Nigeria shall apply in writing through the Central Bank to the Commissioner for the grant of a licence and shall submit the following, that is—

(a) a copy of the memorandum of association and articles of association or other instrument under which the company is incorporated duly verified by a statutory declaration made by a director, secretary, or other senior official of the company;

(b) a copy of the latest balance sheet of the company; and

(c) such other particulars as may be called for by the Central Bank.

(2) Upon receiving an application under subsection (1) of this section the Central Bank shall require the Examiner appointed under section 20 of this Decree to carry out a preliminary examination of the books and affairs of such company.

(3) The Central Bank shall consider the application and the report of the Examiner and make a recommendation to the Commissioner stating whether or not a licence should be granted and the conditions (if any) to be attached to the licence.

(4) Upon receiving an application under subsection (1) of this section and the recommendation of the Central Bank under subsection (3) thereof the Commissioner may in accordance with the recommendation of the Central Bank grant a licence, with or without conditions, or refuse to grant a licence.

(5) If the Commissioner, notwithstanding the recommendation of the Central Bank, is of the opinion—

(a) that it would be undesirable in the public interest that a licence should be granted; or

(b) that it would be desirable that a licence should be granted, he shall make a report of the circumstances to the Federal Executive Council who may direct him to refuse or grant a licence, as the case may require; and where an application is refused, the Commissioner need not give any reason for the refusal.

(6) Where a licence is subject to conditions, the licensed bank shall comply with those conditions.

(7) Any licensed bank which fails to comply with any of the conditions of its licence shall be guilty of an offence and shall be liable to a fine not exceeding £50 for each day during which the condition is not complied with.

3. (1) The Commissioner may, at any time on the recommendation of the Central Bank, vary or revoke any of the conditions of a licence or impose such conditions or additional conditions as he may deem necessary.

Power to vary conditions of licences.

(2) Where the Commissioner proposes to vary, revoke or impose conditions in accordance with subsection (1) of this section, he shall before exercising such power give notice of his intention to the licensed bank concerned, and shall give the bank an opportunity to make representations to him and to submit reasons why the bank's licence should not be so amended.

(3) Any licensed bank which fails to comply with any conditions as varied or imposed by virtue of subsection (1) of this section shall be guilty of an offence and shall be liable to a fine of £1000.

Supplemental

4. No person licensed to carry on banking business in Nigeria may, after the coming into force of this Decree, open or close branch offices anywhere in Nigeria or outside Nigeria except with the consent in writing of the Central Bank.

Opening and closing of branches.

5. Every licensed bank shall inform the Commissioner through the Central Bank of—

Restriction as to amalgamation, etc.

(a) any proposed agreement, or arrangement, for any sale or disposal of its business by amalgamation or otherwise;

(b) any proposal for reconstruction, and the Commissioner may on the recommendation of the Central Bank approve or withhold approval of such agreement or arrangement or proposal for reconstruction.

6. (1) No bank shall hold or be granted licence, unless—

Requirements as to minimum paid-up capital.

(a) as respects a bank which is not directly or indirectly controlled from abroad, its paid-up share-capital is not less than £300,000; and

(b) as respects a bank which is directly or indirectly controlled from abroad its paid-up share Capital is not less than £750,000.

As amended by
S. 1 (a) Banking
(Amendment)
Decree No. 3,
1970
(2) The Central Bank may, in consultation with the Commissioner, prescribe the minimum ratio which licensed Banks shall maintain between their respective paid-up capital and statutory reserves on the one hand and their loans and advances on the other;

(3) In subsection (1) of this section, a bank shall be deemed to 'be controlled from abroad—

(a) if the composition of its board of directors consists wholly or mainly of persons who are not citizens of Nigeria; or

(b) where the majority voting rights of that company are held by persons who are not citizens of Nigeria.

(4) Any failure to comply with any of the foregoing provisions of this section shall be a ground for the revocation of the licence of the bank under this Decree.

Certain savings
as to licences
validly granted
under the repea-
led enactment.
Cap. 19.
7. (1) Where any person carries on banking business under a licence validly granted under the Act repealed by this Decree, and the licence was in force immediately before the commencement of this Decree, that person shall not later than 6 months thereafter comply with the provisions of section 6 of this Decree relating to the minimum paid-up capital required for the purposes of that section.

(2) Any failure to comply with the provisions of subsection (1) of this section shall be a ground for the revocation of the licence under this Decree.

Revocation of
licences.
8. (1) The Commissioner may on the recommendation of the Central Bank by order published in the Federal Gazette revoke any licence—

(a) if the holder thereof ceases to carry on in Nigeria the type of banking business for which he was licensed or goes into liquidation or is wound-up or otherwise dissolved; or

(b) if the holder thereof fails to fulfil the prescribed conditions and regulations ; or

(c) in the circumstances and in the manner where under this Decree failure to comply with any provisions thereof is a ground for revocation of licence.

(2) Where the Commissioner proposes to revoke any licence in accordance with subsection (1) of this section, he shall before revoking any such licence give notice of his intention to the licensed bank and shall give the bank an opportunity to make representations and to submit reasons why its licence should not be so revoked.

PART II
DUTIES OF LICENSED BANKS
General

9. Every licensed bank shall maintain a reserve fund and shall, out of its net profits each year and before any dividend is declared—

Maintenance of reserve fund.

(*a*) transfer to the reserve fund, where the amount of the reserve fund is less than the paid-up share capital, a sum equal to not less than twenty-five *per centum* of such profits; or

(*b*) transfer to the reserve fund, where the amount of the reserve fund is equal to or in excess of the paid-up share capital, twelve-and-a-half *per centum* of the net profits of the bank, but no transfer under the fore-going provisions of this section shall be made until any past losses have been made good.

10. (1) No licensed bank shall pay any dividend on its shares until—

Restriction on dividends.

(*a*) all its preliminary expenses, organization expenses, shares selling commission, brokerage, amounts of losses incurred and other capitalized expenses not represented by tangible assets have been completely written off; and

(*b*) after adequate provision for bad and doubtful debts has been made to the satisfaction of the Central Bank.

(2) For the purposes of this section, an issue of bonus shares out of profits shall be deemed to be a payment of dividends.

11. (1) Every director of a licensed bank who is in any manner whatsoever, whether directly or indirectly interested in an advance, loan or credit facility or proposed advance, loan or credit facility, from that bank shall as soon as practicable declare the nature of his interest to the board of directors of the bank, and the secretary of the bank shall cause such declaration to be circulated forthwith to all directors.

Disclosure of interests by directors.

(2) The requirements of subsection (1) of this section shall not apply in any case—

(a) where the interest of the director consists only of being a member or creditor of a company which is interested in an advance, loan or credit facility from the licensed bank; and

(b) if the interest of the director may properly be regarded by the Central Bank as not being a material interest.

(3) For the purposes of subsection (1) of this section a general notice given to the board of directors of a licensed bank by a director to the effect—

(a) that he is an officer or member of a company or firm specified in the notice; and

(b) that he is to be regarded as interested in any advance, loan or credit facility which may, after the date of the notice, be made to that company or firm, shall be deemed to be a sufficient declaration of interest in relation to any such advance, loan or credit facility, if—

    (i) the notice specifies the nature and extent of his interest in a company or firm so specified;

    (ii) such interest is not different in nature to or greater in extent than the nature and extent so specified in the notice at the time any advance, loan or credit facility is made; and

    (iii) the notice is given at the meeting of the directors or the director takes reasonable steps to ensure that it is brought up and read at the next meeting of the directors after it is given.

(4) Every director of a licensed bank, who holds any office or possesses any property whereby, whether directly or indirectly, duties or interests might be created in conflict with his duties or interests as director, shall declare at a meeting of the director of the licensed bank the fact and the nature character and extent of the conflict.

(5) The declaration referred to in subsection (4) of this section shall be made at the first meeting of directors held—

(a) after he became a director of the licensed bank; or

(b) if already a director, after he commenced to hold office or to possess the property.

(6) The secretary of the licensed bank shall cause to be brought up and read any declaration made under subsection (1) or (4) of this section at the next meeting of the directors after it is made, and shall record any declaration made under this section in the minutes of the meeting at which it was made or at which it was brought up and read.

(7) Any director who contravenes subsection (1) or (4) of this section shall be guilty of an offence and shall be liable to imprisonment for a term not exceeding 3 years or to a fine not exceeding £5000 or to both such imprisonment and fine.

12. (1) Every licensed bank shall maintain a holding of cash reserves, specified liquid assets, special deposits in the Central Bank and stabilization securities as the case may be, not less in amount than as may from time to time be prescribed by the Central Bank by virtue of section 40 of the Central Bank of Nigeria Act.

Minimum holding of cash reserves, specified liquid assets special deposits and stabilization securities, by licensed banks. Cap. 30.

(2) Where there are both assets and liabilities due by or to other licensed banks, they shall be offset accordingly, and any surplus of assets or liabilities shall be included as specified liquid assets or demand liabilities as the case may be:

Provided that in the case of long term advances to a licensed bank or by an overseas branch or office of a licensed bank, the advances may with the approval of the Central Bank be excluded from the demand liabilities of the licensed bank.

(3) Every licensed bank—
(a) shall furnish within a reasonable time any information required by the Central Bank to satisfy the Central Bank that the licensed bank is observing the requirements of subsection (1) of this section;
(b) shall not allow its holding of cash reserves, specified liquid assets, special deposits and stabilization securities to be less than as from time to time prescribed by the Central Bank; and
(c) shall not during the period of such deficiency, grant or permit increases in advances, loans or credit facilities to any person without the prior approval of the Central Bank.

(4) Any licensed bank which fails to comply with any of the provisions of subsection (3) of this section shall be guilty of an offence and shall be liable to a fine of £50—

(a) for every day during which a default under paragraph (a) thereof exists;

(b) for every day during which a deficiency under paragraph (b) thereof exists; and

(c) for every offence under paragraph (c) thereof, and the Central Bank may also during the period when the licensed bank fails to comply with any of the requirements of subsection (3) as aforesaid withdraw any privileges or facilities that are normally accorded to the licensed bank.

(5) For the purposes of this section "specified liquid assets" provided they are freely transferable and free from any lien or charge of any kind shall, without prejudice to the provisions of section 2 of the Central Bank of Nigeria Act (Amendment) (No. 3) Decree 1968, consist of all or any of the following, namely—

1968 No. 50.

(a) notes and coins which are legal tender in Nigeria;

(b) balances at the Central Bank;

(c) net balances at any licensed bank (excluding uncleared effects) and money at call in Nigeria;

(d) Treasury Bills and Treasury Certificates issued by the Federal Government;

(e) inland bills of exchange and promissory notes rediscountable at the Central Bank.

13. (1) A licensed bank shall not—

Restriction on certain activities of licensed banks

(a) grant to any person any advance, loan or credit facility or give any financial guarantee or incur any other liability on behalf of such person so that the total value of the advances, loans, credit facilities, financial guarantees and other liabilities in respect of such person is at any time more than thirty-three and one-third *per centum* of the sum of the paid-up capital and statutory reserves of the bank:

Provided that the provisions of this paragraph shall not apply to transactions between licensed banks or between branches of a licensed bank, or to the purchase of clean or documentary bills of exchange, telegraphic transfers or documents of title to goods the holder of which is entitled to payment for exports from Nigeria or to advances made against such bills transfers or documents; and for the purposes of this paragraph, all advances, loans or credit facilities extended to any person shall be aggregated and shall include all advances, loans or credit facilities extended to any subsidiaries and associates whatsoever of that person;

(b) grant any advances, loans or credit facilities against the security of its own shares;

(c) grant or permit to be outstanding unsecured advances or loans, or unsecured credit facilities, of an aggregate amount in excess of £500—

    (i) to its directors, or any of them, whether such advances, loans or credit facilities are obtained by its directors jointly or severally;

    (ii) to any firm, partnership or private company in which it is or any one or more of its directors is interested as director, partner, manager or agent, or to any individual, firm, partnership or private company of which any one of its directors is a guarantor;

    (iii) to any public company in which it or any one or more of its directors jointly or severally maintains interest either directly or indirectly;

(d) grant or permit to be outstanding to its officials and employees unsecured advances or loans, or unsecured credit facilities, which in aggregate amount for any one official or employee exceed one year's salary of such official or employee;

As amended by S. 1 (b) of Banking Decree No. 3, 1970.

(e) engage, whether on its own account or on a commission basis, in the wholesale or retail trade, including the import or export trade, except insofar as may exceptionally be necessary in the course of the banking operations and services of that licensed bank or in the course of the satisfaction of debts due to it;

(f) acquire or hold any part of the share capital of any financial, commercial, agricultural, industrial or other undertaking, except—

(*i*) such shareholding as a licensed bank may with the prior approval of the Central Bank acquire in the course of satisfaction of debts due to it which shareholding shall, however, be disposed of at the earliest suitable moment,

(*ii*) any shareholding approved by the Central Bank in any statutory corporation set up for the purpose of promoting the development of a money market or securities market in Nigeria or of improving the financial machinery for the financing of economic development,

(*iii*) all shareholdings approved by the Central Bank in other undertakings the aggregate value of which does not at any time exceed twenty-five *per centum* of the sum of the paid-up capital and statutory reserves of that bank;

(*g*) own any subsidiary company which is not carrying on a banking business; provided that the provisions of this paragraph shall not apply to any nominee company of a licensed bank which deals in stocks and shares for or on behalf of the bank's customers or clients;

As amended by
S. 1 (*c*) Banking
(Amendment)
Decree No. 3,
1970.

(*h*) remit, either in whole or in part, the debts owed to it by any of its directors or past directors without the approval of the Central Bank;

(*i*) purchase, acquire or lease real estate, except as may be necessary for the purpose of conducting its business, including provisions for foreseeable future expansion or housing of its staff, or other exceptional circumstances, where the agreement of the Central Bank is obtained;

(*j*) sell, dispose or lease out any real estate, except with the prior approval of the Central Bank: Provided that a licensed bank may secure a debt on any real or other property, and in default of repayment may acquire such property and exercise any power of sale, or as may be provided for in any instrument, or by law prescribed, immediately upon such default or soon thereafter as may be deemed proper.

(2) In paragraphs (*c*) and (*d*) of subsection (1) of this section, the expression "unsecured advances or loans, or unsecured credit facilities" means advances, loans or credit facilities made without security, or in respect of any advances, loans or

credit facilities made with security, any part thereof which at any time exceeds the market value of the assets constituting the security, or where the Central Bank is satisfied that there is no established market value, the value of the assets as determined on the basis of a valuation approved by the Central Bank.

(3) In paragraphs (c) and (h) of subsection (1), the expression "director" includes the wife, husband, father, mother, son or daughter of a director.

(4) All directors of the bank shall be liable jointly or severally to indemnify the bank against any loss arising from any unsecured advances, loans or credit facilities, under paragraph (c) of subsection (1) of this section.

(5) Any licensed bank which after the commencement of this Decree enters into any transaction inconsistent with any of the provisions of paragraphs (a) to (h) of subsection (1) of this section shall be guilty of an offence and shall be liable to a fine of £50 for every day during which any such transaction continues.

(6) Nothing in this section shall be construed as permitting a licensed bank to grant to any marketing board established under any written law in Nigeria any advance, loan or credit facility, or to give any financial guarantee, or to incur any other liability on behalf of such board.

14. (1) The rate of interest charged on advances, loans or credit facilities or paid on deposits by any licensed bank shall be linked to the minimum rediscount rate of the Central Bank subject to stated minimum and maximum rates of interest, and the minimum and maximum rates of interest when so approved shall be the same for all licensed banks; provided that differential rates may be approved for the various categories of banks to which this decree applies;

Rates of interest on advance, etc.

As amended by S. 1 (d) Banking (Amendment) Decree No. 3, 1970.

(2) The interest rate structure of each licensed bank shall be subject to the approval of the Central Bank.

Books of Account

15. (1) Every licensed bank shall cause to be kept proper books of account with respect to all the transactions of the licensed bank.

Keeping of books of account.

(2) For the purpose of subsection (1) of this section, proper books of account shall not be deemed to be kept with respect to all transactions if such books as are necessary to explain such transactions and give a true and fair view of the state of affairs of the licensed bank are not kept by the bank.

(3) The books of account shall be kept at the principal administrative office in Nigeria of each licensed bank in the English language or any other language approved by the Federal Executive Council on the recommendation of the Commissioner.

(4) If any person—

(a) being a director or officer of a licensed bank fails to take all reasonable steps to secure compliance with any of the provisions of this section; or

(b) has by his own wilful act been the cause of any default by the bank therefor, he shall be guilty of an offence under this section and shall be liable to imprisonment for a term not exceeding 6 months or to a fine not exceeding £500 or to both such imprisonment and fine.

(5) In any proceedings against a person under sub-section (4) of this section, it shall be a defence to prove that he has reasonable grounds to believe that another person was charged with the duty of seeing that any of the requirements was complied with and that that person was competent and in a position to discharge that duty.

16. (1) Every licensed bank shall submit to the Central Bank—

Delivery of returns, etc. to Central Bank. First Schedule.

(a) not later than 28 days after the last day of each month, a statement in the appropriate form set out in the First Schedule to this Decree;

(b) such other periodical returns as may be prescribed by the Central Bank; and

(c) on request, such information as may be required by the Central Bank.

Second Schedule

(2) Every licensed bank shall submit to the Central Bank a statement in the form set out in the Second Schedule to this Decree giving an analysis of advances and other assets of its office and branches

in Nigeria within such period following the end of each month as the Central Bank may from time to time determine.

(3) The Central Bank may require a licensed bank to submit such further information as the Central Bank may deem necessary for the proper understanding of the statements furnished by that bank under subsections (1) and (2) of this section, and such information shall be submitted within such a reasonable period as the Central Bank may require.

(4) Any licensed bank which maintains branches or offices outside Nigeria shall produce to the Central Bank such statements relating to its offices or branches outside Nigeria in such form and at such times as the Central Bank may require.

(5) Any bank which fails to comply with any of the requirements of subsections (1), (2), (3) and (4) of this section shall in respect of each such failure be guilty of an offence under this Decree, and shall be liable to a fine of £50 for each day during which the offence continues.

(6) It shall be the responsibility of the Central Bank to prepare and to publish consolidated statements aggregating the figures in the statements furnished under subsection (1) of this section for each class of banks licensed under this Decree.

(7) The statements submitted by each licensed bank under subsection (1) or (2) of this section and any information submitted under subsection (3) or (4) thereof shall be regarded as secret other than as between that bank and the Central Bank.

Provided that the Central Bank—

(a) shall furnish any such information required by the Commissioner, and shall inform the Commissioner if at any time in its opinion there is need for an examination of any licensed bank; and

(b) may in support of its opinion convey to the Commissioner such information as it possesses concerning the state of the affairs of that bank.

17.—(1) Not later than 4 months after the end of any financial year of a licensed bank, the licensed bank shall—

(a) cause to be published in a daily newspaper printed in and circulating in Nigeria;

(b) exhibit in a conspicuous position in each of its offices and branches in Nigeria; and

As amended by S. 1 (e) of Banking (Amendment) Decree No. 3, 1970.

Publication of profit and loss account and balance sheet.

(c) forward to the Commissioner and the Central Bank, copies of its balance sheet and profit and loss account duly signed and containing the full and correct names of the directors of the bank.

Third Schedule. As amended by the Banking (Amendment) Decree No. 3, 1970

(2) The balance sheet and profit and loss account of the licensed bank shall bear on their face the report of an approved auditor and shall contain statements as to the matter mentioned in the Third Schedule to this Decree.

(3) For the purposes of subsection (2) of this section an "approved auditor" is an auditor who is approved for the purposes of section 19 of this Decree.

(4) Any licensed bank which fails to comply with any of the requirements of this section shall in respect of each such failure be guilty of an offence and be liable to a fine of £100.

Contents and form of account

18. (1) Every balance sheet of every licensed bank shall give a true and fair view of the state of affairs as at the end of every financial year of such bank and every profit and loss account shall give a true and fair view of the profit or loss of such bank for the financial year.

As amended by S. (1) (9) Banking (Amendment) Decree No. 3, 1970

(2) Every balance sheet and every profit and loss account of every licensed bank forwarded to the Commissioner and the Central Bank in accordance with the provisions of Section 17 (1) (c) of this Decree shall comply with the requirements of the Third and Fourth Schedules to this Decree.

As amended by S. (2) (h) Banking (Amendment) Decree No. 3, 1970.

(2a) Every balance sheet and every profit and loss account of every licensed bank shall be published or exhibited in accordance with the provisions of Section 17 (1) (a) and (b) may be so published or exhibited in abridged form agreed with the Central Bank;

(3) Any person being a director of any licensed Bank who fails to take all reasonable steps to secure compliance as respects any account required under the provisions of this section shall in respect of each offence be liable to imprisonment for a term not exceeding 2 years or to a fine of £500 or to both such imprisonment and fine.

(4) In any proceedings against a person in respect of an offence under this section, it shall be a defence to prove that he had reasonable grounds to believe and did believe that another person, who is competent and reliable, was charged with the duty of seeing that the said provisions were complied with and was in a position to discharge that duty.

(5) A person shall not be sentenced to imprisonment for an offence under this section unless, in the opinion of the court, the offence was committed wilfully.

19. (1) Every licensed bank shall appoint annually a person approved by the Commissioner, in this section referred to as "the approved auditor" whose duties shall be to make to the shareholders a report upon the annual balance sheet and profit and loss account of the bank and every such report shall contain statement as to the matters mentioned in the Third, Fourth and Fifth Schedules to this Decree.

Appointment and powers of auditors.

(2) No person—

(a) having an interest in a licensed bank otherwise than as a depositor; or

(b) who is a director, officer or agent of a licensed bank; or

(c) which is a firm in which a director of a licensed bank is interested as partner or director, shall be eligible for appointment as the approved auditor for any licensed bank, and any person appointed as such auditor—

Third, Fourth and Fifth Schedules.

(i) who subsequently acquires such interest ; or

(ii) becomes a director, officer or agent of that bank; or

(iii) subsequently becomes a partner in a firm in which a director of a licensed bank is interested as partner or director, shall cease to be such auditor.

(3) If any licensed bank—

(a) fails to appoint the approved auditor under subsection (1) of this section; or

(b) at any time fails to fill a vacancy for such person, the Commissioner shall after consultation with the Central Bank appoint "the approved auditor" and shall fix the remuneration to be paid by the bank to such auditor.

(4) Every auditor of a licensed bank shall have a right of access at all times to the books and accounts and vouchers of the bank, and shall be entitled to require from the directors and officers of the bank such information and explanation as he thinks necessary for the performance of his duties.

(5) The report of the approved auditor shall be read together with the report of the board of management at the annual general meeting of the shareholders and two copies of each report together with the auditor's analysis of doubtful advances on the form provided in the Fifth Schedule

As amended by S. 1 (1) of the Banking (Amendment) Decree

to this Decree shall be sent to the Central Bank who shall transmit a copy of such each report to the Commissioner;

(6) For the purposes of this section, the approved auditor shall be an auditor who is a member of one of the professional bodies for the time being declared by the Commissioner by notice in the Federal Gazette to be approved for such purposes.

(7) No auditor shall be approved for the purposes of this section unless—

(a) he is resident in Nigeria; and

(b) he is carrying on in Nigeria full-time professional practice as a public accountant and auditor.

PART III

POWERS OF THE CENTRAL BANK

Appointment and powers of Examiners.

20. (1) There shall be an Examiner, who—

(a) shall be an officer of the Central Bank appointed by the Bank with power to examine periodically, under conditions of secrecy, the books and affairs of each and every licensed bank;

(b) shall have a right of access at all times to the books and accounts and vouchers of the bank; and

(c) shall be entitled to require from the officers and directors of the bank such information and explanation as he thinks necessary for the performance of his duties,

and the Examiner shall be given and shall have access to any accounts, returns or information regarding banks licensed under this Decree that are in the possession of the Federal Ministry of Finance.

(2) There may in the same manner be appointed one or more fit persons as Deputy or Assistant Examiner who shall have and may exercise the powers of an Examiner under this Decree.

(3) In examining the affairs of any licensed bank in accordance with subsection (1) of this section, it shall be the duty of the Examiner at all times to avoid unreasonable hindrance to the daily business of that bank and to confine the investigation to matters strictly relevant to the examination.

(4) Every licensed bank shall produce to the examiners at such times as the examiners may specify all books, accounts, documents and oral information which they may require.

(5) If any book, account, document or information—

(a) is not produced in accordance with subsection (4) of this section; or

(b) is false in any material particular, the licensed bank shall be guilty of an offence, and shall be liable—

(i) in the case of an offence against paragraph (a) of this subsection, to a fine of £50 in respect of each day in which the offence continues, or

(ii) in any other case under paragraph (b) thereof, to a fine of £500.

(6) The Examiner shall forward a report of his findings to the Governor of the Central Bank, who shall forward a copy of the Examiner's report to the Commissioner and inform the Commissioner of any circumstances in which the Commissioner may exercise any powers under section 22 of this Decree.

21. (1) The Commissioner may at any time require the Governor of the Central Bank to require the Examiner appointed in accordance with section 20 of this Decree, or one or more other qualified persons whom the Governor shall appoint, to make a special examination under conditions of secrecy of the books and affairs of any licensed bank— *Special examination.*

(a) where, after consultation with the Central Bank, the Commissioner has reason to believe that a licensed bank—

(i) may be carrying on its business in a manner detrimental to the interest of its depositors and other creditors, or

(ii) may have insufficient assets to cover its liabilities to the public, or

(iii) may be contravening the provisions of this Decree.

(b) where application is made—

(i) by shareholders holding not less than one-third of the total number of shares for the time being issued and paid-up, or

(ii) by depositors holding not less than one-half of the gross amount of the deposits of the bank:

Provided however that the applicants under this paragraph submit to the Commissioner such evidence as he may consider necessary to justify an examination, and provided also that they furnish adequate security for payment of the costs of the examination;

(c) where the licensed bank suspends payments or informs the Commissioner or the Governor of the Central Bank of its intention to do so.

(2) Where a licensed bank considers—

(a) that it is likely to become unable to meet its obligations; or

(b) that it is about to suspend payments,
it shall forthwith inform the Central Bank of its intention to do so, and any failure to make such report shall be an offence under this Decree.

(3) As soon as may be after the conclusion of an examination under this section, the Examiner shall submit a full report thereon to the Governor of the Central Bank who shall forward a copy of the report together with his comments to the Commissioner, and the Commissioner may at his discretion communicate to the Head Office of the licensed bank concerned or to the applicants such information arising from the report as the Commissioner deems fit.

(4) The Commissioner shall have power to order that all expenses of and incidental to an examination shall be paid by the bank examined, and shall also have power in respect of examination made under paragraph (b) of subsection (1) of this section to order that the expenses shall be defrayed by the applicants.

Power after
Examination

22. If, in the opinion of the Commissioner, an examination shows that a licensed bank is carrying on its business in a manner detrimental to the interests of its depositors and other creditors, or has insufficient assets to cover its liabilities to the public, or is contravening the provisions of this Decree, the Commissioner may take such one or more of the following steps from time to time as may seem to him necessary, that is to say—

(a) require that the licensed bank shall, forthwith, take such steps as the Commissioner may consider necessary to rectify the matter, and these may include any or all of the following steps, that is—

(i) require that the bank shall call meeting of its directors for the purpose of considering any matter relating to or arising out of the affairs of the bank, or require that an officer of the bank shall discuss any such matter with an officer of the Central Bank,

(*ii*) require that the bank shall make, within such time as may be specified, such changes in the management as the Commissioner may consider necessary,

(*iii*) appoint a person who in his opinion has had proper training and experience to advise the licensed bank in the proper conduct of its business and fix the remuneration to be paid by the licensed bank to such person; or

(*b*) report the circumstances to the Federal Executive Council which, unless satisfied that the bank is taking adequate measures to put its affairs in order, may direct the Commissioner to make an order—

(*i*) revoking the bank's licence and requiring its business to be wound-up, or

(*ii*) requiring the Central Bank to assume control and carry on the business of the licensed bank,

except that the Commissioner shall not so report the circumstances without giving the bank reasonable prior notice of his intention to do so and an opportunity of submitting a written statement in reply.

23. (1) Where the Central Bank has assumed control of the business of a licensed bank in pursuance of paragraph (*b*) of section 22 of this Decree, the Central Bank shall, subject to subsection (2) of this section, remain in control of, and continue to carry on, the business of that bank, in the name and on behalf of the bank until such time as— *Control of licensed banks.*

(*a*) the deposits with the bank have been repaid or the Central Bank is satisfied that suitable provision has been made for their repayment; and

(*b*) in the opinion of the Central Bank, it is no longer necessary for the Central Bank to remain in control of the business of the bank.

(2) Where the Central Bank has assumed control of the business of a licensed bank as aforesaid, the High Court may—

(*a*) upon application by the licensed bank; and

(*b*) if the High Court is satisfied tha it is no longer necessary for the protection of depositors of the bank that the Central Bank should remain in control of the business of the licensed bank, order that the Central Bank shall cease to control the business of the bank as from a date specified in the order.

(3) Where the Central Bank has assumed control of the business of a licensed bank as aforesaid or ceases to control the business of a licensed bank in accordance with this section, the Central Bank shall notify that fact in the Federal Gazette.

Licensed bank under control of Central Bank to co-operate with Central Bank.

24. (1) Where the Central Bank has assumed control of the business of a licensed bank in pursuance of paragraph (b) of section 22 of this Decree, the licensed bank shall submit its business to the control of the Central Bank and shall provide the Central Bank with such facilities as the Central Bank requires to carry on the business of that bank.

(2) Any licensed bank which fails to comply with subsection (1) of this section or with any requirements of the Central Bank under the said section 22 of this Decree shall be guilty of an offence and shall be liable to a fine not exceeding £100 for each day during which such default continues.

25. (1) Where by section 22 of this Decree, the Commissioner makes an order revoking the licence of a bank and requiring the business of that bank in Nigeria to be wound up, that bank shall within 14 days after the making of the order apply to the High Court for an order winding up the affairs of that bank under supervision of that court and the court shall take up the hearing of the application in priority to all other matters.

(2) If the bank fails to apply to the High Court within the time prescribed by subsection (1) of this section, the Commissioner may in his discretion—

(a) apply to the High Court for any necessary order; or

(b) without waiting for the expiration of the time prescribed, appoint the official receiver (within the meaning of section 395 of the Companies Decree 1968) or any other fit person to be a provisional liquidator, and the provisional liquidator shall have the powers conferred by and be deemed to have been appointed a provisional liquidator by the High Court for the purposes of that Decree.

(3) The provisions of this section shall have effect, and section 209 of the Companies Decree 1968 shall be construed, as if the making of an order under section 22 of this Decree to revoke the licence of a bank had been included as a ground for winding-up by the High Court under that section.

(4) The liquidator of a licensed bank shall forward to the Central Bank copies of all returns which he is required to make under the Companies Decree 1968.

(5) The Central Bank may, at any time by notice in writing require the liquidator of a licensed bank to furnish, within such time as may be specified in the notice or such further time as the Central Bank may allow, any statement or information relating to or connected with the winding-up of the bank, and it shall be the duty of every liquidator to comply with such requirements.

PART IV
GENERAL AND SUPPLEMENTAL

26. (1) Save with the consent of the Commissioner and subject to subsection (2) of this section, no person other than a licensed commercial bank shall—

> (*a*) use or continue to use the word "bank" or any of its derivatives, either in English or in any other language, in the description or title under which such person is carrying on business in Nigeria;

Use of the word "bank" in company's name. Section 26 (1) (b) delete by virtue of Section 1 (i) of Banking (Amendment) Decree No. 3, 1970.

(2) Every licensed commercial bank shall use as part of its description or title the word "bank" or some one or more of its derivatives, either in English or in some other language.

(3) Subsection (1) of this section shall not apply to any association of licensed banks formed for the protection of their mutual interests.

(4) Any licensed commercial bank which acts in contravention of this section shall be guilty of an offence and shall be liable to a fine of £50 for every day during which the offence continues.

(5) In this section, the reference to a "licensed commercial bank" is a reference to a bank that is licensed as a commercial bank within the meaning of this Decree.

27. (1) No person other than a licensed bank shall, after the commencement of this Decree, issue any advertisement inviting the public to deposit money with it.

General restriction as to advertisement for deposits.

(2) Where any licensed bank proposes, after the commencement of this Decree, to issue any advertisement for deposits of money with it, then the bank shall deliver to the Central Bank the text of the proposed advertisement and the bank's latest published accounts, and shall thereafter comply with such directives and conditions as the Central Bank may prescribe, and such texts shall be regarded as confidential information.

(3) Any person who issues an advertisement in contravention of any of the foregoing provisions of this section shall be guilty of an offence and shall be liable to imprisonment for a term not exceeding 2 years or a fine not exceeding £200.

(4) Any person who in the ordinary course of his business issues an advertisement to the order of another person, being an advertisement the issue of which by that other person constitutes an offence under this section, shall not himself be guilty of the offence, if he proves that the matters contained in the advertisement were not (wholly or in part) devised or selected by him or by any other person under his direction or control.

(5) In this Decree "advertisement" includes any form of advertising, whether in publication or by the display of notices or by means of circulars or other documents or by an exhibition of photographs or cinematograph or by way of sound broadcasting or television or loudspeakers or other public address systems, and references to the issuing of an advertisement shall be construed accordingly; and for the purposes of this Decree, an advertisement issued by any person by way of display or exhibition in a public place shall be treated as issued by him on every day on which he causes or permits it to be so displayed or exhibited.

(6) For the purposes of this Decree, an advertisement which contains information calculated to lead directly or indirectly to the deposit of money by the public shall be treated as an advertisement inviting the public to deposit money.

(7) For the purposes of this Decree, an advertisement issued by any person on behalf of or to the order of another person shall be treated as an advertisement issued by that other person; and for the purposes of any proceedings under this Decree, an advertisement inviting the public to deposit money with a person specified in the advertisement shall be presumed, unless the contrary is proved, to have been issued by that person.

Strikes

28. No licensed bank shall incur any liability to any of its customers by reason only of failure on the part of that bank to open for business during a strike: Provided that the said bank has, within 24 hours of the continuance of the strike, obtained the approval of the Central Bank for any continued closure of the bank.

Prohibition of receipt of commission by staff.

29. Any director, officer or employee of a licensed bank or other persons being persons receiving remuneration from such licensed bank, who asks for or receives, consents

or agrees to receive any gift, commission, emolument, service, gratuity, money, property or thing of value for his own personal benefit or advantage or for that of any of his relations, from any person other than from the bank—

    (*a*) for procuring or endeavouring to procure for any person any advance, loan or credit facility from the licensed bank; or

    (*b*) for the purchase or discount of any draft, note, cheque, bill of exchange or other obligations by that bank; or

    (*c*) for permitting any person to overdraw any account with that bank, shall be guilty of an offence and shall be liable to imprisonment for a term not exceeding 3 years or to a fine not exceeding £1000 or to both such imprisonment and fine.

30. (1) Any person who is a Director, Chief of Banking Operations, Secretary or other officer concerned in the management of a licensed bank shall cease to hold office—

Exclusion of certain individuals from management of licensed banks.

    (*a*) if he becomes bankrupt, suspends payments, or compounds with his creditors; or

    (*b*) if he is convicted of an offence involving dishonesty or fraud.

(2) No person who has been a director of, or directly concerned in the management of, a licensed bank which has been wound up by a High Court shall, without the express authority of the Commissioner, act or continue to act as a director of, or be directly concerned in the management of, any licensed bank.

(3) Any person acting in contravention of subsection (1) or (2) of this section shall be guilty of an offence and shall be liable to imprisonment for a term not exceeding 3 years or to a fine not exceeding £1000 or to both such imprisonment and fine.

PART V
MISCELLANEOUS

31. (1) Where any offence against any provision of this Decree has been committed by a company, firm, society or other body of persons, any person who at the time of the commission of the offence was a director, manager, secretary or other similar officer thereof or was purporting to act in such capacity shall be deemed to be guilty of that offence, unless he proves that the offence was committed without his consent or connivance and that he exercised all such

Offences by companies, etc. and by servants and agents.

diligence to prevent the commission of the offence as he ought to have exercised, having regard to the nature of his functions in that capacity and to all the circumstances.

(2) Where any person would be liable under this Decree to any punishment or penalty for any act, omission, neglect or default, he shall be liable to the same punishment or penalty for every such act, omission, neglect or default of any clerk, servant or agent, or of the clerk or servant of such agent:

Provided that such act, omission, neglect or default was committed by such clerk or servant in the course of his employment, or by such agent when acting in the course of his employment in such circumstances that had such act, omission, neglect or default been committed by the agent his principal would have been liable under this section.

Penalties : directors and managers.

32. Any person who, being a director or manager of a licensed bank—

> (*a*) fails to take all reasonable steps to secure compliance by the bank with the requirements of this Decree; or

> (*b*) fails to take all reasonable steps to secure the correctness of any statement submitted under the provisions of this Decree,

shall be guilty of an offence under this Decree and shall be liable to imprisonment for a term not exceeding 2 years or to a fine of £500 or to both such imprisonment and fine.

Penalties for offences not otherwise provided for.

33. Any licensed bank which contravenes or fails to comply with any of the provisions of this Decree for which no offence or penalty is expressly provided shall be guilty of an offence and shall be liable to a fine not exceeding £1000.

Powers as to offences and the Attorney-General's fiat.

34. (1) The Governor of the Central Bank may compound any offence punishable under this Decree by accepting such sums of money as he thinks fit, not exceeding the amount of the maximum fine to which that person would have been liable if he had been convicted of the offence.

(2) Any monies paid to the Governor pursuant to subsection (1) of this section shall be paid into the Consolidated Revenue Fund of the Federation.

(3) No prosecution in respect of any offence under this Decree shall be instituted without the consent in writing of the Attorney-General of the Federation.

35. Notwithstanding the provisions of any other written law, a Chief Magistrate's court shall have jurisdiction to try any offence against this Decree and to impose the full penalty prescribed.

36. (1) Neither the Government of the Federation nor the Central Bank, nor any officer of that Government or body, shall be subject to any action, claim or demand by or liability to any person in respect of anything done or omitted to be done in good faith in pursuance or in execution of, or in connection with the execution or intended execution of, any power conferred upon that Government, the Central Bank or such officer, by this Decree.

(2) For the purposes of this section, a Commissioner and any public officer shall be deemed to be an officer of the Government of the Federation, and the Governor and the Deputy Governor of the Central Bank and any director or employee thereof and any person holding any office therein or appointed by the Central Bank under paragraph (a) of section 22 of this Decree shall be deemed to be an officer of the Central Bank.

37. Where a licensed bank becomes unable to meet its obligations or suspends payments, the assets of such bank in the Federation shall be available to meet all deposit liabilities of the bank in the Federation, and such deposit liabilities shall have priority over all other liabilities of the bank.

38. (1) The provisions of this Decree shall not apply to—

(a) the Central Bank established under the Central Bank of Nigeria Act;

(b) the fund established under the National Provident Fund Act 1961;

(c) the Nigerian Industrial Development Bank Limited;

(d) the Post Office Savings Bank established under the Savings Bank Act.

(e) the Nigeria Housing Development Society Limited.

(2) The list of exceptions in subsection (1) of this section may be amended, by such additions or omissions as may be deemed necessary, by the Commissioner by order published in the Federal Gazette.

39. The provisions of this Decree are without prejudice to the provisions of the Companies Decree 1968, insofar as they relate to banks and to winding-up by the court:

Provided that where any of the provisions of that Decree is inconsistent witn any provision of this Decree this Decree shall prevail.

Regulations.

40. The Commissioner may in consultation with the Central Bank make such regulations as may be required from time to time for carrying into effect the object of this Decree, and he may by order published in the Federal Gazette amend, alter or vary the Schedules to this Decree.

Interpretation.

41. (1) In this Decree, unless the context otherwise requires, the following expressions have the meanings hereby assigned to them, respectively, that is—

"bank" means any person who carries on banking business, and includes a commercial bank, an acceptance house, discount house and financial institution; and in this definition—

    (*a*) "commercial bank" means any person who transacts banking business in Nigeria and whose business includes the acceptance of deposits, withdrawable by cheque,

    (*b*) "acceptance house" means any person in Nigeria who transacts banking business and whose business mainly consists of granting acceptance facilities or whose operations are, in the opinion of the Central Bank, those of an acceptance house,

    (*c*) "discount house" means any person in Nigeria who transacts banking business and whose business mainly consists of trading in and holding commercial bills of exchange, Treasury Bills and other securities, or whose operations are, in the opinion of the Central Bank, those of a discount house, and

    (*d*) "financial institution" means any person in Nigeria who transacts banking business but who is not a commercial bank, an acceptance house or a discount house;

As amended by Section (1) (*k*) Banking (Amendment) Decree No. 3, 1970

"banking business" means the business of receiving monies from outside sources as deposits irrespective of the payment of interest and the granting of money loans and acceptance of credits or the purchase of bills and cheques or the purchase and sale of securities for account of others or the incurring of the obligation to acquire claims in respect of loans prior to their maturity or the assumption of guarantees and other warranties for others or the effecting of transfers and clearings.

and such other transactions as the Commissioner may, on the recommendation of the Central Bank, by order published in the Federal Gazette designate as banking business;

"Central Bank" means the Central Bank of Nigeria established under the Central Bank of Nigeria Act;

"Commissioner" means the Federal Commissioner charged with responsibility for matters relating to banking;

"deposits" means monies lodged by the general public with any person for safe-keeping or for the purpose of earning interest or dividends whether or not such monies are repayable upon demand, upon a given period of notice or upon a fixed date;

"director" includes any person by whatever name he may be referred to, carrying out or empowered to carry out substantially the same functions of a director in relation to the direction of a company registered under the Companies Decree 1968;

"licence" means a licence granted by or under Part I of this Decree authorising the carrying on of banking business in Nigeria;

"licensed bank" means a bank holding a valid licence by or under Part I of this Decree;

"prescribed" means prescribed by this Decree or by the Central Bank of Nigeria Act, or by regulations made under this Decree or that Act.

(2) For the purposes of this Decree, the following expressions, namely—

(a) "commercial bank" ;

(b) "acceptance house" ;

(c) "discount house" ; and

(d) "financial institution",

have the meanings given respectively in the definition of "bank" in subsection (1) of this section.

(3) For the purposes of this Decree, a person shall be deemed to be receiving monies as deposits—

(a) if that person accepts, from the general public deposits as a feature of its business or if it issues an advertisement or solicits for such deposits; and

(b) notwithstanding that it receives monies as deposit which are limited to fixed amounts or that certificates or other instruments are issued in respect of any such amounts providing for the repayment to the holder thereof either conditionally or unconditionally of the amount of the deposits at specified or unspecified dates or for the payment of interest on the amounts deposited at specified intervals or otherwise, or that such certificates are transferable.

(4) Notwithstanding anything contained in this section to the contrary, the receiving of monies against any issue of debentures offered to the public in accordance with any enactment in force within the Federation shall not be deemed to constitute receiving of monies as deposits for the purposes of this Decree.

Citation, extent
and repeal
Cap. 19

42. (1) This Decree may be cited as the Banking Decree 1969 and shall apply throughout the Federation.

(2) The Banking Act 1958 is hereby repealed, and any reference in this Decree to "the Act repealed by this Decree" shall be construed accordingly.

FIRST SCHEDULE

Name of Bank..

Monthly Statement of Assets and Liabilities as at......

(To be submitted in accordance with

LIABILITIES   £   £

1. CAPITAL

   Authorised

   Issued, paid-up and outstanding

2. RESERVE FUND

3. DEBENTURES

4. BALANCES HELD FOR

   (a) Other banks in Nigeria

   (b) Offices and branches of this bank outside Nigeria

   (c) Other banks outside Nigeria

5. DEPOSITS

   (a) Repayable on demand

   (b) Savings Accounts

   (c) Other deposits repayable as from the date of this return

       (i) within 3 months

       (ii) between 3 and 6 months

       (iii) between 6 and 12 months

       (iv) later than 12 months

   of which, in total, by Governments   (....................)

6. LOANS AND ADVANCES FROM

   (a) Other banks in Nigeria

   (b) Offices and branches of this bank outside Nigeria

   (c) Other banks outside Nigeria

   (d) Other creditors

       (Contingent liability in respect of bills rediscounted) (....................)

       (Other contingent liabilities)   (....................)

7. Acceptances on account of customers (*as per contra*)

8. Confirmed documentary credits (*as per contra*)

9. Guarantees, endorsements and other obligations on account of customers (*as per contra*)

10. Other liabilities

    Net External Assets   £....................

    Net External Liabilities   £....................

Details should be given, on an attached sheet, of any assets which are not freely transferable to Nigeria or which are subject to a lien or charge of any kind.

N.B.— A company shall be deemed to be a subsidiary of a bank if that bank either is a member of it and controls the composition of its board of directors or holds more than half in nominal value of its equity share capital or if a company is a subsidiary of any company which is a subsidiary of that bank. (By equity share capital is meant the issued share capital of the company excluding any part thereof which neither as respects dividends nor as respects capital carries any right to participate beyond a specified amount in a distribution).

APPENDIX - 1

........................day of..**19**..........

Section 16 of the Banking Decree, 1969)

ASSETS

	£	£

1. CASH IN HAND
   - (a) Notes
   - (b) Coin

2. BALANCES HELD WITH
   - (a) Central Bank of Nigeria
   - (b) Other banks
     - (i) In Nigeria of which remittances in transit and uncleared effects
     - (ii) Outside Nigeria (including foreign currencies and coins)

3. MONEY AT CALL IN NIGERIA

4. TREASURY BILLS IN NIGERIA/OUTSIDE NIGERIA

5. TREASURY CERTIFICATES

6. BILLS DISCOUNTED
   - (a) Payable in Nigeria
     - (i) From banks in Nigeria
     - (ii) From non-bank sources
   - Comprising bills
     - (i) maturing as from the date of this return
       - (a) within 3 months
       - (b) between 3 and 6 months
       - (c) later than 6 months
     - (ii) past-due (unpaid and unaccepted)
       - (a) Payable outside Nigeria

7. LOANS AND ADVANCES FOR
   - (a) Other banks in Nigeria
   - (b) Other banks outside Nigeria
   - (c) Other Customers
     - (i) Subsidiary companies of this bank in Nigeria
     - (ii) Governments in Nigeria
       - (a) Federal
       - (b) State
       - (c) Local
     - (iii) Other Customers
       - Repayable from the date of this return
         - (i) within 3 months
         - (ii) within 6 months
         - (iii) within 12 months
         - (iv) later than 12 months

   - Securities
     - (i) Unsecured
     - (ii) Secured against real estate
     - (iii) Otherwise secured

     Total outstanding

8. INVESTMENTS
   - (a) Government Securities
   - (b) Stocks Bonds
   - (c) Public (Statutory Corporations)
   - (d) Subsidiary of this bank
   - (e) Others

9. FIXED ASSETS
   - (a) Bank premises (including land and buildings)
   - (b) Furniture and Fixtures
   - (c) Other Real Estate
   - (d) Other Fixed Assets

10. OTHER ASSETS INCLUDING GOLD

11. CUSTOMERS LIABILITIES (PER CONTRA)
    - (a) Liabilities of customers for acceptances
    - (b) Liabilities of customers for confirmed documentary credits
    - (c) Liabilities of customers for guarantees, endorsements and other obligations

12. OTHER ASSETS

We declare that this statement is made up from the books of the bank, and that, to the best of our knowledge and belief, it is correct.

_____   _____
      General Manager   *Chief Accountant*

SECOND SCHEDULE

Section 16 (2)

REPORT ON LOANS AND ADVANCES

(To be submitted in accordance with Section 16 of the Banking Decree 1969)

As at ....day of.................................19.........

Name of Reporting Bank..

Address ....

SECTION A

Loans and Advances analysed by Sector Borrowers:

CODE

Major Minor

0. AGRICULTURE, FORESTRY, FISHING, ETC.
    01 Agriculture (including live-stock, poultry, etc.)   ...   £...............
    02 Other   ...   .
    03 Timber (logging)   ...   .
    04 Fishing   ...   .   £...............

1. MINING AND QUARRYING
    01 Coal   ...   .   £...............
    02 Metallic mining (tin ore, iron, zinc and lead)   ...   ...
    03 Crude petroleum and gas   ...   .
    04 Other non-metallic mining (including quarrying and
        sandpits)   ...   .   £...............

2. MANUFACTURING
    01 Flour milling and bakeries   ...   .   £...............
    02 Meat and other food processing, canning and cold storage   ....
    03 Beverages, tobacco and tobacco products   ...   ...
    04 Textile and apparel (including spinning, weaving,
        finishing textiles and tailoring)   ...   .
    05 Footwear (excluding rubber footwear)   ...   .
    06 Woodproducts (including furniture)   ...   .
    07 Paper and paper products   ...   .
    08 Printing, publishing, etc. ...   .   £...............

3. 01 Manufacturing of rubber products (including rubber
        footwear) ...   .
    02 Soaps, oils and detergents ...   .
    03 Petroleum and coal products   ...   .
    04 Building materials, pottery, ceramics and glass   ...
    05 Other non-metallic products   ...   .
    06 Basic metal products (including smelting and
        fabricating)   ...   .
    07 Miscellaneous manufacturing and processing   ...   .   £...............

4. REAL ESTATE AND CONSTRUCTION
    01 Owner occupied property ...   .   £...............
    02 Commercial property:
        02.1 Residential   ...   .   £...............
        02.2 Non-Residential   ...   .   £...............   £...............
    03 Public construction   ...   .
    04 Other   ...   .   £...............

Major Minor

5.   PUBLIC UTILITIES
   01   Electricity, water, harbour, etc. ...   .   £...............

GENERAL COMMERCE

A. Exports

Minor		
01	Cocoa	£...............
02	Groundnuts and groundnut oil	....
03	Palm produce	....
04	Cotton	....
05	Hides and skins	....
06	Rubber and products	....
07	Timber and products	....
08	Other agricultural exports	....
09	Non-agricultural exports	....

B. Imports and Domestic Trade

Minor		
10	Imports	£...............
11	Domestic Trade	....
01	Wholesale merchant	....
02	Retail merchant	£...............

7.   TRANSPORTATION AND COMMUNICATIONS

Minor		
01	Rail transport	£...............
02	Road transport	....
03	Water transport	....
04	Air transport	....
05	Other Communications	£...............

8.   CREDIT AND FINANCIAL INSTITUTIONS

Minor	
01	Commercial banks and Acceptance Houses ... ...
02	Hire-purchase finance companies ... ...
03	Insurance companies ... ...
04	Building societies, finance co-operatives, real estate companies ... ...
05	Other financial institution ... ...

9.   GOVERNMENT

Minor	
01	Federal Government ... ...
02	State Governments ... ...
03	Local Governments ... ...

10.   GENERAL

Minor	
01	Personal and professional ... ...
02	Miscellaneous loans and advances ... ...
03	Total Section A. ... ...

SECTION B

11.   MONEY AT CALL AND BILLS DISCOUNTED

A. Money at Call

Minor			
01	Call money scheme	£...............	
02	Finance companies	....	
03	Commercial banks :		
	03.1 In Nigeria	£...............	£...............
	03.2 Abroad	£...............	£...............
04	Other	£...............	£...............

Major Minor

    B. *Bills Discounted*

05	Produce paper	£..................
06	Other commercial paper:	
	06.1 Payable in Nigeria	£ ....
	06.2 Payable abroad	£.............. £..................
07	Total Section B	£..................

SECTION C

12.   **LOANS AND ADVANCES BY TYPE OF SECURITY**

01	Documentary bills	£..................
02	Plant, equipment and other real estate	....
03	Time and savings deposits, life insurance policies and other cash deposits	....
04	Corporate, and government securities and other financial assets	....
05	Personal guarantee	....
06	Otherwise secured	....
07	Unsecured	....
08	Total Section C	£..................

SECTION D

13.   **LOANS AND ADVANCES BY MATURITY**

01	On Call	£..................
02	Maturing within 3 months	....
03	Maturing between 3 and 6 months	....
04	Maturing between 6 and 12 months	....
05	Maturing between 1 and 5 years	....
06	Maturing after 5 years	*..................
07	Total Section D	£..................

    07.1 *Of which past-due and uncollected   ...   ... £............

SECTION E

14.   **LOANS AND ADVANCES BY METHOD OF REPAYMENT**

01	Overdraft	£..................
02	Repayable by specifically agreed instalments	£..................
03	Repayable in one single payment...	£..................
04	Total Section E	£..................

Major Minor

SECTION F

15. LOANS AND ADVANCES BY AMOUNT NUMBER AND TYPE OF BORROWERS

Amount	Total Amount to Indigenous Persons	Total Amount to Others	Total Amount £	No. of Borrowers Indigenous Others
01 Up to £50				
02 Over £50 and up to £100 ...				
03 Over £100 and up to £500				
04 Over £500 and up to £1,000				
05 Over £1,000 and up to £5,000				
06 Over £5,000 and up to £10,000				
07 Over £10,000 and up to £50,000				
08 Over £50,000				
09 TOTAL				

Name and address of person to contact if questions arise concerning this report:

....

....

....

Signature of Authorised Officer

Title...

Date...

THIRD SCHEDULE   Sections 17, 18 and 19

ACCOUNTS

Preliminary

1.   Paragraphs 2 to 11 of this Schedule apply to the balance sheet and paragraphs 12 to 16 apply to the profit and loss account.

GENERAL PROVISIONS AS TO BALANCE SHEET AND PROFIT AND

LOSS ACCOUNT

Balance Sheet

2.   The authorised share capital, issued share capital liabilities and assets shall be summarised, with such particulars as are necessary to disclose the general nature of the assets and liabilities, and there shall be specified—

(*a*) any part of the issued capital that consists of redeemable preference shares and the earliest date on which the person has power to redeem those shares;

(*b*) the amount of the share premium account;

(*c*) particulars of any redeemed debentures which the person has power to re-issue.

3.   There shall be stated under separate headings, insofar as they are not written off—

(*a*) the preliminary expenses;

(*b*) any expenses incurred in connection with any issue of share capital or debentures;

(*c*) any sums paid by way of commission in respect of any shares or debentures;

(*d*) any sums allowed by way of discount in respect of any debentures.

4. (1) The following shall be classified under headings appropriately itemised:

(*a*) Cash in hand,

(*b*) Balance due to and from other banks,

(*c*) Short-term investments falling within the terms of section 12 (5) (*d*) and (*e*) of this Decree,

(*d*) Other Investments,

    (e) Loans and Advances,

    (f) Fixed Assets,

    (g) Other Assets,

    (h) Deposits,

    (i) Borrowings,

    (j) Other Liabilities,

    (k) Provisions and Reserves,

    (l) Capital,

    (m) Liabilities for Acceptances, Guarantees, etc.

    (2) The method or methods used to arrive at the amount of each item of fixed assets shall be stated.

5.   Loans and Advances shall be shown gross less the amount of provisions made in respect of debts doubtful or recovery. Where no provision is considered necessary a note to that effect shall appear on the balance sheet.

6.   In respect of Balances due to and from other banks, a distinction shall be made between balances held in Nigeria and outside Nigeria.

7.   Demand deposits, savings accounts and time deposits shall be itemised under the heading "Deposits".

8.   In respect of investments shown under "Other Investments" in paragraph 4 (1) (d) above, a distinction shall be made between the quoted and unquoted investments.

9. (1) The method of arriving at the net amount of any fixed assets shall be the difference between—

    (a) its cost or, if it stands in the person's books at a valuation, the amount of the valuation; and

    (b) the aggregate amount provided or written-off since the date of acquisition or valuation, as the case may be, for depreciation or diminution in value.

For the purposes of this paragraph the net amount at which any assets stand in the person's books at the commencement of this Decree (after deduction of the amounts previously provided or written-off for depreciation or diminution in value) shall, if the figures relating to the period before the commencement of this Decree cannot be obtained without unreasonable expense or delay, be treated as if it were the amount of a valuation of the said asset made at the commencement of this

Decree, and, where any of those amount less the assets are sold, the said net amount of the sales shall be treated as if it were the amount of a valuation so made of the remaining assets.

(2) The foregoing sub-paragraph shall not apply—

(a) to assets for which the figures relating to the period beginning with the commencement of this Decree cannot be obtained without unreasonable expense or delay; or

(b) to assets the replacement of which is provided for wholly or partly—

(i) by making provision for renewals and charging the cost of replacement against the provision so made; or

(ii) by charging the cost of replacement direct to revenue.

(3) For the assets under each heading the amount of which in each case is arrived at in accordance with sub-paragraph (1) of this paragraph, there shall be shown—

(a) the aggregate of the amounts referred to in paragraph (a) of that sub-paragraph; and

(b) the aggregate of the amount referred to in paragraph (b) thereof.

10. The aggregate amounts respectively of statutory reserves, capital reserves, revenue reserves and provisions (other than provisions for depreciation, renewals or diminution in value of assets) shall be stated under separate headings:

Provided that the Central Bank may direct that a separate statement of the amount of provisions, shall not be required where the Central Bank is satisfied that such a statement is not required* in the public interest and would prejudice the person, but subject to the condition that any heading stating an amount arrived at after taking into account a provision (other than as aforesaid) shall be so framed or marked as to indicate that fact.

11. The matters referred to in the following sub-paragraphs shall be stated by way of note, or in a statement or report annexed, if not otherwise shown—

(a) the amount of any arrears of fixed cumulative dividends, on the person's shares and the period for which the dividends, or if there are more than one class of them, each class of them are in arrears, the amount to be stated before deduction of income tax, except that in the case of tax free dividends, the amount shall be shown free of tax and the fact that it is so shown shall also be stated;

(b) the general nature of any other contingent liabilities not provided for and, where practicable, the aggregate amount or estimated amount of those liabilities;

(c) where practicable the aggregate amount or estimated amount of contracts for capital expenditure so far as not provided for;

(d) the basis on which foreign currencies have been converted into £N, where the amount of the assets or liabilities affected is material;

(e) the basis on which the amount, if any, set aside for Income Tax is computed;

(f) the amount of the net External Assets or Liabilities of the person;

(g) the amount of deposits, if any, held by persons not ordinarily resident in Nigeria;

(h) the total amounts respectively of loans and advances secured against real estate, otherwise secured and unsecured;

(i) except in the case of the first balance sheet of the person after the commencement of this Decree, the corresponding amounts at the end of the immediately preceding financial year for all items shown in the balance sheet;

(j) the market value of the investments.

Profit and Loss Account

12. There shall be shown—

(a) the amount charged to revenue by way of provision for depreciation, renewals or diminution in value of fixed assets;

(b) the amount charged to revenue by way of provision for debts doubtful of recovery;

(c) the amount of bad debts written-off where such amount is not charged to a provision created as in sub-paragraph (b) above;-

(*d*) the amount of the interest on the person's borrowings, distinguishing between interest paid in respect of borrowings from banks and other creditors respectively in Nigeria and that paid in respect of borrowings from banks and other creditors respectively outside Nigeria;

(*e*) the amount of the charge for Nigerian income tax and other Nigerian taxation on profits, including, where practicable, as Nigerian income tax any taxation imposed elsewhere to the extent of the relief, if any, from Nigerian income tax;

(*f*) the amount, if any, provided for redemption of loans;

(*g*) the amount set aside or proposed to be set aside to, or withdrawn from, reserves;

(*h*) the aggregate amount of the dividends paid and proposed;

(*i*) the remuneration of the auditors if such remuneration is not fixed by the person in general meeting, the amount thereof shall be shown under a separate heading, and for the purposes of this paragraph, any sums paid by the person in respect of the auditors' expenses shall be deemed to be included in the expression "remuneration";

(*j*) (*i*) the aggregate amount of directors' emoluments;

    (*ii*) the aggregate amount of directors' or past directors' pensions; and

    (*iii*) the aggregate amount of any compensation to directors or past directors in respect of loss of office.

For the purposes of this sub-paragraph the expression "emoluments", in relation to a director includes fees and percentages, any sums paid by way of expenses allowance insofar as those sums are charged to Nigerian income tax, any contribution paid in respect of him under any pension scheme and the estimated money value of any other benefits received by him otherwise than in cash.

13. The earnings of the company shall be classified under the headings, "INTERESTS", "TRANSFER CHARGES", "FOREIGN EXCHANGE", "OTHER INCOME".

14.　　The matters referred to in the following sub-paragraphs shall be stated by way of note, if not otherwise shown—

(a) the basis on which the charge for Nigerian income tax is computed;

(b) except in the case of the first profit and loss account laid before the person after the commencement of this Decree, the corresponding amounts for the immediately preceding financial year for all items shown in the profit and loss account;

(c) any material respects in which any items shown in the profit and loss account are affected—

(i) by transactions of a sort not usually undertaken by the person or otherwise by circumstances of any exceptional or non-recurrent nature; or

(ii) by any change in the basis of accounting.

FOURTH SCHEDULE
Sections 18 and 19

MATTERS TO BE EXPRESSLY STATED IN AUDITORS' REPORT

The auditors' report shall indicate the following matters—

(a) whether they have obtained all the information and explanations which, to the best of their knowledge and belief, were necessary for the purposes of their audit;

(b) whether, in their opinion, proper books of account have been kept by the person licensed under this Decree, at Head Office, and at each of the person's branches, and in such form as explain, and give a true and fair view of, all the transactions of the person;

(c) whether they have examined the books of the person at Head Office, and at each of the person's branches, and whether proper returns adequate for the purposes of their audit have been received from branches not visited;

(d) whether, to the best of their knowledge and belief, there have been any contraventions of the Banking Decree 1969 and other related legislation during the period covered by the audited accounts and whether every such contravention has been reported to the Central Bank as required by law;

(e) whether, in their opinion, the assets of the person have been properly valued, and whether adequate provisions have been made for losses and diminution in the value of the person's assets;

(f) whether, in their opinion, and to the best of their information, and having regard to the explanations given to them, the audited accounts of the person are in agreement with the books of account kept and give the information required by this Decree in the manner so required, and also give a true and fair view—

(i) in the case of the balance sheet, of the state of the person's affairs as at the end of its financial year;

(ii) in the case of the profit and loss accounts, of the profit or loss for its financial year.

APPENDIX - 1

Section 19

FIFTH SCHEDULE

AUDITOR'S ANALYSIS OF DOUBTFUL ADVANCES (LIMITED TO ADVANCES OVER £2,000) AS AT ....

Name of Customer	Date Advanced or Last Instalment of Advances Drawn	Original Amount of Advances	Rate of Interest (Insert X if Interest Stopped)	Date of Last Repayment	Balance Outstanding		Efforts made by the Bank to recover Advances	Realisable Value of Security Held (if any)	Estimate of Bad and Doubtful Debts		Remarks
					Capital	Interest Accumulated			Doubtful	Loss	
SECTION 'A'											
SECTION 'B'											
SECTION 'C'											

NOTE:

SECTION 'A'   Advances which have not been fully recovered because of insufficient efforts on the part of the bank.

SECTION 'B'   Advances which may either be fully or partly irrecoverable by reasons of the known financial position of the debtors.

SECTION 'C'   Others (Advances granted to deceased persons and defunct companies should be included here).

Made at Lagos this 7th day of February, 1969

MAJOR-GENERAL Y. GOWON,
Head of the Federal Military Government,
Commander-in-Chief of the Armed Forces,
Federal Republic of Nigeria.

PUBLISHED BY AUTHORITY OF THE FEDERAL MILITARY GOVERNMENT OF NIGERIA
AND Printed By Central Bank Press, Lagos

APPENDIX 2

BANKING (AMENDMENT) ACT, 1979

(formerly Banking (Amendment) Decree, 1979

Reprinted from the original

[*28th September* 1979]

Commencement.

THE FEDERAL MILITARY GOVERNMENT hereby decrees as follows :—

1. The Banking Decree 1969 is hereby amended as follows :—

(*a*) in section 2, subsection (4) thereof shall be deleted ;

(*b*) in section 3, for subsection (1) thereof, there shall be substituted the following new subsection—

Sundry amendments to the Banking Decree 1969. 1969 No. 1.

"(1) The Commissioner may at any time on the recommendation of the Central Bank and with the approval of the Federal Executive Council, vary or revoke any of the conditions of a licence or impose such conditions or additional conditions as the Commissioner may deem necessary." ;

(*c*) for section 6 there shall be subtituted the following new section :—

"Requirements as to minimum paid-up capital.

6.—(1) No bank shall hold or be granted a licence unless—

(*a*) as respects a bank which is not directly or indirectly controlled from abroad, its paid-up share capital is not less than ₦600,000 ;

(*b*) as respects a bank which is directly or indirectly controlled from abroad, its paid-up share capital is not less than ₦1,500,000 ; and

(*c*) as respects a merchant bank, its paid-up capital is not less than ₦2,000,000.

(2) The Central Bank may, after consultation with the Commissioner, specify the minimum ratio which licensed banks shall maintain between their respective paid-up capital and all retained earnings on the one hand and their loans and advances on the other.

(3) The Central Bank shall, as respects merchant banks, from time to time specify the ratio of—

(*a*) deposits and call money held for other banks to be maintained in liquid assets ;

(*b*) loans and advances to the bank's total assets ;

(*c*) total loans and advances that may be repayable within one year.

(4) Except with the prior approval of the Central Bank, a bank which fails to maintain any ratio specified pursuant to subsection (2) or (3) of this section may not increase its loans and advances.

(5) For the purposes of subsection (1) of this section, a bank shall be deemed to be controlled from abroad—

(*a*) if the composition of its board of directors consists wholly or mainly of persons who are not citizens of Nigeria ; or

(*b*) where the majority voting rights of that company are held by persons who are not citizens of Nigeria.

(6) Any failure to comply with any of the foregoing provisions of this section shall be a ground for the revocation of the licence of the bank under this Decree." ;

(*d*) in section 8, for subsection (1) thereof there shall be substituted the following new subsection—

"(1) The Commissioner may on the recommendation of the Central Bank and with the approval of the Federal Executive Council by order published in the *Gazette*, revoke any licence—

(*a*) if the holder thereof ceases to carry on in Nigeria the type of banking business for which he was licensed or goes into liquidation or is wound up or otherwise dissolved ; or

(*b*) if the holder thereof fails to fulfil the prescribed conditions and regulations ; or

(*c*) in the circumstances and in the manner where under this Decree failure to comply with any provisions thereof is a ground for revocation of licence." ;

(*e*) in section 10 (1) thereof, the word "and" at the end of paragraph (*a*) shall be deleted, for the full stop at the end of paragraph (*b*) there shall be substituted a semi-colon, and immediately after paragraph (*b*) there shall be inserted the following new paragraph—

"(*c*) it has complied with any direction given by the Central Bank pursuant to subsection (2) or (3) of section 6 of this Decree." ;

(*f*) in section 12 (5) thereof, for the full stop at the end of paragraph (*e*) there shall be substituted a semi-colon and immediately after that paragraph there shall be inserted the following new paragraphs—

"(*f*) stocks issued by the Federal Government with such dates of maturity as may be approved by the Central Bank ;

(*g*) negotiable certificates of deposit approved by the Central Bank ;

(*h*) such other negotiable instruments as may from time to time be approved by the Central Bank for the purposes of this subsection." ;

(*g*) in section 13—

(*i*) for subsection 1 thereof, there shall be substituted the following new subsection, that is—

(1) A licensed bank shall not, without the prior approval of the Central Bank—

(*a*) grant to any person any advance, loan or credit facilities or give any financial guarantee or incur any other liability on behalf of such person so that the total value of the advances, loans, credit facilities, financial guarantees and other liabilities in respect of such person is at anytime more than thirty-three and one-third *per centum* of the sum of the paid-up capital and statutory reserves of the bank; and in the case of a merchant bank, more than the sum of its paid-up capital and statutory reserves :

Provided that the provisions of this paragraph shall not apply to transactions between licensed banks or between branches of a licenced bank or to the purchase of clean or documentary bills of exchange, telegraphic transfers or documents of title to goods the holder of which is entitled to payment for exports from Nigeria or to advances made against such bills, transfers or documents ; and for the purposes of this paragraph, all advances, loans or credit facilities extended to any person shall be aggregated and shall include all advances, loans or credit facilities extended to any subsidiaries of that person ;

(*b*) grant any advances, loans or credit facilities against the security of its own shares ;

(*c*) grant or permit to be outstanding, unsecured advances or loans, or unsecured credit facilities, of an aggregate amount in excess of ₦1,000—

(*i*) to its directors or any of them, whether such advances, loans or credit facilities are obtained by its directors jointly or severally ;

(*ii*) to any firm, partnership or private company in which it or anyone or more of its directors is interested as director, partner, manager or agent, or to any individual, firm, partnership or private company of which any of its directors is a guarantor ;

(*iii*) to any public company in which it or any one or more of its directors jointly or severally maintains an interest either directly or indirectly ;

(*d*) grant or permit to be outstanding to its officials and employees, unsecured advances or loans, or unsecured credit facilities, which in aggregate amount for any one official or employee exceeds one year's emoluments of such official or employee ;

(*e*) engage, whether on its own account or on a commission basis, in the wholesale or retail trade, including the import or export trade, except in so for as may exceptionally be necessary in the course of the banking operations and services of that licensed bank or in the course of the satisfaction of debts due to it, so however that nothing in this paragraph shall be construed as precluding a merchant bank from undertaking equipment-leasing business or debt factoring ;

(*f*) acquire or hold any part of the share capital of any financial, commercial, agricultural, industrial or other undertaking, except—

(*i*) such shareholding as a licensed bank may, with the prior approval of the Central Bank, acquire in the course of satisfaction of debts due to it, which share-holding shall, however, be disposed of at the earliest suitable moment,

(*ii*) any shareholding approved by the Central Bank in any statutory corporation set up for the purpose of promoting the development of a money market or a securities market in Nigeria or of improving the financial machinery for financing of economic development,

(*iii*) all share-holdings approved by the Central Bank in other undertakings the aggregate value of which does not at any time exceed twenty-five *per centum* of the sum of the paid-up capital and statutory reserves of that bank,

(*iv*) all share holdings acquired by a merchant bank while managing an equity issue : Provided that the aggregate value of such acquisition does not at any time exceed the sum of the paid-up capital of that merchant bank or 10 *per centum* of its total assets excluding contra items, whichever is the higher ;

(*g*) remit, either in whole or in part, the debts owed to it by any of its directors or past directors : Provided that the provisions of this paragraph shall not apply to any nominee company of a licensed bank which deals in stocks and shares for or on behalf of the bank's customers or clients or majority interests acquired by a merchant bank in a company while managing an equity issue ;

(*h*) own any subsidiary company which is not carrying on a banking business ;

(*i*) purchase, acquire or lease real estate, except as may be necessary for the purpose of conducting its business, including provisions for foreseeable future expansion or housing of its staff or other exceptional circumstances, where the agreement of the Central Bank is obtained ;

(*j*) sell, dispose or lease out any real estate, except with the prior approval of the Central Bank : Provided that a licensed bank may secure a debt on any real or other property, and in default of repayment may acquire such property and exercise any power of sale or as may be provided for in any instrument, or by law prescribed, immediately upon such default or soon thereafter as may be deemed proper." ;

(*ii*) immediately after subsection (5) thereof, there shall be inserted the following new subsections—

"(6) A merchant bank shall not—

(*ii*) accept any deposit withdrawable by cheque except from its corporate clients ;

(*b*) accept from any depositor total interest-bearing deposit of an amount lower than ₦50,000 ;

(*c*) except with the prior approval of the Central Bank, hold for more than six months any equity interest acquired in a company while managing an equity issue.

(7) Any merchant bank which acts in contravention of or fails to comply with any of the provisions of subsection (6) of this section shall be guilty of an offence and liable to a fine of ₦100 for each day during which the offence continues." ; and

(*iii*) the existing subsection (6) shall be renumbered as subsection (8) ;

(*h*) in section 16 (1), immediately after the word "Decree" in paragraph (*a*) thereof, there shall be inserted the words "or as modified, in the case of a merchant bank, by the Central Bank ;"

(*i*) in section 26 (1), the words "and subject to subsection (2) of this section" occurring in the first line shall be deleted ;

(*j*) in section 41—

(*i*) in the definition of bank in subsection (1) thereof, for the words "and financial institution" in the second and third lines thereof, there shall be substituted the words", financial institution and merchant bank ;", the word "and" at the end of paragraph (*c*) shall be deleted and immediately after paragraph (*d*) of that definition there shall be inserted the following new paragraph—

"(*e*) "merchant bank" means any person in Nigeria who is engaged in wholesale banking, medium and long term financing, equipment leasing, debt factoring, investment management, issue and acceptance of bills and the management of unit trusts" ;

(*ii*) in subsection (2) thereof the word "and" at the end of paragraph (*c*) shall be deleted and immediately after paragraph (*d*), there shall be inserted the following new paragraph:—

"(*e*) merchant bank ;".

2. This Decree may be cited as the Banking (Amendment) Decree 1979. Citation

MADE at Lagos this 28th day of September 1979.

GENERAL O. OBASANJO,
Head of the Federal Military Government,
Commander-in-Chief of the Armed Forces,
Federal Republic of Nigeria

EXPLANATORY NOTE

*(This note does not form part of the above Decree but is
intended to explain its purpose)*

The Decree amends the Banking Decree 1969 *inter alia* to extend the
application of its provisions to the operations of merchant banks.

PUBLISHED BY AUTHORITY OF THE FEDERAL MILITARY GOVERNMENT OF NIGERIA
AND PRINTED BY THE MINISTRY OF INFORMATION, PRINTING DIVISION, LAGOS

APPENDIX 3

MONETARY POLICY CIRCULAR No. 16 CENTRAL BANK CREDIT GUIDELINES FOR 1983 FISCAL YEAR

PART I — BANKS

Monetary expansion moderated considerably in 1981 and 1982 after the accelerated expansion in the preceding two years. As in 1981, the moderation in the expansion of money supply in 1982 was due to a decline in foreign exchange earnings from exports, especially oil export, and continued high level of outflow of funds to the external sector to finance imports. The resultant low level of foreign reserves at the end of 1982 has rendered the moderate rate of monetary expansion in the year even excessive in relation to its foreign reserves backing. The rate of inflation declined during 1982 compared with 1981.

Against this background, the monetary and fiscal policies for 1983 are formulated mainly to achieve a substantial improvement in the balance of payments; accelerate the rate of domestic production and thus further restrain price inflation, mobilize domestic savings and attract foreign capital into more productive economic activities. They are designed also to promote a more efficient allocation of productive resources, and ensure that the financial needs of small scale enterprises are adequately catered for.

Banks are again hereby enjoined to pay special attention to the prescribed overall credit ceiling and to the sectoral distribution of their loans and advances particularly to agriculture, housing and small-scale industries in 1983, so as to ensure the attainment of Government socio-economic objectives. The penalties prescribed for non-compliance in the previous two fiscal years will be retained in 1983 and will be strictly enforced.

Guidelines for 1983

1. Aggregate Credit

In order to foster the financial environment considered conducive to the attainment of the Government's macro-economic objectives for 1983, credit expansion during the year should be moderated. On the basis of individual commercial and merchant bank's aggregate loans and advances (as per sections A and B of the Second Schedule Returns) outstanding as at 31st December, 1982 each bank's aggregate loans and advances shall not rise by more than 25 per cent during 1983 fiscal year. However, small banks with loans and advances not exceeding ₦100 million as at 31st December, 1982, may be allowed to exceed the 25 per cent ceiling up to 35 per cent, or

60 per cent of their total deposit liabilities (excluding government deposits maturing earlier than six months) whichever is higher. Loans granted for the purchase of shares by Nigerians under the Indigenisation Scheme, and for buying motor cars by workers both in the public and private sectors, are to be excluded from the credit ceiling. Also to be excluded are loan facilities granted for agriculture and residential building construction over and above the minimum prescribed under the Sectoral Distribution of Loans and Advances. Loans for residential buildings shall be for a minimum period of fifteen years except at the instance of the borrower.

Banks are required to supply as an attachment to their monthly returns information on the following items:

(i)   Loans and advances to purchase shares under the Indigenisation Decree;

(ii) Loans to employees in the private and public sectors for purpose of buying motor cars; and

(iii) Loans and advances to small-scale enterprises, classified as specified under section 4 of this guideline.

Such information shall be supplied in the form shown below:

Name of Bank . . . .

Reporting Month . . . . .19 . . . .

SEE TABLE OPPOSITE

2. Sectoral Distribution of Loans and Advances: Commercial Banks

The sectoral credit allocations prescribed for 1982 are retained for 1983 with the following adjustments:

(a)   allocation to agricultural production is raised from 8 to 10 per cent;

(b)   allocation to Exports is reduced from 3 to 2 per cent;

(c)   allocation to domestic trade is reduced from 11 to 10 per cent.

Thus allocation to the Production Sectors is increased to 61 per cent from the prescribed 59 per cent in 1982.

Purpose of Loans (1)	Total amount outstanding as at end of the preceding month (2)	Loans granted during the month (3)	Repayments made during the month (4)	Total amount outstanding as at the end of the reporting month (5)
1. Purchase of shares				
2. Purchase of motor cars				
3. Small-scale Enterprises: Categories: A B C D E				

In 1983, allocation of each commercial bank's total loans and advances to various sectors/sub-sectors of the economy will therefore be as stated below:

Commercial Banks

A. Preferred sectors/sub-sectors	Minimum Percentage Share
(i) Production	61.0
Agricultural Production	10.0
Mining	2.0
Manufacturing	36.0
(a) Agro-allied industries	(3.0)
(b) Other manufacturing	(33.0)
Construction	13.0
(a) Residential building	(6.0)
(b) Others	(7.0)
(ii) Services	12.0
Public utilities	3.0
Transportation and Communications	9.0
(iii) Exports	2.0
(iv) Development Finance Institutions[1]	1.0
TOTAL (A)	76.0

[1] The development oriented finance institutions for the time being are:

(a) Nigerian Industrial Development Bank Limited.

(b) Nigerian Bank for Commerce and Industry.

(c) O'dua Investment Company Limited.

(d) Northern Nigeria Investment Limited.

(e) New Nigeria Development Company Limited.

(f) Central Investment Corporation.

(g) Investment Companies owned by State Governments.

In view of the fact that development Finance Companies are expected to engage in long-term investment, loans granted to any qualified institutions must satisfy two conditions before such loans could qualify for classification under A (iv);

(i) the maturity of the loan should not be less than five years and with a minimum grace period of two years before repayment of principal starts;

(ii) the rate of interest on the loan should not be more than two percentage points above the Minimum Lending Rate of the Central Bank of Nigeria.

B. Less Preferred Sectors/Sub-sectors — **Minimum Percentage Shares**

(v) General Commerce — 16.0
Imports — 6.0
Domestic trade — 10.0
(vi) Others — 8.0
Credit and financial institutions — 1.0
Government — 3.0
Personal and professional — 4.0
TOTAL (B) — 24.0
TOTAL (A) + (B) — 100.0

Note: Percentage shares in sectors and sub-sectors A(i), (ii), (iii) and (iv) should be regarded as MINIMA while those for the sectors and sub-sectors B(v) and (vi) should be regarded as MAXIMA. In other words, banks may exceed the targets for the preferred sectors within the overall ceiling.

The guidelines in respect of the sectoral allocation of the merchant banks' loans and advances in 1983 shall be the same as in 1982. With effect from January 1983, the share of the "Preferred Sectors" shall not be less than 79 per cent while that of the "Less Preferred Sectors" should not exceed 21 per cent.

The prescribed sectoral distribution of merchant banks' loans and advances for 1983 are as follows:

Merchant Banks

A. Preferred sectors/sub-sectors — **Minimum Percentage Share**

(i) Production — 69.0
Agriculture — 5.0
Mining — 3.0
Manufacturing — 41.0
(a) Agro-allied industries — (5.0)
(b) Other manufacturing — (36.0)

<u>Construction</u>	20.0
(a) Residential building	(6.0)
(b) Others	(14.0)
(ii) <u>Services</u>	7.0
Public utilities	3.0
Transportation and Communications	4.0
(iii) Exports	3.0
TOTAL (A)	79.0

B. Less Preferred sectors/sub-sectors	Maximum Percentage Share
(iv) <u>General Commerce</u>	14.0
Imports	8.0
Domestic trade	6.0
(v) <u>Others</u>	7.0
Credit and financial institutions	3.0
Government	2.0
Miscellaneous	2.0
TOTAL (B)	21.0
TOTAL (A) + (B)	100.0

Note: Percentage shares in sectors and sub-sectors A(i), (ii) and (iii) should be regarded as MINIMA while those for the sectors and sub-sectors B(iv) and (v) should be regarded as MAXIMA. In other words merchant banks may exceed the targets for the preferred sectors within the overall ceiling.

The existing guidelines, designed to ensure a desirable structure of merchant banks' portfolio of financial assets are retained for 1983 as follows:

(a) A minimum of 40 per cent of total loans and advances shall be of a medium and long-term nature with maturity of not less than 3 years.

(b) A maximum of 20 per cent of loans and advances shall be of short-term nature, i.e. maturing within 12 months.

(c) A maximum of 15 per cent of total assets shall be in equipment leasing.

3. Penalties for default

Banks should note that failure to comply with the guidelines stipulations in respect of: (1) ceiling on aggregate loans and advances, and (2) sectoral distribution of such loans, will continue to attract the penalties stated below:

Where a bank's monthly aggregate of loans and advances, excluding loans for the purchase of shares under the Indigenisation Scheme, facilities to workers for purchase of cars and loans to Agriculture and Residential Building Construction over and above the minimum prescribed under the guidelines on sectoral allocation of bank credit, rises by more than 25 per cent or 35 per cent as the case may be or its credit to import sub-sector and the less preferred sectors in general, exceeds the prescribed percentage, the bank shall receive a warning on the first default. For any subsequent default or continuation of a default, the bank shall pay to the Central Bank a stipulated penalty on the excess credit as follows:

1st default — warning.
2nd default — payment of 1/16 per cent of the excess credit.
3rd default — payment of 1/8 per cent of the excess credit.
4th default — payment of 3/16 per cent of the excess credit.
5th default — payment of ¼ per cent of the excess credit.
6th default — payment of ½ per cent of the excess credit.

Banks shall not in any way pass such penalties to their customers.

Where a bank's total monthly loans and advances to agriculture and residential building construction fall short of the guideline's minimum ratios of 10 and 6 per cent, respectively, for commercial banks; and 5 and 6 per cent, respectively, for merchant banks, such banks shall be required to deposit the amount of the shortfall with the Central Bank. The refund of such money to the banks may not be automatic if later the banks meet the minimum ratios. such deposits lodged with the Central Bank shall not count as part of the specified liquid assets, and shall also not attract any interest.

4. Loans to Indigenous Borrowers

The minimum proportion of total loans and advances that should be given to indigenous borrowers was raised to 80 per cent in 1982. This proportion is retained for 1983. Thus each bank's minimum credit allocation to indigenous borrowers in 1983 should be 80 per cent of the total. The share of this 80 per cent that should be reserved exclusively for small-scale enterprises wholly owned by Nigerians must not be less than 16 per cent thus leaving 64 per cent to other indigenous borrowers. Distribution of the 16 per cent among such enterprises will continue to be based on their annual business turnover as follows:-

A.	Up to ₦25,000	— 1.6 per cent
B.	Over ₦25,000 — ₦50,000	— 2.0 per cent
C.	Over ₦50,000 — ₦100,000	— 3.2 per cent
D.	Over ₦100,000 — ₦200,000	— 4.0 per cent
E.	Over ₦200,000 — ₦500,000	— 5.2 per cent

A breakdown of loans to small scale enterprises wholly owned by Nigerians shall be supplied as an attachment to the Second Schedule as specified under Aggregate Credit (above).

5. Loans to Rural Areas

In order to enhance the contribution of the on-going rural banking scheme to the development of the rural areas, banks are required in 1983, as in the past year, to lend not less than 30 per cent of the total deposits collected through their rural branches to customers in those rural areas.

6. Capital Funds

Except with the approval of the Central Bank, a commercial bank may not apply its funds for payment of dividends to its shareholders in 1983, unless such a bank maintains a ratio of not less than one to twelve (1:12) between its adjusted capital funds and its total loans and advances, (that is the former should not be less than 8⅓ per cent of the latter). Provisions for bad and doubtful debts would be netted out of loans and advances before the calculation of the ratio.

7. Reserve Requirements

(i) Cash Reserve Requirement

Each commercial bank shall continue to maintain a minimum amount of cash deposits with the Central Bank of Nigeria at its Head Office in

Lagos. The cash deposit shall be expressed as a ratio of each bank's total demand deposit liabilities. As in 1982, the prescribed minimum ratio for each of the four classes of banks, based on total deposit liabilities, shall be as detailed below:

Class	Total Deposit Liabilities	Ratio of cash to demand deposit (per cent)
A.	₦300 million or more	5.0
B.	₦100 million or more but less than ₦300 million	4.0
C.	₦30 million or more but less than ₦100 million	3.0
D.	Less than ₦30 million	2.0

(ii) Compulsory Advance Deposits for Imports

The regulations regarding Compulsory Advance Deposits against imports which came into effect from the 21st of April, 1982 as amended in CBN Circular of October 27, 1982 shall continue to be in force in 1983 as follows:-

Items	Percentage deposits relative to the value of Imports Per cent
Raw materials	10
Spare parts	15
Food (except rice)	50
Medicaments	50
Building materials	50
Capital goods	50
Books	50
Motor vehicles and Trucks	200
Motor cars	250
Other goods	250

(a) Imports under letters of credit

In the case of imports under letters of credit, banks must demand and obtain the required percentage advance deposits for the particular imports before opening the letter of credit. All such deposits are to be kept in a separate account and deposited with the Central Bank of Nigeria within three days following the end of each month, interest free. Where, for its own purposes, a bank collects advance deposits in excess of the prescribed percentage, the whole of the advance deposits so collected by that bank must be deposited with the Central Bank in all cases, interest free.

(b) Imports under Usance Bills, Bills for Collection and Payments on Account

(i) As regards imports under Usance Bills of less than six months' maturity from the date of shipment of goods to Nigeria, and for Bills for Collection and Payments on Account of less than six months' duration from the date of shipment of goods to Nigeria, importers are required to make advance deposits for imports, in the required percentages, not later than ten days before the vessel carrying the goods arrives at any Nigerian port. Where, for its own purposes, a bank collects advance deposits more than the prescribed percentage, the whole of the advance deposits so collected by that bank must be deposited with the Central Bank in all cases, interest free. All advance deposits are to be kept in a separate account and deposited with the Central Bank of Nigeria within three days following the end of each month, interest free. The schedules relating to the deposits should be classified into Usance Bills, Bills for Collection and Payments on Account, as well as their maturities. Failure by importers to make the advance deposits for each consignment within the specified period will mean that no foreign exchange will be provided for the imports.

(ii) In the case of imports for which credit facilities of more than six months from the date of shipment have been obtained, no advance deposit is required. However, the importers are required to register with the Exchange Control Department of the Central Bank through their bankers such credit facilities of more than six months' maturity from the date of shipment of any particular consignment for which foreign exchange will subsequently be required for settlement. Registration must be made by the importer seven days before the arrival of the goods at any Nigerian port. In this connection, every bank is required to submit to the Central Bank within three days following the end of each month the following information in respect of such credit facilities for imports obtained by its customers:

(i)   Name and address of the importer

(ii)   Name and address of the overseas supplier

(iii) Name and address of the overseas bank

(iv)   Date of registration of Form M

(v)   Registered number of Form M

(vi)   Value of import stated on Form M

(vii) Description of goods

(viii) Date of shipment of the particular consignment

(ix)   Date and number of bill of lading

(x)   Value of the particular consignment

(xi)   Expected date of arrival of the consignment

(xii) Amount of credit granted for the consignment

(xiii) Payment due date.

(c) Advance deposits for imports shall not count for purposes of meeting the liquidity requirements of banks.

(iii) Liquidity Ratio

The minimum specified liquidity ratio shall remain at 25 per cent in 1983. As in the preceding years, deposits made with the Central Bank in respect of Compulsory advance deposits for imports and shortfalls of loans to agriculture and residential building construction, and cash holdings for meeting cash requirements shall not count for the purpose of computing liquidity ratio.

8. Interest Rates

The following interest rates shall continue to be in force in 1983.

			Interest Rate (%)
(i)	Minimum Rediscount Rate	...	8
(ii)	Treasury Bill issue rate	...	7
(iii)	Treasury Certificate (1 year)	...	7½
(iv)	Treasury Certificate (2 years)	...	8
(v)	Federal Government Stock	...	9-9¾
	4 - 8 years maturity	...	9
	9 - 14 years maturity	...	9¼
	15 - 20 years maturity	...	9½
	21 - 25 years maturity	...	9¾
(vi)	Deposit Rates (Commercial Banks)		
	Savings Deposit	...	7½
	Time Deposits with 7 days notice	...	6½
	" " for 1 month	...	7
	" " for 1 - 3 months	...	7¼
	Time Deposits for 3 - 6 months	...	7½
	" " " 6 - 12 months	...	7¾
	" " " over 12 months	...	8
(vii)	Lending Rates: Minimum	...	9½
	Maximum	...	13
	(a) Preferred sectors maximum	...	11½
	(b) Less preferred sectors maximum	...	13
	(c) Agricultural Credit Guarantee Scheme		6 - 7
	(d) Residential Housing Costing not more than ₦100,000		7
	(e) Agricultural production	...	7
(viii)	Specialised Institutions		
	(a) Fed. Savings Bank-Savings Deposit Rate		7½
	(b) Nigerian Ind. Dev. Bank (Lending Rates)		10½ - 13
	(c) Nig. Bank for Commerce and Industry (Lending Rates)		10½ - 13
	(d) Nigerian Agricultural Bank (Lending Rates for Agricultural production) For Agric. Commodities marketing	...	10 - 13
	(e) Fed. Mortgage Bank — Savings Rate		7½ - 8½
	Lending Rates	...	7 - 13
	(i) Residential Housing	...	7
	(ii) Commercial Property	...	9½ - 13

The range of lending rates for the preferred sectors/sub-sectors for loans maturing within 3 years is 9½ to 11½ per cent; but loans to those sectors maturing after 3 years could carry interest rates up to a maximum of 13 per cent.

Only the Reducing Balance Method shall be used to calculate interest charges on loans payable in agreed instalments. The use of any other method such as the Discount Method or Simple Interest (straight line method) for loans payable in agreed instalments results in charging more than the contracted rates and would amount to a breach of Central Bank's directives on interest charges.

Interest on savings accounts shall be calculated on the balance existing on the customer's account on the 15th of each month. Entries of interest earnings on such accounts should be made at least once a quarter, i.e. four times a year.

The Inspection Department of each bank shall have the responsibility to check on the bank charges and interest payable on deposit accounts. Where the Inspection Department of a bank discovers the non-payment or under-payment of interest on deposits or other entitlements or excessive bank charges, a return shall be made to the Central Bank. The under-payment and excessive charges shall be refunded with interest at the minimum lending rate along with a letter of apology within two weeks to the customer. Any bank which fails to refund excess charges or under-payment of interest on deposits within two weeks shall be liable to a penalty of 5 per cent of the amount involved which shall be credited to the Consolidated Revenue Fund of the Federal Government.

Loans for residential building construction shall be for a minimum period of fifteen years.

9. Mid-month Supply of Statistics

The supply of mid-month returns on certain financial data of the commercial and merchant banks shall continue in 1983. Each bank shall submit within 10 days after the 15 of each month; and if the 15th falls on a non-working day, then on the succeeding working day in respect of:

A. Total loans and advances _____

　　1. Total loans and advances
　　　　(Including bills discounted) _____

　　2. Money at call outside CBN _____

　　3. Investments

　　　　(a) Treasury Bills _____

　　　　(b) Treasury Certificate _____

　　　　(c) Eligible Development:

　　　　　　 Stocks _____

　　　　(d) Others _____

B. Total Deposit Liabilities _____

　　1. Private Sector _____

　　　　(a) Demand deposits _____

　　　　(b) Savings deposits

　　　　　　(i) Others　　　　(　　)

　　　　　　(ii) Accounts not more
　　　　　　　　　than ₦20,000　(　　)

　　　　(c) Time deposit _____

　　　　(d) Others _____

　　2. Federal and State Governments _____

　　　　(a) Demand deposits

　　　　(i) Federal Government　(　　)

　　　　(ii) State Government　(　　)

　　　　(b) Others _____

　　　　(i) Federal Government　(　　)

　　　　(ii) State Government　(　　)

C. 1. Foreign Assets _____

　　2. Foreign Liabilities _____

D. Total Liquid Assets _____

　　of which (1) Vault Cash _____

　　　　　　　(2) Balance with the CBN _____

The report shall reach the Director of Research of the Central Bank within 10 days of the reporting date. Since the re-introduction of this report in January 1978, a few banks have persistently failed to render their returns promptly. The banks are, therefore, enjoined to observe strict compliance in the current fiscal year. The penalty for default to render returns will apply.

10. Revision of Section A (01 – 04) of the Second Schedule Returns

The breakdown of loans granted to Agriculture as per section A (01 – 04) of the Second Schedule Returns shall continue to be as follows:-

SECTION A

LOANS AND ADVANCES ANALYSED BY SECTOR BORROWERS

Code:

Major Minor Agriculture .... ₦

    01 Food crop (such as grains, tuber, citrus, vegetables, etc.) ₦

Major Minor

      02 Other crops (such as cotton, cocoa, groundnuts, oil seeds, palm produce, rubber, tobacco, etc.) ₦

      03 Poultry .... ₦

      04 Other livestock .... ₦

      05 Forestry .... ₦

      06 Fishing .... ₦

      07 Others .... ₦

This new format of reporting on loans to agriculture should be provided as a separate attachment to the second schedule returns.

PART II — INSURANCE COMPANIES

With effect from April 1978, insurance companies were required to report on their lending operations monthly to the Central Bank. However, reports from the companies have continued in most cases to be irregular and delayed, such that information provided have not been useful for purpose of current policy formulation. All insurance companies are required to ensure that they submit their reports within the stipulated time which is within 30 days from the end of the reporting month.

Loans for residential building construction shall be for a minimum period of fifteen years. The guideline regarding interest charges by insurance companies in the 1983 fiscal year shall be as follows:-

Lending Rates	1983 per cent
(a) Preferred Sector — Manufacturing	7 – 13
Agriculture, Mining, Building and Construction	9½ – 11½
(b) Favoured Sector — Residential Housing costing not more than ₦100,000 and Agricultural Production	7
(c) Less preferred sector — General Commerce	10½ – 13

The penalty stipulated for default on the rendering of required returns (See Central Bank of Nigeria Act (Admendment) Decree 1967 Section 19A, paragraph 1 - 3) shall be strictly enforced on all insurance companies.

A. AHMED
GOVERNOR

31st December, 1982.

SELECTED BIBLIOGRAPHY

Books

1.	Chandler L. Y.	*The Economics of Money and Banking* Harper Int'l Edition, New York 1973
2.	Lipsey R. G.	*An Introduction to Positive Economics,* English Language Book Society, 4th Edition 1975.
3.	Cox D.	*Success in Elements of Banking* John Murray, 1981.
4.	Nwankwo G. O.	*Basic Economics* Cambridge University Press 1977
5.	Laidler D. E. W.	*The Demand for Money* Harper & Row 2nd Edition 1977.
6.	The Economist	*Money & Finance 1981* The Economist, 1981.
7.	C.B.N. Research Dept.	*Twenty Years of Central Banking in Nigeria 1959 – 79* 1979
8.	Nwankwo G. O.	*The Nigerian Financial System* Macmillan 1980.
9.	Sheldon H. P.	*Practice & Law of Banking,* MacDonald & Evans 1958.
10.	Mather L. C.	*The Lending Banker* Waterlow & Sons 1972.
11.	Adeniji O. A.	*The Law & Practice of Banking in Nigeria* University of Ife Press, 1981.
12.	Crocket A.	*Money: Theory, Policy and Institutions* Thomas Nelson & Sons, 1979.
13.	Perry F.	*The Elements of Banking* Methuen.
14.	Ojo A. T. & Adewunmi W.	*Banking & Finance in Nigeria* Graham Burn 1982.
15.	Dyer L. S.	*A Practical Approach to Bank Lending* Institute of Bankers, London 1977.
16.	American Bankers Association	*Financial Statements Analysis Bk i – iv*
17.	Havrilesley T. M. & Boorman J. T.	*Current Perspective in Banking* 2nd Edition (Harlan Davidson) 1981.
18.	Hutchinson H. H. & Dyer L. S.	*Interpretation of Balance Sheets* The Institute of Bankers, London, 1979
19.	Clemens J. H. & Dyer L. S.	*Balance Sheets and the Lending Banker* Europa 1979.
20.	Watson Alaisdair	*Finance of International Trade* 2nd Edition, The Institute of Bankers, London, 1981.
21.	Ajayi S. I. & Ojo O. O.	*Money and Banking* George Allen & Unwin, 1981.
22.	Dufey G. & Giddy I	*The International Money Market* Prentice Hall, 1978.

Articles, Seminar Papers and Official Publications

1. Falegan S. B.   *Instruments of Monetary Policy: Their Application and Effectiveness in Nigeria* A paper presented at the symposium of "Role of Monetary Policy in Developing Countries", February 1978 at Banjul Gambia.

2. Fisher J. L.   *Report on the Desirability and Practicability of establishing a Central Bank of Nigeria for promoting the economic development of the country* Government Print Lagos, Nigeria 1953.

3. Nwankwo G. O.   *"British Overseas Banks in* Developing Countries" *Institute of Bankers Journal June 1972.*

4. Hugo Colje   *"How much capital is adequate" The Banker, June 1982*

5. Paton G. D.   *Report on Banks and Banking in Nigeria* Government Printer, 1948.

6. CBN   *Exchange Control Instructions Manual*

7. CBN   *Annual Reports*

8. World Bank   *Annual Report 1981*

9. Adekanye F. A.   *"Borrowing from your Bank" Management in Nigeria, April 1978.*

10. Adekanye F. A.   *"Banks Profitability versus Liquidity vis-a-vis New Economic & Monetary Measures".* A paper presented at the 17th Annual Banking Seminar — 21st – 26th November 1982, at the University of Lagos Conference Centre.

ELEMENTS OF BANKING

Banking in Nigeria: A practical guide.

Name: --Date: --

Address: --

(If you prefer not to give your name and address, this will not prejudice the respect which your replies will be given.)

This questionnaire is designed to secure reader opinions on the adequacy and relevance of the text. Your comments, both positive and negative, will influence the design and content of future editions.

Thank you for your assistance.

----

1. BACKGROUND INFORMATION

A. I am a ☐ Lecturer   ☐ Student   ☐ Other -----------------------------------
                                                    (please specify)

B. Highest educational attainment:
   ☐ WASC; GCE   ☐ Some College   ☐ First Degree/Professional Qualification

   ☐ Advanced Degree

C. I am a (an): ☐ Officer   ☐ Non-Officer   ☐ Non-Bank Employee

D. My major job responsibility is ---

E. I am pursuing an AIB diploma: ☐ Yes   ☐ No

F. I am pursuing a Banking/Finance Course in a Polytechnic, College of

Technology or University: ☐ Yes   ☐ No

2. THE MATERIALS

Please rate the book according to the criteria below. Check the box that most closely corresponds with your opinions.

<u>Thoroughness:</u> ☐ covers too little of subject   ☐ covers sufficient content   ☐ covers too much un-related content

<u>Difficulty Level:</u> ☐ Too basic   ☐ Appropriate for level of course/interest   ☐ Too difficult

<u>Interest Level:</u> ☐ Dull and un-interesting   ☐ Acceptable   ☐ Very interesting

<u>Organisation:</u> ☐ Sequenced logically   ☐ Not in logical sequence

<u>Timeliness:</u> ☐ Most content was current   ☐ Most content was outdated

<u>Practicality:</u> ☐ Too theoretical   ☐ Has sufficient prac-tical application

Please rate the overall effectiveness of the book by circling the number which represents your opinion.

Very effective as a learning aid   Ineffective as a learning aid

5   4   3   2   1

3. COMMENTS

A. Can you make any suggestions for improving the book?
(use additional sheet if necessary)

B. Would you recommend this book?

☐ Yes   ☐ No

Please return the completed questionnaire to:-
Femi Adekanye, F.I.B; F.C.I.S.
Savannah Bank of Nig. Ltd.,
Inspection/Examination Dept.,
P.O. Box 2317,
Lagos, NIGERIA.